C000044703

EUROPE

EUROPE
UNITE, FIGHT, REPEAT

ANDREW P. HYDE

AMBERLEY

For Wynter, Tayjah, Cloe, Deandre and Nasya Rae

First published 2019

Amberley Publishing
The Hill, Stroud
Gloucestershire, GL5 4EP

www.amberley-books.com

Copyright © Andrew P. Hyde, 2019

The right of Andrew P. Hyde to be identified as the Author
of this work has been asserted in accordance with the
Copyrights, Designs and Patents Act 1988.

All rights reserved. No part of this book may be reprinted
or reproduced or utilised in any form or by any electronic,
mechanical or other means, now known or hereafter invented,
including photocopying and recording, or in any information
storage or retrieval system, without the permission in writing
from the Publishers.

British Library Cataloguing in Publication Data.
A catalogue record for this book is available from the British Library.

ISBN 978 1 4456 9342 2 (hardback)
ISBN 978 1 4456 9343 9 (ebook)

Typeset in 10.5pt on 12.5pt Sabon.
Typesetting by Aura Technology and Software Services, India.
Printed in the UK.

Contents

Introduction

Suffering Europeans looking to the prospering United States for salvation, 1914-1918. (Library of Congress)

The departure of the United Kingdom from the European Union has been widely interpreted as a watershed in the long history of the continent. During the preceding referendum campaign 'Remainers' and 'Brexiteers' had been at pains to convince their audiences of the merits of their respective cases. For one group membership was anathema to democracy and sovereignty, while to the other it was an article of faith, the holy grail of European integration. Along the way a new vocabulary had entered the lexicon of political debate. Phrases such as 'free movement', 'hard border', 'frictionless trade', 'regulatory alignment', 'convergence', 'people's vote' and 'Brexit bill' found their way into everyday conversation. Similarly, far-reaching issues had achieved a significance that few had appreciated prior to the vote. It soon became evident that membership of the EU had entwined Britain and its European colleagues in a dizzyingly complex arrangement of interrelated matters of mutual importance. Hence the impasse over the border between the Irish Republic and the United Kingdom, free movement and the rights of EU minorities in the UK, or of British expats in the EU.

It has been argued that both British and European security is at stake as a consequence of Brexit, while others claim that remaining would inevitably lead to Britain's defences being subsumed into a European army. Those who defended the European Union claimed that it alone could be credited with the reconciliation of nations that had been intermittently at war with one another for hundreds of years, a claim challenged by others who assign this fortune to international bodies such as NATO. Such conundrums gave politicians and civil servants alike many sleepless nights as they tried to square the circle of conflicting opinions and overlapping points of view. It is therefore understandable that the average bystander might assume, judging from the heated exchanges in the Westminster village, the media and perhaps even in the public bar of the proverbial 'Dog and Duck', that the dilemma in which Europe subsequently finds itself is somehow unique, perhaps even an aberration. In fact, one only needs to examine the longer history of the continent to appreciate that these issues bear comparison with both the recent and more distant past.

Similar challenges have vexed power brokers and influencers almost from antiquity, and as a consequence Europe has been reconciled and rent asunder many times. Borders have been fluid, soft and hard, and within them nations have been subject to regulatory alignment, single markets, free trade and free movement; they have welcomed and resisted with equal vigour rule from distant capitals. Territory has been used as a bargaining counter or a means of coercion, and entire populations have even been asked to decide their fates in people's votes or referenda. As guarantees against bad faith, ill-will or cliff-edge outcomes, backstops have been employed; and frequently states have been obliged to pay large cash sums to one another in order to conclude and underwrite treaties. Examples can be seen to have concentrated minds at various times, vaguely remembered constructs such as the Holy Roman Empire, Napoleon Bonaparte's Continental System, the short-lived Congress System, the Confederation of the Rhine, and their successors the German and North German Confederations. Each offered blueprints designed to unite various nationalities in one combination or another as super-states under a single government. They can be seen, too, through the prism of the subsequent German and Austro-Hungarian empires, and more recent attempts during the First World War to unite the continent under the Orwellian sounding *Mitteleuropa* and *Ober Ost*. The architects of these projects had sought to bring about a form of political and economic unification totally at odds with the more peaceful versions advocated by prophets elsewhere. The calamity of 1914–1918 also placed upon the German and Austro-Hungarian empires the greatest tests of their integrity, which they ultimately proved incapable of passing. On the other hand, their adversaries, most significantly Britain and France, by agreeing upon a process of cooperation and deeper integration had, for the duration of the war at least, demonstrated the benefits of working together for mutual benefit.

The monumental Treaty of Versailles, which concluded the aforementioned conflict, largely decided the direction of the continent up to the Second World War and beyond. It also had a significant role in reshaping Europe and producing the impasse we face today. It was instrumental in dissolving the two great continental single markets of Germany and Austria-Hungary, and establishing the 'successor' states of Poland, Czechoslovakia, Yugoslavia, Austria and Hungary. These experiments in statehood laid bare the consequences of dismantling successful models and replacing them with untried alternatives. Post-war optimists vainly encouraged a new era of European reconstruction, reconciliation and eventual unification. However, these formerly integral parts of interdependent political and economic unions encountered new barriers to trade, commerce and free movement. Internally, their governments faced the challenges of establishing new currencies, balanced economies, social regimes and national identities out of peoples who had previously belonged to entirely distinct cultural and political systems. More than this, they faced them at the same time as hostile neighbours endeavoured to undermine and corrupt them from without. Disputes over borders and minorities plagued their existence during a critical period when goodwill and a spirit of cooperation was in short supply. They vainly persevered until, within the relatively short space of twenty years, the crushing weight of combined pressures saw these nascent states come crashing down. In the meantime, a resurgent Germany slowly regained its strength, and took advantage of the weakness of its neighbours to gradually extend its power and influence over the continent in pursuit of its own plan for European union, the ominously entitled Großraumwirtschaft (large-area economy).

The subsequent catastrophe, beginning in 1939, heralded the most grotesque version of a Europe under one government, inflicting incalculable misery on millions of people. Those who survived this obscene experiment were left with a continent shattered by war and with calls for reconciliation drowned out by demands for retribution. Only gradually, and with some reluctance, did the nations of the West concede that a sense of combined purpose was the one thing that could help them rebuild, while those of Central and Eastern Europe, some willingly, others less so, pursued a separate path. There followed nearly fifty years of a Europe divided between communist East and capitalist West, separated by what became known as the 'Iron Curtain' and which served, with its barbed wire, watchtowers and armed border guards, as a stark symbol of this division. Many of those countries which formed the so-called Eastern Bloc were the same as those which had sought their freedom from the two older, imperial systems, and they found life under Soviet tyranny far worse than under the Hohenzollerns and the Habsburgs. Yet, within years of freeing themselves from the iron grip of Moscow, they would seek to join yet another union, that created by the Treaty of Rome in 1957. Britain, meanwhile, struggled to reconcile itself to an organisation subject to increasing criticism and hostility. With a significant section of both the population and their politicians proving unable or unwilling to make the necessary adjustments to life inside the European Union, the Westminster Parliament finally succumbed to demands for a 'people's vote'. This resulted in a majority decision to leave.

An uncertain future follows for both the UK and the EU, but as with so many epochal events in history, past events can serve as a signpost for the future. I have endeavoured in this account to shed light upon which of those signs best indicate the direction of travel and how we might reflect upon the generations of statesmen, soldiers and diplomats who have sought to resolve similar challenges. Their endeavours have been motivated by greed, philanthropy, a craven lust for power, hubris or a genuine desire to secure peace and prosperity. Some met with varying degrees of success; others plunged Europe into chaos.

Only time will tell what the latest twist in this perpetual narrative will bring, but I hope that what follows will help the reader to put it into some perspective.

1

I Find Myself Shoring up Crumbling Edifices

Emperor Francis-Joseph of Austria-Hungary, the cement that kept a fractious empire together. (Library of Congress)

At the turn of the twentieth century, Europe was dominated by two large single markets. Austria-Hungary was languishing under its aged Habsburg emperor, Francis-Joseph, while Germany prospered under the Hohenzollerns' unpredictable Kaiser, William II. However, both men headed but the most recent renderings of a lineage stretching back almost a thousand years to the once grandly named Holy Roman Empire of Charlemagne. A Catholic appointee of the Pope, the Holy Roman Emperor ruled as its remote titular head, but it was not an empire which would have been recognised by either his German or Austrian descendants. Despite its size it had evolved into an archaic, ad hoc and piecemeal arrangement, with an eclectic mix of local princes and dukes levying their own direct and indirect taxes upon a peasantry they ruled with virtual autonomy. The lesser nobility and clergy often exempted themselves from such onerous burdens, and their vested interests and local power politics hampered the empire's development into the kind of effective political and economic union that would have been recognised by nineteenth-century commentators. There was a centralised government of sorts, the Imperial Diet, but it was an informal affair, where matters of mutual interest were discussed and debated, and decisions taken through consensus rather than the will of the emperor.

The Diet seemed to work, sitting until 1806, although by then few of those eligible to participate in this ineffective debating chamber troubled to do so. A European Court of sorts had also been established in 1507, to adjudicate on matters raised by the princes and dukes, but again it was somewhat makeshift and lacked executive power. Much of this was due to the fact that the empire was in a state of perpetual flux, with each successive emperor finding himself presiding over different lands to those of his predecessor. This ebb and flow continued throughout much of its existence, until some continuity was established with the coming of the Habsburgs. When the Duke of Babenburg, who had owned extensive lands in today's Bavaria and northern Switzerland, died without an heir in 1246, his estates fell into Habsburg hands. This ambitious dynasty was to further its holdings over the ensuing years through dynastic marriages and inheriting titles from across Europe's ruling houses. The title of Holy Roman Emperor would eventually become the preserve of the Habsburgs from the fifteenth century, and at one time or another during the middle part of the sixteenth century it would embrace the lands and titles of Austria, most of the Kingdom of Burgundy and Brabant, the Netherlands, Naples, Sicily, Bohemia, Hungary and Spain. In 1556, the House of Habsburg was split into Austrian and Spanish branches, held together only by an increasingly slender dynastic union. This peculiar arrangement continued in its rather nebulous and ill-defined way for much of the rest of Habsburg rule.

Approaching the end of the eighteenth century, the empire consisted of some 1,800 territories of various sizes with a combined population of approximately 26 million. This the French philosopher Francois

Voltaire contemptuously dismissed as an 'agglomeration which was called, and which still calls itself the Holy Roman Empire [but] was never holy, Roman, nor an empire'. His dismissive evaluation was shared by many fellow Europeans, most of whom considered the entire rambling institution to be well past its time, and due for root-and-branch reform. Others felt the empire ought to disappear entirely. As we shall see, it was the tumultuous effects of the Napoleonic Wars that would provide a chance for the latter outcome to materialise. In the meantime, the Habsburg's future nemesis, Prussia, was entering stage left.

Beginning in the thirteenth century as a small, forested community to the east of the Vistula, Prussia remained a medium-sized member of the Holy Roman Empire for many years. As the dynamics of the empire changed so did the fortunes of Prussia, and by the time of the Habsburgs Prussia had grown to become a duchy of the Hohenzollerns, in 1618 passing to the Electors of Brandenburg. Prussia's acquisition of Cleve and Mark in 1614 had already formed the nucleus of its future power in the Rhineland, but the Thirty Years War around this time gave France a foothold in Alsace, checking Prussia's ascendancy for the next few decades.

The proclamation of the Kingdom of Prussia in 1701, with its capital in Berlin, saw further expansion during the course of the century. Under arguably its most famous and successful monarch, Frederick the Great, who became king in 1740, Prussia rose to become a dominant regional player. When Austria's Maria Theresa succeeded as Holy Roman Empress, its right to rule was challenged by Charles Albert, Elector of Bavaria, Philip V, King of Spain, and Augustus III, Elector of Saxony, provoking the War of the Austrian Succession. Frederick threw his hat into the ring too, but with a different motive. He saw in the ensuing chaos the opportunity to claim Austria's province of Silesia, which he seized during 1740–41. Crucially for Frederick, when Prussia left the war in 1742, the territory and its abundance of natural wealth remained in his possession.

The Seven Years War followed in 1756, providing Prussia with another opportunity to weaken Austria. Frederick faced a combination of enemies including Austria, but again emerged victorious, establishing Prussia as the dominant state in northern Germany. France nevertheless remained a threat, with Louis XIV consolidating French possessions on the Alsatian Rhine and his successor, Louis XV, annexing Lorraine in 1766. When the French seized the left bank of the Rhine from Prussia in 1801, the ground was laid for these key territories to remain focal points for a century of hostility and competition between the two countries.

Prussia's eastern expansion was not confined to Silesia; it also came at the expense of Poland. German colonisation here was nothing new, and internal schisms within the country had been exploited for settlement even before the Middle Ages. The German language and German laws were widespread here, and a number of cities enjoyed semi-autonomous status. In 1697 the

Electors of Saxony assumed the title of King of Poland, further diluting Polish sovereignty. Such privileges had been largely within the gift of the local princes, who conducted their affairs with scant regard to the edicts of central government. Years of civil war further weakened Poland, until by 1772 it was on the verge of disintegration. This dire situation led to the Polish *Sejm*, the lower parliamentary chamber, signing away virtually a third of its territory in the First Partition of Poland, by which Austria gained Galicia and Prussia acquired Ermland, which allowed it to unite the territories of East Prussia and Brandenburg. Russia, too, made some modest gains. Another partition followed in 1793, and then its third dissection in 1795, from which Russia received the lion's share. As a result of this final partition, 83,000 square miles of land disappeared, with Russia incorporating Courland, all Lithuanian territory east of the River Niemen and the last of the Volhynian Ukraine. Prussia acquired the remainder of Mazovia, including Warsaw and a slice of Lithuania west of the Niemen; for its part Austria took the remaining section of Lesser Poland, from Krakow north-east to the bend of the northern Bug River.

Prussia and Austria, however, along with much of the rest of the continent, faced their biggest tests as a consequence of the two decades of war which resulted from the French Revolution of 1789. Threatened by the overthrow of the French monarchy, Prussia and Austria formed a coalition in 1792 hoping to suppress the revolutionaries and reinstate the status quo. Instead, revolutionary France retook the Saar, along with the entire west bank of the Rhine. Great Britain, Sardinia, the Netherlands, Spain, the Kingdom of Naples and the Papal States then joined together against France, but they had reckoned without the determination of the French insurgents to defend their revolution at all costs. Prussia was quickly defeated, followed by Spain, and in quick succession Sardinia, Naples and the Papal States. Austria dropped out of the fighting in 1797, and then Russia, Portugal and the Ottoman Empire jumped into the fray. Fighting paused briefly when peace was signed with the Ottomans, Austria, Naples and eventually Great Britain. Napoleon Bonaparte had come to power in France around this time, and in 1804 he crowned himself emperor and embarked upon yet another war. Britain, Austria, Russia, Sweden and Naples formed a further coalition, a decision which would have dramatic consequences for the Holy Roman Empire.

August 1804 saw the latest incumbent of the Holy Roman Emperorship, Francis II, assuming the title Emperor Francis I of Austria and King of Bohemia and Hungary. Nevertheless, these overlapping roles were not to last for much longer, particularly given that Francis had earned Napoleon's ire by taking up arms against him. Austria's subsequent defeat by Napoleon resulted in the humiliating Peace of Pressburg of 1805, by which Francis had to make territorial concessions and pay an indemnity of 40 million gold Francs. On 6 August 1806, Francis finally dissolved what was left of the Holy Roman Empire. What lands remained to him after Napoleon's seizures – Austria, Bohemia, Hungary, Croatia, Transylvania, Galicia and some Italian territories – thus transitioned into the Habsburg Empire.

Napoleon, meanwhile, had plans of his own. He created the Confederation of the Rhine on 12 July 1806 as a buffer between France and Prussia. Initially comprising sixteen states, with its capital at Frankfurt am Main, by 1810 it had expanded to thirty-nine members, covering an area of 135,000 square miles and with a population of 14.5 million. It was a considerable political and economic bloc, and Napoleon intended to use it in his war against Britain. He imposed a blockade, prohibiting any trade between the confederation and his enemy across the English Channel. When he was finally persuaded that this strategy was doing more harm to France than Britain, he imposed heavy tariffs on British goods, hoping instead to restrict imports and stimulate exports. Nevertheless, the Continental System, as Napoleon's strategy was called, devalued Britain's trade with Europe by between 25 and 55 per cent during the eight years in which it operated. Although it demonstrated the effectiveness of combined action against a third-party state, it was nevertheless a relatively short-lived experiment in economic coercion.

While these developments were taking shape, Prussia and Russia were being trounced. In 1807 Napoleon created the Duchy of Warsaw out of the central provinces of Prussian Poland. In all, Prussia lost half of its territory; as well as Poland, all its land west of the River Elbe was taken by the French dictator. In 1808 he ordered the invasion of Spain, resulting in the Peninsular War, where his later nemesis, Sir Arthur Wellesley, would confront his armies for the first time. Austria foolishly re-entered the war in 1809, but was again defeated. Driven by hubris and single-mindedness, Napoleon went one step too far when he invaded Russia in 1812 in retaliation for its reneging upon undertakings not to trade with Britain, among other things. This folly proved his downfall, resulting in the destruction of his Grande Armée of nearly a million men and camp followers. He could not hope to recover from such a loss as the Russian, Prussian, Swedish, Austrian, Spanish, British and allied German states forced him to abdicate in May 1813. Although he returned to power the following year, he was finally and decisively beaten at the Battle of Waterloo in June 1815. This time the Allies were taking no chances, and Napoleon sailed to his exile and early death on the British island of St Helena in the middle of the Atlantic Ocean. With Napoleon no longer able to threaten the peace of the continent, the victorious powers could sit down and redefine the frontiers and governance of the continent for a generation.

The subsequent Congress of Vienna largely sought to restore Europe to its state before the upheavals of revolution and war. France returned to its pre-1792 borders, but there were many other changes. The Austrian Netherlands were absorbed by the newly created Kingdom of the Netherlands, in exchange for which the Habsburgs gained control of Lombardy, Venetia,

Tuscany, Parma and the Tyrol. France's ally Denmark was punished by the loss of Norway to Sweden, and the Pope was restored to the Vatican and the Papal States. The Bourbons were established in the Kingdom of the Two Sicilies, and Napoleon's Grand Duchy became Congress Poland, with the Czar of Russia as its king. Napoleon's final defeat also brought immense benefits to Prussia on its western borders. The peace awarded Prussia the Ruhr, which would prove invaluable later, and France's frontier on the Rhine returned to the Alsatian zone. North of Alsace, the Palatinate was brought under the administration of Bavaria. North-west of the Palatinate were some other minor German enclaves, but north of these the whole west bank as far as Cleve, together with Julich and Aachen, also became Prussian. As a result of the largesse of the peacemakers, Prussia also regained possession of the coal-rich Saar, which was incorporated into the Province of the Rhine. Prussia now stretched unbroken from the River Niemen in the east to the Elbe, and governed other scattered lands further west.

This dismantling of Napoleon's grandiose plans nevertheless left intact perhaps his most lasting legacy, the Code Napoleon, a Europe-wide legal system which endures to this day. The revolutionary government of the National Assembly had sought to rationalise and standardise the myriad of laws which governed different parts of France from as early as 1791, but it was Napoleon who oversaw its realisation. Whereas Roman law dominated the south of the country, Frankish and German elements applied in the north, alongside local customs and various other archaic usages. These were abolished after 1804 with the adoption of the structure which bore Napoleon's name. It reformed commercial and criminal law, and divided civil law into property law and family law, giving greater equality in matters of inheritance. Although it also denied rights to illegitimate heirs and women, and reintroduced slavery, it enshrined in law that all free men were recognised as equal, with inherited rights and titles abolished. It was far from perfect, but it reflected Napoleon's worldview and once adopted was applied to nearly every territory and state dominated by France. Defeat in 1815 did not see his brainchild abandoned or reconfigured like his territorial acquisitions; indeed, elements of this legal template were widely adopted during the course of the following century, by a unified Italy in 1865, Germany in 1900 and Switzerland in 1912, all of which passed statutes echoing his original system. And it was not only Europe which appreciated the merits of the Code Napoleon; many of the newly independent states of South America also incorporated it into their constitutions.

Possibly the most politically significant outcome of the end of the Napoleonic Wars was an agreement, sadly short-lived, to create a structure preventing a similar catastrophe occurring again. It emerged in part from the earlier efforts of British foreign secretary Lord Castlereagh to forge the coalitions or alliances which ultimately brought about Napoleon's downfall. At the Peace of Paris in 1815, Castlereagh sought to limit the terms against France and avoid the sort of peace which would foster resentment and provide the conditions for another war. This was to become the so-called Concert of Europe, underwritten by a series of treaties which called upon the signatories to convene at regular intervals to ensure that the continent's collective security was guaranteed against another conflict. Nevertheless, despite these high-minded intentions it soon appeared to the British that the co-signatories Russia, Prussia and Austria, joined in 1818 by a rehabilitated France, instead saw the system as a mechanism for repressing internal dissent and interfering in the domestic affairs of recalcitrant populations. Castlereagh explained his government's position:

> ... [Whilst] it is the province of Great Britain to encourage peace by exercising a conciliatory influence between the powers, rather than put herself at the head of any combination of courts to keep others in check ... it is not my wish to encourage on the part of this country, an unnecessary interference in the ordinary affairs of the continent...[1]

He had made it explicit, therefore, that the British did not propose any proactive involvement, and as a result the Concert was likely to wither on the vine. Although the 1818 congress held at Aachen was successful enough, dealing with the accession of France now that it had paid off the 700 million Franc indemnity imposed at the end of the war, later congresses grew more and more obsessed with defending the status quo, even if that involved waging war on troublesome neighbours. The Congress of Verona met in 1822 to discuss intervention in the Spanish and Greek revolutions, but once again the British opposed any direct involvement. When the French decided on their own to march into Spain to crush the republicans and re-establish the monarchy, the Congress System, only recently conceived and with so much potential for European unity, passed into obscurity. Britain would go its own way, and it remained for France, Prussia, Austria and Russia to resolve continental matters of mutual concern between themselves for the most part.

One means by which resolutions might have been achieved was through the auspices of the German Confederation, another child of the Congress of Vienna and intended to succeed the Holy Roman Empire. Consisting of broadly the same members as Napoleon's Confederation of the Rhine, it now enjoyed the additional muscle afforded by the inclusion of Prussia and Austria. Its federal Diet also remained in Frankfurt, and Austria's emperor, Francis, was appointed its first president, remaining in post until 1835. From its inception, one of the key topics for discussion among the German Confederation was just how far and how deep the states were prepared to go in developing their relationship, both economically and politically. There was, for example, considerable resistance to calls for a federal army and constitutional harmonisation, and there was clearly a difference in emphasis between the largely Protestant northern states and their Catholic neighbours to the south. Furthermore, the smaller members were wary of measures which might find them subsumed within a greater Prussia. Fortunately, they were protected from such ambitions by a system of majority voting, which ensured that they could use their veto to block any reforms that they opposed. Prussia naturally resented the disproportionate influence exercised by the smaller members, some of whom were no larger than a city, as their presence necessitated either going at the speed of the slowest members or accepting a two-speed Europe. Nevertheless, if the Confederation was to succeed in whatever form, agreements would have to be made that bound its members more closely together than a loose association of separate independent states would permit.

For the Prussians the first step to harmonisation was an all-embracing customs union, or *Zollverein*, in which a single market could operate. This would enable the free movement of goods and services between its members and levy a common tariff on imports from third parties outside the Confederation. There had been some bilateral customs unions in operation between members from as early as 1818, but in theory non-signatories were third parties and may have to pay tariffs to export to them. Over time these arrangements were expanded and consolidated, so that by 1834 a tax union or *Steuerverein* was in existence, first between the Duchy of Brunswick and the Kingdom of Hanover, and then joined by the Duchy of Oldenburg. In 1854, Hanover and Oldenburg became members of the larger Deutscher *Zollverein* and the *Steuerverein* was dissolved. The tariffs imposed on third parties outside of these customs areas were collected centrally and then shared out among member states on a per capita basis. The scheme spread until only the Hanseatic League, the two Mecklenburgs and the Austrian Empire remained outside. Despite its importance to the Confederation, Austria opted out due to a mix of protectionism and concern on the part of Chancellor Klemens von Metternich. A highly cautious man, von Metternich saw serious implications for Austria's sovereignty if an agreement was made to pool such important powers as setting tariffs. It was just one of a number of ways in which Austria set itself apart from the rest of the Confederation, particularly Prussia.

Part of the reason for the contrast between Prussia and Austria was the fact that the Habsburgs appeared settled and unambitious compared to their Prussian neighbours. Austria's Ruritanian complacency was evident as early as the Confederation's inception. In 1817, one French ambassador concluded that the Austrian Empire 'keeps going by its own size ... the government has no energy, and none is to be found anywhere ... there is here neither will nor authority, everyone does more or less as he wishes.'[2] Von Metternich shared such sentiments and admitted he faced an uphill struggle if the empire was to form a viable counter to Prussian power. In 1822, as he fought to manage an empire apparently unable or unwilling to stamp its will upon its various nationalities, he had to concede, 'I find myself shoring up crumbling edifices.'[3] The single largest cause of this was the continual state of penury in which the empire found itself, preventing efficient management. Nor was Austria as united as its emperor might have wished. The main bones of contention were to be found among the Czechs, the Slovenes and particularly the Magyars of Hungary, the largest of the Habsburg domains. As the second-largest ethnic group within the empire, the Magyars were in a perpetual state of discord and resentment at being subject to rule from Vienna.

Hungary had been a restless and unwilling appendage ever since Austrian troops conquered the country and ejected the Turks in 1699. The proud and chauvinist Magyars were not reconciled to exchanging one master for another and staged a series of rebellions which were only finally suppressed in 1711. In 1740, the Magyar nobles succeeded in extracting concessions from the newly installed Empress Maria Theresa, who was distracted by the War of the Austrian Succession. These concessions placed the Magyars in a privileged position compared to others in the empire, granting them the right to convene their own Diet and exemption from paying tax. Such largesse was short-lived, however, as Maria Theresa's successor, Joseph II, did not share his predecessor's predilection for such arm's-length government. He subsequently revoked nearly all of the concessions when he assumed the emperorship in 1780. Understandably, this caused considerable rancour among the Magyars until Joseph's successor, Leopold II, restored the concessions, forestalling another revolt and securing Magyar support against the French during the Napoleonic Wars. This truce would prove to be temporary, however, as Magyar nationalism was still a seething cauldron, waiting for a chance to boil over. In the meantime, Austria had to overcome the challenges of war with Napoleon and, as we have seen, face the consequences of the end of the Holy Roman Empire.

Francis II's tenure, arguably the most turbulent of all to date, was followed in 1835 by that of Ferdinand I, a man whose character and demeanour had long been a source of disquiet in his court. It eventually became evident that Ferdinand was unsuited to the demands of ruling an empire, and particularly dealing with such complex issues as recalcitrant Magyars. This was largely due to his epilepsy, which at the time was mistaken for stupidity. In an age when a king had to exude strength and authority, Ferdinand was deemed to be severely lacking in both qualities. As a consequence, soon after Ferdinand's nephew Francis-Joseph was born in 1830, it was decided to prepare him to rule the empire in his uncle's stead. Submitted to a highly demanding regime of education for up to sixteen hours a day in languages, etiquette, history, philosophy and a raft of other subjects, by the time Francis-Joseph came of age he was fully trained in the art of kingship. He was also to prove staunchly conservative, and more than willing to assist his chancellor in shoring up the crumbling edifices of his inheritance.

Chancellor von Metternich had ensured Francis-Joseph was completely convinced of the dangers of liberalism and constitutionalism, and prepared to confront the perils of the Magyars head-on. The wisdom of preparing Francis-Joseph was vindicated by the resurgence of Magyar nationalism under men such as Louis Kossuth, who used his influence and oratory to urge his fellow countrymen to demand concessions from Vienna. Born in 1802, the son of a landless Magyar aristocrat, Kossuth was educated in fervently anti-Habsburg and nationalistic Hungarian schools, in which he became imbued with the cause of Magyar liberation. Upon leaving university he went on to practise law before entering politics, where he found a ready outlet for his views. He also came under the influence of Count Istvan Szechenyi, who further radicalised him in the cause of Hungarian independence. Kossuth soon became even more extreme than his mentor, landing him a prison sentence in 1837. Freed in 1840 following a general amnesty, Kossuth then returned to the political arena, becoming leader of the opposition in the Hungarian Diet.

When revolution swept the continent in 1848, reaching Vienna and then Budapest, Kossuth and his colleagues seized the opportunity to make a practically unilateral declaration of independence by passing the so-called March Laws, a raft of constitutional reforms which would have made Hungary a de facto sovereign state. The reforms gave Hungary its own parliament, cabinet, civil service, army and militia, and enshrined the primacy of the Magyar language in administration and education. Finally, Hungary's separate status would be entrenched by the installation of a viceroy sitting in Budapest as the emperor's representative. In September 1848, Ferdinand, who might have been expected to acquiesce to these demands, instead sanctioned an invasion of Hungary from Croatia. Assisted by the Russians, who feared a successful Hungarian revolution would inspire their equally restless Polish subjects, the Austrians crushed the rebellion and Kossuth fled to Turkey. In exile, he continued to promote his idea of a Danubian Federation until his death.

Inevitably, the revolution found another high-profile victim in the person of Emperor Ferdinand. Despite Ferdinand having overseen the suppression of the revolt, his courtiers and ministers decided this was the ideal opportunity to implement the long-planned palace coup. Having assumed the throne, Francis-Joseph's first step was to suppress the March Laws and instead embark upon a policy of wholesale centralisation. The suppression of the Hungarian rebellion and Francis-Joseph's subsequent actions led to more of a unitary state than existed before or after. Hungary's county assemblies were abolished and replaced by Czech and German officials who administered most of the country directly. A single legal system was imposed, and taxation codified, with the privileged position enjoyed by the aristocracy set aside. This ever-closer union was confirmed in June 1850, when the tariffs between Hungary and the rest of the empire were abolished and a single commercial system was applied throughout the monarchy.[4]

Prussia, in the meantime, saw the recent revolutions as an opportunity to assert itself, and sought to reconfigure the Confederation so that it could sit at its pinnacle, at least on a par with Austria. To this end, asserting that the German Confederation had ceased to exist because of the revolutions, Prussia's chief minister, Joseph Maria von Radowitz, convened a conference in Erfurt on 20 March 1850. He invited representatives from every member state and proposed a new union in which Prussia and Austria would enjoy equal billing. Although Saxony and Hanover initially gave their backing, the proposal was rejected by the other members, most significantly Bavaria and Württemberg. The Austrians, appalled at the implications should the Erfurt Union succeed, insisted that, contrary to popular misconceptions, the former German Confederation was still in existence and that the status quo had not and would not change. With the support of the Russians, Vienna was able to quash the new plan and demand that von Radowitz be dismissed. Faced by both Austria and its protector Russia, the Prussians were forced into a humiliating climbdown, which was confirmed by the so-called Punctation of Olmutz on 29 November 1850. Nevertheless, despite the victory, Vienna's days as top dog were numbered, particularly as Francis-Joseph had not counted upon the emergence of Prussia's Otto von Bismarck. Bismarck's genius for statecraft would determine the shape of the continent for decades to come.

Born to a noble family near Berlin in 1815, Otto von Bismarck won admission to the Prussian civil service after attending university. Finding life in the corridors of power unappealing, he decided to return home to help his father manage the family estates for a few years. In 1847, considering his familial duties fulfilled, Bismarck returned to politics and entered the Prussian legislature, where his work ethic and efficiency attracted notice. In 1851, the Prussian king, William IV, appointed Bismarck Prussia's representative at the Frankfurt Diet. Having fulfilled his duties in that capacity with distinction, he was then invited to act as Prussian ambassador to Russia, and then France, where he further enhanced his growing reputation as an effective diplomat and administrator. His star was clearly in the ascendant, and in 1862 he became Prussia's minister-president. Once ensconced in this powerful position, Bismarck demonstrated that he was a man on a mission. He was to play a prominent role in blocking Austrian membership of the *Zollverein*, and would manoeuvre to secure a final parting of the ways. He knew there was not enough room for both Prussia and Austria to dominate the Confederation, and as early as the mid-1850s had urged the 'harnessing of German nationalism as a means of destroying the Austrian influence within Germany'.[5] The extent to which Bismarck designed Austria's estrangement has long been debated by scholars. In any event, a series of critical circumstances would hand him the means to achieve his goal.

Austria's political fortunes waned considerably in the period between the Punctation of Olmutz and Bismarck's emergence as Chancellor of Prussia. This was largely due to the personal ineptitude of Francis-Joseph, who had decided early on that he would play a greater part in the government of his empire than even von Metternich might have considered wise. He proceeded to make or agree to a series of foreign policy decisions which seriously undermined the integrity of his realm. Perhaps the most significant was his decision to favour Britain and France against Russia in the Crimean War, which estranged the one country that still had the power to act as Austria's guarantor. Nicholas I of Russia saw this Austrian policy as an unforgivable betrayal.

Then, in 1859, the emperor went to war with the Kingdom of Sardinia to protect his territories in Lombardy. Not only did he lose this war – largely because France became involved – and have to cede the province to the Sardinians, but he reignited latent nationalism in Italy as a whole. This would come back to haunt him, as the country was stirred to reunite under the leadership of men such as Giuseppe Garibaldi and Comilio de Cavour, creating constant tension in his southern realms. By the time Francis-Joseph summoned the Congress of Princes in Frankfurt in 1863 to discuss the future direction of the Confederation, the full extent of Austrian decline was evident, and the King of Prussia did not even bother to attend. For Bismarck, it was clear that the balance of power between the two had all but reversed, and that it was only a matter of time before there was a showdown.

This confrontation drew another step closer thanks to an obscure crisis brewing in Schleswig-Holstein. These two autonomous duchies to the south of Denmark, nominally under the sovereignty of their northern neighbour, suddenly rose to prominence in 1864. Holstein was mostly German and a member of the Confederation while Schleswig was more mixed, but Germans in both duchies had long held the view that the two duchies were inseparable. In 1848 the Danish had tried to take advantage of the upheaval of the revolutions to annex Schleswig outright, but the German population resisted, and Prussian troops were all set to intervene when Anglo-Russian mediation defused the situation.

The issue nonetheless remained an open sore to German nationalists, and was as much a burning issue when it reared its head again in 1864 as it had been sixteen years earlier. The threat of Danish annexation remained, accompanied by suggestions that precipitate action could be expected at any time. Therefore, on 30 March 1863, when Denmark's King Christian IX unilaterally announced a new constitution which abolished Schleswig's parliament and imposed a de facto union with Denmark, alarm bells began to ring. In response, troops from the German Confederation marched into Holstein to shield the territory from a similar fate. Something of a stand-off ensued until an impatient Bismarck issued an ultimatum to King Christian on 16 January 1864, giving him forty-eight hours to rescind the new constitution. While he awaited a reply, Bismarck colluded with Austria to take joint action in the event of Denmark's expected rejection of the ultimatum. Bismarck's pessimism proved justified, and a combined Prussian–Austrian force invaded and occupied both duchies. Forced to retreat in the depths of winter, the Danish army was finally overcome and had no choice but to agree to the terms of the Treaty of Vienna on 30 October, by which they ceded the duchies, along with Lauenberg, to Prussia and Austria.

As a consequence of his rash decision to take on two of Europe's major powers, Christian IX was forced to surrender 40 per cent of the land and 38 per cent of the population of his kingdom, about 1.6 million people. In a final desperate act, Christian offered to join the German Confederation if the two duchies were restored to their previous status. Bismarck rejected the proposal, as this would have removed the basis for the next stage of his scheme. For their part, under the terms of the Convention of Gastein, signed on 14 August 1865, the victorious allies agreed to a provisional division, with Austria taking Holstein and Prussia receiving Schleswig and Lauenberg. However, this was no more than a backstop for Bismarck. As part of his longer-term strategy to alienate Austria from the Confederation entirely, he sought to press for sole Prussian control of the duchies in the hope of antagonising Vienna and forcing a confrontation.

War with Austria held few fears for Bismarck in any case; the recent fighting against Denmark had further highlighted Austria's weak military situation. Not only did Bismarck's armies outperform Francis-Joseph's in the field of battle, but Austria's problems in trying to suppress an uprising in Venetia at the time had been noted. As a screen for his real motives, Bismarck had offered to assume responsibility for the duchies and to support Austria in Venetia. However, such an admission of weakness would be an affront to the prestige of the Austrian empire, so Francis-Joseph declined. The Austrian emperor's recalcitrance was especially irksome because his military weakness was self-evident. Compounding Austria's foreign policy disasters was the perpetual agitation from within, as the various nationalities pushed for greater autonomy. These were loudest among his ever-restless Hungarian subjects, tempered by more moderate nationalists such as Ference Deak. As Bavarian prime minister, Ludwig von der Pfordten observed in October 1865, 'Austria, financially bankrupt, in a state of political anarchy, is at the moment incapable of action. We cannot now nor for a long time count on Austria.'[6]

Habsburg rule in Holstein proved far more benevolent than the repressive regime imposed upon Schleswig by the Prussians, to such a degree that refugees were fleeing Prussian-controlled Schleswig and seeking asylum in Austrian-held Holstein. This state of affairs was infuriating for Bismarck, and with relations at a low ebb it was clear that there would be no better opportunity to brings things to a head. At a meeting of the Prussian Grand Council, it was agreed that war with Austria was now inevitable. However, Bismarck needed a pretext, so in

April 1866 he introduced a motion for limited reforms in the Federal Diet. He did so quite cynically, and in the full knowledge that Austria was bound to reject them. Francis-Joseph duly obliged, and in response Prussia mobilised its army.

Despite its relative weakness, Austria was not without influence, friends or allies. Many of the smaller German states still feared Prussian dominance in the Confederation, and only the two Mecklenburgs, the Thuringian states, Oldenburg, Hamburg, Bremen and Lubeck expressed solidarity with Prussia. In anticipation of this, Bismarck had made strategic plans of his own, and signed an alliance with Italy, who would draw part of the Austrian army away from the Prussians should war actually break out. Confident that the odds were in its favour, on 11 June 1866, Austria summoned the majority of the German Confederation to mobilise in its support. In response, Prussia declared the Confederation to be dissolved, and on 15 June its troops marched across the border.

Unfortunately, the Confederation members' faith in Austria all too soon proved misguided. The war, which lasted for only six weeks, ended in ignominy on 23 July when Francis-Joseph's armies were defeated at Sadowa, while Prussia also crushed Bavaria and the other states that had allied with Austria. This humiliation finally signalled the end of Austrian pretensions to be the paramount power in the now-defunct Confederation. France intervened and brokered a truce, which was followed by a preliminary peace, signed on 26 July at Nickolausburg, confirmed a month later by the Treaty of Prague. As a consequence, Bismarck secured control of Schleswig-Holstein and annexed Hanover, Hesse-Kassel, Nassau and Frankfurt. Austria was also forced to concede Venetia to Italy. Bismarck had Austria at his mercy, but instead he counselled against humiliating Francis-Joseph further. His reasons echoed Lord Castlereagh's policy towards France after 1815:

> ... we had to avoid wounding Austria too severely ... we had to avoid leaving behind in her any unnecessary bitterness of feeling or desire for revenge; we ought rather to reserve the possibility of becoming friends again...[7]

Francis-Joseph instead had to face the domestic humiliation that defeat brought. The bloody nose suffered by Austria persuaded Ference Deak and his fellow Hungarian nationalists that the time had come to reopen the issue with Vienna. Though he sought a more moderate solution than Kossuth had, the result was the despised *Ausgleich* or Compromise, and its conditions, agreed in 1867, were much the same as those briefly extorted twenty years previously, and which Francis-Joseph had so ruthlessly reneged upon. No longer the Austrian Empire, his realms were henceforth to be known as Austria-Hungary, demonstrating to the world that his Magyar subjects were no longer mere appendages but equal partners. The Compromise, furthermore, was more than a simple branding exercise, as it created a physical and geographic half-way house. As Emperor of Austria, Francis-Joseph's domains – known as Cisleithania – formed an arc from Istria in the south, up through the Tyrol and Austria proper to Bohemia and thence Galicia in the north-east. His separate, Hungarian kingdom constituted the eastern half – known as the Lands of the Crown of St Stephen, or Transleithania – and was roughly kidney-shaped, incorporating among others Hungary, Transylvania, the former Voivodeship of Serbia and the internally self-governing kingdom of Croatia-Slavonia. Francis-Joseph would therefore remain Emperor of Austria but only King of Hungary, a point emphasised by the adoption of the nomenclature Kaiserlich und Königlich – Imperial *and* Royal.

The Magyars would waste little time in exploiting the new constitution to project themselves as distinct from Austria in all but name, their association represented solely through their participation in a handful of joint ministries and common institutions. They could not even agree on the design of a common coat of arms until the coming of the First World War, by which time such expressions of unity were entirely academic. The only link between the two halves that Hungary was prepared to acknowledge was Francis-Joseph himself, but they insisted that he be crowned in a lavish ceremony in June 1867, in order to underline the point. In this new capacity he was to spend several weeks a year in Budapest, where he would issue and grant his approval to statutes passed in his Hungarian Diet, and the remainder of the year in Vienna, overseeing his realms in that half of the empire. This new structure also exposed its contradictions. When some of Francis-Joseph's Hungarian subjects attempted an audience with him in Vienna, they were left understandably perplexed when he replied that as Emperor of Austria, he was unable to entertain appeals from subjects of the King of Hungary.[8]

Each half of the Dual Monarchy therefore had their own premiers and parliaments in their respective capitals, where they legislated on matters of purely domestic concern, and from where they administered their various territories. In addition, the Compromise had confirmed the validity of the three joint ministries which had existed since the Pragmatic Sanction of 1713. These reflected the pooling of sovereignty in the areas of foreign relations, defence and finance, liaising via regular written contact with delegations from the two parliaments. In addition, the three central ministries sat alongside the two premiers in a joint council chaired by the single imperial foreign minister. The king-emperor, for his part, attempted to keep as much power as possible to himself by chairing his Crown Council, through which he succeeded in maintaining considerable influence over foreign policy on behalf of both Austria and Hungary.

This already flawed and unwieldy system revealed significant shortcomings in the implementation of the joint ministries. While Austria's sixty representatives to the delegations included members of its other nationalities, the Hungarian deputation was exclusively Magyar. Not only did this allow next to no dissent, they only had to exploit disagreements among the Austrian delegation to manoeuvre support for their own position. The Magyar leaders were also not averse to bullying the Crown by threatening to block the ten-year renewal of the Compromise or by holding back money from the military budget. They also succeeded in negotiating a better financial arrangement, for although Hungary had 40 per cent of the population, it was only required to contribute a third of the empire's tax revenue. Although this proportion increased slightly later, it further underlined the advantages they were to glean as the party prepared to walk away from the table if they did not get their way.

Nevertheless, some common ground was possible, such as common postage and coinage, and in 1878 a national bank was created. Full merger would have to wait nearly twenty years, however, again because of the complicated negotiations necessary to satisfy Hungarian demands. One of these was over the conversion to the gold crown from the silver florin, which was not completed until 1900, and until then Hungary issued its own banknotes. Nevertheless, once established the institution proved a success and survived until the monarchy was dissolved in 1918. A far greater symbol of the empire was its eyewatering melting pot of nationalities and religions, which both Austria's Germans and Hungary's Magyars dominated only by employing great deftness and skill.

Despite respectively constituting 23 per cent and 20 per cent of a population of roughly 50 million by 1900, German and Magyar hegemony over all the other nationalities was largely the consequence of smoke and mirrors. Francis-Joseph's Slav subjects alone – 12.5 per cent Czech, 10.8 per cent Polish, 7.9 per cent Ruthene, 5.3 per cent Croat, 3.8 per cent Slovak, 3.8 per cent Serb and 2.6 Slovene – together outnumbered the Germans and Magyars by a factor of two to one. Both would therefore pursue the age-old policy of divide and rule by perpetuating an 'equilibrium of discontent',[9] and were ruthless in protecting their interests in other ways. The 1867 Austrian Constitution, and the Fundamental Laws particularly, were supposed to afford absolute parity among the member nationalities of the Austrian half of the empire. All Austrian subjects were afforded equality before the law, and freedom of religion. Clause 19 particularly could not have been more explicit:

> ... all ethnic groups in the nation have equal rights, and each ethnic group has an inalienable right to preserve and cultivate its nationality and language.[10]

However, when Francis-Joseph attempted in 1871 to extend representation in his Austrian lands by settling a similar constitutional arrangement on the Czechs as that negotiated with Hungary, intense lobbying by the Germans and Magyars scuppered it almost at once. Furthermore, this mutual competition between Austrians and Magyars to dominate all other nationalities was vividly demonstrated by their joint management of the so-called Common Army. It was the most significant institution to emerge from the Compromise, whose ranks included recruits from every corner of the Dual Monarchy. Moreover, the fact that national interests were supposedly secondary to those of the empire as a whole were emphasised by each man's personal loyalty to the person of the king-emperor.

According to statistics compiled in 1911, out of every 1,000 soldiers there were on average 267 Germans, 233 Hungarians, 135 Czechs, 85 Poles, 81 Ukrainians, 67 Croatians and Serbs, 54 Romanians, 38 Slovaks, 26 Slovenes and 14 Italians.[11] The officer corps unsurprisingly reflected the domination of the empire as a whole, with Germans constituting 76.1 per cent and Magyars 10.7 per cent. Czechs provided just 5.2 per cent, and the rest of the empire between them just 8 per cent.[12] Naturally, commands were given in German, but in order to avoid confusion these were kept to a bare minimum of sixty words, and during basic training recruits also employed their native tongue.[13] In addition every officer had to be well-versed in two other languages in addition to German while non-commissioned officers also acted as interlocutors. As individual units comprised men of the same nationality who often used their own language as well, a very complex system of command and control emerged, requiring a considerable degree of efficiency and discipline. Nationalism was also adding to the confusion, with troops in Hungary often receiving commands in Magyar, contrary to regulations but axiomatic of their relentless determination to emphasise the differences between themselves and the Austrians.

Moreover, the Magyars, who were never comfortable participating in such joint ventures, demonstrated scant enthusiasm for the institution from its inception. This was partly due to an underlying paranoia that the army could be used, as in 1849, to overthrow the Compromise, reassert Austrian hegemony, and bring the Hungarians back under the absolute control of the monarch. Such sentiments manifested in a reticence to fund the army properly. Despite reaching a total budget of £34 million by 1914, military expenditure was still little more than Britain's £28 million, although the British lavished much of this on their beloved Royal Navy.[14] Moreover, it was far behind Germany's £78 million and Russia's £76 million. It was also largely due to the Hungarians that the Austro-Hungarian army received the smallest annual intake of conscripts of any European power. Until 1912 Budapest stubbornly opposed any appreciable increase[15] and kept rigidly to the quotas set by law in 1868. This stood at 94,400, of which 54,400 were drawn from Austria and

40,000 from Hungary, with a further 20,400 allocated to their respective national militias. Pressure from both politicians and the military itself did see this figure rise to 103,000 in 1889, and modestly increase thereafter, until by 1913 it stood at around 136,000.

These steps reflected the growing tensions in the Balkans, and it was planned to incrementally increase annual conscription to 154,000 by 1914 and 159,000 by 1915. To sugar the pill slightly – and to save money – conscripts would be required to serve for two years instead of three, and remain in the reserves for ten.[16] Despite this increase, the pool of reserves available in wartime was severely limited compared to Germany, Russia and even France. In July 1914 the standing army would be a relatively modest 36,000 officers and 414,000 men, not even double that fielded by the United Kingdom.

Hungarians were not alone in resenting the demands of military service. Ultranationalist Pan-Germans also begrudged the high proportion of their countrymen serving in the army. Their newspapers jibed that only the German regiments could be trusted in combat because 'one wouldn't dare use the Czech regiments, and the Polish ones stay at home, they have to be treated gently'.[17] Some critics even went so far as to call upon their compatriots to refuse to pay this 'utterly burdensome [human] tax of constantly sacrificing to the army the strongest and most beautiful years of every fellow German'.[18]

Due to its comparatively miserly budget, the Austro-Hungarian Army was kept scandalously short of good weaponry and equipment right up to 1914, despite the world-famous Skoda works producing artillery of the highest quality. One of these was the magnificent 305mm Morser M11 siege gun. This was so highly regarded that the Austrians would loan eight of them to Germany for its invasion of Belgium. Its own forces, however, were often left with field pieces dating back to the 1880s, many of which were obsolete steel-bronze models, both heavier and of a shorter range than those with which neighbouring armies were equipped. For example, the highly regarded French 75s had a rate of fire nearly four times that of the standard Austro-Hungarian gun, and they had fewer of them, with thirty-eight guns to every division compared to Serbia's fifty-four.[19] To further compound their problems, those guns with which they were supplied had fewer rounds per unit than comparable armies, ranging from a third to two-thirds compared with the French and the Germans.

Even in small arms the Austro-Hungarian had initially been seriously disadvantaged by shortsightedness and penny-pinching. As far back as 1851, so-called experts pronounced the recently introduced breech-loading rifle an unnecessary luxury and one which would simply encourage wasteful expenditure of ammunition. After all, Vienna contained a perfectly good arsenal capable of producing much cheaper muzzle-loaders which, it was claimed, were just as effective; these had served the infantrymen quite well up to then. The war with Prussia in 1866 soon disabused even the most diehard stick-in-the-mud of this illusion and forced the adoption of the breech-loader. This gun alone would not have changed the outcome of the 1866 conflict, but it would certainly have allowed Austria's infantry to acquit themselves far more effectively against the so-called 'Needle-Guns' of the opposing Prussians.

These shortages prompted the chief of the General Staff, the irascible Conrad von Hotzendorf, to oppose signing up to the Hague Disarmament Conference in 1907. He cynically remarked that 'the present condition of our army has already an appearance of permanent limitation of armaments',[20] and claimed he could not imagine how much further its army could be denuded of its capacity to wage war. This was not lost on Germany either, and despite having achieved a rapprochement since 1866, and signing a landmark treaty to that effect in 1879, there were voices in Berlin challenging the value of any pact. One politician had even asked whether 'it really pays us to bind ourselves so tightly to this phantasm of a state which is cracking in every direction',[21] and another asked if Germany was simply maintaining the alliance out of a sense of 'diplomatic inertia'.[22] Such was the extent of this lack of faith that the German field marshal, Count Schlieffen, designed his famous plan so that France should be attacked first in the event of a future conflict partly because Austria-Hungary could not be relied upon to move in time.[23] In order to maintain even a modest level of funding, however, the finances of the empire had to be sufficient to allow the government to approve its budgets. Here fortunately, the joint finance ministry appeared to have met with some success.

Since the early days of the Confederation and the turmoil of 1848, various reforms and widespread liberalisation in trade and investment had lain the groundwork for an improvement in the empire's economic situation. A spur to this had been a commercial treaty signed with Prussia in 1853, under the provisions of which it abolished the majority of its import duties and lowered its tariffs in return for more advantageous access to the *Zollverein*. The opening in Vienna of the Credit Anstadt by Anselm Rothschild in 1855 gave the empire the added fillip of access to further capital and investment, which it could use to build up infrastructure and fund other projects. In 1873, to showcase such progress, Vienna hosted the most ambitious trade fair to date, at least five times larger than the previous one held in France. Over 12 hectares it offered 194 pavilions for 35,000 exhibitors from thirty-five countries. Attracting 7 million visitors, this initiative was intended to project the image of a vibrant, outward-looking and cosmopolitan nation succeeding perfectly well outside the German single market with its own highly successful self-contained economy. Although it made a loss, the publicity generated by the event was considered to have made it worthwhile.

Though perhaps some way behind the economies of the United Kingdom, Germany and France, Austria-Hungary was gradually catching up. Pig iron consumption increased four-fold between 1881 and 1911, and railways, in which industry Austria-Hungary had at one time led Germany, expanded likewise between 1870 and 1911.[24] By 1913, Austria-Hungary produced 44 million metric tonnes of coal; just over 1 million metric tons of petroleum, in which it was almost self-sufficient; 3.3 billion metric tons of iron ore; 2.6 million metric tons of crude steel;[2] and 4,000 tons of copper,[26] running a budget surplus in 1889 and by 1913 experiencing annual growth of 4.8 per cent.[27] As impressive as this performance may have been, Austria-Hungary still accounted for only 5.6 per cent of all European exports in 1910, compared to 20.4 per cent for Germany and even 8.9 per cent for its 'backward' neighbour Russia. Such figures seem to reflect Austria-Hungary's underlying insularity. Within its unwieldy political and customs union, each component served as a seamless exporter or importer of goods and services to or from other parts of the empire: iron, coal and manufactured goods from Bohemia and Moravia, oil from Galicia and agricultural produce from Hungary and Croatia. As the Austrian philosopher Robert Musil reflected, 'There was no ambition for world markets or world power ... ruinous sums were spent on the army, but only just enough to secure its position as the second weakest among the Great Powers.'[28]

Economic growth was accompanied by associated social costs as workers flooded into the cities of the empire to seek employment. They frequently experienced substandard housing and even worse conditions in the factories, mines and foundries. Rising awareness among the working class resulted inevitably in further restlessness on the shop floor. Fear of the consequences of such agitation led to an anti-terror law in 1884, and two years later anti-socialist legislation was introduced. Those brought to trial on charges of sedition would not face an impartial judiciary, either. After 1886, juries were dispensed with in political trials, with all the implications that had for due process. However, seeing the merits of a more compliant workforce and the advantages of undermining the platforms of more liberal political parties, Vienna thought it prudent to address some of the root causes of working-class unrest. A series of legislative measures were undertaken, delivering a reduction in working hours and restrictions on the use of child and female labour in factories and mines. Sickness and accident insurance were also introduced in 1887 and 1888 respectively to provide some sort of safety net for those prevented from working through no fault of their own. These measures only applied to workers in the cities, however. In the countryside, where the prospect of civil disorder was more remote, the landowners were left to carry on much as they wished. Nevertheless, such legislation alone could not quell growing and persistent manifestations of disquiet. In 1911, a demonstration in Vienna, organised by the Social Democrats in protest at living and working conditions, turned into a riot. Many were killed and injured when the authorities panicked and mobilised the cavalry, sending sabre-wielding troopers into the crowd.[29]

Although the Dual Monarchy was undergoing considerable change, it was still to Vienna, the old centre of the Austrian Empire, that most of its Cisleithanian subjects looked for a sense of continuity and reassurance. It was also where the emperor felt most at home, with the unchanging nature of the royal court shielding Vienna's 2 million citizens from the stark realities of the threatening world beyond.[30] The city's role as an oasis of stability also led to a reputation as something of a sleepy-hollow, however. One commentator claimed that 'Vienna has no night life',[31] and as late as 1906 Austrian playwright and critic Herman Bahr remarked how 'in Europe one knows of Vienna, the place where it is forever Sunday'.[32] Others were kinder. British journalist and historian Henry Wickham Steed observed lyrically how the city's 'combination of stateliness and homeliness … the comparative absence of architectural monstrosities and the Italian influence everywhere apparent, contribute … to charm the eye and ear of every travelled visitor'.[33] Russian revolutionary Vladimir Lenin was also beguiled; despite it representing everything he despised about capitalism and monarchy, he thought Vienna was a 'beautiful and vivacious' city in which to plot the overthrow of his Czar.[34]

For so long aloof and detached, by the turn of the century Vienna's quaint isolation was threatened by hundreds of thousands of visiting tourists. Many came to witness such opulent ceremonies as Corpus Christi Day, when the devoutly Catholic emperor piously observed the veneration of the Eucharist. The procession was a stunning spectacle, glowingly described one year by Francis-Joseph's aide-de-camp. The emperor ostentatiously processed to St Stephen's Cathedral in a state coach drawn by six horses, with

> … the archdukes preceding him in state carriages drawn by four horses … the wagons made of glass and full of gold ornaments, the stallion's precious harnesses – magnificent Spanish-bred white horses – the coachmen, lackeys and servants holding the horses in their gold embroidered black rococo dresses, with white stockings, shoes and buckles, and wigs under the large tricorns and bicorns decorated with gold braid and ostrich feathers…[35]

Another tourist was the destitute young artist Adolf Hitler, who appreciated that such grand imperial centres, with all their pomp and show, served another purpose:

> … the little man who arrives in a big city, who arrives in the imperial capital, he shall have a sense of that's where the king, the sovereign lives…[36]

According to August Kubizek, a friend of Hitler's from the time, he was in such awe of the opulent architectural treats offered by the capital that he became 'downright intoxicated' by them.[37] The foundations of such lavishness began in the 1850s, when the city walls were dismantled and work began on the Ringstrasse or Ring Boulevard. It was largely completed by 1865, and when Hitler visited the vast complex of classical structures, he remarked that they were the 'most beautiful line of streets that has ever been built'.[38] The Vienna Academy of Fine Arts was also situated here. Founded in 1692 as a private institution, it was relocated in 1877 to a grand new structure designed by Theophil Hansen. Hitler would apply to study here in 1907, and again in 1908, suffering rejection on both occasions.

More drastic – and, to some, startling – changes were gradually being introduced, exemplified by the work of the revolutionary Viennese architect Adolf Loos. He designed the eponymous Loohaus in Michaelplatz, one of the central features of Viennese Modernism. His more conservative critics called it 'the house without eyebrows' because Loos eschewed what he considered architecturally superfluous window lintels. Indeed, he had declared that 'ornaments are crimes', and felt that those responsible for the Ring Boulevard had committed an 'immoral act'[39] with their entablatures, Corinthian columns, cornices and, of course, lintels.

Francis-Joseph, appalled by innovations such as the Loohaus, could take comfort from some of the more traditional and familiar structures of the capital, such as the Vienna Court Opera House, completed in 1868 by the Czech Joseph Hlavka. Hitler believed it to be 'the most magnificent opera house in the world'.[40] Architects Gottfried Semper and Karl Freiherr von Hasenauer, followed it with their Burgtheatre, finished in 1888 as part of the emperor's sprawling Ring Boulevard.

The metropolis was facing change in other ways. Its Jewish population had been growing exponentially as a result of migration from the far more repressive Russian Empire since the 1880s. By 1910 the Jewish population in Vienna stood at 175,000, smaller than that in Prague or Budapest but nonetheless subject to increasing suspicion and discrimination. These seemingly strange newcomers were distrusted, feared and resented by the introvert Viennese, frequently derided as destitute pedlars who refused to integrate and whose commercial and professional prowess engendered jealousy and envy. Karl Lueger, the city's controversial mayor from 1867 to 1910, was reported to have warned menacingly that 'should the Jews threaten our homeland they would suffer',[41] and during the 1895 mayoral election he referred to them as the 'Jewish threat'.[42] There were even more extreme elements, especially the Pan Germans, who sought to expunge such 'undesirables' from their midst entirely. Landowner and politician Georg Ritter von Schonerer advocated for those he deemed unwelcome under the monarchy to be removed in order to preserve the empire's purity, and saw anti-Semitism as 'a keystone of the national idea'.[43] The Richard Wagner Association in Vienna was founded specifically to 'free German culture of all its fake and Jewish elements',[44] and Professor of Medicine Theodor Billroth, widely lauded as the father of modern abdominal surgery, held similar views:

> ... no Jew, just like no Iranian, Frenchman or New Zealander, or an African can ever become a German ... Jewish Germans are nothing but Jews who happen to speak German...[45]

It was seen as the duty of the extremist German press to join in with such calumnies. In 1908, the *Deutsches Volksblatt* carried an editorial in which it claimed that the Jews were literally the manifestation of everything evil in society. It asserted that they 'ruin peoples and destroy states' and that 'all national property has fallen into Jewish hands'.[46] Even Francis-Joseph was reported to have casually asked, 'We do everything we can to protect the Jews, but who really is not an anti-Semite?'[47] Despite every sort of discrimination, insult and humiliation that men such as Schonerer, Lueger and Billroth could heap upon them, however, the Jews remained a feature of Viennese life – and an expanding one at that. The Viennese Jewish contingent even felt confident enough to successfully host the eleventh annual Zionist Conference in September 1913.

While the Jews of Vienna were subject to discrimination, in other parts of the empire the authorities were mostly allowed to treat minorities as they wished, even if they were theoretically afforded the protections of the Fundamental Laws. The privileged Poles of Galicia were fully aware of the treatment meted out to their compatriots in German or Russian Poland,[48] but they were content to offer fealty to Francis-Joseph as long as they were left to exploit their Ruthene peasants in shameless collusion with their Magyar neighbours.[49] In 1861 Galicia was granted the autonomy denied to Bohemia and Moravia, but of course the attendant privileges were largely restricted to the Poles, and guaranteed by voting qualifications which gave landowners and industrialists virtual veto over the decisions of the *Sejm*. Subsequent reforms were made to education in Galicia, and some light industries were established, including food processing, sugar refining and oil production, but the region remained backward due to the resistance of the landowners to meaningful change. Agriculture also remained neglected, and widespread poverty persisted throughout the region, but many Ruthene peasants were becoming increasingly disinclined to continue with the status quo. As discontent festered, more hard-line elements began to dominate the political landscape, until in 1898 the Polish governor of Galicia was assassinated. Galician nationalism, as the Polish overlords feared, was also becoming more pro-Russian, and many were agitating for union with their Ukrainian cousins.

Nor were such expressions of dissatisfaction restricted to the farther reaches of the empire. The Czechs, too, resented being treated less favourably than their German neighbours and both had long vied for greater influence. The prospect of the Czechs having the upper hand was, however, deplored by men such as the German liberal Ernst von Plener, who was at pains to explain that 'we can sacrifice the Ruthenes to the Poles, the Slavs and Romanians to the Magyars, because Ruthenes and Slovaks can be Polonised and Magyarised ... but Germans can't be Czechised'.[50]

In an attempt to secure their predominance, and in response to electoral reforms enacted in 1882 in the Bohemian Diet, the Germans responded in 1884 with demands of their own. They wanted German to be recognised as the 'state language', a privilege enjoyed by the Magyars in Hungary, but this was rejected. Then, in 1886, the Czechs managed to secure the recognition of their native tongue as the 'internal language' in Bohemian and Moravian high courts in Prague and elsewhere. Although these concessions still did not go far enough for groups such as the radical 'Young Czechs', they riled the Germans. These younger agitators had ousted the last of the more moderate 'Old Czechs' from the *Reichsrat* by 1891, a move heralding an even more extreme form of nationalism and bringing clashes with other minorities even closer.

The previous year, Chancellor Taaffe had sought some middle way, and had managed to get the Czechs and the Germans to compromise on some functions of the province, especially with regards to the judiciary, but these were scuppered by the Young Czechs and radical Germans. By the 1890s, disputes between the two communities over the recognition of equal status created endless problems. Much of the intercommunal violence endemic during this period came from this issue. Finally, in 1893, martial law was declared in Prague when the police felt unable to cope with the deteriorating situation. This led to countless arrests and the trials of alleged ringleaders, who faced terms of imprisonment of up to eight years. In 1897, Taaffe's successor, Count Badeni-Lang, made another flawed attempt to give Czechs and Germans equal standing. Due to obstruction by German deputies, it failed to pass through the *Reichsrat*. With more violence in the streets, the reform had to be abandoned in 1899.

This perpetual squabbling was holding up other business in the *Reichsrat*, and between 1897 and 1904 much essential legislation had to be passed by decree. Otherwise debates were reduced to shouting matches, and because there was no single official language in the chamber, up to ten dialects could be spoken at once as deputies constantly interrupted and spoke over one another. Furthermore, there were no interpreters. With the minutes only taken in German, educated guesses had to be made as to what was being said. This chaos led, in the words of one commentator, to 'less a legislature than a cacophony',[51] and meaningful debate was all but impossible. Representative Wilhelm Ellenbogen was appalled, asking, 'Why [is] the Austrian Parliament...

[the] most vulgar in the world... with its... rude manners ... and ... boyish yelling and screaming?'[52] The state of anarchy into which the *Reichsrat* had descended even reached the ears of media moguls in the United States, prompting *Harper's Weekly* to despatch the author Mark Twain to Vienna late in 1897 to see for himself.

Senior ministers came to accept that the best way to address such obstructionism was to broaden the franchise in the hope that this would make room for moderate voices on all sides.[53] A series of electoral reforms had been attempted over the last few decades, but the *Reichsrat* remained woefully unrepresentative of its people. The Germans, in particular, despite their resentment of the Czechs, actually held more seats than was justified by their share of the total population, undermining the very basis upon which the democratic process and the Fundamental Laws of 1867 were supposedly founded.

Consequently, universal adult male suffrage quotas for each national group were introduced in time for the *Reichsrat* elections of 1907. When the new parliament of 515 seats was elected under the new system, Ruthenes, Poles, Czechs and Slovenes had more seats, while the Pan Germans and Radicals lost some.[54] Nevertheless, the Germans still had the lion's share with 241 while the Czechs had ninety-seven and the Serbs had just three. Translated into party allegiances, the main left-wing party, the Social Democrats, consisted of fifty Germans, twenty-three Czechs, seven Poles, five Italians and two Ruthenes.[55] This formula suggests that politics, rather than ethnicity, largely dictated party structures.

The reforms did little to instil any greater sense of decorum, however, and the chamber was now host to thirty different parties, still barracking one another in unintelligible tongues. When a draft bill was brought before parliament in the spring of 1909 there was such pandemonium that pacifist and Nobel Laureate Bertha von Suttner was driven to distraction by the shenanigans: 'whistles, drums, foghorns ... swinging fists, torn off coat collars, bitten fingers ... it really is as if Parliament is trying to commit suicide.'[6] Ironically, an ordinance insisting that interpreters be employed was not introduced until 1917. With the *Reichsrat* having only a year left to run, this was to prove far too little and far too late.

By contrast, Hungary's Diet in Budapest faced few of the challenges encountered by its sister parliament in Vienna. This was quite simply due to the fact that the Magyars had no intention of sharing power with any others. Just as they dominated the Delegations to the three shared ministries, they wielded disproportionate influence in parliament. By blatant manipulation, they controlled 90 per cent of the 400 seats;[57] if representation had been proportionate, the Slovaks would have had forty-five deputies instead of just three, and the Romanians sixty-eight rather than five.[58] As early as 1866, Magyar magnate Julius Andrassy went so far as to insist that 'the Slavs are not fit to govern, they must be ruled', and consequently racial divisions were even more engrained here than in Austria. The Magyars would foil any attempt to sabotage their special status. A bill legalising the marriage of Jews and non-Jews was thrown out by the Hungarian Diet in 1883 for fear that it would dilute Magyar bloodlines.

The Magyars were helped in their exercise of power by the fact that the writ of the Fundamental Laws which offered protections to Francis-Joseph's Austrian subjects did not apply in Hungary. Instead, his coronation oath set out his eastern kingdom's own interpretation of human rights. Consequently, the king solemnly undertook to 'uphold the rights, privileges, liberties, patents, laws, and good and approved ancient customs of inhabitants of all ranks, religious and secular ... [and to maintain intact] ... the rights of Hungary and its associated lands, its constitution, lawful independence and territorial integrity'.[59]

Moreover, unlike the empire as a whole, Hungary was declared a unitary state, to which all people of whatever ethnic group belonged. Although the use of regional languages was permitted at local level in courts of law, the administration and higher education, in the national Diet, educational institutions and the civil service only Magyar was allowed.[60] This automatically excluded anybody who could not speak Magyar, and the language was far from easy to learn. This situation would persist right up until the end of the Dual Monarchy, and by 1913 over 95 per cent of government officials were Magyar, as were 92 per cent of county officials, 89 per cent of doctors, and 90 per cent of all judges.[61] Such inequality could only be addressed through legislation, as was attempted in the *Reichsrat*, but that would require a more representative government and fewer vested interests. A solution was only barely touched upon by the half-hearted electoral reforms introduced in 1908. This theoretically conceded universal suffrage, but property qualifications, literacy tests and plural votes for the nobility kept power firmly in the hands of the wealthy.[62] A further reform, adopted in 1913, added another 800,000 people to the electoral roll, but this was partly negated by the voting age being raised from twenty-one to twenty-four. Consequently, just 6.5 per cent of the population had the vote even by 1914, almost all of them Magyars.

It was not only in government that the Magyars sought to impose their will. The three Slovak secondary schools were closed down in 1874, and in 1879 it was made compulsory that all primary school lessons were taught in Magyar. The last fourteen non-Magyar secondary schools were placed under supervision in 1883, and all remaining secondary schools had to teach lessons in Magyar. Later, in 1907, even more draconian regulations were introduced, extending state control to church schools and requiring teachers to take an oath of loyalty. Those who failed to ensure their pupils had reached the required standard of Magyar could be fined, and any textbooks, maps and globes used in teaching had to refer not to Austria-Hungary but to Hungary and Austria.

Such had been the Magyar determination to eradicate the identities of their minorities that of the 1,971 Slovak primary schools in existence in 1874, just 327 remained in 1919, and out of 353 teaching Ruthenian in 1871, none whatsoever remained by 1915.[63] By 1913 over 80 per cent of the students graduating from high school were Magyar,[64] and of all the newspapers read throughout a theoretically multicultural Hungary some 85 per cent were in Magyar.[65] Little wonder, then, that literacy rates were appalling throughout Transleithania. In Bukovina, 513,000 out of 730,000 were unable to read and write, while illiteracy rates among Ruthenes, Serbo-Croats and Romanians stood at 60 per cent.

Language and culture were key weapons of repression, of course, but they were also vital factors in fuelling the fires of discontent. Such was the ingrained nature of this racial inequality that one commentator was moved to observe quite late in the empire's existence that the 'poorest Magyar, even though he be a landless man, [considers] himself to be the superior, though he be in rags, of the non-Magyars'.[66]

The wealthier Magyars used their social and political advantages to govern the country much as a colonial landowner would, enjoying a comfortable lifestyle while the peasants toiled in the fields. Thus, despite being a largely agrarian society, small landowners were relatively few and far between in Hungary. Less than one-third of the land was owned by those cultivating their own properties, and most of these properties consisted of less than 20 acres. Instead, most peasants were wage labourers on the great *latifundia*, of which over 300 averaged in excess of 40,000 acres. One, the Esterhazy estate, consisted of 500,000 acres, and one bishopric alone covered more than 250,000 acres.[67] The economic stranglehold enjoyed by the elite was reinforced by a tax system which only reflected the interests of Hungarian landlords, despite this hindering commercial and industrial progress. As a result, many an ambitious or 'energetic Magyar peasant'[68] had little alternative than to seek a better life elsewhere. Despite the ruthless way the Magyar landowners preserved their status, they could nonetheless present to the casual observer an urbane and civilised persona. One remarked that 'the Magyar noble is a cultured and pleasant gentleman ... courteous, hospitable and genial',[69] an evaluation that would not perhaps have passed muster with Ruthene or even Magyar peasants.

By the 1860s, 90 per cent of exports to Austria were made up of agricultural goods, increasingly feeding the factory workers in burgeoning complexes like the Skoda factories in Bohemia, but they would come to face stiff competition from other countries. Diversification seemed to be the answer, and by 1880 there were 800 breweries, 120 sugar factories, and 400 distilleries, as well as sawmills, paper factories, coalmines, hotels and spas.[70] By 1913, manufactures would account for 44 per cent of its exports to the rest of the empire.[71] Nevertheless, even in 1918 one visitor was to note that 'the Magyar disdains trade or industry', content to leave such important aspects of the economy to others.[72] They were more interested in thinking up new ways to 'neglect ... subject peoples of small account, such as the Ruthenes' and pursue the 'oppression of others of greater political influence, such as the Slovaks'.[73]

The contrast between the 2 million-strong German community in Hungary and their counterparts in Austria could not have been starker. As Austria pushed eastwards following the defeat of the Ottoman Empire towards the end of the seventeenth century, it was the Germans who first went to defend and then colonise these newly acquired lands. Incentivised with lucrative grants of land, generous loans and other sweeteners, they eventually grew into a significant part of the ethnographic and economic landscape. Other than Budapest, the Germans lived mainly in small, isolated enclaves no bigger than villages, where they largely kept to themselves but enjoyed a special and privileged status. This changed with the rise of the Magyars, especially after 1867, and saw 'both German influence and German population decline'.[74]

Increasingly marginalised and resented, the Germans in Hungary became even more insular, maintaining the 'purity of their race by a calculated disdain of the other[s] ... living in groups of villages ringed round with non-Germans who [the German] despises and at times dreads'.[75] Many others chose to vote with their feet, embracing the prospect of a better life in the United States.[76] Such departures left whole communities without 'German place names [and] without a single German inhabitant', which the Magyars eagerly erased 'from the official registers'.[77] In the meantime, the remaining Germans experienced similar discrimination to their peers, and it was found that in the west of the country German schools made up 3 per cent, 'even though 17 per cent of the population was German'. This was all part of the policy of 'Magyarising the country's children' and eradicating their German roots,[78] but despite such efforts the Germans resisted, with illiteracy rates among the Germans still at just 3.12 per cent.[79] They also proved surprisingly stubborn. In 1911, considerable pockets of ethnic Germans clung on in their ancestral homes, mostly in the north around Budapest, on the banks of the Danube to the south, in the Banat and in eastern Transylvania, with a smattering in Slovakia.

For both halves of the Dual Monarchy there was one group which, above all, posed the greatest threat to the integrity of Francis-Joseph's empire, and it was those peoples known collectively as the Southern Slavs. Discounting the Poles, the only minorities with a semblance of autonomy were the people of Croatia-Slavonia. However, it would still prove too little to meet their aspirations. Admittedly, the provincial Sabor (parliament) of Croatia-Slavonia, granted by the Magyars in 1868 under an agreement known as the *Nagodba*,[80] offered Croatia-Slavonia limited self-government and access to some representation in the National Diet.[81] However, the governor was appointed by the king on the advice of his Hungarian prime minister and was responsible to the Magyar-dominated parliament. His role was essentially to keep an eye on the procedures of the Sabor and ensure its activities did not exceed its remit, especially as the national government controlled 55 per cent of the Sabor's budget and could react to any unwelcome measures by cutting off its funds.

Predictably, not all Croats were satisfied with this limited autonomy. In 1905, a conference of Croat politicians in Fiume demanded further reforms. One solution was the union of all southern Slavs in both halves of the Dual Monarchy in a single self-governing province. Such an idea went much too far for the Magyars, who had no intention of relinquishing any more autonomy than had already been devolved through the *Nagodba*. Nor did the proposal go anywhere near far enough for many Croats. Moreover, for arguably the most discontented minority in either half of the empire, the Serbs, it was a travesty. For many, the only acceptable solution was incorporation into the neighbouring Serbian kingdom.

A vassal of the Ottomans until achieving independence under Russian protection in 1830, Serbia reached full nationhood in 1878 following the Russo-Turkish War, which also gave Austria-Hungary control of Bosnia-Herzegovina. By 1900 many Serbs were actively eyeing their ethnic cousins – 100,000 in Dalmatia, 500,000 in Hungary, and 650,000 in Croatia-Slavonia – as potential components of a Greater Serb state.[82] This prospect may have appealed to fellow Serbs, but it did not endear itself to all the Slavs of the empire, no matter how discontented they may have been with the status quo. As we shall see later, with their different culture and outlook, these communities were wary of their more Orthodox cousins in Serbia and felt little sense of affinity.[83] Nevertheless, Francis-Joseph's heir apparent, Francis-Ferdinand, whose more enlightened views sounded alarm bells within the empire's higher echelons, was among those who felt that a devolved Southern Slavic province would ease tensions and counter the pull of Serbia. Von Hotzendorf, however, feared it was just a first step to Austria losing its southern provinces entirely, and thus almost its entire coastline; he warned gravely that such a development would ultimately 'relegate the monarchy to the status of a small power'.[84]

A constant fly in the ointment was Bosnia-Herzegovina. It had been administered jointly by Austria and Hungary since its detachment from the Ottoman Empire in 1878, but it remained technically under Turkish rule. Instability in the wider Balkan region led to fears that Bosnia-Herzegovina might fall within the orbit of one of its neighbours, so Vienna took the unilateral decision in 1908 to annex it outright. Such an addition to the territory of the empire perhaps ought to have been welcomed by those of an imperialist bent, but many Pan-German newspapers were instead forthright in their condemnation of the action. One, the *Alldeutsches Tagblatt*, complained angrily that 'any strengthening of Slavdom means a weakening of Germandom'[85] in the empire, a fear shared by the Hungarian government with regard to their own special status. Furthermore, these additional Slavs would be closer to Budapest than Vienna, and a potential source of agitation for separatism. Indeed, Serbia was now geographically closer to Austria-Hungary proper than ever before, and this fact could make collaboration between Slav nationalists and Belgrade even easier. These worries were vindicated by reports that Croat students were openly visiting Belgrade, and to the hardliners in Vienna and Budapest this could have only one purpose.

The annexation provoked widespread outrage, particularly in St Petersburg, which saw itself as the Slavs' protector, but also in Constantinople where the move was seen as a provocation. In response to the annexation, Turkey imposed a trade embargo which was copied by other Balkan states. Serbia understandably viewed the annexation with trepidation, as the province had now been officially absorbed into the neighbouring empire, making the prospect of a Greater Serbia more distant than ever. Joining in the chorus of disapproval, Belgrade imposed sanctions on goods from Austria-Hungary, and Vienna imposed a counter-embargo on Serbian agricultural imports. Serbia found alternative markets for its produce in Greece and Germany, however, and the impact of Vienna's tactics proved minimal.[86] Instead, Serbia proceeded to collude with nationalists inside the empire and conspired to sow further discord and disunity among the Southern Slavs. Thus the running sore of instability within the region persisted, and even an event which ought to have been one of the greatest celebrations of its existence could not mask the growing estrangement felt by various groups within the Dual Monarchy.

In 1908, the sixtieth year of Francis-Joseph's reign, a huge party was to be hosted in Vienna to celebrate this milestone and recognise the imperial unity which he embodied. His court planned to mark this momentous event with festivities and expressions of fealty to the aging emperor, but instead the proceedings emphasised the underlying divisions and rancour permeating the monarchy. The Pan-Germans wanted instead to pay homage to one of the honoured guests, the Kaiser,[87] while the Magyars claimed that as far as they were concerned his reign over them only began in 1867, not 1848, and they had already had their forty-year anniversary the year before. On the day of the parade, the conservative-leaning nationalist Hungarian daily newspaper *Budapesti Hirlap* wished Francis-Joseph 'happiness, well-being and blessing' but added sullenly that no one from Hungary would take part because the Austrians were behaving 'rudely, antagonistically and contemptuously towards us'.[88] The Czechs also refused to participate in the parade over another perceived slight by Vienna's mayor, Lueger,[89] and Italians noses were put out of joint by their billing in the parade. The Croats, too, found cause for offence over what they considered to be insulting aspersions made about them, although an apology did eventually bring them back on board.[90]

The committee formed to organise the event had funds available so that those from the empire's farthest reaches could attend the celebrations, and in spite of the brickbats being exchanged many did. However, the impressions some of the visitors made shocked many of their hosts, whose observations were often less than complimentary. Author Karl Klaus remarked upon their 'ugliness', while the architect Loos was even more disparaging, commenting how 'the parade included peoples who even during the migration of nations would have been considered backward.'[91] It was hardly surprising, then, with such opinions prevalent among their hosts, that the Czechs and Croats felt so affronted. The militaristic nature of the parade managed to raise eyebrows too. Although it was inevitable that the empire's Common Army would take centre stage, Bertha von Suttner called it 'a raise-the-arms circus ... glorification of any imaginable savagery'.[92]

Nevertheless, 12,000 people, 4,000 in historic costume and 8,000 in national dress, managed to bury their differences and dutifully march past the dais from which the seventy-eight-year-old emperor in field marshal's uniform took the salute. Nonetheless, having provoked so much animosity, many must have felt the anniversary celebrations could not end soon enough. Mercifully, events came to a close on 2 December, with the ringing of church bells all over the city and a firework display. Even what ought to have been a joyful conclusion to the festivities produced a dark side, when the tightly packed crowds started pushing and shoving one another. A panic broke out, and in the ensuing melee four died and 106 were crushed.

Meanwhile, the Czechs and Hungarians found another means by which to cock a snook at the empire. That year, they sent their own teams to the London Summer Olympics, determined to emphasise their individual national credentials. As there was no opportunity to participate as a unified Austro-Hungarian team, Austria was left with little choice but to do the same. The Czechs for their part marched into the opening ceremony under the banner 'Boheme' waving a red-and-white flag. The Hungarian and Austrian teams likewise had their own flags and team names. The Czechs participated in athletics, fencing, gymnastics, tennis and wrestling, losing 9–7 against Hungary in the men's team sabre event. The Czechs left with two bronze medals in fencing; Hungary won three gold, four silver and two bronze; Austria left with a single bronze medal in a swimming event. Hitler's judgement of this 'old mosaic, the cement binding the various little stones together [but which] had grown old and begun to crumble'[93] therefore appeared to be vindicated.

Even at this late stage, there remained among the Dual Monarchy's nationalities those not yet ready to see it put out of its misery. During the bitter acrimony experienced between Czechs and Germans in the 1890s, leading Czech nationalist Tomas Masaryk had expressed his conviction that 'we want Austria to remain a great power, but we also wish that Austria should be great and powerful inwardly.'[94] Twenty years later, in 1913, with the empire having just five years left to run, he remained convinced that he would seek 'to strengthen the whole' rather than see it dissolve entirely.[95] Foreign observers also detected a reluctance to rent the empire asunder quite yet. Henry Wickham Steed wrote, 'I have been unable to perceive ... any sufficient reason why, with moderate foresight on the part of the dynasty, the Habsburg Monarchy should not retain its rightful place in the European community.'[96]

Furthermore, in spite of the rancour which accompanied his anniversary in 1908, deep residual respect and affection remained among the majority of the peoples of the empire for their aging monarch, and it was in essence this sense of loyalty which bound them together. Ultimately, the empire's death knell would be struck following the assassination of Archduke Francis Ferdinand. Despite being a sponsor of Slav unity, albeit within the empire, he and his wife would perish at the hands of Bosnian Gavrilo Princip on an official visit to Sarajevo, the capital of Bosnia-Herzegovina, on 28 June 1914. Encouraged by ministers in Belgrade, he provided the catalyst for the First World War and the ultimate destruction of the empire. The strains of the subsequent war would finally bring the Dual Monarchy to its knees.

2

A Sudden, Blessed Opportunity

Bismarck, the man who created the German Empire in 1871. (Library of Congress)

We left Bismarck at the top of his game, having secured the parting of the ways with Austria in 1866, which left Prussia dominating the new North German Confederation. His next step was to entrench and codify the new union, producing a constitution which bound its members ever more closely together. The final document took two months of debate and required the ratification of every state parliament, but it was finally adopted on 1 July 1867 and embraced a raft of provisions for which the new Reichstag, or parliament, and *Bundesrat*, or Federal Council, would now take sole responsibility. These would include the right to free movement and settlement, naturalisation, commerce and navigation, customs and taxes, weights and measurements, coinage, banking, copyright law, and the regulation of railways and waterways, along with matters relating to criminal, contractual and commercial law, plus the army, navy and militia. States would also have to agree to the judgements of the *Bundesrat*, which served as the Federation's de facto court of justice. There was now a *Zollbundesrat*, or Federal Council of Customs, consisting of representatives from the states, and a *Zollparlement*, which it was hoped would encourage closer cooperation with the southern states, because although they were not yet full members of the Federation, they would be permitted to send delegates.

Despite the presence of delegates, Prussia would nevertheless exercise most of the leverage. This entire system effectively served to extend its influence in countries that were yet to be drawn closer by political means. The federal presidency was also to be permanently within the gift of the Prussian king, who was to have wide-ranging powers including the right to declare war and make peace, to negotiate treaties with third-party states outside of the federation and to introduce legislation. The federal president was also vested with the right to appoint or dismiss military officers, and to assemble or dissolve the Reichstag or the *Bundesrat*, although the Reichstag could not be dissolved without the *Bundesrat*'s agreement. On paper, the new constitution was widely perceived to be the model of democracy, respecting human rights and liberties, even comparing favourably with that of the United States. However, as we shall see later, Bismarck's cunning was deployed to ensure that true power and authority resided in Prussia alone.

Nevertheless, that situation was a few years away yet. Bismarck had to tread warily for now, as he was still not quite strong enough to push through all the reforms he had planned. He also had to bear in mind that the war against Francis-Joseph had polarised the German states, and many, including Saxony, Bavaria, Württemberg and Hanover, had allied themselves with Austria. Prussia's victory was down to its own power rather than the support of states such as Oldenburg, the Mecklenburgs and Brunswick. Consequently, when in 1867 Bismarck suffered a veto over his proposed extensions to the *Zollverein* to complement the creation of the North German Confederation, he had to stay his hand. Some of the southern states in particular feared that the proposals would be used as a stepping stone to even deeper integration with Prussia.

In Württemberg, the liberal-leaning People's Party was particularly wary of the Prussians. It led the campaign against Bismarck's plans, insisting that closer ties would mean higher taxes, conscription, and 'keeping your mouth shut' for fear of incurring the wrath of the bigger neighbour.[1] Such doubters did, however, concede that closer military cooperation was in their national interest as an insurance against renewed French aggression. Consequently, a number agreed to reform their armies to model them more along Prussian lines and follow a common rulebook for organisation and training, plus the establishment of a joint mobilisation plan. However, the varying extents of engagement between Prussia and the other states of the Confederation did not sit well with the principle of complete integration. For instance, Baden, feeling most exposed to France, adopted Prussia's model almost without exception. Württemberg, meanwhile, adopted Prussian regulations and equipment but not its uniforms, while Bavaria accepted the principle of conscription but insisted on keeping its own weapons, uniforms and tactics.[2]

Bismarck, naturally enough, had wanted a more extensive integration, and had submitted ideas for a joint war cabinet or Federal War Ministry, but these proposals were not warmly received.[3] Instead, the armies of the states were linked to the Prussian War Ministry by separate conventions, and Hesse, Saxony, Brunswick and Mecklenburg also retained extensive autonomy. Nevertheless, Bismarck had secured the nucleus of a unified army, and with the Prussians at its core it had the makings of a formidable fighting machine. Indeed, by 1870, even without the complete participation of all the states, it could call upon 15,000 officers and 715,000 men, and could be augmented with 6,500 reservist officers and a further 201,000 men if required.[4] Nor would it be too long before it was put to the test. If tightening the scope of the customs union was not a strong enough draw, Bismarck needed something else with which to hasten the closer union of the German states. A timely coup in Madrid in 1868 was to provide him with that.

In Spain's Glorious Revolution of 1868, Queen Isabella II had been deposed. With the throne empty, there was no shortage of nominations from neighbouring states for a new ruler. Bismarck obviously preferred the installation of one amenable to Prussia, and he saw this in the person of Prince Leopold of Hohenzollern-Sigmarinen. Emperor Napoleon III of France understandably saw a Prussian king as contrary to French interests, and applied pressure to have the Prussian nomination withdrawn. Despite Bismarck appearing to back down, the hostile environment that had been engendered seemed to be too good an opportunity for Bismarck to let pass. French emotions were running high, and he believed that the increasingly febrile atmosphere offered all the ingredients necessary to provoke an escalation. If Napoleon III was shown to present a threat, then Bismarck might just have the opportunity he needed to unite the German states in another war.

With mobs in both Paris and Berlin crying 'To the Rhine',[5] he concocted a scheme which he felt would bring about the results he sought. He doctored an innocuous note from the Prussian king – the so-called 'Ems Telegram', which had simply discussed the Prussian candidature – into an incendiary document guaranteed to exploit French sensitivities and provoke an equally aggressive reaction. Napoleon fell for the ruse, saw the contents of the document as an outright challenge and rashly declared war on 15 July 1870. The German states, too, fell for Bismarck's clever sleight of hand; convinced that the French posed a clear and present danger, they threw in their lot with Prussia. Napoleon however, had bitten off more than he could chew. Having fallen into Bismarck's trap, it was soon obvious just how completely outclassed his army was. It was but a shadow of the war machine which Napoleon Bonaparte had led to victory after victory against a coalition of enemies over fifty years before, and the weakness of the French army in the face of the Prussian war machine was even more stark than that of the Austrians in 1866. The outcome was almost a foregone conclusion, and French hopes of victory were crushed. Even Napoleon's personal intervention proved counterproductive; he was no Bonaparte, and his generals came to refer to him as 'our golden ball and chain'.[6] His troops were equally unimpressed by his martial prowess and responded to the traditional calls of 'Vive l'Empereur', with a less than respectful 'Un, deux, trois – Merde!'[7] A series of routs culminated in the Prussian victory at Sedan in September 1870, and in January of the following year Napoleon finally conceded defeat. On 10 May 1871, the two parties concluded peace with the signing of the Treaty of Frankfurt.

Like Austria five years before, France was left at the mercy of a German diktat. Whereas the price Austria had to pay for defeat was mainly its humiliation and loss of prestige, the cost to France was to be far more severe and long lasting. Once more that bone of contention – security – was to prove the hallmark of the subsequent settlement. To this end, Bismarck demanded that France cede the whole of Alsace, with its provincial capital at Strasbourg on the Rhine, and the northern section of Lorraine, with its capital of Metz on the Moselle. He claimed that Prussia needed the provinces, renamed Elsass-Lothringen, as insurance against future French aggression, insisting that it had been attacked by its neighbour thirty times in two hundred years and was thus entitled to take drastic preventative measures: 'An enemy whose honest friendship can never be won, must at least be rendered somewhat less harmful.'[8]

In any case, to many Germans this was not annexation but the restoration of German lands seized by Louis XIV years before. German philologist Friedrich Max Muller insisted that the people of Alsace and Lorraine were 'all German by blood, many by language, and, what is most important, they are still German by the simplicity and honesty of their religion'.[9] Heinrich Trietschke, an historian and Reichstag deputy, insisted that the population must have no say in their fate should they prove unwilling to join the Reich. He urged that, if necessary, 'against their will we shall restore them to their true selves.'[10] Indeed, one of the Prussian king's closest military advisers had urged that Prussia should go further and seize all of France up to the River Marne,[11] whereas Bismarck would have preferred a slightly less punitive peace. He wanted to leave Metz in French hands, but under pressure from the king, who said that too much blood had been spilt besieging the city to return it, and a domestic press which also insisted that it be annexed,[12] he acquiesced.

The loss of territory was not the only humiliation imposed upon France. A fine of 5 million Francs was also levied, and it had to be settled before the army of occupation would leave the country.[13] In the event, the French were so determined to be rid of the hated Prussians that the money was found and the debt paid off in just over two years. However, this fine, like the fate of the two provinces, was something neither country wanted to forget. As a young student, Prince William – later to become Kaiser William II – was discussing the war with his French tutor and the subject of the indemnity came up. William suggested that France was so prostrate at the end of the war that Germany could have demanded even more. Taunting his teacher, he added, 'Well, next time!' His tutor responded ominously, 'Next time, it will not be we who shall have to pay.'[14]

The territorial losses and financial exactions, however, were tempered by the realisation that France, like Austria before it, remained an important European power, and one with which Germany would need to do business in the future. Trade would remain a strong tie binding the two countries, and to this end the treaty contained the critical Article XI, which stated:

> The Treaties of commerce with the different States of Germany having been annulled by the war, the French Government and the German Government will adopt as the basis of their commercial relations the system of reciprocal treatment on the footing of most favoured nation ... [with respect to] import and export duties, transit dues [and] customs formalities...[15]

The Germans could have insisted that France bestow this 'most favoured nation' status upon them while denying the same benefit to their defeated foe, but the obvious economic benefits outweighed the pleasure of imposing further humiliations. It also served to broaden the scope of the *Zollverein*, benefitting the future German Empire as a whole and reflecting a policy of encouraging cordial relations, now that Bismarck had achieved his aims. This approach was underlined by Article XII of the treaty, which provided for the mutual recognition of rights for German citizens resident in France, and those French citizens domiciled in Germany. Thus he ameliorated as best as he could the possibility of renewed friction between the two countries, with the notable exception of Alsace-Lorraine. Bismarck could now turn his attention to completing his long-held ambition.

The Prussian chancellor had been able to exploit the war as 'a sudden, blessed opportunity to complete the work of national unification',[16] which may otherwise have taken much longer to realise. Prussian victory had also made it clear to those southern states – Württemberg, Bavaria, Baden and Hesse – which still resisted inclusion in the German Confederation that the cost of remaining outside – 'political isolation, economic decline and military uncertainty'[17] – was far too high a price to pay. It was now Bismarck's task to draw up the marriage papers for a union far tighter than even the Confederation had been.

This would involve negotiating individually with each of the members' leaders, most significantly their kings, princes, dukes and grand dukes. To this end, he invited them to Versailles, persuading or bribing them into joining the new imperial family. He had to use the most unscrupulous tactics and chicanery to achieve his ends, offering all kinds of special privileges, including the offer to the King of Bavaria of an annual pension of £15,000.[18]

Once Bismarck had achieved this final step, it then fell to the Reichstag of the North German Confederation to debate its own dissolution and the creation of an empire. Although some deputies were opposed as they feared it might lead to more war with France, the motion was voted through. Amid great fanfare, the Second Reich was officially declared by its first emperor, William I of Prussia, on 18 January 1871 in the Galerie des Glaces, Versailles. This new empire, the culmination of eight years of calculation and war, had transformed a customs union and free market into an extensive trading bloc of 41 million people, overwhelmingly dominated by Prussia, which possessed two-thirds of the land area and population, practically all the industrial capacity and eighteen of the twenty-one army corps which constituted what was now the Imperial German Army.[19] Four kingdoms, five grand duchies, six duchies, six principalities, three free cities and one imperial territory comprised the rest.[20] Having thoroughly eclipsed both France and Austria, a massive economic and military power had entered the European stage. Predictably, this seismic event in European politics was widely acclaimed by German nationalists. Trietschke welcomed unification as 'a great resurrection', and Max Muller exclaimed that Germans 'could breathe again more freely than before',[21] the empire's modernity and ambition comparing favourably with the perceived stagnation of Austria and the exhaustion of a France that was a shadow of its imperial past.

Yet this novel experiment still brought with it the baggage of semi-feudal rites, shrouded in ancient traditions that would not have been out of place in the arcane court of Francis-Joseph. These were still practiced in the Imperial Palace in the centre of Berlin, once home of the Electors of Brandenburg, then the Hohenzollern kings and now the emperor. From here he presided over protocols passed down from the Holy Roman Empire, which relied almost exclusively upon privilege and venal practices. In deference to these arcane customs, ancient rules of precedence based upon some fifty categories of nobility were obeyed, even though many had long fallen into disuse and existed in title only.[22] Nevertheless, because the emperor and below him the emperor were invested with extraordinary powers, any ambitious or aspiring noble had to be here, for it was within the confines of the palace that imperial favours and indulgences were dispensed, and lucrative sinecures granted.

Below the imperial court stood the upper house of parliament, the *Bundesrat*, and the lower house, the Reichstag, essentially the same as those designed by Bismarck in 1867 as the federal parliament of the North German Confederation. Under Bismarck's new Imperial German Constitution of 1871, parliament would go on largely unchanged, with the *Bundesrat* containing representatives from each of the twenty-five states, and the 397-seat Reichstag occupied by deputies elected through secret ballot by all males over twenty-five. However, not all of the states represented in the *Bundesrat* had the same number of votes. With seventeen, the Prussians held eleven more than the next largest state, Bavaria, and sixteen more than the smallest states, who only had one vote each. This gave Prussia a virtual veto over any constitutional changes of which Bismarck did not approve.

Moreover, the rural constituencies created in 1867, and again in 1871, dominated 67 per cent of the parliament. This was a deliberate ploy on the part of Bismarck because he believed the population in the countryside was more conservative and would therefore vote for equally traditional parties. Furthermore, in smaller rural constituencies it would be far easier for the Junker landlords and officials to manipulate and influence elections. Bismarck calculated that this should prevent any serious opposition to his policies, but new parties would emerge to challenge this comfortable assumption. Indeed, to hold on to power he would have to deliver things like pensions, workers' insurance and medical cover. These, like the bread and circuses of ancient Rome, were intended to keep the masses quiescent, and deter them from challenging the status quo for fear of losing their privileges.

Bismarck had other built-in safeguards intended to preserve his control over legislation. Deputies in the Reichstag could question the chancellor about his policies, but on the matter of foreign affairs, arguably the most important aspect of government business, much like in Francis-Joseph's monarchy they were hardly given a voice. Moreover, although both the Reichstag and the *Bundesrat* had to agree to bills, if the *Bundesrat* approved legislation it rarely went to the Reichstag for consent. Furthermore, instead of creating disciplined parties intended to form governments, the deputies generally functioned more as individuals, special interest groups or lobbyists.[23]

This lack of cohesion would have serious consequences for the effective scrutiny of legislation, in addition to making opponents easier to isolate or marginalise and reducing their capacity to bring the executive to account. Nor could the chancellor be dismissed in any case; if he met with more opposition from the deputies than he was prepared to tolerate, he could simply dissolve parliament and order new elections to be held,[24] a prospect few politicians ever relish. This situation, as Bismarck intended, relegated parliament to little more than a 'rubber stamp' for imperial legislation.[25]

The differences in structure between the imperial and Prussian parliaments also helped Bismarck manipulate proceedings. In Prussia's domestic parliament, the lower house was elected under a restricted three-tier voting arrangement which gave the wealthiest 15 per cent of the population (largely the landowning Junkers) the right to choose 85 per cent of the deputies. Therefore, even though the imperial parliament, with its universal male suffrage, at least gave the potential for more liberal government, the Prussians could simply fill the *Bundesrat* with conservatives and vote down legislation. Moreover, irrespective of the outcome of any election, government ministers like the chancellor were appointed by the emperor and owed their loyalty to him alone. Coming from the ranks of the civil service and the military, and with at least 40 per cent of them wealthy or of noble birth, they had little practical experience of either government or foreign affairs. In effect, like the deputies in parliament, the ministers were little more than functionaries in a complex matrix of government which effectively ruled by edict.

Perhaps a less conceited and more rational emperor might have borne in mind the extent of the power invested in his office, and installed ministers whose advice and council might temper his decisions. But William II, who ascended to the throne in 1888, would tolerate no such limitations on his sovereignty, especially as the existing arrangement perfectly suited his taste for autocratic government. This overlapping and conflicting system of government was, as he admitted when still Crown Prince, an 'ingeniously contrived chaos'.[26] It allowed Bismarck to dominate the government, but even he could not resist the growing popularity of liberalism forever. In 1890, despite an attempt to ban the Social Democratic Party, the Centre, Social Democratic and Progressive parties won half of the seats in the Reichstag.

The imperial government's powers were only slightly limited, at least in the early days, by each state retaining its own parliament, or Landtag, and controlling a range of domestic issues relating to justice, education, health and taxation.[27] The constitution allowed the imperial government to take the proceeds from customs and internal duties on staples such as salt, tobacco and other consumables, plus the income from the various postal and telegraph systems, but each state levied its own income tax and then passed a proportion of these revenues on to Berlin. Still, as far as it was within the gift of the imperial parliament, the new empire was to acquire as many of the characteristics of a single unitary political and economic entity as possible. German was the empire's official language, and was compulsory in civil administration, business and education. The year 1871 saw the establishment of a national currency, new commercial infrastructure including common weights and measures, a central bank and a uniform legal formula[28] – all essential to the prosperity of the inheritor of the German and North German Confederations.

Bismarck then embarked upon a series of incremental steps in foreign policy designed to consolidate and entrench the new empire, and he met with far more success than the Austrian emperor had. In 1873 he negotiated the so-called Three Emperors League with Russia and Austria-Hungary, while the signing of the Dual Alliance with Austria-Hungary in 1879, as we shall see, strengthened ties and rapprochement between the two. In 1882 Italy joined the latter arrangement, transforming it into the Triple Alliance. Bismarck had achieved his ultimate aim, consolidating German power and avoiding further conflict while underpinning the unity of the empire. This move could also be interpreted as an attempt to resurrect the long-abandoned Concert of Europe, compelling the monarchs of the most significant powers on the continent to take joint action against any threat to the status quo. However, these measures would be secondary to, and in many respects dependent upon, the empire's most significant creation.

Arguably the single most distinctive feature of imperial unity was the Kaiserliche Heer, or Imperial German Army. No longer a federal but an imperial military machine, each member was bound by his personal oath of allegiance to the Emperor. Its roles and responsibilities were enshrined within Article XI of the Imperial Constitution, by which every German male from the age of seventeen could be called up, and from the age of twenty up to forty-five-years could provide actual military service. Each recruit had to serve in the active army and army reserve for a total of seven years, of which two (or three in the case of the cavalry or horse artillery) had to be with the colours. Then he would serve three or four years in the reserve, during which time he was liable for training with his corps twice for a maximum of two months. The Imperial Constitution confirmed that the army would be modelled upon that of Prussia with respect to tactics, training, uniforms and equipment, and abide by the Prussian Penal Code of 3 April 1845, which covered all aspects of military law and discipline. These requirements were strengthened by the Military Laws of 1851 and 1874, which were designed to further unify the army, although for the time being both Bavaria and Württemberg were granted opt-outs from deeper integration, and along with Saxony were permitted their own war ministries, uniforms and training.

The one great advantage the German Imperial Army had over Austria-Hungary was its homogeneity, and therefore its ability to field a completely unified force, with none of the drawbacks dogging the army of the neighbouring monarchy. The most significant element here was language – generals down to the humblest private soldier knew and understood what was being conveyed without the need for a complicated system of translators or reliance upon basic words of command. Despite every effort at homogeneity and uniformity, however, the German officers, and even the emperor, could not order the members of the different states to like one another. There may have been none of the racial tensions prevalent in the Austro-Hungarian army, but there was still a considerable vein of rivalry, especially between Bavarians, Prussians and Saxons. This was particularly so because the Prussians were perceived to be the most aggressive within the army, the Bavarians coming a close second and others such as the Saxons proving to be the least warlike of all. Naturally, the Prussians, constituting the bulk of the empire in terms of geography, population and of course their contribution to the Imperial Army, harboured a considerable sense of superiority and seniority over their compatriots. Religion too, played a part in inter-unit rivalry, with Bavarians being overwhelmingly Catholic, compared to the Saxons who were almost exclusively Protestant. The Prussians were mostly Protestant themselves, but with a significant minority of Catholics, and Bismarck's later campaign against the Pope and the Roman Catholic clergy would prove a bitter reminder of his suspicions of the loyalties of those believed to look to Rome as their spiritual home.

The army's officer corps – elitist and drawn overwhelmingly from the highest echelons of society – was instrumental in binding the army to the state and maintaining a close affinity to the emperor, the Supreme War Lord.[29] Although the emperor had the power to appoint, demote or dismiss officers, the highly selective recruitment process was so riven with snobbery and class consciousness that candidates had to be approved by their brother officers as well as the army hierarchy before they could receive admission through its hallowed portals. Despite the army's size, progress was surprisingly slow; a junior officer could wait eighteen to twenty years for promotion, while even captains could languish for up to thirty years in the same rank. Whatever their position, however, these monocle-sporting, heel-clicking and punctiliously polite officers and gentlemen loved to assume a distinctive bearing and demeanour that made them appear distant, aloof and intimidating. To those critical of the militarism they personified – side-lined liberals and national minorities – they represented the worst of the new regime. Visiting Polish Marxist Rosa Luxemburg referred to them as 'darling arrogant Prussians, everyone looking as if he has swallowed the stick with which he had just been beaten'.[30]

The significance of the army to national life was further emphasised by the special status it enjoyed. Ominously, and perhaps unknown to people such as arch critic Rosa Luxemburg, the constitution did not allow for scrutiny or even oversight by the executive of any aspect of the army's administration or actions. Being answerable to the emperor alone, and even free to advise him on political matters, the Imperial German Army was effectively a state within a state and acted outside of the lax rules applicable even to the other arms of imperial government. In the absence of a national police force, the army repaid this indulgence by serving in another capacity. The constitution gave the 'princes of the Empire', that is its kings and dukes, the right to employ in a policing role not just their own troops but those from other contingents of the army, which may be stationed within their jurisdictions. Such a highly disciplined body was ideally placed to ruthlessly engage in strike-breaking or to suppress other perceived manifestations of dissent.[31]

This situation, combined with the right of the emperor to declare martial law should 'the public security of the Empire demand it', provided the emperor with a terrifying organ through which to protect the interests of the state. In 1874, a Press Law gave the government the right to imprison editors found to be printing what was considered 'sensitive' information,[32] as a result of which any journalist could find himself behind bars.[33] The determination to root out such sources of criticism saw few limits. In 1880 Hamburg, Berlin and other cities found themselves in virtual lockdown as the authorities ransacked their bookstores for decades-old works of the highly influential social critic and dissident writer Heinrich Heine.[34]

As late as 1904, the government, nervous that strikes and demonstrations might grow beyond the capacity of the civilian police to contain them, issued a memorandum in which the deployment of the army was permitted should 'the demeanour of the working-class population ... reach such a stage of ferment that it is to be feared that violent activities could take place to a much larger degree... [and] it is no longer likely that the civilian police will be able to rein in the passions'.[35]

By 1910, the army's peacetime strength was set at a million men. But with its massive cadres of reservists, accrued incrementally over many years, this number could be increased to an eyewatering 7 million in time of war. The Laws of 1912 and 1913 raised the peacetime strength of the army still further, and it was calculated that by the third week of a major war, full mobilisation could yield 633 battalions of infantry, 410 squadrons of cavalry and 574 batteries of artillery. The army was in fact becoming so large that the Prussian minister of war complained in 1912 that there was no more barrack space to accommodate the recruits being sent for training.[36] The cost of maintaining such an entity would have been prohibitive without the political will to push through the necessary funds, so in 1880 and 1887 Bismarck had succeeded in passing military budgets to cover seven-year periods. By 1912 the government debt stood at 489 billion Marks; a year later, despite some economies, it still exceeded 400 billion.[37] A good portion of that debt had been incurred to meet the voracious needs of this vast military organisation.

The primary factor enabling Germany to sustain such a deficit and finance such an enormous military machine was its massive industrial power. Between 1848 and 1857, pig iron production in the *Zollverein* had increased by 250 per cent, coal production by 138 per cent, and iron ore and coalmining by a third.[38] The creation of the empire would only have exponentially accelerated this growth. By 1880 Germany was one of three countries outside the United Kingdom renowned for coal production, an industry reaping the advantages of the empire's acquisition of the Saar, Ruhr and Silesia. By 1910 the Ruhr alone would be responsible for 60 per cent of the empire's total coal output,[39] and it also shared the large iron deposits of the Saar basin and Lorraine.[40]

Goethe had written in 1826 that 'railways, express mails, steamboats and all possible means of communications are what the educated world seeks',[41] and his vision was vindicated by the huge strides that his country achieved in the succeeding fifty years. By the 1890s the railways were synonymous with German power, and with an eye to future developments many were constructed only if they conformed to strict military criteria.[42] Freight traffic on the Prussian railways had already increased sevenfold between 1850 and 1860,[43] while ships of 2,000 tons would be able to navigate the Rhine as far as Mannheim by 1905.[44] In 1914, Germany would have 20 per cent more electrical output than Britain, France and Italy combined, in addition to supplying a third of the world's electrical goods[45] and operating the largest cotton industry on the continent.[46] In 1881 it enjoyed the benefits of the world's first electric trams, and a telephone network more advanced than anywhere on the continent;[47] Berlin signed up its first 200 subscribers as early as 1880.[48] By 1900, Germany would be producing 80–90 per cent of the world's dye and quintupling production of sulphuric acid.[49] It would also dominate Europe in synthetics by the start of the First World War, producing plastics, drugs, explosives, anaesthetics and rubber, in most of which it was practically self-sufficient.[50]

A large domestic population supplied both the manpower needed for the factories and the consumers for the goods produced. Germany's population, growing at the rate of 800,000 a year,[51] was almost 50 million in 1890 and 65 million by 1910.[52] Nevertheless, despite such meteoric industrialisation, a third of the labour force was still working the land in 1914,[53] and the agricultural labourer's life was a tough one. Many depended on seasonal employment, and in East Prussia, to make their lives even harder, their meagre incomes were undercut further by the employment of cheap labour from Russia and Austria-Hungary. Such factors drove workers off the land to seek a more prosperous life in the cities. This potential westward migration prompted fears of a commensurate influx of foreigners from the east, as landowners sought to find alternative sources of labour. A British royal commission on Central Europe in 1893 reported fears that 'unless some means can be adopted for checking the outflow of the German population [from the east] there is every reason to fear that their places will be supplied by an inroad of Slavs'.[54]

Such scaremongering would in turn encourage nationalists who viewed with trepidation and hostility the prospect of Germany's eastern lands being eventually subsumed by non-Germans. This constant movement of people nevertheless ensured a regular supply of relatively cheap labour, and Germany's agricultural industry continued to expand. Between 1880 and 1912, a further million acres came under the plough; by 1914, German agriculture was among the most productive in the world.[55]

Many of those migrating from the east to find work in industry made their way to Berlin. By 1870 over 80,000 people were moving to the capital each year, and the population was to grow from 658,000 to 964,000 between 1865 and 1875 alone.[56] By 1910 it exceeded two million.[57] Bismarck was determined that Berlin, as the seat of this new empire, would reflect its new-found importance. He envisaged a city at least the equal of Paris, emulating grand avenues like the Champs Elysees. But alongside planned projects, there would be much ad hoc and speculative development, resulting in a 'helter skelter' of jerry-built housing, tightly packed into the limited space available.[58] Such developments were needed to accommodate the demands of the working class of the city but did not make for a humane environment. More than 100,000 people existed in absolute squalor, mainly in the eastern and northern parts of the city. Dank, fetid, insanitary basements were breeding grounds for nearly every conceivable evil to public health, from rheumatism to tuberculosis. In 1870, each small block or apartment of around five or six stories held an average of fifty-three people, and by 1900 population density had reached 1,000 people per hectare,[59] with one commentator referring to the 'long corridors of dismal streets'.[60]

This situation was compounded by the working conditions, which had to be endured for up to ten to twelve hours a day. Men could hope to earn no more than 18 to 25 Marks a week and women about half that,[61] out of which they would be expected to pay extortionate rents for the privilege of living in a disgusting hovel. Many instead opted for life in one of the huge illegal squatter camps which sprang up in the poorest sections of the capital.[62] With the authorities concerned by the potential for popular insurrection, sword-wielding troops frequently intervened to smash up these squats and evict their occupants.[63] The problem could only get worse as the city relentlessly industrialised and the demand for labour grew, so much so that by 1900 the working class comprised 55–60 per cent of the population, compared to 43 per cent in London and 38 per cent in Paris.[64] Aware of the potential dangers of a discontented working class, Bismarck embarked upon a series of ground-breaking social reforms. They were promulgated less out of a sense of philanthropy than an acceptance that his great project could be severely compromised by a repeat of 1848. Old-age pensions and health insurance were introduced in 1883 and 1884 respectively,[65] and by 1911 nearly 14 million Germans would be insured against sickness or disability.[66]

To go some way towards addressing the conditions endured by the workers, legislation was introduced in 1884 to regulate factories and hospitals, establish schools and build sewers.[67] These reforms came none too soon. The extent of working-class discontent can be gauged by demonstrations which were organised in 1884. Workers took to the streets demanding 'Liberty, Equality and Fraternity', better living conditions and workers' rights. An analysis of the situation and its potential for further disorder led to a report by the chief of police, who conceded in 1889 that 'the antagonism between the classes has sharpened'.[68] Statistics compiled for the period 1899 to 1914 show that despite extensive social legislation the working class were far from pacified, with some 4.6 million working hours lost in an average of 2,058 strikes a year.[69]

Such unrest was an acknowledged consequence of the enormous gulf between the haves and the have-nots, who now lived almost parallel lives. While the workers toiled in their factories, their employers would be setting up home near the Tiergarten, the stylish Wilhelmstrasse or the Grunewald. There would be no shortage of profits to spend on the most ostentatious projects, because by the turn of the century there were dozens of millionaires – forty-five families boasted fortunes in excess of 3 million Marks.[70] These nouveau-riche vulgarians were determined to demonstrate their wealth and good fortune, constructing edifices that were not to everyone's taste. Boleslaw Prus, a Polish part-time insurgent and journalist, described them as 'overloaded with ornaments', and according to Maximilian Harden, an influential journalist and editor, they were designed with the sole purpose of '[showing] off to the people across the road'.[71]

This desire to project the wealth of the city and its citizens was also seen in plans for its public buildings. One such project was the old Prussian State Library's Reading Room. Founded in 1661 and rebuilt in the Baroque style between 1775 and 1785, the existing library only had space for forty researchers, so was greatly expanded into a new, 'monumental palace'.[72] The old parliament, too, was considered in need of a revamp and ten years of works starting in 1884 saw a new Reichstag situated on the Königsplatz. The competition to design the new edifice was won by architect Paul Wallot in 1882, but construction was closely monitored by the emperor, who took a great personal interest in the project. Completed in 1894, it was a suitably imposing structure, as befitted the heart of the empire, and the emperor fully approved of its classical columned porticos, its four wings, two inner courtyards and central plenary chamber topped by an impressive dome.

The city's exponential growth was also making it attractive as a tourist destination. In 1883 it received nearly 352,000 visitors; by 1896 this figure had increased to nearly 718,000, many arriving to view the new Reichstag. By 1906 it had exceeded a million.[73] This booming tourist trade was partly the result of the free movement enjoyed not just by Germans, but also citizens throughout Europe during this period,[74] and to accommodate these guests the great metropolis needed more hotels and restaurants, which sprung up on the Unter den

Linden, the Wilhemstrasse and the Friedrichstrasse. The Berlin Adlon opened in 1907 to compete with such stalwarts as the London Savoy and the Crillon in Paris. It was so lavish and ostentatious, in fact, that when the emperor visited he could not help but remark as to how his own palace paled in comparison.[75] By 1914, such developments had provided Berlin with twelve top-end hotels with a total capacity of 3,355 rooms.[76] Moreover, the emergence of restaurants such as Carisch and Kempinski's gave the city a host of venues in which to meet and socialise. Some people nevertheless failed to see the attraction of Berlin, despite attempts to bring it up to the standard of Paris or Vienna. Even the emperor, not one known to undersell any aspect of his empire, lamented that there was little to encourage a visit of longer than a few days, 'as there is nothing that can captivate the foreigner except a few museums, castles and soldiers'.[77]

The diverse nature of Berlin's visitors had produced an increasingly cosmopolitan place in which to live and work. For some, however, the city's attractions and amenities were entirely irrelevant. They were not only those slaving in the factories, but also the Jewish migrants who, like those in Vienna, had abandoned the east to escape hostility and discrimination, particularly in Russia. However, they found little warmth in Berlin. As early as 1853, French aristocrat Arthur de Gobineau's damning polemic *The Inequality of the Human Races* played into the hands of German racists to justify their attitude towards 'non-Germans' within the empire. Later, a society bearing his name was founded to spread his beliefs.[78] His thoughts were later echoed by the writings of Englishman Houston Stewart Chamberlain, who had made Germany his home. In 1899 he wrote *The Foundations of the Nineteenth Century*, in which he warned against the intermarriage of Jew and 'German'. Convinced that the Germans were predestined to rule the world, he warned that any mixing of their blood would be a fatal impediment.[79]

Even prominent Germans revealed their anti-Jewish credentials. Fredrich Nietzsche wrote in 1885, 'I have not met one German who was well disposed towards the Jews',[80] while Princess Catherine Radziwell went so far as to claim that 'there is no city in the entire world where the children of Israel are more repulsed by society.'[81] Even the emperor was said to have a copy of Houston Stewart's racist tract somewhere in his library. Between 1871 and 1910 the Jewish population rose from 48,000 to 151,000, and attitudes did slowly improve, at least superficially. By 1906 the politician August Bebel felt able to assure an audience that 'anti-Semitism has no prospect of ever exercising a decisive influence on political and social life in Germany.'[82] Nevertheless, anti-Semitism was not the only philosophy espoused by extreme nationalists. Any ethnic groups deemed to threaten the concept of a homogeneous Germanic state faced similar discrimination and marginalisation.

Since the war of 1866 and the break with Austria, Bismarck remained suspicious that many Catholics in south and west Germany retained vestigial loyalty to Vienna rather than Berlin. These suspicions began with the encyclical *Quantra cura*, issued by Pope Pius IX in 1864, which ordained that the writ of papal, not national, law applied to all adherents to the Catholic Church. The devoutly protestant chancellor was outraged and vowed to protect the unity of the German people and the empire itself against this Catholic 'Roman Menace'.[83] He responded to the encyclical with incremental measures which culminated in the May Laws of 1873, which established a Royal Tribunal for Ecclesiastical Affairs, extending state control over wide areas of the Catholic Church and empowering provincial governors to veto the appointment of any parish priest who was considered politically unreliable.

These statutes were followed in 1874 by further measures that permitted the confiscation of dissident priests' endowments and the imprisonment of those bishops with suspect loyalties. As a result, the first four months of 1875 alone saw 241 clergy fined or imprisoned and over 1,000 parishes deprived of their priests.[84] As the campaign, or Kulturkampf, intensified, religious orders were dissolved and civil marriage made compulsory,[85] but after 1878 the campaign eased considerably when a new pope, Leo XIII, ascended to the papacy. He was more liberal minded, with advanced attitudes towards science and civil law – views which chimed more comfortably with those of Bismarck. This rapprochement was sealed in 1880 with the completion of the Cologne Cathedral, the consecration of which was attended by the emperor and all the empire's reigning princes. By 1887 most of the more repressive laws were abandoned, although civil marriage and the state inspection of Catholic schools remained on the statute books.[86]

Germany's Polish, French and Danish minorities, which would number over 4 million by 1910, also proved a cause for anxiety among diehard German nationalists. Their inability – or perceived unwillingness – to integrate and 'Germanise' was seen, as with the Jews and the Catholics, to be a barrier to the integrity of the empire. Many went so far as to advocate that if any minority refused to integrate then they should be thrown out of the empire altogether.[87] For the 2.5 million Poles in the east this meant the full weight of 'Germanisation', a series of measures starting in the 1870s aimed at eliminating any Polish cultural identity in government, law or education.[88] Organisations such as the League for the Furtherance of Germandom in the Eastern Marches continued to advocate ever more punitive policies against the Poles,[89] leading to the passing of the Settlement Law of 1886, which sought to drive them off the land by having estates owned by Poles bought up and settled with German peasants.[90]

This challenge from the 150,000 Germans who were settled in the east galvanised the Poles. They organised their own cooperatives and lending societies which bought land for themselves. Between 1896 and 1914, 71 per cent of the 500,000 hectares of land sold was actually purchased from German landowners.[91] Undeterred, German nationalists persisted, and in 1904 the Law Regarding Limitation of Polish Parcellation Activity was passed, which made the issuing of planning permission mandatory for all private land in the eastern provinces. The law was however, made into something of a proverbial ass when a Pole, Mihel Dryzmala, sought and was predictably refused such permission. Realising that the law only applied to fixed property, he acquired an old circus trailer, moved himself and his family into it, and proceeded to live inside. By shifting it just a few inches a day, he was able to demonstrate that it was not a fixed building and was thus able to circumvent the law.[92]

Such embarrassing reports nevertheless failed to halt further legislation. Under pressure from leading Pan-German agitators such as the wealthy businessman Alfred Hugenberg, the Reichstag passed the Expropriation Law of 1908, which made the sale of Polish estates compulsory. This was done in the face of fierce opposition from both Social Democrat and Liberal deputies, as well as angry protests by Polish, Slovenian and Czech politicians in Austria, who resented this slight against their fellow Slavs. Consequently, recognising that the new law was likely to create more trouble than it was worth, only lip service was paid to it and just a handful of token expropriations were carried out in 1912. After that it was quietly forgotten.[93]

As in Hungary, the field of education was seen as another ideal conduit through which to impose German principles, and in the face of student strikes during 1906 and 1907 the Germanisation of Polish schools was pursued, and the following year the Imperial Associations Law restricted the use of any language except German at public meetings.[94] Such crude undermining of Polish culture simply added to a growing sense of injustice, but those responsible tried to dismiss the measures as perfectly fair and reasonable. Former chancellor Heinrich von Bulow insisted somewhat disingenuously in 1914 that whilst

> ... it is the duty and the right of the Germans to maintain our national ownership in the East of Prussia and if possible to increase it... we certainly do not wish to deprive the Pole of his mother tongue, but... by means of the German language he [will come to] understand the German spirit. In our policy of settlement we fight for German nationality in the east; in our policy with regard to the schools we are really fighting for Polish nationality which we wish to incorporate in German intellectual life. Here again, we cannot proceed without severity...[95]

To some extent, German policy in Poland seems to have been working. Although a study carried out in the town of Posen in 1905 cautioned that 'the lower and middle class ... is becoming more and more Polonised,' it went on to assure its readers that they were at no imminent risk of being overrun by 'the Polish masses'.[96] The success or failure of German policy was in a way academic in comparison to the effect it was having upon the psyche of the Poles themselves. As we have seen, the Poles in neighbouring Austria enjoyed something of a privileged position by comparison to those in Germany, and this could not have gone unnoticed. Germany's Poles, harassed and under siege, would have viewed the situation with some bitterness, and a desire took root either to join with better-treated compatriots elsewhere or to secede entirely.

At the same time, few French speakers in Alsace-Lorraine were reconciled to being German subjects. Their situation was worsened in the eyes of those in both France and the provinces by what were perceived as frequent and persistent provocations by their new rulers. On one occasion in 1887, the Germans provoked a diplomatic incident when a French official was lured across the border and arrested on a charge of spying. The French minister of war, General Ernest Boulanger, urged that the French respond by recalling their ambassador from Berlin and massing 50,000 troops on the border as a tangible expression of French outrage.[97] Statesman Leon Gambetta demanded even more of a response from the government, urging that they exact 'a revenge that will be the protest of right against infamy'.[98] Others preferred more peaceful means by which to articulate French sentiments. In the 1890s, Christian Pfister, a lecturer at the University of Nancy, would take his pupils on tours of the frontier in order to reflect. 'We need to come back to look at this temporary border every once in a while,' he explained. 'We need to turn the knife in our heart a little.'[99] Nevertheless, such mawkish sentimentality was far from widely shared. In 1891, Remy de Gourmont, who worked at the Bibliotheque Nationale in Paris, bravely dissented from the general consensus when he wrote:

> ... it seems to me this has lasted long enough ... this ridiculous image of the two little enslaved sisters, dressed in mourning and sunk to their knees before the frontier post, weeping like heifers instead of tending their own cows ... This new Babylonian captivity leaves me entirely cold...[100]

Nevertheless, many in Alsace-Lorraine felt they had good reason to be angry. A similar policy was pursued here as had been attempted with the Poles, using language as a tool to further Germanisation. The authorities incrementally reduced the number of hours that French was to be taught in schools in the hope that German would inevitably supplant French entirely. The pettiness of imposing the German language was most severely felt in Alsace, with French Christian names being rejected by the civil registrar or exchanged for German equivalents, and the naming of hairdressers as *coiffeurs*, or of chemists as *pharmacies*, being forbidden. For the latter, the Germanic term *apotheke* was insisted upon instead.

The compulsory settlement of Germans was another resented measure with which the authorities persisted, and between 1871 and 1910 some 170,000 moved into the two provinces. To an extent this policy worked, and during roughly the same period around 460,000 displaced and disgruntled inhabitants of Alsace-Lorraine left for France.[101] In Alsace alone, the number of Germans reached between 11 and 14 per cent of the population by the early 1900s, and 39 per cent of the population of Strasbourg by 1910. They also dominated the administration and the judiciary, in the process producing another source of acrimony among the natives.[102] The singing or humming of the French national anthem, shouting *'vive la France'* or displaying the French tricolour were made punishable by a fine or imprisonment.[103] Little wonder, then, that Baron Johann von Dallwitz sensed that he was receiving a cool reception when he arrived to assume the post of governor, or Reichstatthalter, in 1914:

> ... there was no shortage of symptoms arousing certain misgivings. The applause accorded me was too uniform, the decoration of the streets ... too similar to be taken for the spontaneous demonstrations of the people's mood...[104]

He nevertheless seemed little inclined to attempt to mend any fences, and suggestions that Berlin annex the provinces to the Reich completely did little to endear him to the French population. Despite an often tense and confrontational period of office, he remained in his post throughout almost all of the First World War and was not to lose his governorship until October 1918.

A similar atmosphere was created for the Danes, who also found themselves subjected to severe Germanisation policies. For its part, the Danish government feared that following Bismarck's victories against both Austria and France he might decide to annex the whole country,[105] so there was some relief when this did not materialise. But having lost Schleswig and Holstein, a deeper sense of nationalism emerged, something contemporary observers interpreted as the philosophy that 'what is lost outwards must be gained inwards.'[106] There was deep resentment that an undertaking made in 1864 for a referendum on the future of Schleswig-Holstein had been reneged upon,[107] a betrayal which many felt discharged them from any obligations to their new masters. Inevitably, the Germans did not respond well to such recalcitrance and anyone brave enough to resist Germanisation faced at worst deportation, and at best severe restrictions on their free will. The teaching of the Danish language in state schools was suppressed, and a policy called the 'Battle for the Soil' was pursued, with the intention of planting as many German settlers as possible, along the lines of what was being practised in Poland and Alsace-Lorraine.[108] Regardless of the bitterness such policies were engendering, to ardent Pan-Germans they were nevertheless key to establishing a homogeneous state. As General Friedrich von Bernhardi, soldier and writer on military matters, argued:

> ...the importance of Germany will depend on two points: firstly, how many millions of men in the world speak German? Secondly, how many of them are politically members of the German Empire...[109]

Nonetheless, despite these obvious exceptions, the contrast with Austria-Hungary could not have been starker. The majority of ordinary Germans, despite discrete regional differences such as customs, dress, and religion, embraced broadly the same language, value system and loyalties. Consequently, their experience of ever closer union had been reasonably frictionless, a fact largely confirmed in 1898 in a special edition of the *Berliner Illustrierte Zeitung*. This was the year in which the venerated old chancellor, who had been forced to resign eight years before, passed away. Although he is said to have spent his final years embittered by his treatment, he might have been more cheerful had he been aware of the gratitude many of his fellow Germans felt towards him for the legacy he left behind. With the new millennium on the horizon, the newspaper commissioned a questionnaire which asked its readership to offer their opinions on a range of issues. One question asked, 'What was the greatest event of the nineteenth century?' The overwhelming answer: 'The unification of Germany'.[110]

3

A Free Trade Union
Should Be Established

Field Marshal Hindenburg, Kaiser Wilhelm and General Ludendorff, architects of *Mitteleuropa* and *Ober Ost*.

As templates for closer integration and economic cooperation, both the German and Austro-Hungarian empires had long attracted attention. Since the war with Germany, France had sought a trading relationship deeper than the 'most favoured nation' status enshrined in the Treaty of Frankfurt, while other non-German states had also benefited from limited participation in the affairs of both single markets. Luxembourg had been in the *Zollverein* since 1842, and since 1852 Liechtenstein had agreed that Austrian officials would collect customs duties on its behalf. Since 1872, Austrian oversight of the country's economy had also included management of the Vienna–Zurich railway, which passed through its territory, and since 1880 Liechtenstein had also delegated diplomatic representation abroad to the Austrians. In 1879, Gustave de Molinari, free-market economist and editor-in-chief of the *Journal des Economistes,* had proposed merging the German and Austro-Hungarian *Zollvereins* and extending them to embrace France, Belgium, Holland, Denmark and Switzerland.[1] In 1880, Hungarian parliamentarian Guido von Bausznern made a similar proposal which would incorporate Switzerland, Denmark, Holland, Belgium and the Balkan states. He went so far as to communicate his idea to Bismarck, who on 5 March 1880 responded that:

> ... a tariff union between Austria-Hungary and Germany ... [would be] ... the ideal direction of our commercial relations. I do not know whether we can ever reach this ideal but the nearer we approach it the closer will our commercial and political interests correspond...[2]

The possibility of future commercial relations between the two empires was also discussed at the Eighteenth Congress of German Economists in Berlin in October 1880, but the subsequent motion was not encouraging. It was rejected largely because 'it entirely destroys the independence of the individual states of the union so far as the commercial legislation is concerned by making the will of one state dependent upon that of another.'[3] Such reticence was widely shared by their respective governments.

Although Bismarck told his economic experts that 'now as much as ever [he] wished the establishment of a closer commercial relationship between Germany and Austria-Hungary', and that it should be, 'if at all possible, along the lines of a tariff union',[4] the negotiations undertaken during the winter of 1882 and 1883 subsequently foundered due to the opposition of their respective officials. As Austria-Hungary were responsible for less than 5 per cent of Germany's foreign trade, it is not surprising that there was a distinct lack of enthusiasm. Undeterred, other advocates of tariff reform, such as Austria's Baron von Kubeck, also believed that closer economic ties were the means by which to confront the protectionism of Russia and the United States. In 1895, politician and industrialist Dr Alexander von Peez made this clear in an article in which he urged the creation of a Middle European *Zollverein* to counter growing competition from third-party states. He claimed that without such an arrangement western Europe would be at the mercy of both the foreign policy of the United Kingdom and the commercial policy of the United States.[5] Countries further afield were also warming to the concept, and on 25 November 1897, the *Neue Preussiche Zeitung* reported that Spain would also join any combination against American tariff legislation.[6] It was, therefore, a concept that was certainly gaining traction.

Concurrent with such thought, more countries sought to stimulate trade by hosting trade fairs to showcase both their own and the wider world's capacity for closer economic ties. As we have seen, Austria-Hungary had demonstrated the benefits of such extravaganzas, and France's turn came again in 1900. Held in Paris, the fair was to run for 212 days, hosting 83,047 exhibitors from forty-seven countries, nearly half of them representing French companies and organisations. The 543 acres of national pavilions advertised the best their nations had to offer and attracted over 50 million visitors. The centrepiece of the exposition was the 'Palace of Electricity', illuminated by 5,000 lightbulbs, and it was in Paris that German engineer Rudolf Diesel introduced his famous and revolutionary engine, which ran on peanut oil. The fair also saw the opening of the Paris Metro, a demonstration of moving pavements, and the hosting of the first Olympics outside Athens, for which a 40,000-seater velodrome had been constructed. To many Europeans this example of the potential for peaceful coexistence and cooperation made ever closer economic and political ties the logical option. In 1902, American professor H. H. Powers asserted that 'a generation more will see the entire world under the jurisdiction or within the sphere of influence of half a dozen Powers.'[7]

Alongside these ambitious displays, more prosaic bilateral and multilateral treaties had been pursued for many years. They included agreements designed to regulate such matters as post, railways, ports and shipping, the fight against slavery and the prevention of the spread of disease. The Universal Postal Union had been formed in 1875, and in 1886 agreements had been reached regarding the sealing of railway trucks subject to customs inspection, and the standardisation of the railways themselves. In 1891 an agreement had been signed in Madrid to prevent the false indications of the origin of goods and for the international registration of trademarks. The International and Radio-Telegraphic Bureau, the International Railway Bureau, the Danube and Suez Canal Commissions, and the International Office of Public Health had long been in operation, along with an International Maritime Committee founded by private enterprise in 1898, which had facilitated measures for the uniformity of sea law. The coming of the twentieth century saw further advances in international cooperation with the signing of a sanitary convention in 1903, and another in 1906 for the suppression of night work for women. A convention of 1906 also sought to ban the use of white phosphorous in matches, and another in 1910 endeavoured to ban the export and import of pornography.

Even the conduct of war had been codified by common consent, as evidenced by the Hague Conventions, of which Austria's von Hotzendorf had been so scathing. These covered the treatment of prisoners of war and the conduct of armies in wartime and had been signed in the full knowledge that a certain surrender of sovereignty had been involved. Both Germany and France, with their security apparatus particularly preoccupied by the need to monitor, arrest and secure the prosecution of dissidents and revolutionaries, had also pushed for closer cooperation in the field of law enforcement. They wanted to improve extradition arrangements, tighten information sharing and standardise criminal mugshots.[8] The mood music was therefore clearly moving in the direction that men such as von Peez had been long advocating.

However, lurking in the shadows were others far less well intentioned. When Emperor William visited London for the funeral of Queen Victoria in 1901, he attended a dinner party held in his honour at Marlborough House, hosted by Edward VII. During the party he cornered the king and engaged him in one of his characteristic monologues in which he raised the prospect of 'an Anglo-German alliance; you keep the seas while we would be responsible for the land; with such an alliance not a mouse would stir in Europe without our permission'.[9] No doubt taken aback by such an outrageous proposal, Edward politely brushed the idea aside and replied that 'it can't be done'.[10]

Nonetheless, this episode served to highlight the mindset gathering within the increasingly assertive and militaristic state apparatus inside Berlin and Vienna. Even so, it might have been dismissed as just one more of the Kaiser's impetuous, attention-seeking expressions of bombast, had not the concept of Mitteleuropa, something far more radical than a European customs union and single market, been gathering enthusiastic disciples for some time. The idea of German hegemony in Europe to compensate for being denied its place in the imperial sun was one which had its attractions, and inevitably led to a meeting of minds between those seeking economic domination and those aspiring to a political dimension.[11] All that was required was a catalyst, something that would make their ideas appear plausible. This was provided when Europe embarked upon its four-year killing spree in 1914, following the assassination of Archduke Francis-Ferdinand in June.

As early into the war as 10 December, the German economist Dr Francis Oppenheimer stated starkly in the German scientific journal *Das Monistische Jahrhundert*, 'I desire to see a union of states comprising all the civilised nations of Europe [of which] ... Germany should be the leading state.'[12] This idea was endorsed in May 1915 by the eminent German jurist Francis von Liszt. He envisioned a closer union of states after the war, of which Germany and Austria-Hungary were to form the nucleus, and including Belgium, the Netherlands, Luxembourg, France, Spain and Portugal.[13] To others, this was the means by which the country's future viability and prosperity would be guaranteed. On 15 August 1915 the German National Liberal Party resolved that 'the result of the war can only be a peace which enlarges Germany's territories in the East, in the West, and overseas, which secures Germany politically, militarily and economically'.[14] A few months later, former diplomat Freiherr von Mackay wrote somewhat ominously in *Das Grossere Deutschland*: 'Germany must become the centre state of Europe, its organising force, which, owing to its political, economic and moral superiority will become the president of the whole world and give the world rest and peace.'[15]

Basking in the prospect of a complete German victory, highly ambitious proposals were promulgated in the corridors of power. Not least of which were those which emerged from the deliberations of Chancellor von Bethmann-Hollweg. His discussions with other ministers and his own enthusiastic civil servants produced a manifesto which was both far-ranging and troubling for the future of Europe. The September Programme of 1914 proposed that France be forced to cede tracts of its territory in the north, as well as the iron ore mines at Brey and an entire strip of coastline running from Dunkirk to Boulogne. The French would also have to agree a commercial treaty that left them economically dependent on Germany. Echoing Napoleon's plans of a century before, France would also be obliged to end its trading relationship with the UK. In addition, an indemnity of 10 billion Marks would have to be paid, to cover both German war costs and the pensions of its soldiers. Friedrich Naumann generously suggested in *Der Deutscher Krieg* in 1914 that 'France need pay only a war indemnity in respect of their own war, supposing they conclude peace. If they should continue fighting, and if Germany and Austria-Hungary should remain victorious, they would have to pay the Russian war indemnity as well.'[16] Belgium, Luxembourg and the Netherlands would be annexed entirely or at the very least reduced to the status of vassal states and its colonial empire expanded at the expense of France and Belgium.

In any event, a Central European 'economic association' was to be established which would include Germany, France, Belgium, Holland, Denmark, Austria-Hungary, Italy, Sweden and Norway. It would be promoted as an organisation of equals, but in reality would be one of supplicants serving the perpetuation of German predominance.

The true implications of *Mitteleuropa* would be evident to Germany's enemies in the west once they witnessed the eastern version, *Ober Ost*, the political and economic integration of those territories conquered following the defeat of Russia. The conflict on the Eastern Front, perhaps even more frightful than the fighting experienced in the west, finally came to an end in 1917 following the two Russian revolutions and then the coming to power of the Bolsheviks under Lenin. Unlike the Provisional Government of Kerensky, which he usurped, Lenin, having been smuggled back to Russia with Germany's help, promised the masses peace, land and bread. The Russian people, starving and desperate for an end to their suffering, eagerly embraced his strategy for concluding a settlement with the Germans, even if it was to come at a bitterly high cost. Russia would pay an indemnity of 6 billion Marks, renounce sovereignty over Lithuania and Estonia, recognise the independence of Georgia in the

Caucasus and undertake to sell to Germany 25 per cent of the yield of its oilfields in Baku, Azerbaijan.[17] In addition, it was obliged to cede Kars, Ardahan and Batum to Turkey.

In all it surrendered 1 million square miles of territory, 55 million people (a third of its population), the majority of its coal, oil and iron and much of its industrial base. Victory meant that the Germans could realise their blueprint for *Ober Ost*. As General Ludendorff explained, 'the motley population cannot create any *kultur*'[18] of their own, so it was the duty of the Germans to undertake this task on their behalf. In pursuit of their grand plan the occupiers engaged in a programme of ruthless Germanisation via the press and education, while any local publications deemed to be spreading sedition were suppressed. These measures were intended to embrace the creation of order, or *ordnung*, as anticipated in 1916:

> ... the task of the administration is the establishment and maintenance of ordered political and economic circumstances in the occupied territory ... the interests of the army and the German Empire always come before those of the occupied territory...[19]

Of course, before Germany and its ally could comprehensively realise their wartime plans, they needed to emerge victorious. To do so, both empires and their allies would need to harmonise their internal economic and political systems to a degree of efficiency never before attempted. This was a tall order, and even arch militarists were not convinced that it was achievable. General Ludendorff would admit later, 'I was averse to the Central-European economic union; it did not appear capable of realisation, as it postulated too great a position of superiority on Germany.'[20] Nor was he enthusiastic about a proposal made in the autumn of 1916 for the creation of a 'Central Supply Office' to coordinate the procurement and organisation of supplies and war materiel for Germany and all its allies. Ludendorff explained that it could not work primarily 'because the food situation ... depended on circumstances that were fundamentally different' in each country.[21] He added that, as 'equality could never be established',[22] the rest of the Central Powers would have ended up living off German resources. He was, therefore, quite happy when the idea was quietly kicked into the long grass. As Ludendorff predicted, Germany and the Habsburg monarchy would fail to integrate their economies or cooperate in any meaningful way. Instead both would have to exploit their own internal markets as best they could to maximise their contributions for the war effort.

The declaration of war in August 1914 was accompanied in Germany by the announcement of a *Burgfrieden*, effectively a truce between the nation's various political interests in the pursuit of a common front for the successful prosecution of the war. Nevertheless, the strain under which it suffered as the conflict became longer and the sacrifices greater would serve to expose the empire's inherent structural weaknesses and fundamental shortcomings. Initial success, as seen in the startling speed of the Schlieffen Plan in the west and the humiliating trouncing of the Russians early in the conflict, was in large part made possible by the state's highly efficient and utterly uncompromising approach to the prosecution of the war. Early on, the Prussian War Ministry established the War Raw Materials Department (KRA) to manage and coordinate the supply of raw materials throughout the empire. The successful industrialist Walter Rathenau was co-opted to serve as its boss, and under his tutelage it had set up organisations whose function was to purchase metals, chemicals and other important materials, hold them centrally and allocate them as necessary. The actual production of munitions was also coordinated by the Prussian War Ministry in conjunction with the War Committee for German Industry, and it also coordinated the return to work of skilled men who had been conscripted, enabling an efficient war economy to continue without disadvantaging the needs of the battle fronts.

Nevertheless, as competently as this was managed, the deteriorating war situation meant that still more needed to be done. In 1917, in response to growing pressures, the Hindenburg Programme was initiated, named after the empire's venerated field marshal. The idea was to harness the assets and resources of the entire empire and direct them solely toward the pursuit of military victory. Luxuries were curtailed, non-vital industrial production was closed down, and all available manpower, capital assets and finance were redirected to benefit the war effort, along with 3 million additional war workers, a little under half of whom were men exempted from war service.[23] The War Office, too, was granted draconian powers over the wider economy. Scions of Germany's industrial giants such as Carl Duisburg and Gustav Krupp were recruited, and an Auxiliary Service Law was passed which enabled labour conscription to be expanded, particularly regarding women. As a result, the number of female workers had grown to 1.2 million by 1917, and 80 per cent of the workers in agriculture were also women. According to Marie-Elisabeth Lüders, head of the Special Women's Labour Centre inside the War Office, by 1918 400,000 women were working in machine shops, 600,000 in ammunition manufacture and 30,000 were employed by Krupp.[24] Still these measures proved insufficient, and before the war's end matters had become so dire that some 18,000 church bells and countless organ pipes had to be melted down in aid of the war effort.[25]

These harsh measures were not confined to the Reich. Germany's occupation of some of the most productive industrial areas of France and Belgium compensated in part for shortages created by the blockade. France alone lost large swathes of territory, much of which contained assets vital for conducting the war: 3.7 per cent of its land yielded 64 per cent of its pig-iron, 24 per cent of its steel production and 40 per cent of its coal. Belgium's human capital, too, was considered ripe for exploitation. On

12 May 1916, 25,000 Belgian men and women were deported to Germany to work on its farms, releasing German workers for the army, and three days later all unemployed Belgians were faced with a similar fate.[26] With their factories idle, and much of their industrial focus removed to Germany, there appeared little choice if they were to feed their families. In October 1916 compulsory labour was introduced, and by the end of the war some 180,000 had gone to work in Germany. Of these, around 7,500 died due to the conditions in which they worked and lived. When liberated, some weighed as little as 75lb.

Luxembourg was also ruthlessly exploited. It served as both a logistical support centre and Crown Prince William's headquarters, while the duchy's industrial resources were converted to the production of war materiel. Although the occupiers initially appeared to seek an accommodation by allowing their Grand Duchess Marie-Adelaide and her government to remain in control, any semblance of autonomy soon proved to be a sham. When workers throughout the country, oppressed by low wages and dire working conditions, formed unions and threatened to strike, the civil government responded with threats. When they were ignored and the workers walked out, the German army ruthlessly suppressed the strikes and imprisoned their ringleaders. Furthermore, as part of the occupation terms, Luxembourgers were obliged to feed and billet German troops, putting additional strain on limited resources. Although the buying power of the soldiers did initially offset these sacrifices to a certain extent, a disastrous potato harvest in 1916 heralded a serious food shortage which the civilian government was unable to address. Despite imposing rationing and price controls, inflation became rampant and the black market flourished.

The Germans also sought to maximise the resources of their own national minorities, and even the modest manpower available in Schleswig was harnessed. One national leader, H. H. Hanssen, who represented North Schleswig in the Reichstag, did his best to resist demands for men and was arrested and imprisoned. His efforts did not prevent upwards of 35,000 young men being called up, and of those who did not desert and seek sanctuary in neighbouring Denmark, 6,100 were killed, 4,000 wounded and around 4,000 captured. Many more were arrested for sedition and were only released if they promised to stop agitating against the war, while heavy censorship and other controls were imposed on the population.

Conditions were little better for the average civilian, as progressively severe shortages exacerbated by the loss of farm labourers, animal feed and fertilisers reduced many to a meagre diet of little more than 1,000 calories a day by the end of the war. Alsace-Lorraine's equally reticent French speakers were also earmarked for military service, but 15,000 men deemed eligible for conscription into the German army deserted or fought instead for France, and the authorities were forced to keep thousands more under lock and key to stop them from doing the same. In

Poland, however, the authorities were more successful in raising so-called legions to fight for the emperor. Even this initiative had mixed results, however; whereas some men cooperated in the hope that participation might bring them a measure of self-government after the war, others viewed any collaboration with their oppressors as treachery.

Despite all these increasingly desperate measures, then, the War Office failed to live up to expectations. Ludendorff admitted later how 'the hopes I placed in the War Office for obtaining all the available manpower were not fulfilled. Even this office seemed to look at all such questions in the light of domestic politics, instead of putting war necessities first.'[27] Manpower was not the only challenge facing the government.

As Ludendorff conceded, 'our dependence on foreign countries [for certain raw materials] now came home to roost and I attached great importance to the production of substitutes.'[28] This was where Germany's pre-war predominance in chemicals and pharmaceuticals was to pay dividends. They would enable it not only to find substitutes for vital imports curtailed by the Allied blockade but facilitate the development of new weapons of war. As early as September 1914, Carl Bosch, an executive at BASF, attended a meeting with the War Ministry to discuss the dire shortage of saltpetre, or potassium nitrate, vital for the manufacture of munitions, huge quantities of which had previously been imported from Chile. It was hoped that a process could be developed to produce nitric acid from synthetic ammonia, which was also used in the production of saltpetre. When this proved feasible, a plant began operating in 1915, and a second factory had to be opened in 1916 to meet demand. By the end of 1917 the two plants had between them manufactured 90,000 tons, helping to keep the dream of Mitteleuropa alive for another year.

With the Allies and the Central Powers increasingly deadlocked in trench warfare, it was also agreed towards the end of 1914 that attempts needed to be made to return to a war of movement. To this end the War Ministry accepted an idea by Major Max Bauer, one of the army's foremost experts in artillery, to appoint a commission to investigate the possibility of adapting the noxious by-products from the dyestuff industry to make poison gas. The commission was chaired by chemist and industrialist Carl Duisberg at Bayer, and included Walter Nernst, a chemistry professor at the University of Berlin. Another key personality in the project was Fritz Haber, a chemist who had earlier developed the means by which nitrogen could be converted to produce fertiliser. At the urging of the army, Haber and his team commenced work on producing poison gas as an effective weapon, believing that the shock effect upon an unsuspecting enemy would cause a breach in their lines and allow German troops to exploit the confusion. As a result, chlorine gas was manufactured in large quantities and first used in April 1915 at Ypres. Bayer and later BASF then produced the more effective phosgene, followed by mustard gas, which could penetrate clothing and be absorbed through the victim's skin. As the Allies developed countermeasures, and then copied the Germans by producing their own gas, the initiative was lost, and the weapon was soon relegated to that of just another in a litany of failed projects which proved incapable on its own of changing the course of the war.

While Ludendorff and his scientists sought new ways of inflicting death and destruction on the enemy, the challenge of feeding a nation at war also had to be addressed. Like most western societies, Germany had all but abandoned self-sufficiency in food to concentrate upon its industrial development, and by 1914 was importing one-third of its fodder, food and fertiliser. Furthermore, much of its agricultural output came from large estates in the north of the country and from 4 million small farms scattered around the empire, dependent upon an increasingly overstretched railway network to supply produce to the towns and cities. As the military commandeered more and more of the nation's rolling stock, and as it became worn out, the ability to transport food became seriously compromised.

Germany's highly efficient military machine also saw thousands of farmers swept up and taken into the army, seriously exacerbating an already grave situation. Shortages of fodder also prompted the precipitous slaughter of a third of the country's pigs, but this drastic measure would of course have serious implications for the availability of pork later in the war. Consequently, as the shortages of fodder, feed, fertiliser and manpower began to take their toll, farm production would drop by approximately 70 per cent by 1918, despite the use of approximately 900,000 prisoners of war and forced labourers from the occupied territories.

As the effects of these developments began to bite, the outwardly disciplined German public became increasingly less so. Riots and demonstrations were witnessed in several cities as early as 1915, and these could only increase as shortages worsened. In April 1916 potatoes were rationed as the result of a poor harvest and substituted with turnips; butter and sugar followed that May, with meat in June and then eggs, milk and fats in November. This translated into a weekly ration of 160–220 grams of flour, 120 grams of fish, 100–250 grams of meat, 60–70 grams of fats, 200 grams of sugar, 270 grams of jam, 0.7 litres of milk and one egg, assuming these commodities could be found.[29] Those who produced most of these necessities naturally saw to it that their own families and friends were provided for first, but the conviction that the farmers were stockpiling food for themselves rather than releasing it to the public soon provoked resentment. One Regional Army Commander reported in 1917 that in his particular area 'the whole town, whether rich or poor, looks with envy at conditions in the countryside, where the products that townspeople particularly miss, such as butter, milk, eggs and pork, are still said to be available.'[30]

The farmers, however, were not the only ones to engender the anger of the general public. Despite the cohesion that had been achieved in many areas of life, the residual autonomy left to member states led to wide variations in the way the system of rationing and food distribution was applied. As news leaked out that one authority was more generous than another, tempers frayed, further exposing the latent regional jealousies which underlay the empire's growing fragility. Bavarians, Saxons, Württemburgers and Prussians, up to now accustomed to thinking of themselves as Germans, fell back upon tribal loyalties and self-interest. Had the government taken matters in hand and applied greater centralisation, some of these problems may have been avoided or at least ameliorated; instead, as the war progressed these disparities became more pronounced. By 1918, a third of food was sold only through the black market as farmers wanted to get as high a price as they could for their produce and circumvent the government's highly unpopular price controls.

Combined with the British blockade and the loss of agricultural production, consumption would fall to just 12 per cent of 1914, with 750,000 Germans starving to death. In a desperate attempt to try to establish a fairer system of food distribution, 357 towns had set up soup kitchens by 1916, rising to 472 the following year, with over 2,000 in all by the war's end. In Hamburg alone by 1917, 20 per cent of the population was dependent upon such facilities for their survival, and the inevitable malnutrition also reduced resistance to diseases such as influenza and tuberculosis, increasing by up to 90 per cent in some towns and cities. The deteriorating situation was graphically described by Evelyn Princess Blucher, an English woman living in Berlin and married to a German aristocrat. In January 1917 she noted in her diary how 'we are all growing thinner every day, and the rounded contours of the German nation have become a legend of the past. We are all gaunt and bony now, and have dark shadows round our eyes, and our thoughts are chiefly taken up with wondering what our next meal will be.' Others noted how 'anaemic Berliners, dragging their feet along the hard and unsympathetic pavements'[31] could be seen, indifferent to their environment and lethargically going about their business in an almost trancelike state. As the war entered its final months, the writing was on the wall.

Across the board, exhausted and hungry workers struck for better pay and conditions, including hundreds of thousands of Krupp workers, 75,000 miners and a further 149,000 in other vital industries. In Cologne, even forced labourers from Belgium and Russia felt emboldened to engage in rioting and looting for food.[32] Such incidents grew in intensity as shortages increased, compounded by the lack of good news from soldiers on leave from the front. Inspired by the revolution in Russia, which swept aside the monarchy and brought peace and food, similar mumblings of discontent grew, culminating in the mutiny of the German High Seas Fleet on 3 November 1918. This was to serve as the spark which ignited the spread of further uprisings throughout the empire and the end of the emperor and the war. William's great war machine finally lost faith in him, and its loyalty could no longer be depended upon. His abdication was only a matter of time, and as he slipped into ignominious exile his empire conceded defeat. The empire's dissolution would come in the same Hall of Mirrors at Versailles in which it had been founded less than fifty years before.

But if a homogeneous society succumbed to the stresses and strains of war, what of an even older institution, one whose subjects could not even cooperate on their monarch's jubilee, or agree to send the same team to an international sporting event?

The division of responsibilities in Austria-Hungary was managed through the emergency laws promulgated under the auspices of the Kaiserlich und Königlich, which spawned the Kriegsüberwachungsamt (KUA), or War Surveillance Office. It had its roots as far back as 1867 and provided for emergency measures to be taken in the event of war, such as press and post censorship, trade restrictions, and the internment of dissidents. Although it was supposed to be a monarchy-wide body, its writ never really extended further than the Austrian half. As we have seen, the terms of the *Ausgleich* specifically marked defence and foreign affairs as a joint responsibility, and it would have been simple common sense for both governments to liaise and cooperate closely in their mutual interest. Instead, Budapest opted to jealously safeguard its autonomy and freedom of action, and from the outset it circumvented the organisation to enact and operate its own war powers legislation. In fact, the Hungarian prime minister, Istvan Tisza, announced blithely that any decrees issued from Vienna had no validity in Hungary. When the state of emergency was announced, a liaison officer was duly despatched from Hungary to coordinate the work of the KUK, but he would find little to do, receiving few if any instructions from Budapest.

To underline the divisions, the governor of Bosnia-Herzegovina, for whom both halves shared responsibility, proceeded to exercise his own set of emergency powers for the province. Moreover, whereas the Austrian parliament and provincial Diets throughout Cisleithania had been prorogued for the duration of the war, the Hungarian parliament remained in session, passing laws and regulations which caused further divergence between the two governments.

The implications of such a situation for effective administration and coordination did not escape the Germans. General Ludendorff would later blame Austria-Hungary's shortcomings on a very 'clumsy Austrian [*sic*] system of administration'.[33] Another effect of the emergency laws was to magnify the monarchy's underlying divisions. Those suspected of harbouring sympathies for their ethnic brothers fighting with the Allies immediately came under the scrutiny of the authorities. This was not simple paranoia. In Prague, the declaration of war against Serbia was greeted along racial lines, largely welcomed by the Germans but with indifference at best by the Czechs. Women were even heard to implore their menfolk setting off to the front not to 'shoot your Slav brothers'. One town councillor confided in his diary how 'people are grumbling out loud now, although any criticism is strictly forbidden.'[34] Such resistance was also detected among sections of Czech soldiers in the army, which Francis-Joseph told his chancellor Karl von Sturgkh was the fault of 'unhealthy political conditions' on the home front.[35] In response to these manifestations of discontent, Sturgkh declared,

> We will have to oppose those elements ... who for political reasons ... in such decisive and fateful times for the fatherland adopt an indifferent or indeed hostile attitude towards the armed forces and the state...[36]

The kind of manifestations of discontent witnessed at the outbreak of the war compelled the imposition of martial law throughout Bohemia during the winter and early spring of 1915. Prague itself, increasingly seen as a hotbed of sedition, became the most closely monitored and surveyed of the empire's major cities in wartime Europe. Such was the atmosphere of suspicion and distrust that prominent Czech politicians such as Karel Kramer and Alois Raisn found themselves arrested and sentenced to death, although these severe sentences were later commuted. Serbs in Bosnia, Ruthenes in Eastern Galicia and Slovenes in Carinthia and Styria found themselves monitored, imprisoned, deported and in some rare cases executed. By September 1914 a thousand suspects had been deported from Bosnia and in Galicia upwards of 3,000 individuals were either moved westwards or had been incarcerated in Lvov. When Italy joined the war against the Central Powers in 1915, the monarchy's Tyrolean subjects found themselves likewise falling under suspicion.

The Austro-Hungarian High Command – Armeeoberkommando, or AOK – was understandably concerned that such sentiments of discontent, and the actions that had to be taken to suppress them, would be reflected in a refusal to respond to mobilisation orders. They were pleasantly surprised therefore when, with few exceptions, men responded to their call-up in an atmosphere of patriotism and loyalty to the king-emperor. Many largely Slav units had been transferred to the Italian front in May 1915, and for the most part they fought well. Even ethnic Italians in the Austro-Hungarian army fought loyally for their monarch against their fellow compatriots serving the Italian king, and there were few reports of significant desertions by troops until the war situation became untenable.[37] However, morale did take an early and almost fatal knock when the campaign plans of von Hotzendorf were implemented and resulted in almost immediate disaster. The consequences of Austria's neglect of its army, largely at the behest of the Hungarians, were to come home to roost.

In order to fulfil its primary war aim – punishing Serbia and ending its constant meddling in Austria's internal affairs – Austria immediately launched a two-pronged invasion across Serbia's northern frontier on 12 August 1914. To the astonishment and humiliation of the invaders, the Serbs completely outfought them along a 30-mile front, driving the Austrians back and inflicting 40,000 casualties. A further attempt two weeks later proved equally unsuccessful, but a third assault in November finally forced the Serbians to evacuate Belgrade, which was occupied on 2 December. However, the following day the Serbs, inspired by their king, Peter I, launched a furious counterattack which repulsed the Austrians and forced them to abandon all of their gains. Despite entering the war full of arrogance and confidence in a swift victory, they were sent packing after suffering a total of 273,800 casualties. Only when a further offensive was launched in 1915, employing overwhelming force in coordination with Germany and Bulgaria, could the Austrians save face and force the Serbs to retreat to the Adriatic Sea, where they continued their resistance along the bitterly contested Salonika Front.

On the Eastern Front, too, Austria was found seriously wanting. The attack on Serbia, as disastrous as it turned out to be, was still only intended as a secondary offensive. The main thrust was meant to be against the Russians in Galicia. However, von Hotzendorf, who took personal command of the three armies earmarked for this campaign, was caught off guard by a pre-emptive Russian offensive. Austria managed to just about hold its own in the north, but to the south they met strong opposition and were thrown back by vastly superior forces. When a breach in the lines appeared, the Russians took full advantage of it to throw the Austrians back a hundred miles. This farcical operation, requiring rigid compliance with pre-set directions in appalling weather conditions, resulted in the loss of 350,000–400,000 men and 300 guns. These losses equated to two-thirds of the combined forces that had started the war on this front, and the inadequate Austro-Hungarian Common Army was completely ill-equipped to absorb them. By the end of the first year alone 33,310 full-time and reserve officers had been sacrificed, amounting to half of the original headcount with which it entered the war, the cream of the old army.

We have seen how such a complex polyglot organisation needed the careful and skilful management of experienced officers and NCOs, but these had been sacrificed in the first few months of the war. Once these officers and NCOs became casualties and could not be replaced, the consequences for morale and unit cohesion were almost immediately felt. For example, in the spring of 1915 lack of sound organisation led to the 28th and 36th Infantry Regiments surrendering almost *en masse* in the face of determined Russian assaults. Unfortunately, because these regiments were mainly comprised of Czech recruits, it suited both the military high command and nationalist agitators to attribute their failure to a lack of loyalty. In fact it was almost certainly due to inadequate communications and poor leadership, factors which would continue to play a key role in the slow diminution of the army's operability. In any case, as a result of its military disasters, Austria-Hungary would never again be able to take to the field without considerable German reinforcement.

The year 1918 was when the really serious ruptures made themselves evident. Following the Treaty of Brest-Litovsk, by which Russia made peace with the Central Powers, men released from Russian POW camps were ordered to return to the Front. However, they refused to do so. On 23 May, 1,300 Slovene troops of the 97th Infantry Regiment were arrested after staging a nationalist protest, and by that summer it was reported that there were 40,000 desertions in Galicia and a further 70,000 in Croatia-Slavonia and Bosnia-Herzegovina. These numbers were further compounded by increasing dissent which saw another 60,000 desertions in Hungary, 20,000 in Bohemia and Moravia, and 40,000 in the Alpine and pre-Alpine Regions.[38] Hunger, shortages of equipment and the slow realisation that victory was beyond reach were undoubtedly key to the army's eventual collapse. But most telling was an army report passed up the line of command in November 1917 warning that 'poor training' was now seriously compromising the quality of both commissioned and non-commissioned officers.[39]

Despite its many shortcomings, the Dual Monarchy did attempt to manage and coordinate its war effort. On 26 July 1914, under the remit of the emergency decrees, the War Performance Law was invoked which granted draconian powers to the military to oversee large swathes of industry for war production. The state was empowered to take control of and direct the human and material assets of the country as required, impose strict limitations on the activities of trade unions and maximise productivity. In an attempt to try to address shortages in raw materials, the War Ministry also assumed responsibility for scarce commodities like nickel, chromium, vanadium, molybdenum and tungsten. Despite their best efforts, however, demand outstripped supply to the extent that arsenals were compelled to compromise on the quality of their arms as a result. This led, for example, to bronze and nickel for guns having to be replaced by steel, although the need for this substitute would mean that the country could only meet 27 per cent of its steel needs by the end of 1914, and in 1917 had to import 210,000 tons from Sweden.[40]

Although a net producer of coal, the hard variety needed for heavy industry was one in which the empire was also in short supply. Even before the war it had to import 43 per cent of its requirements, and with the war multiplying demand, it found itself almost wholly dependent upon Germany.[41] Oil was one product in which the country was almost self-sufficient before the war, but this too became a critical problem when the Galician oil wells were put out of action by the fighting, resulting in the loss of some three-quarters of its production.[42] Consequently, the empire's capacity to produce the munitions and arms needed at the front was seriously compromised. By 1918 shell production plummeted from a height of 60,000 a month to just 29,000. In October 1917 the number of machine guns produced stood at 1,900 but by February 1918 this had fallen to only 350.[43] In December 1917, out of sheer desperation, the government announced, as had been necessary in Germany, that all church bells were to be surrendered so that they could be melted down and used to manufacture munitions.[44]

As in Germany, it was essential to manage the empire's food production and supply effectively. Again, however, historic inconsistencies which might be tolerated in peacetime were to prove disastrous under wartime conditions. As we have seen, it was from within the Hungarian half of the empire that two-thirds of the bread grain and nearly half of the maize was produced, in addition to half the pigs and a third of the cattle. The Austrians were not entirely beholden to the Hungarians, however, and in dairy products Austria could almost provide for itself. Nevertheless, the quid pro quo between the two had long been that Austria was the industrial side and Hungary the agricultural, cooperating in the common interest. The war would put this arrangement to the test, as a 'perfect storm' of militating factors came into play. In areas close to war fronts such as the Tyrol, Galicia and the Bukovina, farmers would suffer substantial losses of stock and cereals due to largescale requisitioning by the army, while a third of the empire's grain production was lost because of the occupation of key areas of agriculture by Russian troops. Furthermore, vast areas were turned into battlefields, and remained unproductive for most of the war. This situation naturally acted against the maintenance of adequate supplies. The subsequent shortfall was felt more severely in Austria, with a 48 per cent drop compared to Hungary's 34 per cent.

Attempts to address these problems resulted in the creation of the War Grain Distribution Institution in 1915, but it was hamstrung by the constitutional setup and the divisions within the monarchy, and further undermined by competition for what was available, pushing up prices and stimulating the black market. Food agencies introduced in 1916 were another failure, and even a Joint Food Committee created in 1917 did not have the muscle to address the situation effectively. Sensible measures such as the introduction of price controls to protect consumers also proved counter-productive, as the situation simply mirrored that in Germany, with farmers hoarding their produce and selling it on the black market rather than to approved government buyers. Naturally this compounded both the problem of distribution and the resentment this engendered. Rationing was introduced in 1915, and as the war progressed it embraced more and more commodities, but with inefficient distribution and the black market people were invariably short of even the meagre amounts this would have yielded. In 1916, Landwehr von

Pragenau, chairman of the Joint Nutrition Committee, estimated that the shortfall in flour inside the Dual Monarchy was equivalent to 100 wagons a day and rations were reduced to 120 grams a week.[45] Yet again, Austrians fared worse, having to manage on 30 per cent less than that to which their Hungarian counterparts had access. Those who possessed the financial means, usually the Magyars and the Austrians, could also feed themselves better than the Czechs and Poles, further dividing the haves and have-nots along racial lines.

Vienna, with its population of 2 million, was a microcosm of all that was flawed in the imperial system, being completely dependent upon the outside world for most of its needs. With the war adversely affecting not just production but transportation, the Allied stranglehold on imports for fertiliser exacerbated an already dire situation. Vienna also became the target for hundreds of thousands of refugees from the war fronts in Poland and the Tyrol who needed to be fed. Their presence was yet another example of the empire's dismal failure to pull together, because many of these people had been refused help by the Hungarians, who simply moved them on. As a result, by May 1916 the city was experiencing food riots, despite soup kitchens feeding some 54,000 people a day.[46] Ethel Snowden visited the city at the end of the war and recalled how she felt compelled to 'share my meals with strangers whenever it was possible without hurting their pride',[47] so distressed was she by their haggard and starved appearance. Snowden also recorded how the once proud Viennese had been reduced to penury, observing 'porters at the railway stations in worn cotton uniforms... [army] officers [selling] roses in the cafes ... delicate women in faded finery [begging] with their children at street corners'.[48]

Hungary also became less productive because it lost so many of its farmers to conscription into the army. In 1915 it could export to Germany as well as Austria, but the strain of war soon made quotas impossible to fill. In June 1915 flour rationing had to be introduced, and the disorder this provoked prompted Tisza to admit that under such conditions he doubted if the war could last for more than another eight months.[49] It was inevitable that Hungary would prioritise feeding its own once the effects of the war began to bite. In spite of an agreement whereby the Common Army was to be provided for out of the resources of both halves of the Monarchy, it was soon evident that the Hungarians would have to bear the lion's share, but this ate into the supplies available for their civilian population. It also meant that the conflicting interests of Austrians, Hungarians, Czechs and others would engender growing animosity. As Ludendorff recalled:

> The food situation in Austria-Hungary was always exceedingly strained. Hungary had enough. She did ... undertake the supply of a very considerable part of the Austro-Hungarian army, but she gave no

assistance to starving Austria. In the latter country, the Czech cultivators refused to supply the poorer districts inhabited by Germans.[50]

Such sentiments were expressed by senior members of the Austrian military. Field Marshal Svetozar Boroevic insisted that the shortages being endured by his men on the Italian front were causing both 'the rapid decline in the physical prowess of the fighting troops and the dwindling of their morale'. He also believed he knew where the fault lay, claiming that 'it is known that in the monarchy there are still extensive regions with unexhausted food supplies,'[51] by which he was clearly implicating Hungary. Matters could only get worse, and late in 1917 Archduke Eugen also wrote from the Italian Front warning:

> ... the food situation is at the moment worse than critical... I have fed the three armies under my command from the occupied territory ... [but] supplies from the hinterland are irregular and scarce ... almost no tobacco ... bread is bad and only half the ration...[52]

By August 1917, with nearly every basic commodity in short supply, from bread and potatoes to fruit, the empire faced more serious riots, strikes and even sabotage. Ethnic Germans, Czechs, Hungarians, Poles, Jews and Italians turned against one another in competition for food and fuel as age-old jealousies boiled to the surface. The Head of the Austrian Food Office, Hans Loewenfeld-Russ, was reporting that the situation had become 'utterly desperate'.[53] A secret army memorandum of 21 January 1918 admitted that 'we are living from hand to mouth', referring to 'exhaustion and malnutrition among the personnel, shortage of coal ... shortage of doctors'.[54] In May, Colonel-General Rudolf Freiherr von Stöger-Steiner warned that there were only twenty-four days of coal supplies left in Austria and just eleven days in Hungary, while the empire could now produce only 33 per cent of its petroleum needs.[55] By October 1918, Viennese doctor Arthur Schnitzler was writing of the 'complete incapacity of the rulers, absolute demoralisation and disorganisation [and] general insecurity',[56] enveloping the monarchy. The chimera of imperial unity was fast unravelling, and its utter dissolution was only a matter of time. As in neighbouring Germany, the authority of the monarch and his administration was swept aside on a tide of nationalism in which, one by one, the former empire's constituent parts looked to secure their own futures.

For the Allies, and particularly the isolationist British, the war brought home the fact that they too needed to adapt to the new realities of modern warfare. Unlike the rest of Europe, Britain had remained largely aloof from calls for closer economic cooperation, but the demands of so-called total war were to force a drastic change of heart, albeit a temporary one. In addition, Germany's invasion and occupation had deprived the French of vital natural resources, and it soon became evident that only cooperation with the British would ameliorate the situation. As André Tardieu, French delegate to the peace conference, would later explain:

> ... the industrial destruction committed by Germany in France was especially directed against the coal and industrial zone of the Departments of the Nord and the Pas-de-Calais. Two-thirds of the surface, as well as of the production of this zone, have been systematically destroyed by the invader ... the flooding of the Lens Basin [resulted] in an annual loss of 8,000,000 tons of coal ... the destruction of the Courrieres Basin, and of Dourges, resulting in an annual loss of 4,000,000 tons ... the general destruction of the districts of the Departments of the Nord, resulting in an annual loss of 8,000,000 tons...[57]

Lacking the contiguous borders of Germany and Austria-Hungary, France and Britain needed to cooperate to circumvent these disadvantages. Germany and Austria-Hungary had to take measures to evade the Allied blockade, but Britain and France also had to confront the challenges posed by the German submarine menace. Britain was France's nearest and most obvious potential collaborator but had its own problems, importing 60 per cent of its food. Furthermore, with no 1940s style Lend–Lease to rely upon, the two Allied nations had to pay hard cash for goods purchased from largely unsympathetic markets, where they had been competing for supplies and inflating prices as a result. Since these purchases were largely financed by loans from the UK Treasury, the effect of all this counterbidding was felt primarily in Britain.[58] It did not take very long for some visionaries to appreciate that this way of working had no long-term future. A young Frenchman by the name of Jean Monnet, a relatively unknown former cognac salesman, was living in the UK in 1914 when he learnt that both the British and French were basically employing a *laissez faire* approach to sourcing their supplies, and were not pooling their efforts. This approach was probably understandable in the early weeks of the conflict, when it was still widely believed that the war would be over within the year, but would it become disastrous in a long, grinding and seemingly endless life-or-death conflict.

Convinced that something urgently needed to be done, Monnet managed to secure an interview that September with the French prime minister, Rene Viviani. Monnet explained to the minister the need for the Allies to create joint bodies to first assess their combined needs and then obtain and allocate them to an agreed plan, sharing the costs accordingly.[59] Viviani was impressed by the proposals and sent Monnet to the war minister, Alexandre Millerand, who in turn was persuaded by the idea, and he sent him to work at the French Civil Supplies Service in London. Here he would subsequently meet and foster a long and productive collaboration with Arthur Salter, who was employed at the Admiralty. However, the two men were not alone in pursuing routes to closer harmonisation of effort.

On 5 August 1914 the French ambassador in London approached the Foreign Office to discuss the possibility of the British purchasing supplies of flour, grain and meat in the United States on behalf of the French army. The two sides explored the advantages of such an arrangement, and it was agreed that an international purchasing board should be set up to obtain supplies on behalf of both governments. As a result, the Commission Internationale de Ravitaillement, or International Commission of Supply, comprising representatives of the French government, the Admiralty, the War Office and the Board of Trade, was set up on 17 August. Although Monnet called the ICR 'a meagre reality' with little more than an 'ambitious title', he did give it credit for being the 'first stage of a more solid cooperation',[60] and it expanded its responsibilities as the needs of the war dictated. Later, the French decided to transfer responsibility for their meat imports to the Board of Trade, which also took on purchases for the Italian, Serbian, Portuguese and even the Japanese armies.[61] As Lord Walter Runciman, president of the Board of Trade, explained to the House of Commons shortly after its establishment, its function was to

> ... prevent harmful competition in the same markets and a consequent inflation of prices; to place the French government in communication with firms who are capable of carrying out orders satisfactorily and at a reasonable price, and to spread the orders in such a way as to distribute employment, and thus accelerate delivery...[62]

Perhaps an even greater potential coup was to persuade the Russians to join the organisation as well, mainly due to the fact that exclusion might prompt them to undermine Allied efforts. As Runciman commented:

> If the Russian government would make its purchases by the same method as the French government, in conjunction with our Admiralty and War Office, we should by that means avoid competing against each other to our mutual detriment. We could moreover give [the Russians] full detailed information and suggestions as in the case of French purchases.[63]

Russia accepted the invitation and sent a commercial attaché with their military and naval counterparts to sit on the committee. There was still more to do, however, and in February 1915, at a conference of finance ministers, the British and French governments agreed to also create a 'gold pool' to secure the common use of their gold reserves. In the meantime, Britain became the alliance's banker, due to the importance of London as the centre of the international money markets. In August 1915, it was agreed to raise a joint loan in the US, instead of a British loan from which advances would be made to France, and $200 million in gold was transferred to New York to promote the transaction.[64] Furthermore, the Allied governments agreed to collaborate closely in matters such as the granting of credit to the other Allies, the floating of joint foreign loans and the establishment of close liaison between central banks.[65] Further cooperation came as Britain agreed to arrange loans from the USA and then transfer some of them to France. The French also sold some of their gold reserves to Britain to finance purchases from abroad and loaned gold reserves to the Bank of England for use as guarantees.[66] A high degree of financial interdependence developed, until gold started to run out at the end of 1916 and Allied credit neared exhaustion. Total bankruptcy was only avoided by the entry of the US into the war in April 1917,[67] and then it took over as the alliance's financier.

Other commodities came to be included in joint purchasing arrangements as poor practices were revealed. In its eagerness to buy sugar supplies at any price, the British Commission on Sugar Supplies outbid its Allies and cost the country £2 million during the month of June 1915 alone.[68] Consequently, in February 1916 it was agreed that the commission should buy sugar for France and Britain, and supply France with 29,000 tons a month.[69] Agreements were also signed to increase British exports of coal to France and Italy. On 1 June 1916, the Board of Trade limited the price of coal and maritime freight, and the Bureau Nationale de Charbons centralised its importation and sent it to a British Coal Controller, who in turn delivered the coal using colliers which were instructed as to the ports in which they should load and unload their shipments. Jean Monnet pushed for a joint purchasing agency for wheat in the same year, and in November the first inter-Allied agreement was signed to apportion and transport wheat on behalf of the Allies.[70] The executive eventually decided how much to buy, where to buy it, how to transport it and where to send it. In effect:

> ... with its enormous resources and powers of bargaining and negotiation, it was a large factor in eliminating normal interplay of supply and demand, and hence normal registration of price, in the world wheat market...[71]

Such was its significance to Monnet that he wrote in his memoirs that 29 November 1916, the date of the signature of this agreement would be the 'first step on the long road that led me gradually, to discover the immense possibility of collective action'.[72] In August 1917, the minister of commerce, Etienne Clémentel, proposed creating an inter-Allied body for the central control of raw materials along the lines of the Wheat Executive, an idea discussed during the Paris Economic Conference of June 1916. In November 1917, the various Allied nations agreed to the creation of a pool of ships. Through this arrangement, ships would be allocated not by individual governments but by an inter-Allied agency, and an Inter-Allied Maritime Transport Council was created which met in March 1918.[73] On it sat the four ministers for trade of the UK, US, France and Italy, who would decide how to use the ships, and the new system seemed to work quite well. Monnet somewhat cryptically called it 'a service with limited powers yet extraordinary power'. Clementel referred to its creation as 'a decisive stage in the economic history of the war'.[74] Salter was just as positive as his French colleagues, but somewhat more matter of fact, when he explained that it

> was not a separate organisation but the relevant parts of the national administrations themselves, integrated into an instrument of common action for common purposes ... it was a novel, notable and successful experiment in the technique of Allied administration...[75]

There was therefore no overarching authority, but decisions relied upon discussion, debate, consensus and majority agreement. As the major powers, Britain and France naturally had more say, but they could not override the will of the rest. When the US became a member of these various bodies in October 1918, it greatly strengthened their authority and scope. As welcome and productive as these various measures were, they were nevertheless fallible. Sugar rationing had to be introduced in Britain in June 1917, when it was claimed there was only ten days' supply left, and in April 1918 the rationing of meat, tea, butter and margarine was imposed. The population, sorely tested by the demands of wartime life, responded using the one avenue open to them: they withdrew their labour. Despite the best efforts of the government to assuage the worst effects of the war on the home front, a total of 6 million working days were lost as a result of strikes and other disruption. The French experienced particularly serious disturbances in May and June 1917, and on 5 February 1918 bread shortages resulted in protests and looting by a mob of 3,000 in the Loire town of Roanne. Similar examples of civil unrest were witnessed in May 1918, as agricultural output plunged by 40 per cent. Nevertheless, neither Britain nor France witnessed anything like the shortages or the complete breakdown in social cohesion that preceded the collapse of the Central Powers. Their willingness to experiment with different approaches to fighting the war, and their readiness to work and operate in collaboration, proved to be a significant force multiplier.

Monnet was convinced that organisations such as those established to prosecute the war had made a considerable contribution to Allied victory. So much so that he saw no reason why they ought not be retained to help assist in ensuring the peace and direct European post-war reconstruction.[76] His French compatriots, most notably Clementel, were not averse to the idea, and many in the British establishment hoped to 'transform the economic agencies of the wartime coalition into semi-permanent reconstruction and Relief Councils'.[77] They would have authority over Allied resources, regulate neutral and enemy competition, control enemy shipping, and organise commercial and raw material arrangements among the victors, including the 'joint development of underdeveloped regions'.[78] But the Americans were much less enthusiastic and were instead keen to return to normal peacetime competition and free enterprise. Herbert Hoover, who headed the wartime Food Administration, wanted the inter-Allied Councils dissolved as soon as possible. Monnet also found few among the delegates at the Paris conference who wanted to 'be bothered with [the] regulating mechanisms' so painstakingly constructed during the war.[79] For many, the very concept of an 'organised peace' was generally considered too close to the kind of centralised planning that was to be pursued in Communist Russia.[80] Such reticence gave way instead to facing the pragmatic realities of a post-war Europe piecemeal, particularly the immediate problems created by the dissolution of the two great empires and single markets.

There were largely unforeseen consequences for those European nations which previously had close economic relations with Germany and Austria-Hungary. Because Germany was to renounce all its rights over Luxembourg's railways and dissolve the customs union which had existed between the two countries since 1842, the tiny country had no choice but to seek similar arrangements with another state.[81] One option was a customs union with Belgium, which the Belgian government favoured as a means by which to assist its own recovery. Foreign minister Paul Hymans had stated on 11 February 1919 that his country 'counted … upon the [Great] Powers to aid in establishing closer relations between Belgium and the Grand Duchy'.[82]

It was indeed evident that order and stability needed to be restored, as since its liberation Luxembourg had experienced widespread unrest. Although she was retained as little more than a figurehead monarch alongside her collaborationist government, most of the country's woes were put down to Grand Duchess Charlotte, rather than the actions of the Germans. Indeed, the country had been so devastated by the German occupation that a short-lived Communist uprising had broken out in 1918, with workers' councils being formed across the country. Even its tiny army had mutinied and declared itself the army of the republic. It was beyond dispute that economic recovery was an essential element in the restoration of political and social stability, but the solution was not so cut and dried as Hymans appeared to imply. Luxembourgers erred more towards some sort of arrangement with their much larger and stronger neighbour, France, than Belgium. Unfortunately, in 1917 the French government had assured Belgium an economic free hand in Luxembourg after the war, as partial restitution for the damage inflicted upon it by the German occupation. To muddy the waters further, some French politicians were now saying that they too favoured closer ties with Belgium, potentially leaving the tiny duchy friendless and out in the cold. However, as André Tardieu explained, although 'M. Clemenceau … attached peculiar importance to the realisation of … union [with Belgium]',[83] he felt obliged to honour the country's wartime undertakings. In the face of this confusion, it was agreed that the only practical solution was for the people of Luxembourg to decide their fate in a plebiscite.

A referendum was subsequently held on 28 September 1919, and the vote unsurprisingly showed two-thirds of the electorate to be in favour of France. Nevertheless, in spite of this unequivocal outcome, the French still felt that they had to honour their wartime undertakings. A customs union between Luxembourg and Belgium followed on 25 July 1921, and not for the first time the voice of the people was to be put to one side in the interests of wider European power politics. The convention was not dissimilar to the arrangement that Luxembourg previously had with Germany, but it included closer political ties and gave Luxembourg more power over decisions. In addition, the treaty turned the economic frontier into an open border, and the two currencies were to share a fixed parity, revised in 1935 and 1944. The union was to remain in force for a period of fifty years, and then be automatically renewed every ten years unless one or other of the signatories gave a year's notice of their intention to withdraw. In the event, it was to remain in force until 2002.

Luxembourg was not the only country which needed to secure compensatory arrangements following the dissolution of their former ties. Tiny Liechtenstein – technically neutral during the war – had been as closely aligned to Austria-Hungary as Luxembourg had been to Germany, and the extent of their integration had persuaded the Allies to treat it as a hostile power. It thus suffered alongside its neighbour from embargoes and economic blockade, seriously harming its economy and causing considerable suffering, especially as donations of food from the Swiss were also prevented from getting through. The loss of Austria-Hungary as an economic partner and political guarantor left the country out on a limb and badly in need of a substitute. It therefore entered into negotiations with the Swiss, with whom it concluded similar diplomatic and customs arrangements as had existed with Vienna, also accepting monetary union and adoption of the Swiss Franc.

These and other loose ends from the defeat of the Central Powers demonstrated that the consequences of the victory were not simply military. The economic and political ramifications of ending two great continental empires had left the victors with a raft of other problems to resolve. It was evident to men like Monnet and Salter, along with President Wilson's adviser Edward House and the economist John Maynard Keynes, that the new Europe to be created by the Great Powers in Paris could only prosper by embracing much closer economic and political ties. The example of Luxembourg and Liechtenstein convinced House that:

> There is one thing that seems essential, and that is some understanding regarding customs, postal service, and the monetary unit. Without such an understanding, it is difficult to see how these small states can live in comfort and happiness... If a monetary unit is adopted and there is no barrier to trade, it will probably not be long before some sort of

federation will here and there come about. Then, and not until then, will those small states assume a position of importance and ... wield an influence commensurate with their aspirations.[84]

Maynard Keynes was a man who would also prove influential in the subsequent peace negotiations, a role for which he was eminently qualified. Born into a middle-class family in 1883 and the son of an economist, Keynes studied at Cambridge University before taking a post in the prestigious India Office in London. After a brief return to academia, he joined the Treasury in time to accompany the British delegation to Paris. His subsequent experiences, however, and the chicanery that he witnessed, shook his faith in politics and in the outcome of the conference. He would emerge from the whole debacle convinced that a new system of European governance was needed that would not just help the major nations but also get states farther afield back on their feet:

A free trade union should be established under the auspices of the League of Nations of countries undertaking to impose no protectionist tariffs whatever against the produce of other members of the union. Germany, Poland, the new states which formerly composed the Austro-Hungarian ... empire[s] ... should be compelled to adhere to this union for ten years, after which time adherence would be voluntary ... It would be objected, I suppose, by some critics that such an arrangement might go some way in effect towards realising the former German dream of Mitteleuropa. If other countries were so foolish as to remain outside the union and leave to Germany all its advantages, there might be some truth in this. But an economic system, to which everyone had the opportunity of belonging and which gave special privilege to none, is surely absolutely free from the objections of a privileged and avowedly imperialistic scheme of exclusion and discrimination.[85]

Only time would tell if Keynes's words would be heeded, although Czech nationalist Tomas Masaryk appeared to see merit in the idea. In October 1918, he expressed his opinion that a democratic mid-European union was needed 'to replace the German plan of Mitteleuropa by a positive plan of organisation of the many smaller nations located between the Germans and the Russians'.[86] However, such innovative thoughts were still well to the back of most European thinkers' minds. If there was any possibility of bringing about European reconciliation and closer cooperation, it was a distant one.

Fortunately, another possible option was available, courtesy of the President of the United States of America.

4

A General Association of Nations Must Be Formed

Jan Smuts, well-respected supporter of the League of Nations. (Library of Congress)

The experience of the First World War had led to a broad consensus that something should be done to prevent such a calamity being repeated. Britain, France and their allies had demonstrated the advantages of united effort in a common cause, and these did not diminish with the coming of peace. The war also served to revive the idea, dormant for some time, of creating an international body to guarantee peace not just in Europe but throughout the world. Balfour told the Imperial Conference in 1911, 'I have always been a League of Nations man,'[1] using a term increasingly in vogue to describe the kind of organisation many envisaged. Although too much weight ought not to be placed on such utterances, it suggests that an organisation of some sort along these lines had at least been discussed. Had the war not come they might have remained speculative notions as none of the conflicts of recent years had provided the catalyst. Of course, the colonial wars undertaken by the European powers in Africa and Asia might have come under very unwelcome scrutiny had such an organisation existed, although the scramble for Africa might simply have been modified to a slightly more orderly and prescribed partition.

Closer to home, however, the frequent Balkan wars and the Austrian annexation of Bosnia-Herzegovina might have been a whole different kettle of fish had there been an international body, even one as loose and informal as the short-lived Concert of Europe, to turn to and ask to adjudicate. As it still technically had sovereignty over the province, Turkey might have been able to appeal to such an organisation to protest Austria's arbitrary action. So, too, might St Petersburg and Belgrade, rather than each taking unilateral and ultimately calamitous decisions. Such hindsight might of course also be applied to the cataclysm which had been allowed to occur in 1914, and how differently the powers of Europe might have been compelled to behave if a referee had been in existence to calm things down. Cementing peace in Europe would also have a knock-on effect upon the wider world stage as the conflict on the continent had soon escalated to embrace the world and draw in other countries, including, of course, the United States itself. So, when US president Woodrow Wilson set sail for the peace negotiations in Paris, he was single-minded about one issue above all else. Indeed, British prime minister David Lloyd George would later admit that the creation of a League of Nations was the only thing Wilson 'really cared much about'.[2] The last of Wilson's Fourteen Points, proposed on 8 January 1918, had certainly made no secret of his intentions:

A general association of nations must be formed under specific covenants for the purpose of affording mutual guarantees of political independence and territorial integrity to great and small states alike.

Bearing in mind that Europe had long been the scene of the kind of carnage to which he wished to see an end, it needed little imagination to infer which 'great and small states' Wilson was referring to. Nor was it the first time he had mooted such an ambitious project. On 27 May 1916, he addressed the ambitiously named League to Enforce Peace, founded in Philadelphia in 1915 to encourage the establishment of an international body to promote a more peaceful world. He urged the creation of

... a universal association of the nations to maintain the inviolate security of the highways of the seas for the common good and unhindered use of all nations of the world, and to prevent any war begun either contrary to treaty covenants or without warning, and full submission of the causes of the opinion of the world – a virtual guarantee of territorial integrity and political independence...[3]

From May 1916 onwards, Wilson frequently repeated this mantra, declaring himself variously the champion of a 'concert of nations', a 'concert of power' or a 'co-operative peace'. In 1917, world-famous science fiction author H. G. Wells put his weight behind the concept, having expanded Wilson's idea to one of creating free republics aimed at ending 'not only ... this German imperialism ... but also ... British imperialism and French imperialism'.[4] Wells' notion may well have chimed with some like-minded socialists but would have met with an icy response from the British and the French. They were not enamoured by suggestions they should relinquish their empires in the interests of world peace, but Wilson received a more positive reaction to his ideas. Civil servant Sir William Tyrell and Sir Ralph Paget, ambassador to Serbia between 1910 and 1913, had considered the subject in August 1916. They specifically had the Germans in mind when they advocated:

> ... the creation of a League of Nations that will be prepared to use force against any nation that breaks away from the observance of international law ... such an instrument will [not] become really effective until nations have learnt to subordinate their personal and individual ambitions and dreams for the benefit of the community of nations...[5]

In October of that year, Undersecretary of State for Foreign Affairs Sir Robert Cecil circulated some ideas of his own, under the wordy title 'Memorandum on Proposals for Diminishing the Occasion of Future Wars'. In essence he appeared to be advocating the resurrection of the system so unceremoniously abandoned in 1822 when Lord Castlereagh turned his back on the Concert of Europe. Cecil propounded the need for a body created by treaty to 'substitute for war some way of settling international disputes' through 'arbitration and conference of European Concert', and felt that 'a provision that all the powers shall combine to punish by force of arms a breach of the treaty will probably by itself be effective'.[6] He then proceeded to wonder rhetorically:

> Suppose in July 1914 it had been possible for the Entente Powers to say to Germany and Austria, unless the ultimatum to Serbia is modified or a conference is called we will cut off all commercial and financial intercourse from you, it is very doubtful whether the Central Powers should have proceeded...[7]

However, Cecil may have been rather optimistic in proposing that a blockade could have served as a useful antidote to German and Austrian designs; the Central Powers likely wouldn't have felt the effects before they mobilised. Nevertheless, if such a process had been possible, it might have avoided the consequences of 'the dangerous absurdity', as David Hunter Miller, US lawyer and expert on treaties, put it, 'of a telegram about what Vienna had wired to Belgrade, sent by London to Paris, with the hope of averting hostilities between Berlin and Petrograd'.[8] The concept was gaining traction, and on 10 January 1917 the Western Allied Powers expressed 'their wholehearted agreement with the proposal to create a League of Nations which shall assure peace and justice throughout the world',[9] 'backed by the irresistible might of international sanction'.[10]

During a series of Imperial War Cabinet discussions on the subject, it was clear that the precise structure of any League had as yet to be determined, other than the assumption that it ought to be dominated by the victorious European powers. Moreover, questions of sovereignty were at the forefront of any deliberations. While Lord Cecil saw little problem involving the British Empire in the business of other countries, 'he did not believe that matters affecting the vital interests of the British Empire could possibly be submitted to the decisions of an international tribunal'.[11] On 26 April 1917, arch imperialist, veteran diplomat and statesman Lord Alfred Milner, variously colonial governor, secretary of state for war and for the colonies, agreed. He added that 'he did not believe that any attempt to establish an international court would be successful or be a good thing in itself', again because of its implications for British sovereignty. Instead, he thought that the nations who entered in the next Treaty of Peace should agree to 'submitting their cause to a conference' that could be tolerable to all concerned. Signatories, however, should not be subject to 'a court, binding nations who took part in it to enforce its decisions'[12] and the British government for one could not accept any supranational authority. Canadian prime minister Sir Robert Borden went further, suggesting that any form of international arbitration was superfluous. Instead, 'the United States and the British Empire in agreement could do more than anything to maintain the peace of the world,'[13] presumably by acting together in the post-war world as its proverbial policemen.

On 1 May 1917, Cecil returned to the text of his proposal from the previous year. A binding arrangement could be agreed to stipulating that if two countries were at an impasse, with war seemingly likely, 'a conference should be forthwith summoned, and no action taken until that conference had considered the matter, or for three months after the meeting of the conference. Each of the High Contracting Parties should bind itself to enforce this agreement by cutting off all financial and commercial intercourse from an offending power.'[14] South Africa's eminent politician and general Jan Smuts wanted to be less prescriptive, and according to Lloyd George 'suggested that the precise nature of the sanction to be imposed would have to be worked out later. It would be sufficient if the Imperial War Cabinet expressed itself in general terms in favour of the principle of a sanction. The Imperial War Cabinet concurred in this view.'[15] The principle of compulsion and sanction had at least been accepted, so that by the time Wilson came to propose his own, broader concept they would already have outlined their plans. Indeed, in anticipation of Wilson's proposal General Smuts addressed the League of Nations Society on 14 May 1917, where he moved the following resolution:

> That it is expedient in the interests of mankind that some machinery should be set up after the present war for the purpose of maintaining international rights and general peace; and this meeting welcomes the suggestions put forward for this purpose by the President of the United States and other influential statesmen in America and commends to the sympathetic consideration of the British peoples the idea of forming a union of free nations for the preservation of permanent peace.[16]

By this stage Smuts had come to prominence both within and without the British establishment as a solid and reliable ally and adviser. Born in 1870 of Dutch, French and German descent in the then-British Cape Colony, his talents won him a scholarship to Cambridge University in 1891. Graduating with a degree in law, he returned home and entered politics, becoming state attorney in Paul Kruger's Republic of Transvaal, until the Second Boer War found him fighting against the British. Defeat came in 1902, but eight years later, thanks largely to his efforts, the Union of South Africa became a reality and rekindled his loyalty to the Crown. The First World War then saw him fighting the Germans in south-west and east Africa, service which brought him to the attention of Lloyd George, who appointed him minister for air in his government. He soon justified his mentor's confidence and was employed in a variety of key posts, ultimately becoming an almost indispensable confidant and member of the British delegation to the Peace Conference. It was therefore inevitable that he would play a role in something as fundamental to the post-war settlement as the shaping of the League of Nations.

Smuts was conscious that that the world would face many challenges, and that 'the end of this war will be about the most hopeless time imaginable to talk of schemes of lasting peace.' Nevertheless, 'deeper … would be the creation of a better feeling in the hearts of men – the passion which has burnt into millions of minds and hearts that this state of affairs should never be tolerated again.'[17] These and other contributions prompted Lloyd George to claim later that 'it was found that at the date of the Peace Conference that the British Government alone had taken measures to work out a practical scheme for the constitution of a League of Peace. President Wilson had not gone beyond the vague idea and the striking phrase. He had not attempted to develop his thoughts into any concrete plans.'[18] If we take his claims at face value, then it is little surprise that Lloyd George again seemed to anticipate the contents of Wilson's speech when his own War Aims, articulated three days before Wilson's in January 1918, included the prospect of 'some international organisation ... as a means of settling international disputes'. That month a committee was formed under the chairmanship of eminent judge Sir Walter Phillimore to investigate the potential efficacy of such a body. On 20 March 1918 Phillimore reported back, advocating the creation of a somewhat informal body consisting of the victorious powers, who would enter into a sort of gentleman's agreement not to go to war with each other, and allow the organisation to arbitrate on any disputes they submitted to it.

On 11 May 1918, Sir Edward Grey sketched out his own broader vision of the shape a League of Nations might take. He caveated his plans, however, with a warning that such an organisation could only 'be of profitable use [if] we are ready to subject ourselves to some limitations or discipline that may be inconvenient'.[19] He seemed to imply that some level of pooling of sovereignty would be essential to give the League some measure of jurisdiction and be able to act without constant referral to national governments, which may simply veto them. He welcomed Wilson's intervention and the fact that he had stipulated the need for an international forum to preserve peace. He also agreed that the participation of the Americans was critical if the structure of the League was to be completely free of the sort of baggage inevitably brought by the countries who had been in the war from the start:

> President Wilson and his country have had in this matter the great advantage of having been for more than two years and a half, before April 1917, able to observe the war as neutrals, free from the intense anxiety and effort that absorbs all the thought and energy of [its] belligerents...[20]

He was also confident that Britain shared his and others' enthusiasm for such an organisation, having observed that 'in this country at any rate, the project of a League of Nations has met with widespread and cordial acceptance'.[21] He was, however, highly sceptical about how such an idea would be received in a Germany still at war and outwardly, at least, confident of victory:

> ... the military party in Germany are, and must remain, opposed to it ... they can conceive of no development, and even no security, except one based solely upon force ... nothing will change this except a conviction in the German people that the use of force causes at least as much suffering to themselves as to others, and that security based upon law and treaty ... displace the military party and their policy and ideals from power...[22]

Germany would have to be defeated and its domination by warlords and generals expunged; only then could a new Germany arise, democratic and respectful of international law. Grey was much more optimistic about the attitude of Germany's ally Austria-Hungary. He added that 'Austria has shown a disposition to accept the proposal and probably welcomes it genuinely though secretly as a safeguard for its future, not only against old enemies, but against Prussian domination'.[23] This is certainly suggested by the outcome of a secret meeting between General Smuts and two high-ranking Austrian diplomats, Count Albert Mendsdorff and Ottaker Czernin, in Geneva on 18 December 1917. Czernin assured Smuts that he 'was in favour of general disarmament and League of Nations to safeguard the public order of Europe after the war',[24] although he was unaware at that time of the fate that awaited his country as part of that safeguard. The concept was also one that would appeal to the smaller nations. Grey felt, quite understandably, that small European countries, previously at the mercy of bigger neighbours, for example Bosnia-Herzegovina, would welcome the protection offered by a League:

> ... all small states, belligerent or neutral, must naturally desire in their own interest everything that will safeguard small states as well as great from aggression and war.[25]

Grey reiterated, however, that such a massive shift in the dynamics of European power politics would require a sea change in attitudes. Furthermore, smaller countries would perhaps for the first time in history have to be afforded 'rights'[26] that previously could have been ignored or set to one side in the national interest of the transgressor. Henceforth, countries would be bound to arbitration and conciliation, and to make every effort to come to a peaceful settlement. If they did not, 'the other nations must one and all use their combined force against it'.[27] Furthermore, he stated, the other members must be absolutely committed to 'use all the force, economic, military or naval, that they possess' to enforce the will of the League – 'anything less than this is of no value'.[28] Grey may well have had in his mind the rather belated offers of the British government in July 1914 to arbitrate in the early days of the crisis, which Germany and Austria had declined to accept. Would those nations, especially those who had hitherto enjoyed freedom of action, be prepared to make the adjustments required to make it work? 'Are the nations of the world now, or will they be ready after this war, to look steadily and clearly at this aspect of the League of Nations?'[29]

Not surprisingly, neither Wilson's project nor Phillimore's version met with unanimity among his own political colleagues or the Allies. US Congress too, as we shall see, was sceptical, and like the British Cabinet viewed the potential implications for national sovereignty with some trepidation. Such rumblings of discontent did not deter Lloyd George, and he asked Lord Cecil to head a committee to develop ideas for the creation of a League of Nations. He in turn consulted diplomat Lord Eustace Percy, and scholar and historian Alfred Zimmern, and all generally endorsed Phillimore's ideas, but in doing so put much more meat on the bones. On 14 December 1918, a Brief Conspectus of League of Nations Organisation, also known as the Cecil Plan, was published. It proposed an organisation to provide collective security, with the Great Powers meeting at conference annually, and with quarterly meetings of the smaller powers. There would also be special emergency conferences, and all decisions had to be unanimous. As we shall see, however, Wilson would envisage something with even more muscle, and essentially primacy over individual states, whereas Lloyd George would push for a model which preserved the rights of individual nations, and which could not coerce or override national sovereignty. Firebrand Australian prime minister William Hughes was particularly sceptical of the wider Wilsonian vision, claiming with considerable hyperbole how it was 'the great charter of the world that is to be and [Wilson] sees himself through the Roseate cloud of dreams officiating as the High Priest in the temple of which the sarcophagus or Ark containing the body or ashes of this amazing gift of mankind is to rest in majestic conclusion for all time'.[30]

William 'Billy' Hughes was to prove something of an unorthodox influence within the British delegation, having earnt for himself a reputation as a no-nonsense and down-to-earth politician. He was British by birth, emigrating at the age of twenty-two to Australia, where he spent something of a nomadic and often penurious life until he finally settled down and married in Sydney in 1894. There he became a political activist, fighting on a socialist ticket to win election to the New South Wales legislature in 1901. Initially opposed to plans for federation, he eventually took up the idea, but laced his enthusiasm with quite strident views on the need to control immigration and to maintain a 'White Australia' policy. He became prime minister of the Commonwealth in 1915, travelling to London to ensure that his country's interests were served, and was again in the UK when the Fourteen Points were published. Hughes felt the same cynicism for them that he did for the US president who framed them, and he was determined to remain a force within the British and Australian delegations to ensure that Wilson's high-minded visions did not negatively impact upon his country's interests. Hughes did accept, however, that if the idea of a League obsessed Wilson so much, and Britain supported him wholeheartedly in it, 'he will give up all the rest',[31] such as his rather unwelcome liberal views on the future of the German colonies and his attitude towards race. Certainly, Lloyd George desperately needed to maintain good relations with the US, so to this extent Hughes was right.

In the meantime, General Smuts published his polemic *The League of Nations – A Practical Suggestion* on 16 December 1918. Much of it reiterated ideas that had now been in circulation and which had been considered by the Imperial War Cabinet the previous year. He set the scene by suggesting somewhat erroneously that 'today the British Commonwealth of Nations remains the only embryo league of nations because it is based on the true principles of national freedom and political decentralisation.'[32] This claim omitted to mention that a League of Nations based upon this model would be pretty much toothless, as Britain's own waning political influence among its dominions had shown. The British Empire had no structures which could claim to anticipate those envisaged for the League. It had no Imperial Court of Arbitration, and London had few tools at its disposal through which to impose its will, even had it wished to. In practice, the Dominions and India were free to act without recourse to London, and the British monarch was in truth the only mortar which bound it together. That aside, the British Empire had never, and would never, evolve into any kind of judicial body. Nevertheless, on this basis Smuts called upon 'the conference ... [to] look upon the setting up of a League of Nations as its primary and basic task'.[33] Smuts conceded that his proposal was not intended 'to produce a complete scheme ... my object is to sketch a scheme which will be workable in practice',[34] as 'we are only asked to make a beginning, so long as that beginning is in the right direction'.[35]

Although he was adamant that 'we must disregard the idea of a super state which is in the minds of some people',[36] he was also determined that 'we must be equally careful to avoid the mere ineffective debating society at the other end',[37] anticipating early problems with the hierarchy of its constituent members posing an immediate stumbling block. It was clear that the sort of League he envisaged would 'include a few great powers, a large number of medium and intermediate states, and a very large number of small states ... [although] no great power will run [the] risk [of] entering a League in which all have equal voting power ... if its votes need to be unanimous, the League will be unworkable; and if they are decided by a majority, the great powers will not enter it; and if they keep out of it they wreck the whole scheme'.[38] The challenge of squaring that circle, one which Bismarck, as we have seen, resolved by quite drastic means, would require considerable skill.

His solution was to have an essentially bicameral League, consisting of a Conference and a Council. The Conference 'will partake of the character of a parliament, in which public debates of general international interest will take place ...' while a 'small body called the Council ... will be the executive and carry on the ordinary administration of the League'.[39] He believed that 'the Great Powers would have to be permanent members of [the Council] ... with additional members added in rotation,'[40] and Germany would be allowed to join when it had proved itself reformed.

As far as decision-making was concerned, 'more than a two-thirds majority will be required to pass any resolution in the Council.'[41] Smuts was careful, however, to emphasise that the League would not have primacy over the sovereignty of its members, assuring his readers that 'the constitution of the Council is that of a conference of governments, each preserving its own independence and responsible for its own people.'[42]

For this reason, Smuts believed that its members should be the heads of government or foreign ministers of their respective countries, meeting annually, when they would 'review the general policies of the Council'.[43]

Smuts' plan foresaw a League with quite extensive powers to control the national policies of its members, whose admission would be dependent upon them abolishing their conscript armies, accepting arms limitations and the nationalisation of their arms manufacturers. In fact, he went so far as to suggest that the League should be allowed to decide how big an army each member needed for defence, and for the level and extent of its military apparatus to be fixed by the League.[44] He also proposed the remit by which the League would effectively assume responsibility for the territories of the Central Powers, and assign them as mandates to various Allied Powers, who would administer them on its behalf. Surprisingly, however, for a South African of his vintage and political leanings at home, he also advocated that the territories in question should have a voice in which country should administer them. This was because he intended for the mandate system to apply to the former territories of the Ottomans in Africa. It was generally assumed that these would be annexed outright by the British, the French and the South Africans. President Wilson would eventually disabuse him of that fantasy.

The extent to which the League would act in preventing conflict, or in sanctioning those responsible for acts of aggression, were also far reaching. Not only were members to bind themselves not to go to war in the first place, if a dispute arose which might lead to conflict they had to agree to a moratorium before an adjudication could be made. Breaking the moratorium would be deemed an act of war against all other members, who would be obliged to observe the imposition of a range of sanctions. Smuts concluded by commending his ideas, and expressing his confidence that 'whatever its imperfections, I hope it has shown that the project is not only workable but necessary as an organ of the new world order now arising'.[45]

In essence this plan did not depart all that much from either the Paget-Tyrell or Cecil plans, but they failed to chime with the French. Their lack of enthusiasm was due to the fact that they had their own version in mind. They advocated a much more ambitious organisation, which they called the Society of Nations. Foreign minister Stephen Pichon had been working on the concept during spring 1918, and insofar as military, diplomatic, legal and economic sanctions against offending countries were proposed, they concurred with the British. If debate, discussion and coercion failed in resolving a dispute, any of these sanctions might be applied. The French also set forth a proposal for a full-time military structure with a permanent staff that could deploy against any state committing aggression. Furthermore, membership of the society would be open only to those countries willing to act when called upon to do so. It was, in essence, an ill-concealed means by which France might pursue its own top priority, security.

The French take on the League of Nations, containing what in modern parlance would probably be called a 'rapid reaction force', had in mind a mechanism to respond immediately and decisively to any German aggression. This, combined with other tools in their box, might satisfy their obsession, but the concept of an international army to give genuine backbone to any form of league or society of nations was never really on the cards. The British would not countenance the cost of such a force, and the Americans would be far from enthusiastic too, especially in respect to the implication that they would have commit to going to war on the instructions of a third party.

The Germans, too, having requested an armistice based upon the Fourteen Points, had their own views on the subject. Now virtually defenceless, they viewed participation as essential insurance against French retribution. In fact, as Hunter Miller pointed out:

> … the German delegates presented their plan for such an organisation and the absence of any such plan from the treaty would justly have been regarded by Germany as a gross breach of faith; indeed, Germany always vigorously insisted that President Wilson's words, 'a general association of nations', meant not only an association framed by the treaty, but an association of which Germany should be at once and forthwith a member.[46]

Unlike the French and the British, the defeated Germans would have no bargaining position from which to ensure their wishes were considered. They would have to be content with whatever model was agreed by the victors, if one was agreed at all. Another hurdle was the question of conscription. The maintenance of standing armies through compulsory military service was blamed as one of the contributory factors permitting speedy mobilisation and a rush to war in Europe in 1914. We have seen how the structure of the German army, and to a lesser extent the Austro-Hungarian army, meant that they were essentially poised for action not just because they were large standing armies but because they were regularly reinforced by fresh cadres of recruits. Conscription was practised by nearly every sizeable state in Europe apart from Great Britain, however, and it would not be easy to discontinue the practice. Hunter Miller accepted that its abolition was easier said than done, particularly 'owing to... Italian opposition',[47] but nor would the French be persuaded to stand down their army, especially as the League was not to be provided with a full-time military component. Britain, too, fiercely opposed to any measures that spoke of interference in domestic matters, would be unsympathetic.

While these issues were being discussed, a League of Nations Commission was set up by the conference on 25 January 1919. Cecil and Percy were to serve as the British representatives, with Wilson for the US. Cecil's credentials in particular brought considerable weight to the commission and suggested that the British position stood a very good chance of being the one adopted. Hunter Miller regarded him as

> ... undoubtedly one of the commanding figures at Paris. With a character of almost austere simplicity, he had a winning charm of manner and the force which was behind his observations rested largely upon his almost incredible frankness and his obvious sincerity. His mental attitude is an extraordinary combination of the conservative, the practical and the idealistic...[48]

In all the Commission met ten times between 3 and 13 February to discuss the draft, average meetings extending for over three hours as delegates thrashed out the details, until a second draft Covenant was finalised on 14 February, which all the delegates would eventually be willing to sign up to. Among other matters, it was to provide for:

1. An Assembly in which all the powers were represented;
2. A Council to determine policy, consisting of the Great Powers as permanent members, and four non-permanent members appointed by a vote in the Assembly;
3. Guarantees for the territorial integrity of the member states;
4. Recourse to sanctions in order to give weight to its decisions;
5. Membership of all the British Dominions and India; and
6. Mandating of former enemy colonies to the Allies

Inevitably, as Hunter Miller anticipated, 'the text was subject to criticism; both for things omitted and for things contained.'[49] Most significant of these was the potential for Anglo-Saxon domination of the organisation. It gave a seat in the Assembly not only to Britain but also to Australia, Canada, New Zealand and South Africa. India too would be represented, even though it was still technically under direct British rule. These seats, along with that for the United States, certainly skewed the decision-making process toward the Anglosphere. Neither France nor the smaller states were enamoured by this arrangement, especially as no members of the French Empire were to enjoy the same privileges. This might explain the observation made by Harold Nicolson, a diplomat attached to the British delegation, who confided in his diary on 10 February that '[French] feeling against Wilson and the Americans is growing. They loathe the League of Nations.'[50] Perhaps they had good reason, for on matters specific to Europe, Britain might leverage the votes of both itself and its Dominions to outmanoeuvre the French, a prospect which did little to allay its paranoia regarding its own long-term interests.

Other countries, too, were uncomfortable about the disproportionate influence enjoyed by the Europeans, and when the delegates representing minor states met to select their representatives to sit alongside the permanent members – the UK, France, Italy, Japan, and the US – they also smelt a rat. They wanted to be given more seats, something Wilson initially opposed as he was afraid that it would dilute the efficiency of the deliberations. But eventually he assented, and they were allowed to sit in rotation on a par with the permanent members.

The drafting of the League was also dogged by other factors, one of these being the still contentious dichotomy of race in a world dominated by the European powers and based upon their assumption of racial superiority. Britain, France, the Netherlands and Belgium in particular had established and maintained empires founded on this principle. If it were to be admitted now that the legitimacy of one race ruling another was flawed, where would that leave the delicate balance of the world? The Japanese, who had defeated more than one European army in recent years, certainly felt no sense of inferiority, and wanted this reflected in the Covenant. They insisted that the clause providing for religious equality must also include the words 'racial',[51] a prospect which appalled many Europeans, especially Hughes, who insisted that 'no such non sensical theory as the equality of races' should be entertained.[52] Japanese Foreign minister Uchida was eager to point out that his country's request was not intended to imply the universal equality of peoples, including those living under colonial rule, but of those in the League.

This was a highly contentious and divisive proposal, and although it was passed by a majority vote it was not adopted, largely at Hughes's insistence, leaving Lord Cecil 'with an uneasy feeling inside'.[53] Edward House remarked how 'the views of the Dominions had prevailed. Australia had more influence with London than Tokyo.'[54] Consequently, despite being lauded as an international organisation, it had instead been established as a largely Euro-centric club whose various organs, statutes and rules were intended to satisfy the national polices of Britain, France and Italy rather than those of the wider global community. Had this arrangement given Europe a better chance of cooperation and reconciliation, it might not have concerned the rest of the world so much. However, this was not to be the case – the role of the United States as guarantor was to prove short-lived.

Despite its shortcomings, for President Wilson the League was the realisation of a dream. It was clearly flawed, but if it was given enough oxygen to succeed, with America at its helm, it might prevent further conflict on the continent. But when Wilson returned to the US in March, he was confronted by a wall of criticism in the US Senate, which feared participation would result in an unacceptable loss of US sovereignty. Of greatest concern was its direct contradiction of the Monroe Doctrine, drafted by the secretary of state, Quincy Adams, in 1823, which had stipulated unequivocally that the Americas were no longer open to European influence or interference. It was argued that if the League of Nations could impose sanctions on member countries in the Americas, it could supplant the doctrine, which was intolerable. This was an absolute red line for Republicans and Democrats alike, and Wilson was left in no doubt that unless such inference was removed entirely, the whole project was a non-starter. Suitably chastened, Wilson was forced to accept that he would have to go back to the conference and have any such references deleted. This crucial amendment having been accepted, the final draft of the Covenant was presented to the conference on 21 April 1919. It was published five days later, and 'unanimously accepted'[55] by the representatives of the Allied and Associated Powers in plenary session at Paris seven days later. The preamble stated, nobly enough, that the League had been formed 'to promote international cooperation and to achieve international peace and security by the acceptance of obligations not to resort to war'.

The League's fundamental and overriding aim, that of binding its European members never to go to war again, was ostensibly met. Furthermore, although the preamble emphasised 'international', it was only in Europe, and between its nations, that that any significant 'resort to war' on the scale which had just been experienced was likely to take place in the foreseeable future. In the absence of any similar continental apparatus to draw them closer together, Britain, France, Belgium, Greece, Italy, Czechoslovakia, Poland, Romania, Yugoslavia and other sovereign states had accepted the right of the League to exercise supranational authority over several key aspects of their domestic and foreign affairs. Significantly, those held responsible for causing the previous conflict – Germany, Austria and Hungary, the latter now separated – were not to be permitted to join until they satisfied the other members that they had reformed and accepted the norms of law-abiding democratic states. This was an outcome which particularly irked the former Central Powers, as the decision was in direct contravention of the terms upon which an armistice had been arranged. Thus, with their former enemies excluded from the very machinery intended to promote European reconciliation, the Articles of the Covenant proceeded to codify its roles, and particularly those aspects of national sovereignty over which it was to assume responsibility.

Article II stated that 'the action of the League under this Covenant shall be effected through the instrumentality of an Assembly and of a Council, with a Permanent Secretariat', and Article XII 'that the Members of the League agree that, if there should arise between them any dispute likely to lead to a rupture they will submit the matter either to arbitration or judicial settlement or to enquiry by the Council, and they agree in no case to resort to war until three months after the award by the arbitrators or the judicial decision, or the report by the Council. In any case under this Article the award of the arbitrators or the judicial decision shall be made within a reasonable time, and the report of the Council shall be made within six months after the submission of the dispute.' Article XIII stipulated that 'the Members of the League agree that whenever any dispute shall arise between them which they recognise to be suitable for submission to arbitration or judicial settlement and which cannot be satisfactorily settled by diplomacy, they will submit the whole subject-matter to arbitration or judicial settlement'. There followed areas of competence which clearly trespassed upon matters usually the sole prerogative of individual member states or the subject of bilateral treaties. Article XXIII covered worker's rights, conditions of employment and other issues, stating that:

> Members will endeavour to secure fair and humane conditions of labour for men, women and children both in their own countries and in all countries to which their commercial and industrial relations extend, and for that purpose will establish and maintain the necessary international organisations.

None of these obligations carried much weight without a mechanism for enforcement. This was to be found in Article XIV, through which 'the Council shall formulate and submit to the Members of the League for adoption plans for the establishment of a Permanent Court of International Justice ... This implied a legal court outside the jurisdiction of its member states, and with the authority to apply its judicial deliberations upon those countries. In spite of the implications for such far-reaching bodies, even the League's most ardent supporters insisted that its 'founders ... are not fanatics advertising a panacea. They know as well as any critic that they are fallible men working with imperfect instruments.'[56]

Irrespective of such reasoning, by no means was everyone enthusiastic about the new body. Many Americans, not just their politicians, were sickened by the war and tired of European commitments. The US had suffered 116,000 dead and 320,000 wounded, far fewer than their allies but a considerable number, which served to colour the judgment of the average man and woman in the street. They simply wanted to go back to the way things were before, and let Europe get on with it. This point of view was fairly reflected by their representatives in Congress. One of the most vociferous was Henry Cabot Lodge, senator for Massachusetts, who was ideologically opposed to almost anything the liberal Wilson proposed. On 12 August 1919, he tore into the treaty and claimed it fatally impinged upon the integrity, sovereignty, independence and freedom of action of the United States, and did the same to its European signatories. He began by slating the Covenant in no uncertain terms:

> I object in the strongest possible way to having the United States agree, directly or indirectly, to be controlled by a League which may at any time, and perfectly lawfully and in accordance with the terms of the Covenant, be drawn in to deal with internal conflicts in other countries, no matter what those conflicts may be. We should never permit the United States to be involved in any internal conflict in another country, except by will of the people expressed through the Congress which represents them.[57]

He particularly took exception to the term 'any dispute', as this could imply that American troops might find themselves obliged to become part of some European army without the consent of their government. He also raised an issue which in the future would find resonance among Europeans, asking if the League could arbitrarily involve itself in a dispute between the US and Japan over immigration policy, which might lead to the Court finding against the US. He insisted that 'the right to say who shall come into a country is one of the very highest attributes of sovereignty. If a country cannot say without appeal who shall come within its gates and become part of its citizenship it has ceased to be a sovereign nation.'[58] He added that he 'could not consent to putting the protection of my country and of her workingmen against undesirable immigration out of our own hands ... we and we alone must say who shall come into the US.'[59] Cabot Lodge also cast doubt upon the very need for a League of Nations, because historically,

> ... whenever the preservation of freedom and civilisation and the overthrow of a menacing world conqueror summon us ... we shall respond fully and nobly, as we did in 1917 ... but let it be on our own act and not done reluctantly by the coercion of other nations, at the bidding or by the permission of other countries.[60]

He also resented the two-year transition period that had to be served before a member could leave the organisation. He claimed that the proviso that the League alone could decide whether 'all international obligations ... have [first] been fulfilled' would put the United States 'in fetters'.[61] He added that 'we are told we shall "break the heart of the world" if we do not take the League as it stands,'[62] but he was less moved by this prospect than he was by having 'our country's vigour exhausted or her moral force abated by everlasting meddling and muddling in every quarrel great and small, which afflicts the world'.[63] Such opinion-makers undoubtedly did reflect the attitude of a large swathe of American public. A straw poll taken in July 1919 reported:

> The League idea has taken deep roots in the minds and hearts of the people. They are for a League, although they are sincerely anxious that the League finally formed shall not interfere with the [US] Constitution... and that it shall not carry too strong a likelihood of American boys having to go fighting in the Old World again...[64]

League membership, however, was conditional upon ratification of the entire Treaty of Versailles. Its provisions had been predicated upon the virtual assumption of American participation, something Wilson's enthusiasm had appeared to guarantee. Politicians less inclined to dismiss the League recognised this dichotomy, as explained in a speech given by Senator Gilbert Hitchcock of Nebraska on 3 September. He tried to appeal not to US altruism but to its self-interest, in a spirited attempt to secure a change of mind. Much of his dismay was apparently reserved for the Committee on Foreign Relations, which had come out against ratification, accusing them of standing 'before the world unwilling to carry to their whole limit the steps necessary to perpetuate the final victory'.[65] He added that 'fortunately neither this committee nor the senate possesses the power to defeat the treaty. It will go on; it will go into effect; it will be in effect in a few weeks; for its provisions are that when three of the great powers in addition to Germany have ratified it, it goes into operation.'[66]

Hitchcock's argument was that in proposing amendments at this late stage, based on the objections of men such as Lodge, which were bound to be rejected, 'we follow the policy of folly.'[67] He added that should the US not ratify 'it will stand as a deserter ... leaving the nations associated with it to enforce, as they must, the terms of the treaty against Germany.'[68] He went on to describe the necessity of signing for simple US self-interest if no other motive appealed, explaining that failure to do so effectively meant that they had reached an 'unconditional peace with Germany',[69] in which case 'we lose all the benefits and provisions of this treaty ... and Germany will be free to assert against the US, which she undeniably will ... for indemnity ... we would have with Germany, on that account alone for years to come, a controversy which would inevitably in time run into the dangers of war.'[70]

That was not the only drawback, however: 'we have seized from $750 million to $1 billion worth of property belonging to German nationals ... if the treaty is not signed does [this property] still belong to German nationals?'[71] He added that 'there are many other benefits which the US derives under this treaty, and which the majority of the committee ... proposes to sacrifice.'[72] These included the loss of a six-month moratorium on customs duties on imports by Germany, while it would not be entitled to restrict the importing of goods from the US; Germany would not have to give 'most favoured' trading status to the US and could, on the contrary, discriminate against it as regards imports and US shipping in its ports. Germany could also refuse to restore the property of US citizens or to compensate its owners. The US would lose its seat on the Reparation Committee, and have no say in its decisions, nor expect any share in the reparations paid by Germany. He insisted that 'we cannot afford not to be represented.'[73]

If, indeed, America did not want to receive any of the indemnity taken from Germany, he suggested that 'we can if desired be generous and give it back to her, provide we signed the treaty.'[74] He insisted that both the Senate and the 'overwhelming majority of the American people want it ratified',[75] and in any case 'it is too late for us to go to Germany, it is too late to reassemble the Council in Paris, and have the Council undertake to say to Germany, "you must accept this change". Our allies' armies have been demobilised, our army has been brought home, and, even if that were not the case, diplomatic usage and international law will excuse Germany from further concessions.'[76] The future of Europe was, he contended, inevitably linked for the foreseeable future to continued US involvement in its affairs.

Ultimately, it was the arguments of politicians such as Cabot Lodge which would win the day. The US would refuse to ratify membership of the League or put its signature to the Treaty. It meant, as Hitchcock warned, losing out on the other benefits America might have garnered, but it appeared to be a price worth paying. The US and Germany would sign their own, separate peace treaty in 1921, which would rather ironically be lodged with the League of Nations. The terms of the treaty would also afford the US essentially the same rights and privileges which had been ceded to its allies in the Treaty of Versailles but spare it the additional obligations of League membership. Similar treaties agreed with Austria and Hungary brought closure to the whole issue as far as many Americans were concerned, meaning they could move on.

This outcome did indeed leave the League almost exclusively a European club, but one seriously compromised and diminished in the process. In his diary, Nicolson posed a rhetorical but nonetheless important question when he asked, 'What will the new Russia care for the League of Nations? They will argue that it is a rump on the part of the victorious allies.'[77] Indeed, without Germany, Austria, Hungary or the US, it was. The organisation's first deputy secretary general, the still idealistic Jean Monnet, concluded that this was the logical consequence of those who had been instrumental in drafting the Covenant deliberately being 'careful to avoid setting up a genuine authority independent of the member states, or even a first nucleus of autonomous international power'.[78]

Its subsequent performance certainly appeared to vindicate his analysis, although there were also undoubted achievements, as we shall see later. It was in the pursuit of European disarmament that the organisation encountered its most insurmountable challenge. Article III of the Covenant called for the 'reduction of armaments to the lowest point consistent with national safety', but this aspiration was doomed to failure, largely because Britain would not entertain any meaningful reduction to its navy and the French would resist such measures that threatened its huge army. Subsequent German governments also sought to circumvent the restrictions imposed upon it by the treaty while simultaneously pursuing rearmament. To this end it joined other countries who paid lip service to the notion of a continent free of vast military arsenals while simultaneously expanding their military potential. Great Britain would rely too upon bilateral arrangements, such as the Anglo-German Naval Agreement of 1935. Through this it sought to limit the expansion of the Kriegsmarine, ignoring the good offices of the League and undermining Versailles in the process. The League did make some futile attempts to generate meaningful progress, and hosted a series of conferences to this effect, but vested interests undermined every effort. One last try was made in 1932, when a meeting was convened in Geneva, but this achieved nothing meaningful. To those hoping it might promote the idea of closer European integration and peace on the continent, the League proved to be neither an inspiration nor a facilitator.

5

Make Germany Pay

Louis Klotz, the man behind 'Making Germany Pay' in 1919. (Library of Congress)

Hand in hand with brave words about restoring peace, harmony and reconciliation to Europe were starker demands that Germany and its allies atone for their roles in devastating so much of the continent. It was widely accepted that the Central Powers had schemed and connived to bring the war about, and that the conduct of Germany in particular had to be severely punished. As one commentator put it:

> The grim record is damning enough. Civilian hostages shot by the hundreds, villages pillaged and burned to the ground, whole cities sacked and set to the flames, ancient buildings and sacred cathedrals given to wanton destruction, mock surrender to cover treacherous acts;

all these things have been proved against the troops of the Kaiser. The German War Lord, by his orders and his reasons given afterwards, has made himself personally responsible for them.[1]

Sir Edward Grey, who served as foreign secretary until 1916, was convinced in his own mind that the Germans bore final responsibility, and added his own list of crimes to the charge sheet:

> ... The Germans have abrogated all previously accepted rules of warfare. The use of poisonous gas, the firing from the sea upon open undefended towns, the indiscriminate bombing of big cities from the air, were all introduced into the war by Germany...[2]

Added to these indictments was the systematic exploitation of the countries which had been occupied by Germany, and the ruthless enslavement of millions in pursuit of Mitteleuropa. None of these actions lent themselves to the prospect of moderate peace terms; instead calls for restitution and redress were becoming increasingly shrill. Nevertheless in his War Aims speech of 5 January 1918, Lloyd George had insisted that 'there must be reparation for injuries done in violation of international law', and especially 'for the wanton damage inflicted on Belgian towns and villages', but only 'such reparation as *can be* made for the devastation of its towns and provinces', implying that such payments had to be no more and no less than the Germans could afford. The prime minister also appeared to fully endorse a policy of restoration rather than one of punitive reparation. These sentiments resonated with those of Ralph Paget and Sir William Tyrell in their evaluation made as early as August 1916, in which they warned that:

> ... it is evident that Germany's financial situation at the close of the war may be such as to render it difficult if not impossible for her to pay the amount to which Belgium may be found to be entitled in a lump sum, even if spread over a limited number of years...[3]

One assessment, however, had been made with another two years of the war to run, and the other with another eleven months of carnage to follow. There was still time for hearts to harden and positions to become entrenched. Nevertheless, like Lloyd George, President Wilson's Fourteen Points seemed to anticipate a peace based upon rational deliberation rather than revenge. It was also upon these terms that Germany had finally agreed to seek a ceasefire. Wilson had secured an end to the fighting, but he had apparently done so without considering the opinions of his two key allies, for neither Lloyd George or Clemenceau felt that they had been sufficiently consulted either on the drafting or publication of Wilson's announcement. Lloyd George might have been prepared to sound conciliatory, but he seemed somewhat put out that the American president had also taken it upon himself to do likewise. These sentiments were also shared by the French. 'Have you ever been asked by President Wilson whether you accept the Fourteen Points? I have not been asked,' Clemenceau said to Lloyd George. 'I have not been asked either,' he replied.[4] Such indignation so early in the proceedings did not bode well.

The implications of Wilson's statement for the British naturally became the subject of intense scrutiny within the Foreign Office. A memorandum[5] circulated on 12 October 1918 sought to understand what it meant for Britain's negotiating position when they arrived in Paris. In his Fourteen Points he referred to Belgium having to be 'evacuated and restored', and France having the 'invaded portions restored'. It was the interpretation to be placed upon the phrase 'restored' that concentrated minds, as this could only refer to the 'material restoration of all buildings, works etc. which have been destroyed or injured and the restoration of all machinery and property of all kinds which has been destroyed or removed', rather than anything broader such as compensation to those who suffered such damage. The document also pointed out that 'no mention is made of reparation for injuries done to individuals apart from damage to property ... it tacitly excludes indemnity for such acts as the institution of forced labour, the deportation of Belgians to Germany, or physical injury done to individuals during the course of the military operations.'

It made the same observations concerning damage inflicted upon France: 'Here again the clause [restored] is insufficient in as much as it excludes indemnities for damage other than that done to property ... the statement will probably be considered, from the point of view of the Allies, as seriously unsatisfactory in that it includes no reference to reparation.' The memo's authors added that there was 'no mention either to reparation or to punishment for illegal acts such as those committed in submarine warfare'. However, as 'the Germans will certainly make counter claims against the Allies such as compensation for the illegal treatment of German nationals resident in England, and for the ill treatment of German prisoners in France,' it was considered wise not to push this issue too much. The same approach would have to be taken with regards to possible 'claims against Germany for damages caused by illegal methods of warfare arising out of air raids in England', because the Allies had themselves 'resorted to retaliation, and retaliation would necessarily act as a bar to any legal claim for damages'. Germany may have pioneered the policy of dropping bombs on civilians, but the Allies had not resiled from emulating them.

The actual Armistice terms presented to Germany were not much clearer. While Point Nineteen stated that Germany would have to make 'reparation for damage done', it still did not specify what form such reparation should take, and in that sense was as vague as the word 'restoration'. However, the terms did at least contain some financial penalties. It was specified that Germany had to make 'immediate restitution of the cash deposited in the National Bank of Belgium' and in addition 'of the Russian and Romanian gold yielded to Germany or taken by that power', but these were the only specifics contained in the terms presented by the Allies. The vague drafting of both the Fourteen Points and the Armistice terms was compounded by an absence of liaison between the British and the French. The minutes of a Cabinet meeting on 15 October 1918 conceded that although 'a letter [had been] addressed to the British ambassador in Paris endorsing a declaration of the French National Executive Committee for the complete reparation of damage caused by the war ... clarification had been sought from the French as to precisely what they meant by this.'[6]

Lloyd George later reiterated that he had never wanted an outcome which would cripple Germany. He offered as an example of his moderation a speech he gave in Bristol on 11 December 1918:

> I have always said we will exact the last penny we can out of Germany up to the limit of her capacity, but I am not going to mislead the public on the question of the capacity until I know more about it, and I am certainly not going to do it in order to win votes... if Germany has a greater capacity she must pay to the very last penny.[7]

Nevertheless, Lloyd George had called an election in 1918 in which one of the rallying cries referred to 'making Germany pay' and squeezing the German lemon until the 'pips squeaked'. Although not in itself the avowed policy of the government, this clearly resonated with a public who understandably did not care to let economic realities interfere with securing a vindictive peace. Germany was going to be handed a bill, and it was going to settle in full come what may. Punishment was also an outcome sought by some notable British celebrities of the time. Rudyard Kipling, who had lost his own son in the war and who brooded upon his loss until his dying day, penned 'Justice' in October 1918. In it he described 'a people and their king ... through ancient sin grown strong ... but now their hour is past ... evil incarnate held at last ... to answer to mankind.' Perhaps it wasn't one of his most stirring works, but many shared Kipling's belief that the Germans, and particularly the emperor himself, must face the full wrath of the victorious Allies, and that no punishment could be too severe. Such opinions were vehemently opposed by more moderate voices.

John Maynard Keynes put a different interpretation upon Lloyd George's position, citing the 8 December issue of *The Times*, which paraphrased the prime minister to suggest he was in the 'Making Germany Pay' camp. Keynes also later accused Lloyd George of using more intemperate language at the Bristol meeting than he admitted and quoted him as insisting that the British had 'an absolute right to demand the whole cost of the war'. He was certainly well known for being economical with the truth when the need arose, and in Keynes' view he had 'capitulated' to increasingly popular extremist views simply to buy votes.[8] Keynes concluded that 'the ordinary voter was led to believe that Germany would certainly be made to pay the greater part, if not the whole cost of the war,' and that having been so persuaded it ill behoved the prime minister to return from Paris with anything less. In essence, he wrote cynically, 'a vote for a Coalition candidate meant the crucifixion of the Antichrist and the assumption by Germany of the British national debt.'[9]

In truth, Britain had little reason to impose harsh terms because there was little against which it could honestly claim. It had secured most if not all it needed from the war. With its fleet interned at Scapa Flow, Germany was no longer a naval challenge; and with its colonies neutralised, Britain was to secure the plum territories for itself and its dominions. Most importantly, the European balance had been restored, or at least appeared to have been. Not having been fought over or occupied, Britain could expect little gain from any financial penalties that could be imposed; indeed, such indemnities would only make Germany poorer and delay its recovery as a market for British goods. There was perhaps one item of loss against which the country might make a claim, and that was the thousands of tons of mainly British merchant shipping sent to the bottom of the sea by German submarines. Lloyd George put the total cost to the British economy at some £551 million,[10] so Britain could perhaps expect something out of any reparations to make good these losses. It would largely depend upon the American president's interpretation of the terms.

Lloyd George was also well aware that in Paris he would face Belgian and French delegations intent on imposing the severest terms on Germany, and Britain needed to keep the two countries on side. For one, he reminded his cabinet, Britain needed to support them 'with a view to diverting the French from their colonial enterprises', not least of which was the developing spat over the division of the Middle Eastern spoils. The secretary of state for war, Winston Churchill, agreed, and added that 'the first important step for us to take was to come to an arrangement with the French for the safeguarding of our mutual interests,'[11] again no doubt referring to the Middle East, and supporting it over reparations claims was one way of achieving this. The British, of course, also needed the US in a post-war partnership, as its position in 1919 could hardly have been further removed from that of 1914, when it was the greatest maritime, merchant, banking and industrial power. In another meeting, Lloyd George would explain the stark realities of post-war Britain:

> ... the war had made a great change in our position. Before the war we were a creditor nation, and now we were a debtor nation. This was a great change for a commercial people like ourselves ... before the war, although the balance of imports was against us it did not matter, as the difference was paid for by what we called our 'invisible' exports ... the interest from our investments abroad had also been reduced to a figure of £100,000,000 or so ... we were purchasing more than we were paying for, were increasing our expenditure, and were living on capital...[12]

Clearly, the British would have to try to balance a need to placate France with a desperate need to ensure a friendly relationship with the United States. Instead, Lloyd George appeared to have set himself upon a course which would satisfy no one. As Maynard Keynes put it, 'the hopes to which the prime minister had given rise not only compelled him to advocate an unjust and unworkable basis to the treaty with Germany, but set him at variance with the [US] President, and on the other hand with competing interests to those of France and Belgium.'[13] Keynes was right. Led by French prime minister George 'the Tiger' Clemenceau, and ably supported by his right-hand man André Tardieu and finance minister Louis Klotz, the French would fight their corner with the eager collaboration of the Belgian delegates, key among them foreign minister Paul Hymans. Clemenceau is quoted as saying of the Germans, with all that implied, how 'the barbarians of whom history spoke took all that they found in the territories invaded by them, but destroyed nothing, they settled down to share the common existence. Now however, the enemy had systematically destroyed everything that came his way.'[14]

Clemenceau also made abundantly clear the extent to which he was intending to seek redress from the Germans after '[the] bloody catastrophe... [which] has devastated and ruined one of France's richest parts, the broader and finer ought to be the reparation, not only for actual damage – reparation in the vulgar sense – if I may say so, which is due to us, but the more noble and higher reparation which we are trying to bring about.'[15] He was also aware that he had taken with him the high expectations of the greater mass of his people, and this alone gave him little or no alternative than to negotiate the best deal possible: 'We have made formal promises to our people about reparations ... [and] we must keep our word unless it is clearly proved that we cannot do so.'[16]

So, as Lloyd George admitted, 'in 1919 public opinion, both here and in France, was out and out in favour of making Germany pay,'[17] mainly because both he and his counterparts in France had utterly failed to manage public expectations in this respect. For men such as Clemenceau in particular, the attainment of such reparations would make the sacrifices of the French people slightly more palatable. Hardly a single family had been left unaffected, with an average of 900 men perishing each day in the fighting, totalling 1,325,000 by 1918. In addition, the country would have to face the challenge of recovery with a population deficit of another 1.5 million due to death or absence of men who might otherwise have been at home producing children. The French also resented the fact that so much of their farming and industrial land had been wrecked in the invasion, occupation and fighting while Germany's own industrial capacity had emerged almost untouched. For example, Tardieu tells us that in 1920 Germany would have 65 per cent of its blast furnaces in operation, while the French would have only 40 per cent of theirs.[18] If left unaddressed, this fact alone would leave France at a huge disadvantage for the foreseeable future. France's recovery was therefore predicated on the exactions it could secure. Indeed, Louis Klotz was credited with responding to every question of an economic nature by insisting grandly that 'Germany will pay'.[19]

Against them, an increasingly reticent Lloyd George, Wilson and to a lesser extent Italy's Orlando would try to moderate their claims. But President Wilson, having advocated 'peace without victory', still faced a British prime minister who promised in public to punish Germany and a Frenchman who wanted victory to be total and shattering for the Germans. 'Theoretically, peace without victory was within the realm of reason, but practically it was not,' admitted Colonel House, Wilson's adviser at the conference.[20] Harold Nicolson concurred, writing how 'given the atmosphere of the time, given the passions aroused in all democracies by four years of war, it would have been impossible even for supermen to devise a peace of moderation and righteousness.'[21]

Much would come down to the ability of the leading protagonists to find a middle way. Unfortunately, despite their individual qualities, none would prove to have the faculties necessary to come to an equitable arrangement based on logic and reason alone. According to Maynard Keynes:

> ... we knew [Wilson] to be solitary and aloof ... strong willed and obstinate ... a man of lofty and powerful imagination [but] his thought and his temperament were essentially ideological not intellectual ... when it came to practice his ideas were nebulous and incomplete. He had no plan, no scheme, no constructive ideas whatever for clothing with the flesh of life the commandments which he had thundered down from the White House.[22]

James Headlam-Morley, Assistant Director of the Foreign Office Political Intelligence Department, echoed Keynes' sentiments when he spoke of 'people in an extraordinary muddle with regard to all these problems which have inevitably been created by the war and many of which have been very imperfectly formulated by Wilson'.[23] Although Lloyd George said loyally that he thought him 'kindly, sincere [and] straightforward', he also said in private that he considered him 'tactless and vain'.[24] Robert Lansing, nominal head of the US commission to the peace conference, was as ungenerous as Keynes, saying of Wilson that 'even established facts were ignored if they did not fit in with his intuitive sense, this semi-divine power to select the right'.[25] Clemenceau summed up his own evaluation of both the British prime minister and US president when he said wryly that 'I find myself between Jesus Christ on the one hand, and Napoleon Bonaparte on the other',[26] although he did not specify which was which. Nor was he without detractors of his own, some of whom doubted his capacity to secure the best outcome for France. President Raymond Poincaré somewhat damningly called him 'scatter-brained, violent, conceited, bullying, sneering, dreadfully superficial, deaf physically and intellectually, [and] incapable of reasoning, reflecting, [or] of following a discussion'.[27] Harold Nicolson was equally unflattering: 'M Clemenceau was, as a chairman, uncontrolling and uncontrolled ... only roused ... when the interests of France were affected, or the opportunity arose to bully the representative of some smaller power.'[28]

Such inflated egos and personalities did not make for uncomplicated and smooth deliberations. The cliché of the smoke-filled room where conflicting priorities had to be considered to reach compromises which satisfied no one would, as Keynes summarised it, simply lead to 'arid and empty intrigue'.[29] Perhaps to nudge the 'Tiger' towards a more conciliatory approach to the negotiations, Lloyd George used the occasion of his appointment as president of the Peace Conference on 18 January 1919 to flatter and blandish the haughty Frenchman, being confident that 'I am sure M. Clemenceau will not allow useless delays to occur ... his energy and presence of mind have done more than all the acts of us others to ensure victory.'[30] Unfortunately, Nicholson noted little sign of Clemenceau heeding such advice: 'The conference opened officially by Poincaré. Plenary session at Quai d'Orsay at 3:15. Clemenceau rather high handed with the smaller powers. "Y a-t-il d'objections? Non...? Adopte." Like a machine gun.'[31]

One point of unanimity was the need for Germany to admit that its behaviour justified the severity of the peace that was planned for it and its allies, and that they were appropriately contrite. This veneer of legitimacy would demonstrate that indemnities or reparations were legal and fair, so it was agreed that the Germans would have to accept the notorious Article 231:

> The Allied and Associated Governments affirm, and Germany accepts the responsibility of Germany and her allies for causing all the loss and damage to which the Allied and Associated Governments and their nationals have been subjected as a consequence of the war imposed upon them by the aggression of Germany and her allies.

Armed with what would come to be known as the infamous 'War Guilt Clause', the victors could proceed to debate and negotiate the final figure, a matter upon which Lloyd George claimed to have begun work some time before. He tells us that 'at the end of the war, in 1918', he 'set up a small committee to investigate this question'[32] in the hope of taking to the negotiations a basis for sensible discussion on the subject. The subsequent report, perhaps inevitably, would place him in an uncomfortable position, because although 'it proposed that the Central Powers would need to pay an annual reparations payment of £1.2 billion,'[33] totalling some £40 billion plus interest over a period of forty years, in the view of the British Treasury the Germans could pay nowhere near this amount. Whatever amount the accountants or economists came up with, it was widely accepted that the final figure could be little more than conjecture and guesswork. Lloyd George's own committee conceded that they were working with scanty data, and that their calculations could only be a matter of 'forecast and opinion'.[34]

Nevertheless, William Hughes was determined that the British should be as uncompromising as the French and Belgians. He chaired the Committee on Indemnity, which calculated that Germany owed at least £24 billion in damages – less than the figure arrived at by the committee, but still considered widely optimistic by more sober voices, especially of course Maynard Keynes. Hughes was adamant however and insisted that 'some way ... be found of securing agreement for demanding reparation commensurate with the tremendous sacrifices made by the British Empire and her Allies'.[35] He also warned the prime minister that without a substantial indemnity from Germany, Britain would lose out in the coming economic competition with the United States.[36] Nor was he prepared to countenance any weakening in resolve on the part of the British, urging that 'everything is practicable to the man who has strength enough to enforce his views.'[37] So, if even his own advisers, ministers and civil servants could not arrive at an agreed sum, what chance would he have in Paris with at least three other delegations with whom to argue?

The French minister for industrial reconstruction, Louis Loucher, had stated before the French Senate on 17 February 1919, that in order to repair the damage done to the devastated areas of the country, something in the region of £33 billion would have to be spent.[38] This would use up almost the entire sum quoted by the committee in London, leaving little for any for their allies, most particularly Belgium. Equally resolute was André Tardieu. He was to base French demands upon the fact that, if Germany were not to meet its obligations, France 'would be obliged [instead] to borrow about one hundred and seventy million [in gold Francs]'[39] towards the task of rebuilding its shattered country. The prevailing tone, then, was that it was Germany and not France that should foot the bill. However, while Keynes could appreciate that the proceeds from reparations might serve French economic interests as 'they were vital for balancing their budgets,'[40] he was still adamant that extracting them from the defeated foe regardless of the consequences was completely counterproductive.

Despite the figures being bandied about, the French were nevertheless chary of submitting a fixed amount to the Reparation Commission. According to Tardieu, this was because they wanted 'to avoid an arbitrary figure which might in thirty years raise a Germany free from debt, and prosperous at the doors of France'.[41] In other words, France wanted

Germany to pay what was necessary to recompense its victims for the damage done but did not want to impose an amount that later proved to be less than Germany's capacity to pay. Part of France's motive behind reparations was to impose such a financial burden that it would indefinitely preclude Germany from financing its own economic and military recovery. After all, the Prussian indemnity imposed on France after the war of 1871 had been oppressive, but not so much that it could not be paid off in just a couple of years. If Germany demonstrated the same aptitude, where might that leave the victors? Such sentiments also preoccupied British thinking. In a cabinet meeting held at 10 Downing Street on 4 March 1919, Lloyd George echoed Tardieu's sentiments when he suggested that a 'large indemnity would prevent Germany being able to finance a large conscript army'[42] and thus posing a threat for some time. This, however, would mean reneging on his own policy of only seeking what Germany could pay. It was becoming all too evident that while 'France would never get what she hoped for'[43] it was also 'sheer illusion to think that Germany could be appeased by moderate terms'.[44]

Others feared that this obsession with securing a financial settlement was threatening to dominate the conference. Four days after Loucher addressed the French Senate, the secretary of state for India, Lord Montagu, warned the prime minister in somewhat purple prose, 'the prolonged scientific investigations into bills of costs and actual claims which the Reparation Commission is considering are likely to be a work of supererogation, are likely to lead to no practical results, are likely to take much too long, and are likely to lead to unnecessary international disputes.'[45] Nevertheless, during March there was further discussion on the matter and Lord Montagu, presumably having had a change of heart, now wanted to make sure that 'we are not diddled by our allies'.[46] Under siege from all sides, and bombarded by differing opinions, Lloyd George was openly regretting having raised the hopes of the British public in the first place. He professed to Colonel House that 'he needed to find a plausible reason to his people for having fooled them about the question of war costs, reparations and what not. He admitted that he knew Germany could not pay anything like the indemnity which the British and French demanded.'[47] The colonel agreed. He claimed that 'making Germany pay ... was a mad and wholly unwarranted assumption, but the people accepted it as an easy way out of their many difficulties.'[48]

Hoping somehow to achieve a solution to this blind alley, Lloyd George decided in March 1919 to closet himself and his closest advisers away in Fontainebleau just outside the capital. Here, away from the hurly-burly and distractions of Paris, he wanted to look at the options in the cold light of day and present his recalcitrant ally France with a definitive analysis of what was realistic. Accompanied by cabinet secretary Sir Maurice Hankey, his private secretary Philip Kerr, permanent military representative to the Supreme War Council Sir Henry Wilson, and General Smuts, the plan was to thrash out a proposal which would prevent the more excessive ideas starting to circulate in Paris. In essence, the memorandum which emerged from the conference on 25 March was a *crie de Coeur* to those like Clemenceau that a severely punitive peace imposed on Germany would be totally counterproductive. It covered more than reparations, and suggested:

> ... what is difficult ... is to draw up a peace which will not provoke a fresh struggle when those who have had practical experience of what war means have passed away ... you may strip Germany of her colonies, reduce her armaments to a mere police force and her navy to that of a fifth rate power; all the same in the end if she feels that she has been unjustly treated in the peace of 1919 she will find means of exacting retribution from her conquerors ... our terms may be severe, they may be stern and even ruthless but at the same time they can be so just that the country on which they are imposed will feel in its heart that it has no right to complain. But injustice, arrogance, displayed at the hour of triumph will never be forgotten or forgive ... if we are wise, we shall offer to Germany a peace, which while just, will be preferable for all sensible men to the alternative of Bolshevism ... [we must] ... do everything possible to enable the German people to get upon their legs again; we cannot both cripple her and expect her to pay...[49]

The last sentence precisely echoed Keynes' warnings, but if Lloyd George needed further reminding that he was playing both to a domestic audience and to recalcitrant backbenchers in the House of Commons, it came on 9 April 1919. He received a telegram signed by 233 Unionist MPs, insisting that they would tolerate no reduction in any claims made at the conference for reparations and any attempt to do so would be met with the strongest possible consequences.[50] Lloyd George had said one thing to get elected, another to try to stay onside with his allies, and now, having become bitterly disillusioned, he faced huge political repercussions if he went home empty-handed.

One audacious solution to the impasse was proposed by Keynes, but it was far too revolutionary to stand any hope of being adopted. It was that each government simply write off its debts to everybody else, thus allowing everyone to wipe the slate clean and begin anew. Lloyd George predictably expressed sympathy for this rather simplistic but unworkable approach, but Wilson, undoubtedly with an eye on public opinion back home, not to mention Congress, would have none of it. Then, under pressure from Hughes, the prime minister started to ponder how the UK might secure a bigger share of those reparations which might be forthcoming, presumably so as not to be 'diddled' as Lord Montagu so pithily put it. He allowed himself to be persuaded by the rather obscure notion that as soldiers were merely civilians in uniform, injuries to them constituted civilian damage and so their war and disability pensions should be included.[51] By 1920, there would be nearly a quarter of a million war widows arising from the 750,000 British casualties suffered during the war, and as the War Guilt Clause explicitly put the blame for their fate down to the Germans, shouldn't they have to foot the bill, rather than the British taxpayer? Britain was in debt to the tune of over, £7.4 billion due to the war, and much of this was owed to the United States. If there was no possibility of a write-off, and there was no guarantee that shipping losses would be recovered, then maybe the pensions idea could offset part of this sum.

Lloyd George asked Smuts to produce a paper outlining the proposals and this was presented to the US president for his approval. To the astonishment of nearly everyone, Wilson agreed. His advisers were horrified by the idea and believed that including pensions and separation allowances was illogical, not to mention a blatant breach of the pre-Armistice agreement. Wilson clearly resented any such challenge to his authority and characteristically shouted, 'Logic, Logic! I don't give a damn about logic. I am going to include pensions!'[52] Thus the irrational debate continued. However, calculating sums owed and allocating shares to injured parties was one thing; identifying where exactly it was to come from was quite clearly another.

It was widely assumed that the huge sums being discussed were not only to be paid in hard cash, but with the same assets and natural resources that Germany would need in order to survive, such as gold, iron, steel and iron ore. This, however, would mean inflicting possibly irrevocable economic damage upon one of the two largest European free trade areas which had existed in 1914. With their customs unions and common standards, they had constituted the high-water mark of political and economic cooperation and interdependency, and it was not a system from which their neighbours were all of a sudden detached and unaffected. As Keynes explained:

> ... the war had so shaken this system as to endanger the life of Europe altogether. A great part of the continent was sick and dying; its population was greatly in excess of the numbers for which a livelihood was available; its organisation was destroyed; its transport system ruptured, and its food supplies terribly impaired...[53]

Therefore, the exaction of ruthless indemnities could only make this situation worse. Germany had been among Russia, Norway, Holland, Belgium, Switzerland and Italy's best customers before the war. It had been the second-best customer of the UK, Sweden and Denmark, and the third best customer of France. It served as the largest source of supply to Russia, Norway, Sweden, Denmark, Holland, Switzerland, Italy, Romania and Bulgaria, and the second largest source of supply to the UK, Belgium and France. It had therefore clearly been pivotal to the 'economic interdependence' of Europe as a whole,[54] so what, Keynes argued, could possibly be gained from crippling it for possibly decades to come? The same argument stood for its infrastructure and moveable assets. The seizure of railway engines and stock had the effect of seriously disrupting Germany's transport system, a vital component of any healthy economy.[55] Having to absorb the loss of 5,000 locomotives and 150,000 wagons, regardless of how desperately they were needed by the French, the Belgians and the Poles, was a terrible blow. The transportation of the very coal and ore which the Allies would be demanding towards its reparations payments would be hampered, and its own losses of rolling stock compounded the effects of such confiscations.

Another source of exactions was Germany's overseas investments. But among the biggest recipients of these had already been Russia, Turkey, Romania and Bulgaria. By 1918, these would have been almost worthless anyway.[56] As the war progressed, like all the belligerents Germany needed to raise money, and would have resold the best of its investments in American, Dutch, Swiss and Scandinavian securities. The United States, as we have seen, had already confiscated a considerable amount of Germany's US assets. Keynes warned that 'it is not, in fact practicable to take any substantial part without consequence to the German currency system injurious to the interests of the Allies themselves.'[57] Furthermore, he added, once all these factors had been taken into consideration, 'it will be a miracle if much remains for reparation.'[58]

But the humiliations to be heaped upon Germany did not end there. The final settlement would also require Germany to admit imports without quotas from Allied countries free from duty, and it also had to afford 'most favoured nation' status to the Entente powers for five years without reciprocity.[59] These measures would have the effect of opening up its markets to cheap imports, which would inevitably undercut its own producers and further undermine its recovery. This was in clear breach of Wilson's own Fourteen Points, one of which had called for 'the removal, so far as possible, of all economic barriers and the establishment of an equality of trade conditions among all the nations consenting to the peace'. All in all, these provisions, as far as Keynes was concerned, had created 'one of the most serious acts of positive unwisdom for which our statesmen have ever been responsible'.[60]

Harold Nicolson agreed. He felt that the entire arrangement was a complete mess. On 8 June 1919, he wrote to his father that in his opinion, and that of many of his colleagues, the terms were 'punitive and ... abound with what Smuts calls "pin pricks" as well as "dagger thrusts"... [the] reparation and indemnity chapter ... is immoral and senseless ... the only people who approve are the old fire-eaters.'[61] In essence, as Keynes put it, those old fire eaters, among them Clemenceau, Hymans and Tardieu, had created an atmosphere in which it 'became impossible to erect any constructive financial policy which was workable'.[62] Edward House, too, was convinced that the entire approach to the settlement of reparations was wrong. He believed that 'the economic and financial terms of the peace should have been made as soon after the armistice as possible ... failure to do this ... is largely to blame for the present chaotic international situation.' He added that 'it was obviously to our advantage to bring back a normal, healthy economic condition everywhere. We cannot have bankrupt neighbours and continue to prosper for long.'[63] Ultimately, the failure of the US to ratify the treaty meant it was absent from the protracted discussions that decided upon a final sum. With no balance between the demands of Belgium and France on the one hand and the UK on the other, the French were left with the casting vote. The final sum to be paid was not agreed until May 1921, and it was set at £6.6 billion, to be paid in instalments until 1984. Even so, it did not take more than a few months for the whole scheme to unravel as the economic realities began to make themselves felt.

The new Weimar government made an initial payment in August 1921, but this was soon followed by the economic collapse that Keynes had predicted. With hyperinflation gripping the country, plus other economic problems, the second instalment proved impossible to meet. In the same year the government sought a moratorium, which was finally agreed to in May 1922, in the face of fierce opposition from the French, who were dependent upon the payments to meet their own war loan commitments to Britain and the United States. Just as in a latter-day pyramid scheme, the failure of one participant to maintain its contributions had a knock-on effect and ultimately meant its complete collapse. Germany defaulted entirely in 1923, and in January, as punishment, the French and Belgians invaded and occupied the Ruhr. They seized property, plants, manufactured goods and coal in lieu of payment, while their troops treated the civilian population with some brutality. At the behest of the German government, the French and Belgians were faced with passive resistance and strikes, in response to which ringleaders were arrested and workers bussed in from France to work in the mines.

This sorry chapter served to underline the impotence of the League, which did very little but appease the French and the Belgians, who used the dubious argument that their actions were justified under the terms of the treaty. The French realised their actions were counterproductive and left anyway in August, but they left behind them an embittered population and an angry German public. Civil disturbances and demonstrations were staged across the country in sympathy with the Germans of the Ruhr, including uprisings in the Rhineland, and Adolf Hitler's notorious Munich putsch. This was presented as a response to the government's pusillanimous reaction to the French and Belgian actions. Little was achieved by the entire episode but to severely strain relations between the countries involved and further entrench enmity and resentment.

It was also evident that something had to be done about Germany's worsening economic crisis, and in 1924 the Allied Payments Commission, chaired by American financier Charles G. Dawes, met and agreed that the Germans should resume payments on a sliding scale in proportion to its ability to pay. It did not suggest a revised settlement figure, but did make a $100 million loan available to the Germans, to try to stimulate its economy. Germany's ongoing economic problems inevitably resulted in this initiative failing too, and in February 1929, another American banker, Owen D. Young, chaired a committee in Paris to see what could be done. The total sum due from Germany was slashed by 75 per cent, and its repayment schedule extended to 1989, while restrictions on its economy were lifted. The first instalment was made, but again its faltering economy rendered it impossible to continue. Another moratorium had been agreed in 1932, and the following year the key stakeholders met in Lausanne to discuss a way forward. A major factor impeding any progress was that France still depended upon its share of the payments to service its own debts, and the Americans were not prepared to be lenient or generous in the midst of a worsening world economic depression. Despite the impasse, it was obvious Germany could not pay, and the Allies had to reluctantly concede that they were not going to receive anything after all. When Adolf Hitler became German chancellor in 1933, and repudiated the Treaty of Versailles altogether, that became a bitter reality. France would have to manage without its badly needed windfall and Britain would have to pay for its own pensions.

Ultimately the policy of reparations and indemnities had failed, inflicting almost as much damage on the creditors as on the debtor. Keynes, House and Nicolson had been vindicated. Eminent historian A. J. P. Taylor saw the debacle over reparations as symptomatic of much else decided in Paris, that it was due to the fragility and underlying weakness of the Allied position. Essentially, having only the German signature to give it validity, there was no other form of enforcement open to the Allies, and the debacle in the Ruhr demonstrated that force did not work anyway. The German delegation could be forced to sign under threat of renewed hostilities or intensification of the blockade, but once their armies were demobilised and the continent returned to a peacetime regime, there was no tangible means by which to enforce any of the treaty's terms. Furthermore, because the treaty 'lacked moral validity ... it did not enforce itself.'[64] It only needed the force of events beyond everyone's control, such as a depression, to render any agreement null and void.

The intransigence of Germany could also undermine it, as the reparations issue and its response to the invasion demonstrated. As it had acceded to an imposed peace only under extreme duress, 'the German signature ... carried no weight or obligation,'[65] and of course this was a sentiment bitterly articulated by the German representatives themselves.

Nor did the victors assembled in Paris in 1918 appear to see the drawbacks in so humiliating and subjugating those they had defeated, that a burning sense of injustice and desire for revenge would motivate them to do all they could to sabotage the treaty. The head of the German delegation, Count Brockdorff-Rantzau, made the German position clear when he spoke to the conference on 7 May 1919, lamenting that because they had only signed under compulsion:

> A peace which cannot be defended in the name of justice before the whole world would continually call forth fresh resistance. No one could sign it with a clear conscience, for it would be impossible of fulfilment. No one could undertake the guarantee of fulfilment which its signature would imply.[66]

As Keynes had warned, crippling Germany could ruin Europe. Overly punitive peace treaties with Austria in 1866 and France in 1871 would have been equally counterproductive for Germany had it imposed them. Realising this, Bismarck had refrained from inflicting even harsher indemnities and more draconian penalties than he had. Napoleon in his time, and the victors of 1815, had also realised that the economic and political balance of power needed to be maintained. They had for the most part agreed upon equitable peace treaties which largely laid the ground for reconciliation, something forgotten by too many of the peacemakers in 1919. Instead, as Keynes noted later, 'if the General Election of December 1918 had been fought on lines of prudent generosity instead of imbecile greed, how much better the financial prospect of Europe might now be.'[67] In any case, France's appetite for revenge had not been limited to its demands for money; it also had other items on its list. These, too, would have dire consequences for the peace of Europe.

6

France Remains in Perpetual Danger of Invasion

André Tardieu, keen proponent of imposing the severest penalties on Germany in 1919. (Library of Congress)

Apart from exacting every pfennig out of Germany in reparations, the most crucial red line for France at the peace negotiations was the creation of a shield between itself and its Teutonic nemesis. Following the end of the Napoleonic Wars, it was France's neighbours that needed protection from France. Now, having been invaded twice in fifty years, the integrity of the border between France and Germany was the priority. As Paul Cambon insisted on 2 July 1917, 'Germany must have henceforth but one foot across the Rhine',[1] but before such an ambition could be translated into reality its precise nature had still to be negotiated. The options, as they appeared to the French, were a neutral, self-governing buffer state; outright annexation; or military occupation. One way or another, the 'Boche' must be kept at bay. As Harold Nicolson put it so pithily in his diary, the French 'long to create a ditch between themselves and the rest of the world';[2] if not the world at large, then certainly the German world.

Any long-term option was problematic, because the prospect of permanent detachment or occupation would undoubtedly cause tensions and pose insuperable challenges. This was not simply a vast stretch of unpopulated real estate, like the no man's land of the Western Front, which separated the French from the German front lines. The prospect here was the potential detachment of 'a great industrial ... [and] ... military region, rich in munition factories and fortresses and strategic railroads planned to support German military enterprises to the westward'. This explained the French desire to neutralise these assets. Annexation or the creation of a neutral buffer state might achieve this end. However, it was also 'a thoroughly German region in speech and government and economic life, closely bound to the lines beyond the Rhine'.[3] Such a solution was therefore little better than the occupations and expropriations the Germans had carried out. Nevertheless, Francois Aulard, an eminent and highly regarded historian of the French Revolution, insisted brusquely that 'either we annex the left bank of the Rhine and violate principle, or do not annex it and France remains in perpetual danger of invasion.'[4]

He and likeminded compatriots did have a plausible argument to take to the conference. The River Rhine was no English Channel, but conversely there were no bridges linking Dover to Calais across which a hostile force could attack, and the Americans had the entire Atlantic Ocean behind which to consolidate their defence. The French felt that they were asking for no more than a reasonable chance to defend themselves. Nonetheless, it was going to be a hard sell, and a buffer state of any kind had never really been accepted by the British. With Lloyd George's approval, Balfour had expressed his opposition in 1917, stating that the Allies 'must never make another Alsace-Lorraine'.

Undeterred, on 1 December 1918 General Foch and Clemenceau visited London and the issue was raised again, this time with Lloyd George and Andrew Bonar Law, but it again received a somewhat lukewarm response. Lord Balfour considered the very idea of detaching such a large part of the Reich and rendering it into some kind of *cordon sanitaire*, 'a rather wild project' that could never work.[5] The Americans were also opposed, seeing it as against the best interests of the population, as annexation would bring 5.4 million Germans under French rule, an abrogation of the Armistice terms and almost certainly likely to stir up problems again at some time in the future.[6] Wilson, for one, would not countenance what he perceived as naked territorial aggrandisement, especially as the maxim of 'self-determination' was going to become such a watchword of the peace negotiations. Nor, understandably, were there any tangible signs of enthusiasm for separation from Germany among the Rhinelanders themselves.[7] Few, if any, actually viewed with favour any of the options being considered – being detached from their homeland and appended to a foreign state, being forced to become a neutral power like Belgium, or, worst of all, being occupied by foreign troops for perhaps decades to come.

French policy, however, was also predicated upon the fact that before 1914 it could have hoped Russia would draw off German forces in the event of war with Germany, giving the French army more time to mobilise and react to any westward movement. In part the Schlieffen Plan disabused them of this assumption, as Russia's performance in August 1914 had not prevented the invader from sweeping through Belgium and reaching the Marne. The new Russia was even less reliable, and, having been ostracised by its allies, might well become an ally of Germany at some point. It was therefore evident that some other tactic was needed to forestall the prospect of invasion. Without a physical barrier, admittedly cutting it off from Germany but also the rest of Europe, there were few other options available.

There was yet another factor for the French to consider, and one with which Lord Derby sympathised. On 7 March 1919 he wrote to Lord Curzon:

> The French are still in a mortal funk over Germany ... the disparity between the populations of the two countries is a perfect nightmare for them. They are ... determined to get a big buffer between them and Germany and I feel confident that they will sacrifice almost anything to secure our support for that...[8]

Although the German army was likely to be as small as 100,000, and suffering a ban on conscription, it would still possess a pool of millions of men trained in and with extensive experience of war. André Tardieu insisted that this possibility alone justified the maintenance of a defensive barrier.[9] With no neutral zone, no demilitarisation, and no physical defences, there was little to prevent Germany reconstituting a huge force, seizing the Rhine crossings and using them to mount an invasion at some time in the near future. Indeed, the French went so far as to insist that the defence of the Rhine concerned not merely France but all western civilisation,[10] but this claim had little impact and other nations remained unconvinced.

On 10 January 1919, General Foch submitted his own radical ideas to the French government. These called for the maintenance of a permanent garrison on the left bank, which would perforce allow France to control the three strategic bridgeheads which the Germans might be expected to employ in the event of an attack. He also advocated economic integration of the territory with France and Belgium in some form of customs union. His ideas appeared plausible to his audience, and after some debate they were adopted and approved by the French government's Committee on Foreign Affairs,[11] but that was only half the battle. It still had to pass the scrutiny of Messrs Lloyd George and Wilson. Maurice Schwob, editor of the Nantes-based newspaper *Le Phare de la Loire*, or 'Lighthouse of the Loire', proposed something less likely to raise the suspicions of the British and the Americans, which he described later as 'the creation of an autonomous Rhineland-Westphalian state under the protection of the League of Nations'.[12] As could have been predicted, the Allies poured cold water on both proposals. The population of the territory, even if they did belong to a despised and defeated power, could not be treated like bargaining chips. The French, Colonel House despaired, 'do not seem to know that to establish a Rhenish Republic against the will of the people would be contrary to the principle of self-determination'.[13]

Clearly the hurdles confronting any attempt to annex or neutralise the territory were far greater than the French had imagined. Nonetheless, on 25 February, André Tardieu had another try, and proposed 'the fixation of the Rhine as the western frontier of Germany and the inter-allied occupation of the Rhine bridges'.[14] By this plan he explained:

> There is no question of annexing an inch of German soil, only of depriving Germany of her weapons of offence ... France expects from an inter-Allied occupation of the Rhine what Great Britain and the United States expect from the maintenance of their naval forces; nothing more or less.[15]

Furthermore, like Foch, he proposed 'a customs union between France, Belgium and the Rhine country ... [that] would offer advantages in regard to a large number of products, and at least would offer no disadvantages'.[16] Although the question of a customs union between France and Belgium would be settled by the referendum, the inclusion of the Rhineland would bind part of Germany too closely to France for the comfort of many. Moreover, it could be used as a pretext to further extend French influence over its wider neighbours, a prospect which those in Whitehall, or even perhaps Washington, would find uncomfortable. These suspicions understandably perplexed the French. Although Tardieu admitted that his Rhine policy was 'misunderstood by the British',[17] and that 'it was extremely repugnant to our allies',[18] he nevertheless insisted that 'we want no annexation ... but we want our security'.[19] Such exhortations left the Allies cold. Lt-Colonel J. H. M. Cornwall, military attaché to the British delegation, did not believe the French were thinking rationally. On 11 March 1919, he insisted that 'French schemes on the subject ... are short sighted, selfish and quite impractical.'[20]

In any case, the discussions seemed to be getting nowhere, and as a consequence the atmosphere was becoming so soured by the subject that Lloyd George admitted that 'at one time a serious rupture between France and her Allies was threatened.'[21] Tardieu also had to concede that 'it was clear there was a deep difference of opinion between the British and the French governments' over the matter.[22] Philip Kerr also remarked that while 'we quite agree with France as to the object to be attained, we are not sure we agree with her as to the method to be employed.'[23] Regardless, the nagging topic could not yet be put to bed. When the subject was discussed in Downing Street on 4 March 1919, it was accepted that while the French wanted 'a buffer state on the left bank of the Rhine', they had by now accepted French assurances that there were no plans to annex it and that 'its fate must be decided by the peace conference.'[24] This was unlikely to be either annexation or the creation of a neutral state, leaving only the possibility of some kind of military occupation.

However, if the French were not going to be satisfied with anything short of 'control of the bridgeheads, with a permanent military occupation',[25] the problem was now the interpretation of 'permanent'. Foch conceded that another war was highly unlikely for at least twenty years or more, so it was reasonable to infer that France would not 'accept permanently the burden of maintaining a garrison of something like 300,000 men on the Rhine'. Of course, it could finance the occupation from the reparations it hoped to receive, but these were earmarked for reconstruction. Perhaps instead the Rhinelanders themselves could be forced to fund the occupation, maybe out of any proceeds from the proposed customs union. None of these options were likely to be approved by President Wilson, even if suggested to him while he was engaged on one of his flights of fancy.

The issue of who might be expected to provide contingents for an army of occupation was also raised. Now that the war was over, simple economics demanded that demobilisation begin as a matter of urgency. Britain would only be prepared to provide troops for 'the period of occupation prior to the signing of the treaty',[26] after which they would be withdrawn and returned to civvy street. Therefore, any long-term occupation would have to be resourced and funded by the French alone. Perhaps the only practical backstop for French security, then, would be to keep the Rhineland demilitarised, under the supervision of the League of Nations.[27] But this option would take the matter out of French hands, and they would be dependent upon the League to ensure enforcement. While not yet tested, the organisation had not exactly been designed for prompt action, especially as French proposals for a League with a permanent military force were not to bear fruit. This situation was not lost on the Conservatives' own party organ, the *National Review*, which had referred scathingly to the 'League of Nations Fiasco',[28] and thus had already identified its shortcomings.

Nor was the issue lost on Lloyd George. In response, he rather rashly improvised. He wondered whether 'the United States and ourselves would guarantee France against invasion'. He made the proposal despite being dubious as to whether Wilson would even agree to the idea, admitting that he, not to mention the US Congress, 'would not hear of any entangling alliances', as he was still enthusiastic about the League, into which he had 'put his faith'.[29] In that case, what motivated the prime minister to raise such a possibility? It was admittedly the kind of gesture which might assuage French concerns, but it would also be a complete volte-face on the part of Great Britain with regards to its relationship with Europe. British policy since at least the end of the Napoleonic Wars had been to keep the continent at arm's length, and at best to maintain a form of so-called 'splendid isolation'. Apart from being a guarantor of Belgian independence, the UK had not agreed to underwrite the defence of any other state.

The Entente Cordiale of 1904 was primarily an agreement to tie up outstanding colonial issues, placing Britain under no legal obligations, and the Anglo-French conversations which followed were likewise non-binding. Could he really be thinking that the British Parliament would ratify a treaty, against all historical convention, which committed the UK to going to war in defence of a third party? Perhaps it might if the United States could be persuaded to underwrite such a scheme.

Wilson was back in the United States and could not easily be consulted on the matter. Instead Colonel House was made party to the proposal, and he subsequently cabled the president, although his busy domestic schedule did not allow much time to fully digest its implications. Lloyd George clearly could not wait, so in the meantime, on 12 March, Kerr raised the prospect of an Anglo-American guarantee with Tardieu,[30] who appeared to be very receptive to the proposal. Soon after Wilson's ship docked, he, Lloyd George and Clemenceau met informally at the Hotel Crillon on 14 March, in the hope of finally settling the matter. If Tardieu had forewarned Clemenceau, he does not appear to have shown it. Certainly, none of the British Empire delegation seem to have been given prior notice, and apart from raising the possibility at the meeting of the 4th, nor were his cabinet colleagues.

Forewarned or not, Clemenceau welcomed the suggestion, which he hailed as a 'stroke of fortune for France'.[31] In exchange for such an offer he was more than prepared to abandon demands for the Rhineland's separation from Germany, especially as Lloyd George had allegedly promised Clemenceau that he would 'place all our forces'[32] at France's disposal should it be necessary. The British prime minister was even quoted as having undertaken to build a tunnel under the English Channel if necessary.[33] Such vainglorious promises certainly helped to assure the French of his sincerity, although of course agreement among the three did not automatically translate into ratification by the US Congress or indeed approval by the British Parliament. The acceptance of the French chamber, however, could be taken more or less for granted, although the treaty that emerged later would be a seriously diluted version of what had been implied. Nor was it allowed to be quite so straightforward.

Just when everything seemed to have been settled, the French muddied the waters by bringing up the question of Belgium. It was all very well promising to assist France in the event of another attack, but what of its smaller ally? The Schlieffen Plan revealed its exposure to any invasion as much as France. Denied the Rhineland as a base from which to launch an invasion, the next logical point of access was the country for whom Britain ostensibly went to war in the first place. Tardieu later recorded how, 'in our reply of March 17, to the offer of English and American treaties ... [we] expressed the indissoluble unit of French and Belgian interests ... it goes without saying that by act of aggression against France, the French Government understands also any aggression against Belgium'.[34] The British prime minister and the US president agreed, and it was confirmed that Belgium would also be included in the guarantee.

However, it was not lost on observers that the League was already being undermined, a fact the *National Review* inferred by the apparent need for it to be 'bolstered ... by the Triple Pact'.[35] Although the solution to French fears was ostensibly Lloyd George's idea, Wilson did not appear to mind taking credit for the initiative. On 3 April 1919, he allegedly bragged to his personal physician Dr Grayson that he had been 'thinking what would be the outcome if these French politicians were given a free hand and allowed to have their way ... [it] would go to pieces in a very short while'.[36] Whoever was to take the credit for preventing things going to pieces, the solution certainly appeared to give France everything it might need. The reduction of the German army to that of a defence force, and the denial to it of any weapons of aggression such as tanks or military aircraft would make any offensive operations impracticable. For its own part, France, by retaining conscription and a large standing army, and by being free to develop whatever weapons or strategy it saw fit, should be able to maintain an overwhelming superiority well into the future. For Germany, the restrictions imposed upon its potential war-making capacity would be further compounded by Article 180 of the final Treaty, which stated that:

> ... all fortified works, fortresses and field works situated in German territory to the west of a line drawn 50 kilometres to the east of the Rhine shall be disarmed and dismantled ... the construction of any new fortification ... is forbidden...

Furthermore, any withdrawal of the inter-Allied occupation of the West Bank and the three bridgeheads was intended to be conditional on Germany honouring its treaty obligations and making good on its reparations payments. On paper, this further entrenched the likelihood of France's immunity from aggression for some time to come. So much so that Clemenceau said afterwards, 'I have the fifteen years. I now consider that peace is made.'[37] He was further motivated by the conviction that, one way or the other, the fifteen years could be turned into twenty and even more, as he was sure that 'Germany will default, and we shall stay where we are.'[38] This delusion was predicated upon the Allies, backed by the League of Nations, having the will to take whatever action was necessary if Germany did default.

Marshal Foch was scathing of the final settlement, dismissing it as a chimera. On 6 May he explained his reasons to a plenary session of the conference:

> The treaty assures complete guarantees for a period of five years, during which Germany will doubtless be in a position to do no harm. But, from that time on, as German power returns and our danger increases, our guarantees decrease until, at the end of fifteen years they disappear altogether.[39]

He was not alone in his analysis. Maurice Schwob was equally dismissive of any defence guarantees from the British and Americans. The Schlieffen Plan had revealed just how swiftly an invading army could reach French soil on foot. The technical advances made during the war, not to mention those likely to be made in the future, would mean that in all likelihood 'our Allies would arrive on the scene too late, and we should be strangled while they were still deliberating'.[40] Tardieu, nonetheless, felt that the French needed to be pragmatic, admitting that 'the left bank remains German instead of becoming independent. One may regret it. But if we had stuck to the original proposal, it would have meant a break with the Allies.'[41] Moreover, there was the prospect of achieving an even sweeter prize, one which had been at the forefront of French thinking long before possession of the Rhineland had been considered realistic: the recovery of Alsace-Lorraine. This was also assumed to be beyond question, having been specifically guaranteed to France by President Wilson in his Fourteen Points. Tardieu said that, 'like all my compatriots, I was inclined to think that our claims in connection with Alsace-Lorraine called for no discussion whatever and were a foregone conclusion.'[42] He was pretty much right in his assumption.

Since 1871, Alsace-Lorraine had developed into a highly productive territory of 5,600 square miles and 1,694 villages, towns and cities,[43] 'comprising the Departments of Haut-Rhin and the Bas-Rhin, and the *arrondisements* of Metz, Thionville, Sarreguemines, Chateau-Salines and Sarrebourg, with more than a million and a half inhabitants'.[44] Therefore, its return meant ownership of a significant and valuable piece of real estate. In 1913, out of over 28 million tons of iron ore extracted from German mines, some 21 million had been extracted from Alsace-Lorraine.[45] Also, it was not anticipated that any sizeable opposition would come from the inhabitants. As we have seen, neither its population nor many in the French government had reconciled themselves to their fate in 1871. They had been, wrote a commentator at the time, 'incorporated into a nation they detested, to be obliged to serve in its armies, and eventually to fight against those whom they consider their brothers ... [and consequently] ... the twentieth century must redress the greatest iniquity of the nineteenth'.[46]

Nevertheless, the Germans were determined not to be so accommodating. On 24 January 1918, German chancellor Count von Heitling claimed that Alsace-Lorraine had in fact been German until the French began their process of expropriation. All Germany had done in 1871 was to take back 'the district which had been criminally wrested from us. [It was not therefore] a conquest of foreign territory, but rightly and properly speaking what today is called de-annexation.'[47] Unsurprisingly, such sophistry left his Allied listeners unmoved. He nevertheless insisted that at the very least there should be a plebiscite in which the population of the disputed territory could decide its fate. After all, a period of fifty years had elapsed and there was a reasonable chance that this vote might emerge in Germany's favour. Since 1871, at least half a million French men and women had left and almost an equal number of Germans had settled in the provinces. Despite the rationale, this proposal fell on deaf ears as well. Charles Homer Haskins, another of the US delegation's advisers at the conference, dismissed the German's cynical conversion to the concept of self-determination as simple hypocrisy:

Although the Germans had contemptuously refused the self-determination which they had promised the Danes in 1866, although they had ignored the unanimous protest of the deputies of Alsace-Lorraine in 1871, in 1919 they suddenly became enamoured of self-determination as they interpreted it.[48]

Moreover, they had agreed to the return of the provinces when they accepted the Fourteen Points, so they could not have it both ways. Haskins recalled that the Germans 'nevertheless ... put up a last fight for the retention of these territories, tied up as they were with Germany's imperial tradition [and] with her strategic position',[49] which of course was why von Bismarck had annexed them in the first place.

In an attempt to find a middle way, other options were briefly considered. One was to establish a protectorate under the League of Nations, and another was for the territory to become an independent monarchy with a royal house of its own within the German Empire; a third suggested that it be established as an independent and neutral state, like Belgium, owing allegiance neither to France or Germany.[50] None were deemed to be plausible alternatives, and in any case all were in complete contradiction of the Fourteen Points. Subsequently, in keeping with Wilson's undertaking and with the general agreement of the entire conference, the return of the two provinces was approved and enshrined in the final treaty. It became clear, however, that during their occupation the Germans had taken extensive measures to integrate the region economically with the Reich, to the disadvantage of the French. As Tardieu explained, this applied particularly to the port of Kehl:

> ... just opposite Strasbourg and splendidly equipped, [Kehl] had been purposely used to the detriment of the Alsatian port. If, after the signature of peace, Kehl were to be free to compete in any way it chose, Strasbourg would be finally throttled. So, we asked that for a certain number of years Strasbourg should be afforded the possibility of organising itself, and that with this in view the two ports should during this period be placed under a single management.[51]

To become economically viable and reverse decades of decline, the conference subsequently conceded that the two ports should be jointly managed for a period of seven years. There would also be an option to extend the arrangement for another three years if it was considered necessary, and in addition both would be free zones under the international authority of a Central Rhine Commission.[52] The French had thus secured a key war aim, yet the list of French demands had still not been exhausted.

French designs on the Saar were equally voracious but were to prove much more problematic. Having been German for even longer than Alsace-Lorraine and at least as long as the Rhineland, the region was indisputably German in character and substance. Nevertheless, France saw in the defeat of Germany the opportunity to correct another perceived historic injustice as well as increase access to vital raw materials. France, Tardieu insisted, 'needs this basin, not only to furnish Alsace and Lorraine, which consume seven million tons more coal than they produce, but for herself also'.[53] It had, after all, developed under German rule into a rich coal-producing region of 700 square miles with a population of 650,000. The French saw the ownership of its coal mines as no less than they were rightfully due to compensate them, 'as a nation systematically ruined by Germany'.[54] Moreover, according to Tardieu, 'a large part of this territory was inhabited by people French by race, by tradition and by aspiration, which the treaties of 1814 had left to France and which violence alone had torn from her in 1815'.[55]

Keynes could not have disagreed more. He saw no justification whatsoever in the Saar's cession to France, claiming that 'only 100 of 650,000 inhabitants in the Saar in 1918 were French' and that 'the Saar district has been German for more than one thousand years [while] France has possessed the country for not quite sixty-eight years in all.'[56] Such conflicting statistics and counter claims would inevitably mean, Tardieu admitted, that it was an issue 'the American delegates to the peace conference, and the United States as a whole, least understood'.[57] It would also prove to be one of the most intractable.

Charles Haskins, for example, was not alone in insisting that 'the economic claims were the only ones for which a basis could be found,'[58] adding that 'material compensation must not involve the political annexation of unwilling populations.' That said, 'the problem of separating the mines from the people who lived over them was thus created, and it was not a simple one.'[59] On 28 March 1919, Tardieu accompanied Louis Loucher to meet the Council of Four at President Wilson's Paris home. They proposed the political annexation up to the frontier of 1814, with full ownership of the mines in the adjoining districts. While both Lloyd George and Wilson could see no problem in France exploiting the mines to make up for the loss of their own 'for a period that shall be determined',[60] they made no secret of the fact that, like Haskins and Keynes, they harboured serious misgivings regarding the question of annexation. The Frenchmen responded that if annexation was unacceptable, they could accept a larger autonomous state under French protection instead. This suggestion also met with scepticism, so, having reached an impasse, a special committee of experts was established to consider the issue.

The French delegates were understandably despondent. Tardieu conceded that they 'were alone ... fighting without hope of success',[61] all the more so because 'long experience had taught us that reasoning borrowed from the past had little appeal for Mr Wilson.'[62] In other words, even had the French been able to produce irrefutable evidence of the provenance of the territory, the US president would still be singularly unimpressed. Nonetheless, in the interests of fairness, the Council of Four discussed the problem at length between 9 and 11 April. Another option, that of a French mandate under the League, was also rejected, as it was considered to be 'stretching the mandatory principle beyond its proper purpose'.[63] Having considered and dispensed with these options one by one, it was eventually decided that, under League protection, the French could exploit the mines for fifteen years. At the end of this period a plebiscite would be organised, and the population asked whether they wished to return to Germany, become French, or remain under League protection.[64] This seemed to meet everyone's needs – apart from the Germans, of course – but as adviser to the conference Harold Temperley explained, 'The Saar settlement is fundamentally fair in principle, and its practical justice becomes clearer as we see the workings of reparations elsewhere.'[65] Indeed, as he proceeded to describe the arrangement, it would be difficult to see any significant flaws in it:

The people retained their religious liberties, their schools and their language ... they send no representatives to the Reichstag or the

Landtag but have local assemblies of their own. Its male population was not subject to conscription in France, and such were the advantages enjoyed by the population that it was claimed that the populations of neighbouring communes and Cantons in Prussia had petitioned and agitated the League to be incorporated into the Saar.[66]

Furthermore, to forestall any attempt by the French to unduly influence the referendum scheduled for 1935, only those in residence at the time the agreement was made would be permitted to participate.[67] Lloyd George reportedly announced with a sense of achievement, 'Mr President, I think we have got a very good plan here,' to which Wilson immediately responded, 'Well, why don't you apply it to Ireland?'[68] For his part, Temperley firmly believed that the crucial factor in facilitating the agreement was the League of Nations: 'It is difficult to see how the conflicting interests involved could have been reconciled without some serious violation of justice, if the machinery of the League had not been available for a solution.'[69]

Nevertheless, the solution received something of a mixed reception. Henry Wilson remarked to Lloyd George rather sarcastically that 'I wish you luck in persuading Messieurs Clemenceau and Poincaré to accept that they cannot have the Rhineland, that the Saar will be on loan for ten years [*sic*], and that reparations will be both lower than they expect and of limited duration.'[70] Lord Curzon, on the other hand, saw things very differently. He felt the settlement had actually left France with the lion's share of the spoils. Indeed, the conference's decisions had in his view shifted the balance of European power seriously in France's favour, as he warned delegates to the Imperial Conference on 26 June 1921:

> ... with Lorraine, the Saar Valley and the Ruhr [*sic*] in her occupation, she [France] becomes the mistress of Europe in respect of coal, iron and steel, and with those countries under her military command she will also become the military monarch.[71]

As Curzon had cautioned, almost the entire stock of mineral assets of western Europe had been placed in the hands of one state. The Germans inevitably called the solution 'odious', but as 'no secure or acceptable guarantee was offered in its stead'[72] they had to concede that here, too, they had lost the argument. Of course, they had also lost another source of revenue with which they might have been able to meet their reparations commitments. France, on the other hand, had guaranteed its security, regained lost territory, and could shape the economic future of its neighbours for a generation – if the political will to do so existed, that is. Instead, the carefully constructed network of multi-lateral arrangements designed to underwrite the settlement failed to survive more than a few months, due in no small part to the duplicity and backtracking of the British prime minister.

Crucially, Lloyd George made the Anglo-American guarantee conditional upon US participation and had the word 'only' inserted in the drafts, so that the British treaty was not legally enforceable unless the US Senate kept the American side of the bargain. Although he reportedly told the empire delegation that he was 'apprehensive … lest the United States Senate might refuse the guarantee',[73] it is far more likely that he was banking on it. Moreover, the Welshman had diluted the British commitment by insisting that the guarantee was only intended to last for as long as the proposed fifteen-year occupation of the Rhineland. He was also very proscriptive as to how the phrase 'unprovoked aggression' could be interpreted, insisting that the British, not the French, would be the ones to decide if the aggression was unprovoked or not.[74] So if there was to be some sort of spat between the two which might lead to fighting, the British could still refuse to act, claiming that both parties were equally culpable. By the time these caveats were inserted the guarantee was not worth the paper it was written on, but by then it was too late. 'Clemenceau had already accepted our proposals, and he never went back on an arrangement to which he had assented,'[75] Lloyd George bragged, almost proud of his deception.

President Wilson, by now consumed with disappointment by the Senate's refusal to ratify US participation in the League, had lost interest. Ironically, this was one initiative to which Republican senators were minded to give their support. They liked it because it meant assuming the moral high ground by affording France guarantees for its security but without any immediate obligation to back it up with men or money. When the French heard that the treaty had fallen through, they were understandably crestfallen, and many responded with outright panic.[76] A key factor underpinning their future security had been swept away. When Warren Harding succeeded Wilson as president, and the French attempted to inject the project with renewed vigour, he too was lukewarm, and in any case was wary of confronting the 'irreconcilables' in his own party.[77] Consequently, the deal was quietly forgotten, and there was no possibility of the British assuming such an obligation on their own, nor indeed of building any tunnels, at least not for another sixty years.

Instead, in December 1925, French foreign minister Aristide Briand and his German counterpart, Gustav Stresemann, met with the new British prime minister, Stanley Baldwin, and representatives of Belgium and Italy to reconfirm their commitment to pursuing peaceful resolutions to any future disputes. Under the terms of the treaty, named after the city of Locarno in which it was negotiated, Britain offered a guarantee and Germany recognised its western frontiers with Belgium and France. Although the Germans declined to give the same undertaking with respect to those in the east, they did agree to submit any disputes to arbitration and not take any unilateral action. As a quid pro quo, the British and French agreed to end the military occupation of the Rhineland five years ahead of schedule, in 1930, on condition that the region remained demilitarised.

The French were not alone in seeing the war as an opportunity to reverse the perceived injustices of the past. Belgium saw its chance to acquire the two districts of Eupen and Malmedy, which it claimed had been lost to Germany in one of the frequent wars which had dogged the continent. There was certainly some justification for this on ethnic grounds, as of the 60,000 inhabitants some 10,000 were Walloons, and of course Belgium could exploit its martyr status to further support its claims. Belgian troops had in any case occupied the two districts in August 1919, and for Brussels the matter was only raised at the peace treaty to legitimise the new arrangement. The transfer inevitably faced opposition from the Germans, who were angered by the so-called referendum that was supposed to confirm their fate and the means by which it was weighted against them. In effect, if any eligible voters wished to protest the transfer, they had to do so in writing in one of two town halls set aside for the purpose. When only a few hundred of 33,000 eligible voters exercised this right, the Germans understandably protested. Their entreaties were to no avail, however, and the transfer was confirmed in September 1920, with the actual delineation of the new border decided upon by the League in 1922.

Although the Danes had largely resigned themselves to the loss of Schleswig in 1864, its population had not. Their leader, Theophil Hanssen, had begun agitating for reunification almost from the beginning of the war, and in October 1918 a formal demand for reunification was made in the Reichstag. Although the province's demographic and linguistic mix was as complex as it had been in 1864, nationalists realised that there would be no better opportunity to realise their dream. In November, nationalist Eigel Jorgensen declared that 'the Schleswig question is topical again ... we have our own voice'.[78] Before long, matters assumed a momentum of their own. Small soldiers' and workers' councils were formed, declaring independence from Germany and collaborating in the distribution of what little food was still available. The Danish government, which had understandably observed strict neutrality during the war, was now also spurred into action and advanced requests to the peace conference for consideration of the territories' return. The legitimacy of the request was clearly within the remit of 'self-determination', and it was subsequently decided that two referendums should be held, one in the predominantly Danish north (Zone One) and another in the mainly German south (Zone Two). Articles 109 to 114 of the final Treaty confirmed this, and in February 1920 the plebiscites were held. The results were as expected. In Zone One there was a 75 per cent vote in favour of union with Denmark, and in Zone Two an 80 per cent vote for remaining with the Reich. This situation would prove to be unique in post-war decision-making insofar as the Nazis never challenged or attempted to overturn the referendum after they came to power. The same could not be said for the new borders awarded to France.

Another decision which the Nazis had no wish to overturn was the result of the referendum on the future of the Saar, scheduled for 1935. However, whereas under the Weimar government its return could have been considered a foregone conclusion, the emergence of the Nazis changed the political climate in the territory. Communists and Social Democrats had formed a 'united front' and were now urging retention of League of Nations protection, fearing what a return to Nazi Germany would mean. The Saar's Nazis, encouraged by Berlin, had been equally determined that German prestige was dependent upon a vote to return to the homeland, and formed a 'German front' to campaign and, if necessary, intimidate their compatriots to achieve this end. Collaborating with the Saar police and the German Gestapo, they proceeded to cow those campaigning for the status quo. In spite of the safeguards that the original arrangement was supposed to have afforded the population, many anti-Nazis were forced to flee, leaving the field open to the Nazis. Despite being made aware of what was happening, the League was afraid to cancel the vote for fear that it would exacerbate the situation. Encouraged by this inaction, the 17,000 Nazi Saarlanders (who had gone to Germany to join the SA and receive lessons in thuggery) threatened to invade the Saar, circumvent the poll and impose reunification. Only a British offer to send a peacekeeping force to maintain order and preserve the integrity of the vote prevented the danger from being realised.

In the face of continued threats and coercion, the referendum went ahead. The ballot paper would give three options: remain under League protection, join France, or return to Germany. In spite of all the disorder, official observers declared the result valid: over 90 per cent were in favour of returning to the Reich. Honour bound to abide by the result, the League turned the Saar over to Germany, an outcome which Hitler duly lauded as a vindication of his policies and of the right of all Germans to exercise their wish to reunite with the fatherland. Encouraged by the League's reticence to confront the violence instigated during the referendum campaign, he proceeded to undermine more of the Treaty of Versailles.

Secretly, Hitler had already given orders for the army to ignore the limits placed upon it in 1918 and treble in size by October 1934. Similarly, Germany was to build warships larger than those permitted, and to embark upon a programme of submarine construction, all to be undertaken in strictest secrecy. The *Luftwaffe*, too, had seen a renaissance, with pilots and aircrew having been trained surreptitiously in Russia since Weimar times. Then, encouraged by the League's feeble handling of the Saar episode, in March 1935 Hitler decided to seize the moment and authorised the *Luftwaffe*'s head, Hermann Göring, to publicly reveal its existence. There was little to no reaction from Britain and France, and nothing meaningful forthcoming from the League, so a few days later Hitler announced that conscription had been reintroduced, with a target of thirty-six divisions, or 500,000 men. The reaction was limited to murmurings of disapproval, so the chancellor decided that the time must soon be ripe for his first *coup de grâce*, an unequivocal demonstration of Germany's resolve to flout the Treaty entirely. For this he looked, like his predecessors, to the Rhine.

Despite the promises made at Locarno, French paranoia could not be allayed by promises. The realisation that the Rhineland would no longer provide a buffer after 1930 set minds to serious contemplation of an alternative solution. The idea of another form of static defence began to gain currency, having been mooted by French general Philippe Pétain in the early 1920s when the shortcomings of both the Treaty and the League were already becoming evident. It was a return to the strategy credited with the defeat of France in 1871, whereby its troops fought from within fortified cities such as Sedan and the opposing Prussians waited them out. France had then turned to the philosophy of mobility and movement, which cost so many thousands of lives in the early part of the First World War, before resorting yet again to fixed lines of defence. A return to such an approach was frowned upon by officers such as the young Charles de Gaulle, but under the circumstances then prevailing Pétain's appeared to be the only plausible solution. He also enjoyed the backing of minister for war André Maginot, who, alongside his successor Paul Painleve, lobbied for the money to construct a vast line of gun emplacements linked by underground tunnels along France's border with Germany.

In 1929, funding was approved for such a defensive system and construction of this Maginot Line began the following year. By March 1936, the decision appeared to have been fully vindicated. In what was for the Germans a momentous gamble, Hitler had decided to unilaterally breach one of the fundamental tenets of the Treaty and ordered his army to march into the Rhineland. Publicly he justified the action by claiming that the signing of a mutual assistance alliance between France and Russia the previous year had invalidated the promises made by Germany at Locarno. The modest force which undertook the operation had been instructed to withdraw at the slightest sign of resistance, but none materialised. Although France protested loudly at this clear breach of the Locarno agreement, the British refused to speak up. The consensus in the UK was that all the Germans had really done was 'walk into their own backyard', and Stanley Baldwin was fervently against taking any action he feared might result in another European war. He further cautioned that France invoking the treaty it had signed with Russia might lead to turmoil in Germany and the country turning Communist. With Britain unwilling to offer even moral support, France was left in an impossible position. In an election year, the prospect of war would have been incredibly ill-timed, and in any case the generals warned that full mobilisation would be required to have any hope of persuading the

Germans to pull out. This expensive and dramatic manoeuvre would have lost a lot of potential voters. Instead, recourse was made to the League Council, and the government meekly announced that the incident was now out of its hands and that they would abide by any decisions made by the League.

Foch had been right all along. The role of the Rhineland as a barrier had lasted only as long as the Germans were prepared to tolerate its status, and once they chose to stop there was nothing anyone could do. In response, the construction of the Maginot Line was given greater priority and continued until 1940 when the German Blitzkrieg showed it to have been an enormous and very expensive white elephant all along. All it had achieved was to represent the searing embodiment of the failure of reconciliation, unity and trust in Europe, cutting France off from much of the rest of the continent and to serve as a graphic reminder of the utter failure of Versailles.

French obsession with security had, therefore, like its reliance upon reparations, proved short-lived and illusory. The League, set up to act decisively, had failed to do so. As we shall see, this parlous state of affairs did not bode well for other undertakings which the Treaty had initiated, and for which the League was supposed to have acted as guarantor. To examine these issues we must now return to 1919, when the conference was preoccupied with an even more dramatic reshaping of Europe than had been attempted in 1815.

7

Self-determination May Be a False and Monstrous Idea

Tomas Masaryk, the Czech nationalist who ensured the emergence of a Czechoslovak state in 1919. (Library of Congress)

Germany had angrily agreed to reparations, conceded under duress that the Rhineland was to be demilitarised and garrisoned, grudgingly returned Alsace-Lorraine to France, resigned itself to the return of Schleswig and accepted that the Saar's fate was now in the hands of the League of Nations. Resentment at these exactions was compounded by the fact that they had been imposed upon a country which in the eyes of its people bore no relation to the one that had gone to war in 1914. Like Austria and Hungary, its government considered itself to be devoid of responsibility for the actions of its predecessors. Why, they asked, should ordinary Germans pay for the excesses of those who had plunged them into four years of war, from which they had emerged just as devastated and victimised, in their minds, as the citizens of northern France, Belgium or Galicia?

The day after Emperor William abdicated on 9 November 1918, a provisional government had been announced consisting of liberal-minded representatives from the Social Democratic and Independent Democratic Parties. Elections were held in the following month for a National Assembly which was to be entrusted with the task of creating a new parliamentary constitution. On 6 February 1919, the National Assembly convened in the town of Weimar and formed the Weimar Coalition. They then elected SDP leader Friedrich Ebert as the Weimar Republic's first president.

William's abdication had swiftly been followed by those of the other crowned heads of the former empire, all swept away by the revolutions and civil war that had shattered the country. Through the Anif Declaration of 12 November 1918, King Ludwig III of Bavaria discharged all his civil servants and soldiers from their oaths of loyalty, ending the 738-year Wittelsbach dynasty, and he was followed the next day by King Frederick III of Saxony, ending the House of Wettin. William II was also deposed in a palace coup, and his abdication on 30 November 1918 ended the Kingdom of Württemberg.

Thus, a structure of rule which could trace its roots to the Holy Roman Empire, and which had facilitated its transformation under Bismarck from a loose confederation into an empire, was gone. The nation was now a federal republic and the seal was set on the extinction of Bismarck's painstakingly constructed state.

The constitution of the new country made it crystal clear that there was to be no return to the *ancien regime*. Article 17 insisted that every former kingdom, duchy, grand duchy or principality was to have 'the constitution of a free state' and that their representatives 'must be elected in a general, equal, immediate and secret ballot'. The former titles of the nobility, and its dukes and kings, could forthwith only form part of private citizens' surnames. Furthermore, those aspects of the *Zollverein* which had been shared with its former members were to become the sole prerogative of the Reich parliament in Berlin. The state Landtags were now little more than council chambers, whose roles were to nod through legislation passed by the state representatives in the Reichstag. The constitution expressly reserved such matters as nationality, freedom of movement, immigration and management of the national currency to the central government. Moreover, the Reichstag was to manage on behalf of the states the customs service, the union of the customs and trade territory, and the 'freedom of movement of merchandise'. This was explicit in Article 82, which specified that 'Germany forms one customs and trade territory, surrounded by a common customs border' which 'coincides with the border separating Germany from foreign countries'. That Germany had irrevocably moved away from the power politics of the emperor and the Prussian army was underlined by Article 178, which stipulated that 'the constitution of the German Reich of April 15 1871 [is] suspended'.

Monarchists, far-right politicians and nationalist groups alike were aghast at this transformation. Those familiar and still comfortable with the authoritarian rule of the emperor and his military strongmen balked at a democracy elected by proportional representation, and a Reichstag and state presidency which was actually answerable to the people it served. The humiliation of defeat, now compounded by the expunction of its traditional structure to appease the victors, was a stain on national honour and would have to be reversed. They might conceivably take some comfort from the belief that the most egregious of such indignities held the prospect of eventually being overturned, and that the land lost in the west might be repatriated to the Reich in due course. They might even harbour hopes of the return of the monarchy. But in the east, Germany faced the irrevocable loss of cherished ancient lands that had been earmarked to fulfil another of Wilson's promises. This was the recreation of an independent Poland, an undertaking enshrined in the penultimate of Wilson's Fourteen Points:

> An independent Polish state should be erected which should include the territories inhabited by indisputably Polish populations, which should be assured a free and secure access to the sea, and whose political and economic independence and territorial integrity should be guaranteed by international covenant.

It is intriguing to consider that before 1914, indeed even before the war took the turn of events it did, there were few if any calls among Germany and Austria-Hungary's equally imperial neighbours for the salvation of the Poles. No questions were asked in the House of Commons, no expressions of sympathy emanated from the Quai d'Orsay, the Russian Duma or US Congress. The concept of one nation enjoying hegemony over another was never seriously challenged, except of course by the liberal-minded and humanitarian among their citizenry. All this seemed to change after 1914, culminating in Lloyd George calling in his War Aims speech of January 1918 for a Poland 'comprising all those genuinely Polish elements who desire to form part of it'.[1] A few months later, the prime ministers of the UK, France and Italy endorsed these sentiments in their declaration of 3 June 1918. 'Already before the conference assembled,' admitted Robert Lord, one of the members of the commission established to bring this aspiration to fruition, 'the Allied and Associated Powers had in general terms defined their attitude toward the Polish question,'[2] anticipating 'an independent Polish state, including Russian, Austrian and Prussian Poland alike'.[3] There would, nonetheless, be quite a number of hurdles to overcome before this statement of intent materialised into anything more tangible.

As we have seen, since 1795 when Poland was partitioned, the three empires had developed their portions quite differently, and their populations had inherited different customs and traditions. Apart from different laws, systems of administration and cultures, their experience under foreign rule had varied widely in terms of their personal freedoms and civil rights. Germany and Austria, particularly the latter, were comparatively liberal overlords within strict limits when it came to such institutions as education, workers' rights and political participation, as well as limited suffrage. Russia, on the other hand, was governed as a despotic autocracy, with power concentrated at the centre in the hands of the czar.

The desire for complete freedom, as opposed to greater autonomy, also varied depending upon which empire the Poles lived in. German and Austrian Poles were relatively well off compared to those under Russian rule, where enthusiasm for complete independence was more pronounced.[4] In Galicia particularly, Austria's Poles enjoyed a relatively stable and privileged lifestyle, a superior standard of living that they would be in no hurry to abandon. Some aspired to little more than a similar constitutional accommodation as Hungary or Croatia. Russian Poland, by contrast, had long witnessed extensive political turbulence, and as recently as 1905–06 there had been resistance to conscription for the war against Japan, with strike action and acts of sabotage. The actions of the authorities, who responded with harsh measures which forced the strikers back to work and countered the saboteurs at the point of the bayonet,[5] did nothing to address their discontent. It was therefore no surprise that Russian Poland was the source of the most vociferous agitation in the three territories. Two key characters emerged: Joseph Pilsudski, who wanted to seize power through a popular uprising; and Roman Dmowski, who advocated constitutionalism.

Pilsudski had been born in 1867 to an impoverished father of noble descent and a mother who blamed their plight upon the hated Russians. Inspired by her vitriol, the young Pilsudski left home and travelled to Kharkov, where he intended to study medicine. Instead he became a student of rebellion and a marked man. His subversive activities saw him expelled in 1886, and then arrested in 1887 on charges of complicity in an assassination plot against Czar Alexander III. After spending five years in a Siberian prison, Pilsudski returned home and started an underground newspaper, *The Worker*, but in 1900 was again arrested and imprisoned for sedition. In a ploy to secure his release, he succeeded in convincing his captors that he had gone insane, and he then travelled to Japan during the war with Russia, hoping to elicit their support for a

Polish uprising. This proved a fruitless mission, so he returned home. In 1908 he founded the Secret Union of Military Action, which he hoped would form the nucleus of an army of independence. Taking advantage of Austrian hostility to the Russians, he sought and gained their backing for the creation of the Union of Riflemen in 1910. Thereafter he plotted, waiting for his opportunity to materialise.

Roman Dmowski was born in Warsaw in 1864, also becoming active in politics as a student. In 1895 he helped to establish the *All Polish Review*, which sought autonomy within the Russian Empire, a doctrine he pursued as a member of the Russian Duma. However, his approach met with increasing opposition from more radical figures such as Pilsudski, and he was eventually manoeuvred out of his seat. In 1903 he published *Thoughts of a Modern Pole*, and actively resisted Pilsudski's attempts to secure an alliance with Japan against Russia. In 1905 he instead led a deputation to Russian prime minister Sergei Witte, lobbying for changes to the judicial and education systems and the establishment of a *Sejm* in Warsaw, among other reforms. Unsurprisingly, he met with little success.

A number of political groupings had also been emerging at this time. The more moderate National Democrats sought autonomy within the Russian Empire, and the radical Socialists wanted outright independence. By 1914, both men and their supporters were poised to pursue their respective policies through the catalyst of the coming conflict. This further divided the loyalties of the Poles within the partitioned areas, in each of which so-called legions were to serve as distinct formations within their respective armed forces. Some of those who joined harboured the hope that whichever empire prevailed might look favourably upon the loyalty of their Poles and be more amenable to granting greater autonomy.

Beyond Europe, exiles complemented the activities of those on the ground by attempting to influence foreign decision-makers and sell both the legitimacy and inevitability of a free Polish state. One had been the romantic writer Zygmunt Milkowski, who like Pilsudski was opposed to working with the Russians and sought revolution instead. His views led to his exile in 1863, but this did not prevent him predicting as early as 1887 that war between the ruling powers was inevitable and that this would be Poland's opportunity to re-emerge.[6] Another key architect of the cause was fellow exile Ignacy Paderewski, a charismatic and highly talented pianist and composer who was determined to use his art as a means by which to promote the cause. In April 1915, the year of Milkowski's death, he travelled to the US, where 4 million Polish Americans lived, hoping to drum up support and persuade the US government, and particularly President Wilson, of the legitimacy of the cause. At this stage Wilson did not appear to be particularly enamoured by the prospect of Polish statehood and was not yet convinced that it was even feasible. He had written as early as 1902 that he considered the Poles, presumably those in the US anyway, to be largely 'uncouth and lacking energy'.[7]

In the meantime, Dmowski travelled to Europe in November of that year in the hopes of encouraging Allied sponsorship. Ironically, however, it was from their German and Austrian masters that the most encouraging noises were to come. As reports of expatriate Polish agitation and lobbying reached the ears of both emperors, they were prompted to issue a proclamation on 5 November 1916 in which they undertook to jointly establish an independent Polish monarchy once they had emerged victorious from the war. What they envisaged, though, was only a weak tributary dependent upon its erstwhile masters economically and politically, in keeping with Germany's planning for Mitteleuropa. Furthermore, there was no reason to expect them to honour even that undertaking in the event that they did emerge victorious.

A better prospect emerged from revolutionary Russia, following the Bolshevik seizure of power which usurped the Provisional Republican government of Alexander Kerensky. In the euphoria of victory, autonomy was promised for all of the disparate races of the former Russian Empire, which included Poland. A pronouncement on 30 March 1917 reaffirmed this promise,[8] and proposed a new state comprising Poznan, West and East Prussia, Upper Silesia, Minsk, Wilno, Grodno, Volhynia, Cieszyn Silesia and Galicia.[9] This undertaking was then formally confirmed by Article 2 of the Declaration of the Rights of the People of Russia in November 1917, which recognised 'the right of the peoples of Russia to free self-determination even to the point of separation and the formation of a separate state'.

Fortunately, mainly due to the efforts of Edward House and the persuasive Paderewski, Wilson's attitude towards the Poles had changed. Persuaded not only by the justice of their cause but by the diplomatic and political advantages a declaration in their favour would bring, on 8 January 1918 the thirteenth of Wilson's Fourteen Points became established as US government policy.

With such unanimity of purpose secured, it appeared that the end of the war would see a free Poland regardless of the victor. When the Central Powers were defeated, and the Soviets found themselves ostracised by the Allies, it was natural that Poland looked to Britain, France and the USA for the realisation of their dream. Seeing that their time had come, exiled Poles became increasingly vocal in their determination to be represented at the imminent peace negotiations. To this end, preparations had been in hand, and the Polish National Committee (KNP) had been formed on 15 August 1917 with Dmowski at its head, entrusted with the task of negotiating on behalf of their countrymen. A positive development came five days later, when the French government agreed to recognise the KNP as the Poles' official representative, and they were swiftly followed by the British and American governments. With the coming of peace, they could begin their lobbying of the 'Big Three', confident in the knowledge that they had official sanction.

Meanwhile, for those on the ground there was no time for earnest negotiation. In the inevitable chaos and mayhem which accompanied the worsening situation, vacuums developed throughout central and eastern Europe. Committees and pseudo-administrations subsequently emerged, creating power bases and provoking turf wars between the various factions vying for power. Conflicts broke out between those favouring a monarchy along German/Austrian lines, those who wanted to replicate the revolutionary state created in Russia, and some who still advocated remaining within a reformed Austro-Hungarian empire.[10] Fuel was thrown on the fire when, on 10 November 1918, the Germans released Pilsudski. They wanted him to form a provisional government which would negotiate a favourable arrangement with Berlin. As the only contender with an army to back him up, other Poles soon reluctantly recognised him as de facto head of the new state. With the KNP now recognised by the Allies, and Pilsudski sponsored by the Germans, the two groups needed to work together to achieve their common aim. Pilsudski could try to hold things together and establish a functioning administration while Dmowski was in Paris negotiating its longer-term future.

Nor had the Poles been alone in considering their options. When, in 1916, Ralph Paget and Sir William Tyrell were asked to consider the possibilities, they suggested that the new state could either be formed along the same lines as the Grand Duchy of Finland or become a Polish kingdom under a Russian grand duke but 'in every other respect enjoy[ing] complete independence'.[11] Clearly neither would appeal to the Poles. When such outcomes came to be debated later, they did not appeal to the French either. Under the urgings of Dmowski, the French were increasingly attracted to the idea of a new state capable of serving as a buffer between Germany on the one hand and a hostile Soviet Russia on the other. This was recognised by Robert Lord, who realised that 'the tendency of French policy' was 'on the whole extremely favourable to Poland,[12] recalling how French foreign minister Pichon could now be heard repeating the mantra of a Poland '*grand et fort, très forte*'[13] in their discussions on the matter. Clemenceau, too, clearly did not have a Polish principality in mind when he called the disappearance of Poland under partition 'one of the greatest crimes of history'[14] and one it was the duty of the peacemakers to put right. The Americans, on the other hand, 'while very friendly and sympathetic toward Poland, viewed her problems primarily from the standpoint of the general principles involved',[15] which presumably meant no more and no less than fulfilling the spirit of Wilson's Fourteen Points.

The Americans understandably would find the Poles most keen to exploit both the pragmatism and expressed altruism of the French. Unfortunately, their delegates had 'a knack for irritating even their friends'[16] with the zealousness by which they expressed their wishes, and exasperated Wilson with their dogmatic approach. He found dealing with them somewhat 'troublesome'[17] at the very least, and summed up his feelings when he confided to his Allies how he 'met M. Dmowski and M. Padereswski in Washington, and I asked them to define Poland for me ... they claimed a large part of the earth.'[18] To the chief Polish historian of the peace conference, Wilson's reticence could only be interpreted as a determination that 'Poland should get neither too much nor too little, but just what belonged to her.'[19]

The British, especially Lloyd George, as usual found themselves falling between two stools. It was evident that whatever the size, shape and general complexion of any new Polish state, it was unlikely to be of significant strategic importance to the UK. Instead, it would be a client state of France, serving its future interests and furthering its political ambitions. Britain preferred to see Germany regain its position as an important market and trading partner – once the shame of the war had been erased, that is. Carving up Germany to appease France and create a Slav state did not easily fit into that vison or reflect British policy. A Polish state might be unavoidable, but it should be at the cost of the least possible disruption to its neighbours. This attitude was not lost on the other representatives present at the talks, most of whom acknowledged that the British 'did not appear to be particularly concerned that it should be ... large or strong' and consequently that 'the Poles are accustomed to ascribe most of their [subsequent] diplomatic disasters at Paris to Mr Lloyd George.'[20] However, success in securing the guarantee of their new state could hardly have been interpreted as a disaster.

There was another dimension to the problem. Apart from Galicia and the Russian territory liable to be annexed, the lion's share, and the most valuable of the territory likely to become Poland, was currently part of the German Reich. The Germans were clearly not going to lose their eastern provinces without a fight. Lloyd George was also worried about the fate of those German minorities transferred against their will to a new country, especially, as we shall see, given the challenges faced by the commission charged with defining the new borders. Little wonder that Lord Hardinge, permanent under-secretary at the Foreign Office, observed that 'a quick solution is made difficult by the magnitude of the task.'[21] His prescience was well-founded, and Robert Lord readily concurred, later admitting not only that 'the problem of Poland was one of the gravest and thorniest with which the conference had to deal', but more importantly that 'the frontiers of Poland could not be fixed without taking a good deal of territory from Germany; and taking territory from Germany is a very serious business.'[22] He appreciated that 'statesmen, from Bismarck to von Bulow, have been unanimous in declaring that Prussia's very existence depended upon maintaining her established frontier in the east,'[23] and it was Bismarck himself who declared that 'we will never consent to the restoration of Poland. Between Prussia and Poland there is a struggle for existence.'[24]

As Esme Howard, a member of the British delegation, foretold, 'the more contested territories you assigned to it [Poland] the greater were the chances of getting into trouble on its account.'[25] Such sentiments had certainly not abated with the passage of time, nor with defeat. Prince Max Lichnowsky, ambassador to Great Britain in 1914, wrote not long before the Armistice that 'the Polish question constitutes for Germany the gravest question of the war and of the peace, far graver than the fate of Belgium ... with it stands or falls the position of Prussia as a great power, and therefore of the Empire.'[26] Alsace-Lorraine, the Saar and even the Rhineland might have to be sacrificed, albeit temporarily in the case of the latter, but Silesia and Prussia were an entirely different matter. Indeed, many among the British delegation suspected that rather than cede eastern territory, Germany wanted to extend it. Sir Eric Drummond, destined to be the first secretary general of the League of Nations, perceived that 'the Germans are bent on pursuing the policy of securing compensation in the east for any losses they may suffer in the west ... if they succeed in their plan there will be nothing to stop German expansion towards the East and ultimately throughout Russia,' and therefore 'the Allies must help Poland to form a solid national barrier against Germany on the one side and Bolshevism on the other.'[27]

As unlikely as it was that German policy in the east would achieve fruition under the circumstances, there still remained the potential for friction between the plans for Poland on the one hand and demands for national rights on the other. Lord concluded that although 'state boundaries ought, as far as possible to follow the lines of cleavage between nationalities,' he had to concede that 'it may be that the doctrine of the rights of nationality have been enormously exaggerated; self-determination may be a false and monstrous idea; it may be that economic needs or historic rights, or long established political connections ought to be the chief considerations in determining boundaries.'[28] It was upon this dichotomy, and the attempts to reach an equitable and satisfactory conclusion, that negotiations would ultimately depend.

In February 1919 a commission headed by Lord and Jules Cambon, French diplomat and brother of Paul, was established to investigate the claims and report back with its findings. It sat from February to December 1919, meeting at least once a day, trying to formulate a solution to this most vexed of conundrums. 'How difficult that question was can hardly be appreciated,' Lord wrote afterwards, 'without having made a close study of the extraordinary intermixture and interpenetration of Poles and Germans in the former eastern provinces of Prussia.' It was therefore evident that to 'draw a frontier that would separate the two in clear-cut fashion without leaving a large residue to the one nation in the territories of the other is a thing that simply cannot be done.'[29]

Lord found that 'Posen and West Prussia ... [were where] the racial struggle had been hottest in the past half-century. In this case there could be little doubt as to the sentiments of the population, [but] Upper Silesia had been separated from Poland for six hundred years ... the case here was not so clear as in the other two provinces,'[30] while 'in East Prussia there was a large Polish speaking population which had, nevertheless, never been directly under Polish rule at all.' Furthermore, it was largely 'Protestant … [and] had never shown any marked signs of Polish national consciousness'. The commission therefore encountered 'many Poles [who] detested and abhorred Prussian rule, [and] had been badly oppressed under it, and would never be reconciled to it', while there were 'other Poles [who] had no such feelings, and it was not easy to draw the line between such groups'.[31] Clearly, only those with the wisdom of Solomon and the acuity of Albert Einstein would be equipped to cut through the maze of blind alleys with which the commission was confronted on a daily basis.

At the end of March, the commission optimistically proposed that Danzig and Upper Silesia be incorporated into the new state with a corridor to the Baltic separating East and West Prussia.[32] Lloyd George was clearly not impressed with this awkward solution. Nor was he particularly enamoured by the idea of handing over a rich and highly productive area of Germany to an unproven and fledgling state, remarking unflatteringly that in ceding Upper Silesia to Poland 'one might as well give a clock to a monkey.'[33] Wilson, however, had explicitly promised that the new state would have access to the sea, and this was the only way it could be honoured. Without it, Poland would be a stranded, landlocked rump. It also meant twisting the knife into Germany still further, clumsily splitting one part of the country from the other. However, the commission felt compelled to choose between the better of two evils. After all, 'was it to be argued that the interests of the two million Germans in East Prussia in having a land connection with Germany ought to outweigh the interests of twenty-five million Poles in having assured access to the sea?'[34] George Prothero, an adviser to the Foreign Office, was nevertheless vehemently opposed:

> The annexation of West Prussia and Danzig to Poland will create a sense of gross injustice in the mind of Germany which will be fatal for the peace of the world… There comes a point where the cumulative sense of loss becomes unforgettable and intolerable, and this point would, I believe be reached by the mutilation now proposed.[35]

Government adviser and academic James Headlam-Morley shared Prothero's reservations and suggested some other approach be considered. He thought that at a minimum Danzig should be made a free city administered by a League of Nations commissioner, a compromise that would ultimately have to be adopted. Viability was nevertheless the priority. The district of Marienwerder, for example, had to go to Poland in order to guarantee control of both the Lower Vistula and the one direct rail route between Danzig and Warsaw,[36] and so the Germans living there would just have to live with it. Such logic was lost on Lloyd George, who again made his feelings towards the Poles evident when he insisted that 'handing over millions of people to a distasteful allegiance merely because of a railway ... was a mistake.'[37] The commission was persuaded to look again at the status of Danzig, the fate of which was causing considerable rancour. In March 1919 it was agreed that both the city and a small adjacent district be made a free city under League of Nations protection, although it would be included in the Polish frontier for customs purposes and its foreign relations and the protection of its citizens abroad would also be entrusted to Poland. Another concession was that the respective fates of Allenstein and Marienwerder, along with Upper Silesia, would be put to the people in a referendum.

On 7 May 1919, the German government was notified of the commission's deliberations, which was understandably stunned by the draconian measures to be taken. The Labour Party in Britain and others in the United States were also unanimous in their condemnation, believing the awards to Poland were going much too far. If the plebiscite in Upper Silesia went against Germany, it would not only suffer a terrible humiliation but would also lose 23 per cent of its coal, 81 per cent of its zinc, 34 per cent of its lead, and a significant proportion of its steel and iron products.[38] The referendum was scheduled for 20 March 1921, and both sides were permitted to mount campaigns for their respective causes. Predictably, considering how high emotions were running, it soon descended into farce as both the Poles and German Freikorps employed violent intimidation against one another. As matters got increasingly out of hand, the Allies intervened and brokered a ceasefire which created a border roughly along the line of the most serious confrontation. In this tense atmosphere the plebiscite took place, resulting in 717,122 votes for Germany and 483,514 for Poland.

The scattered nature of the population was reflected in the voting patterns, and in some places the outcome was evenly split, and in addition many ethnic and German-speaking Poles voted for Germany. The outcome was so confusing that the British and French disagreed upon where the line of demarcation should go, with the British preferring it to be further east than either the French or the Poles wanted. Dissatisfied, the Poles staged another rebellion, aided by the government in Warsaw, hoping to seize the territory and leave the Allies with a *fait accompli*. Nonplussed by the daunting challenge of resolving the issue, the Allied Supreme Council referred the matter to the League, which despatched a commission to try to untie this Gordian knot. It awarded a third of the country, half the population and 80 per cent of the industry to Poland.

The plebiscites in Allenstein and Marienwerder were staged in July 1920 and the outcome was an almost unanimous decision to remain German. Lord, however, was doubtful as to whether the vote in Allenstein had been entirely fair, having noted that here 'the Polish-speaking majority is a backward, rural population, very much under the control of German landlords, pastors and officials,'[39] and from this we may infer that he felt most if not all of these people had been coerced, blackmailed or otherwise persuaded to vote for Germany. Notwithstanding the outcomes of the referendums, in appraising the challenge faced over Poland Lord had to accept that 'no other part of the territorial arrangements made at Versailles has caused so much anger in Germany as the Polish settlement, and scarcely any other part has been more fervently denounced by the critics of the peace treaties outside Germany.'[40] Lord's evaluation, one that today's politicians might heed, was that 'plebiscites have the drawback of raising national animosities to a fever pitch,'[41] and whoever is the loser is rarely reconciled to the outcome. Rather, they seek other means to overturn the decision of the majority, irrespective of how long it might take.

While the future western borders of a new Polish state were being debated, those in the east were also in the process of being shaped, but this time not based on decisions by commissioners or heads of government sitting in Paris or the councils of the League. As we have seen, General Pilsudski had wasted little time in ensuring the physical integrity of his country, but to many observers the Poles were engaging in disquieting levels of mission creep. Herbert Paton, who had served in the Admiralty Intelligence Section and as a Polish expert for the British delegation, watched with dismay how large tracts of Russian territory were succumbing to Polish expansion. Rather than ensuring their future by taking such huge bites of land, he felt that the Poles were risking quite the opposite outcome:

> The Poles are using the temporary menace of Bolshevism as an excuse for annexing large areas in the east which do not belong to them. They still have to prove themselves capable of ruling over other and bitterly hostile nationalities… If they are to be in conflict with both powers [Germany and Russia] a new partition will be the inevitable result. The only way of securing the future of Poland is by enabling her to develop her natural resources within her proper ethnographical limits.[42]

One of the most contentious subjects to which he was referring was Eastern Galicia, formerly part of Austrian Poland and now also claimed by Ukraine. Here, too, the ethnic complexities rendered anything like a straightforward resolution almost impossible. Lvov and its surrounds were mostly inhabited by Poles, but outside these enclaves the Ukrainians were usually in the majority. The Ukrainians had actually declared an independent republic in 1917, but this simply turned into a free-for-all, with Poles and Ukrainians engaging in open warfare while other splinter groups tried to take advantage. To further complicate matters, at the time Russia was in the throes of a civil war between the Reds and the Whites, and Britain and France were tentatively inclined to support Russian claims so long as it seemed the Whites were going to win. The ultimate victory of the Reds would change the dynamics entirely; as the French had stated many times, if Poland was to be a bulwark against Bolshevism, the bigger it was the better.

On 19 March 1920, Lloyd George discussed the matter with Wilson and Clemenceau, and despite the opposition of the French, it was decided that Eastern Galicia ought to be placed under the protection of the League of Nations. There were to be protections put in place for the 3.5 million Ukrainians there, and a referendum twenty-five years later to decide where they wanted to be placed.[43] This solution, like so many made in Paris, was easier to decide than it was to implement. Instead, the Poles continued fighting and by June 1920 the region was almost completely overrun. They then proceeded to consolidate their gains, refusing to heed the calls from either Paris or the League for restraint, until in 1923 Eastern Galicia was absorbed into the new country.

Still Poland's appetite remained unsated. Teschen, in what was formerly Austrian Silesia, was also territory the Poles sought for their new state. As it contained valuable assets that the Czechs also felt indispensable to their economic viability, with its 'excellent coking coal and its thriving industries',[44] they were not prepared to relinquish it without a fight. The Czechs moved their troops in and managed to secure more or less the entire region, but the League succeeded this time in reversing the outcome, and were able to enforce an award more favourable to Poland. They divided the city of Teschen in two, with the larger eastern portion allotted to Poland and the western part with the railway station ceded to the Czechs. As Robert Lord later recounted, this meant that the economic resources of the area would be allocated in illogical ways, with 'the electric light plant [going] to one state, but the gas works to the other'. As he put it, 'the judgment of Solomon is a curious monument to the wisdom of diplomats.'[45]

The issue was also one of many that some of the peacemakers felt ought to have been resolved without their involvement. Lloyd George found arguing over individual towns and districts increasingly irksome, and remarked irritably, 'How many members have ever heard of Teschen? I do not mind saying I had never heard of it.'[46] Perhaps so, but it was important to the Czechs, and they would not forget the injustice they believed had been inflicted upon them.

It was also almost impossible under these trying circumstances to make any definitive decisions with regards to the Polish border with Russia. In the midst of a civil war, there was no recognised Russian government with which to negotiate, only a statement made by Prince Georgy Lvov in March 1917 recognising the principle of a Polish state. This commitment was nonetheless used to legitimise a provisional border which was defined by the conference on 8 December 1919, encompassing territory with 'an indisputably Polish ethnic majority'[47] and behind what would be known as the 'Curzon Line'. Yet again, however, the Poles disregarded the edicts from Paris. Following a ceasefire between Russia and Poland on 12 October 1920, and the subsequent Treaty of Riga, concluded on 18 March 1921, they established a frontier which exceeded the limits of the Curzon Line, and absorbed a further 4 million Ukrainians, 2 million Jews and 1 million Byelorussians.[48] There was nothing the League or the politicians in the west could do to stop it.

The outcome of the war with Russia did, however, convince Pilsudski to abandon his plan for a Polish, Lithuanian, Byelorussian and Ukrainian federation, and the latter two were instead partitioned between Poland and Russia as part of the deal.[49] Lenin would claim that, had Russia been stronger and 'Poland ... become Soviet, the Versailles Treaty would have been shattered, and the entire international system built by the victors would have been destroyed'.[50] As it stood, the Poles had now made a revanchist enemy of Germany, provoked decades of animosity with Czechoslovakia, and embittered Russia. Not content with this, Pilsudski had antagonised and alienated another neighbour, Lithuania. The town of Wilno had been earmarked for the small Baltic state, but its fate was typical of much of the opportunistic carpetbagging which proliferated after the war. It had a mixed population of Jews, Poles, Russians and Belorussians, but initially the city was subject to fighting between a number of different factions until the Poles entered the city in April 1919. Backed by Moscow, the Lithuanians threw the Poles out, but once they lost the backing of Moscow the Poles moved back in and ejected the Lithuanians. The Poles again sought League legitimacy, but they held on to it in the meantime and used a faux referendum to justify their claim. It was then unilaterally absorbed into the country, prompting the Lithuanians to break off diplomatic relations. Thus, a fourth neighbour had been antagonised in the cause of territorial expansion. As Lord explained:

> As now constituted, the new state is an area of 148,000 square miles ... its population is variously estimated at between 27 million to 32 million ... Poland now ranks as the sixth largest state of Europe, both in size and in population; and it may be considered by far the most important of the new states which the war has produced.[51]

It was, nevertheless, a state that had more in common with Austria-Hungary than, for example, France or Italy. Despite the purpose of the peace conference being to create a unitary Polish state, what emerged instead was a patchwork of competing and unfriendly minorities governed by an unsympathetic centre. This was underlined by a census taken in 1921 which revealed that while 69 per cent of the population was ethnically Polish, 16 per cent were Ukrainian, 3.9 per cent Byelorussian, 3.9 per cent German and nearly 10 per cent Jewish. Some commentators have claimed that in fact the percentage of non-Poles in the country was as high as 40 per cent. Because of the steps that had been taken to create the Poland promised by Wilson, it was built on sand. Had its founders been content with a smaller, more compact country it might have been less of the power-broker France had hoped it to be, but it would have enjoyed more validity and perhaps would have survived longer than twenty years.

8

This Might Be Neither Equitable nor Conducive to Peace

Woodrow Wilson, the US president who found himself trying to arbitrate between vengeful victors and prostrate losers at Versailles in 1919. (Library of Congress)

The future of Austria-Hungary was, if anything, more vexed even than that of its erstwhile ally. While it had not been a foregone conclusion that the empire was to be dismembered, the subsequent decisions taken during the war and then at the peace conference produced a set of circumstances few could have anticipated in July 1914. Charles Seymour, head of the team formed to advise on Austria-Hungary, initially held to the belief that the best outcome would be to leave the monarchy intact, because 'it had become almost axiomatic that the union of Danubian territories was essential to the economic welfare and political tranquillity of southeastern Europe ... there were few who did not recognise the service performed by the Habsburgs in holding together regions naturally interdependent'.[1]

Seymour was among those who also feared, rightly as it transpired, that the breakup of the empire 'would inflame the nationalistic jealousy and ambition of the peoples that had been crushed under the Habsburg yoke',[2] leading to wars and intercommunal violence as they vied for power and territory. Instead, root-and-branch reform within a federal framework, as advocated by the more moderate nationalists, was one option that had found favour. Greater leniency had also been seen as a means to entice the Austrians away from Germany and to a separate negotiated peace. Nor was there unanimous sympathy for the plight of its nationalities yet, or a consensus on the final aims of the war. In December 1916, Lord Cecil wrote that 'nationalism, whether Irish or Slav arouses all the worst passions of my nature,'[3] understandable sentiments perhaps for someone representing a social class which believed strongly in the morality of one race ruling over another. It was nonetheless a sentiment with which imperialists such as Lord Milner, an experienced statesman and colonial administrator, agreed. He concluded that 'we should not go on fighting until their [Czech, Yugoslav and Romanian] aspirations are satisfied, that is till Austria [is] disintegrated.'[4] After all, such precedents would not bode well for the prospects for the British Empire, especially in India and Ireland where increasingly strident demands for self-government were being voiced.

What was of more importance than the fate of the minorities was the need to persuade Austria-Hungary to come to a separate peace – and it was not likely to do so if the threat of the monarchy's dissolution hung over its head. In fact, almost immediately upon his accession to the throne in November 1916 following the death of Francis-Joseph, Karl I started sounding out the prospect of peace with the Allies, and in January 1917 recruited his brother-in-law Prince Sixtus von Bourbon Palma as intermediary. By March 1917, Karl was able to agree in principle to the independence of Belgium and Serbia, and the cession of Constantinople to the Allies, and he also viewed favourably the return of Alsace-Lorraine to France. The Germans would not move on Alsace-Lorraine, and their own September programme of 1914 had made ambitious plans for Belgium. The Italians, too, were making demands with regards to territory, and these Karl refused to entertain. Consequently, at a meeting on 19 April 1917 at St Jean de Maurienne, the prospect of a separate peace received a body blow when the Italians vetoed the idea. An intact Austria-Hungary would clearly deprive it of many of the post-war spoils it was anticipating.

Irrespective of the Italian position, on 9 May 1917 Lloyd George told a cabinet meeting that 'if we fail to induce Austria to make a separate peace [there is] no hope of that sort of victory in the war that we desired,'[5] On 21 June 1917, he further insisted that 'if Russia went out of the war while Austria still remained in we could not win.'[6] If that were the case, then there would be little incentive to stem the nationalism inside the empire, which was the best way to dissolve it and end the war. Nonetheless, some critics felt the prospects for Slav independence were not particularly favourable. In November 1917, Lord Cecil augmented his previous criticism of the empire's nationals in a letter to the editor of the *Spectator*:

> ... [although] we must do all we can for the Poles and the Yugoslavs and the Czechs ... I must add that I cannot look forward with much enthusiasm to the success of our efforts. As far as I can see the Slavs have never shown the slightest capacity for self-government...[7]

Moreover, the question was becoming academic, and the prospect of a separate peace was becoming increasingly distant. Count Ottokar Czernin, a senior Austrian diplomat, explained that such was the dire situation within the Dual Monarchy that they were damned whatever choice they made:

> We could have gone over to the enemy ... we could have fought against Germany with the Entente on Austro-Hungarian soil, and doubtless have hastened Germany's collapse; but the wounds which Austria-Hungary could have received in the fray would not have been less serious than those from which she is now suffering; she would have perished in the fight against Germany, as she has as good as perished in her fight with Germany.[8]

It therefore became evident that Austria could never have betrayed its ally. With that knowledge, Allied planners actively examined the political advantages to be gained from offering its various nationalities the possibility of nationhood. The Paget–Tyrell Memorandum of August 1916 had examined this topic and embraced the principle of self-determination because, in the view of its authors, 'the Dual Monarchy, which in its present composition is a direct negation of that principle ... should be broken up.'[9] Seymour would thus be compelled to concede that its days were numbered, and that 'the integrity of the ancient empire could not be preserved.'[10] Of course, this was not yet Allied policy. Paget and Tyrell, for example, proposed that perhaps the province of Bohemia might become independent on its own, or somewhat crudely 'tacked onto Poland', or, more to some nationalists' tastes, linked 'by some means or other with a southern Slav state'.[11]

Seymour was convinced that whatever the outcome, the new entities that emerged should not simply go their own way. Continued membership of a single market was, Seymour believed, 'essential to the tranquillity and prosperity of southeastern Europe'.[12] On this point at least, he was not alone. On 3 April 1915, Karel Kramer, leader of the Young Czech Party, echoed Seymour in a memorandum to the Entente championing a post-war autonomous Bohemian state incorporated into a greater Pan-Slav federation.[13] At the same time, Tomas Masaryk set down his plans for a post-war settlement just two years after he had expressed his belief in the empire. He proposed a Czech state which would include Bohemia and Moravia, Teschen and also Slovakia, forming a long, snakelike multi-national state.[14] He had already discussed his ideas with historian Hugh Seton-Watson, expert on eastern Europe and a key supporter of such an arrangement. Clearly, these proposals heralded potential problems for the future, especially as a Czecho-Slovak entity was not a solution that was universally welcomed. In the United States the Slovak League of America, led by Albert Mamatej, had been agitating for the creation of their own separate, autonomous Slovakia.

Nevertheless, in October 1915, seeing the advantage of cooperation between two groups with largely similar aims, they merged with the Bohemian Alliance of America to campaign jointly for the 'independence of the Czech lands and Slovakia', and ultimately the union of the 'Czech and Slovak nations' as a sovereign, federal state.[15] If both communities could enjoy large measures of autonomy within such a democratic structure, with mutual respect for their different cultures and traditions, it ought to be possible to accommodate such an arrangement. However, as events were to demonstrate, this was not quite how things worked out. In the meantime, on 14 November 1915, yet another group, the Czechoslovak Foreign Committee, operating from Paris under the leadership of Edward Benes, took it upon themselves to declare war on Austria-Hungary. It was hoped that by distancing themselves entirely from the monarchy, the Czechs would demonstrate to the world that support for total secession among this oppressed minority was widespread and enjoyed popular legitimacy.[16] Furthermore, as an active co-belligerent, the movement would prove to the Allies that they were the true representatives of the Czech and Slovak people. Subsequently, enough Czechs and Slovaks would volunteer to fight on the side of the Allies to enable 'legions' to be created, serving primarily with the French, Italian and Russian armies This demonstrated unequivocally that they were fully fledged co-combatants with the Allies, committed to the defeat of the Central Powers and prepared to shed blood in their common cause.[17]

Masaryk, meanwhile, travelled to Paris to pursue his faction's aims. On 3 February 1916, he secured a meeting with Aristide Briand and impressed upon him the advantages for French security of a strong, stable ally on its flank, and assured the Frenchman that a Czech-Slovak state would play a crucial role in limiting the post-war territorial aspirations of a resurgent Germany. The Allies now held the initiative, and, having decided upon dissolution, declared in January 1917 that one of their key war aims was 'the liberation of Italians, of Slavs, of Roumanians and of Czecho-Slovaks from foreign domination'.[18] Then, on 3 March, the new regime in Russia announced that one of its foreign policy objectives was also the creation of a 'Czecho-Slovakian' state,[19] giving extra vim to nationalists' aspirations.

By no means was the idea of breaking up the empire universally popular, however. Many of its subjects preferred Habsburg rule to the prospect of living as resentful minorities in new, hostile countries. For them, reform within a new federal empire was the answer, as it had only recently been for Masaryk. Emperor Karl could perhaps take some comfort from the fact that when the new parliament was opened in Vienna on 29 May 1917, some deputies expressed their loyalty and support for the new federal empire he advocated.[20] Nevertheless, Wilson at this early stage would not commit to anything other than the pursuit of 'the freest opportunity of autonomous development' within the empire, a sentiment which could not, strictly speaking, be interpreted as secession or outright independence. Regardless of his apparent equivocation, there were growing moves within the monarchy for groups to take the law into their own hands. Two days before he published his Fourteen Points, on 6 January 1918, deputies in the *Reichsrat* in Vienna issued the 'Twelfth Night Declaration' in which they demanded self-determination for the Czechoslovaks.

After something of a hiatus, matters assumed greater momentum when on 29 May the Allies announced their backing for both the 'nationalist aspirations of the Czecho-Slovaks and Yugoslavs',[21] and three days later emigres in the United States issued the 'Pittsburgh Agreement'. In this they called for an 'independent state consisting of the lands of the Bohemian Crown and Slovakia', while the Allies had by now recognised the National Council, which had been formed late in 1915 to represent the Czechs and Slovaks. Later, in July, another group claiming to represent the Ruthenes demanded freedom for, and union with, Greek Catholic Ruthenes in Galicia and the Bukovina.[22] Nevertheless, despite movement clearly being in the nationalists' favour, it was still far from a foregone conclusion. Phrases such as 'autonomous' and 'aspirations' might be interpreted according to the preconceived wishes of the various parties, but it was the increasingly popular phrase 'self-determination' that would vex the negotiators the most, because, as Robert Lansing would later admit, it was a term 'loaded with dynamite'.[23]

When, on 2 September 1918, President Wilson followed the rest of the Allies and recognised the National Council as the 'de facto belligerent government of the Czecho-Slovaks',[24] he provided them with greater legitimacy and enhanced their credentials as negotiators on behalf of their people. The French likewise undertook to build a Czecho-Slovak nation of Bohemia, Moravia, Austrian Silesia, and Slovakia, and promised them representation in any conferences in which their national interests were affected. As a consequence, the phrases 'autonomous' and 'aspirations' were now firmly translating into 'self-determination'; that is, the right to exist as a completely independent, sovereign state with no ties whatsoever to the old monarchy. On 16 October 1918, in a desperate last-ditch attempt to save his dynasty, Emperor Karl issued an abortive 'Imperial Manifesto' formalising his proposal for a new constitution granting autonomy to the nations of the Austrian half of the empire. In his proclamation he promised that:

> ... Austria must, in accordance with the will of its people become a federal state, in which every nationality shall form its own national territory in its own settlement zone ... This reorganisation ... will guarantee the independence of each independent national state ... [but] ... will effectively protect common interests ... I call on the people, on whose self-determination the new kingdom will be based, to cooperate in the great task ... so that the great work of peace that we construct may mean happiness for all my people...[25]

However, because of the constitutional arrangements surviving from the Compromise of 1867, as Emperor of Austria he could not offer the same reforms to his kingdom of Hungary. Their fate still rested with the Diet in Budapest. Perhaps worried that the Allies might change their minds or even be persuaded that a reformed empire was preferable to the upheaval of complete dissolution, Masaryk swiftly made a formal declaration of independence. This prompted Wilson to reiterate his support for the new state and dismiss the 'Imperial Manifesto' out of hand. On 18 October, the document, drafted in Washington and signed by Masaryk, Benes and Dr Milan Stefanik, declared:

> ... Realising that federalisation, and, still more, autonomy mean nothing under a Habsburg dynasty, [we] do hereby make and declare this our Declaration of Independence ... we claim the right of Bohemia to be reunited with her Slovak brethren of Slovakia, once part of our national state...[26]

The signatories promised that their new country would be a democratic republic affording equal civil rights to all men, women and minorities and would embrace universal suffrage, with representatives elected through proportional representation. Instead of a standing army there would be a militia, so as to underline the new country's credentials as a peace-loving state. Furthermore, the declaration assured its audience that its government would carry out 'far-reaching social and economic reforms' and promised 'efficient, rational, and just government', prohibiting special privileges based upon a person's status or class. This utopia clearly offered a much better prospectus for the new society than that of Emperor Karl, and served to further entrench the cause of complete independence.

On 28 October, with what was left of any pro-Karl politicians melting away, a coup led by Antonin Suehla, leader of the Czech Agrarian Party, and Frantisek Soukup, leader of the Social Democrats, resulted in the announcement that they were now in power in Prague and that 'an independent Czechoslovak state had come into being'.[27] In the words of Charles Seymour, having put up little or no meaningful resistance, the 'Habsburg officials and organs of government were not assailed, but simply passed over.'[28] On 31 October, the new government was formed with Masaryk as president and Benes as foreign secretary, but this did not by any means imply that the new regime was unanimously embraced. Four German 'Provisional Governments' rivalling Prague had also claimed sovereignty in the Bohemian Crown lands and were demanding that they be allowed their *own* self-determination, by which they meant union with Germany. The Cisleithanian territories were also fracturing along Czech, German and Polish lines in Silesia, and in Upper Hungary rival Slovak, Magyar, Jewish and Romanian national councils were being set up in competition with one another. As in Poland, turf wars were being fought almost everywhere. When Hungary declared itself independent on 1 November 1918, the Prague government needed to assert its authority and legitimacy in Slovakia, and orders were issued for its occupation before the Hungarians could prevent them annexing the territory. Consequently, on 5 November, five Czecho-Slovak ministers and seventy gendarmes crossed the border to assert sovereignty over the territory and declared it to be an integral part of the 'Czecho-Slovak Republic'.

At last accepting that his dynasty was finished, Emperor Karl issued a final proclamation on 11 November. This time it was to relinquish 'every participation in the administration of the state' of Austria, thus releasing his civil servants and other officers from their oaths of loyalty, and two days later he repeated the exercise for his Hungarian subjects. He declined to abdicate, however, seeing his role of monarch as divinely ordained and thus not in the hands of men. The Habsburg Law of 3 April 1919, passed in the Austrian *Reichsrat*, was required to remind him that his rights to the throne were in fact for his subjects to decide upon. Thus, irrevocably dethroned, he would die a young man of only thirty-four in exile in Madeira, never reconciled to the destruction of his dynasty and the final dissolution of an empire stretching back to the Holy Roman Empire of Charlemagne. On 13 November, Prague issued a provisional constitution with Masaryk confirmed as president. All rival Czech national councils were given notice that they had until the end of December to dissolve themselves or face the consequences.[29] There was still opposition to overcome, however. On 15 November, Hungarian troops finally broke up the Slovak National Council, and on 7 January 1919 it was announced that sub-Carpathian Ruthenia constituted part of the new state.

Right: 1. Lord Castlereagh, cautious sponsor of the Congress System for maintaining peace and stability in Europe after Napoleon.

Below: 2. Belgrade *circa* 1890, capital of Serbia, the thorn in the Habsburgs' side and later centre of the new kingdom created at Versailles.

3. Panoramic view of Budapest, capital of the Hungarian half of the Dual Monarchy, photographed between 1890 and 1900.

4. 'The Enfant terrible of Europe', an 1893 cartoon depicting a nervous Europe scrutinising an unpredictable German Kaiser William II.

5. The Viennese *Reichsrat*, where many of the Habsburgs' various subject nationalities tried to make their voices heard.

6. The Berlin Reichstag, 1900. It was the heart of the expanding German Empire.

7. The Great Bridge, Danzig, 1900. A German city destined to figure large in the destiny of Europe.

8. The highly coveted Croatian port of Fiume in 1900. It was to become a case study in the intransigence of European power politics.

9. Archduke Francis-Ferdinand. His ideas for a more democratic and federal Austria-Hungary died with him on 28 June 1914, when he was assassinated in Sarajevo, Bosnia-Herzegovina.

10. *Momentaufnahme von Europa und Halbasien*, 1914. A stylised German depiction of Europe at war.

Above: 11. Russian prisoners of war in 1915, the detritus of countless battles in highly disputed Galicia.

Left: 12. Austria-Hungary's Count von Hotzendorf, right, in conference with Germany's Kaiser William II.

13. Sir Arthur Salter, instrumental alongside Jean Monnet in fostering closer Anglo-French cooperation during the First World War.

14. A 1916 poster appealing for contributions to the Serbian Relief Fund.

Left: 15. Walther Rathenau, German industrialist and brains behind the formation of the KRA in the First World War.

Below: 16. Krupp Works, Essen, 1917. This was the beating heart of the German war industry.

Above: 17. European leaders including Clemenceau, Wilson and Lloyd George leave the palace after signing the Treaty of Versailles, a document intended to redraw the map of Europe but which proved to be the blueprint for further division.

Right: 18. Raymond Poincaré, who tried but failed to seize the Rhineland from Germany in 1919.

Left: 19. British Prime Minister David Lloyd George, a key architect of post-First World War Europe.

Below: 20. A German poster of 1919 insisting upon sovereignty over Schleswig prior to the referendum on the fate of the province.

21. Henry Cabot Lodge, a staunch defender of national sovereignty and opponent of Europe's plans for the League of Nations.

23. Aristide Briand, one of the earliest proponents of a European Union. 'The European organisation contemplated could not oppose any ethnic group, on other continents or in Europe itself, outside of the League of Nations, any more than it could oppose the League of Nations.'

Above left: 24. Ignacy Paderewski, talented Polish pianist and patriot.

Above right: 25. Roman Dmowski, a staunch patriot who lobbied for the creation of a new Polish state.

25. Josef Pilsudski. His determination to create a greater Poland helped to sow the seeds of its tragic fate.

Above left: 26. Andre Maginot. The French line of forts which bore his name failed to resolve French security fears, and instead added to the division of Europe in the 1930s.

Above right: 27. Adolf Hitler's perverted vision of a United Europe plunged the continent into a six-year-long nightmare.

Right: 28. The youthful Peter II of Yugoslavia, king in his nation's darkest hour and destined to enjoy a tragically short reign.

Left: 29. Free Movement, Nazi style. A 1943 propaganda poster depicts a French mother and her child in occupied France 'overjoyed' that the father is working in Germany.

Below: 30. Auschwitz. Here *Grossraumwirtschaft*'s most tragic victims slaved for German companies such as IG Farben.

Above: 31. British Prime Minister Winston Churchill, US President Harry Truman and Russia's Joseph Stalin. Their post-war decisions and subsequent estrangement decided the future of Europe for the next fifty years.

Right: 32. Henry Morgenthau. In 1945 he would advocate transforming Germany to the status of pastoral backwater.

33. Charles de Gaulle, early and unlikely supporter of a United Europe centred around France and the UK.

34. Jean Monnet, left, meets Konrad Adenauer in Bonn, 1953. (Federal Archives, B 145 Image-F001192-0003 / Unterberg, Rolf / CC-BY-SA 3.0)

All this jockeying for position and advantage was alarming the peacemakers. They envisaged an orderly transition of power within properly and legally defined ethnic and national borders, not a chaotic free-for-all. Lloyd George was highly critical of the chaos that had been unleashed, observing disdainfully that 'small nations, before they have hardly leapt into the light of freedom, beginning to oppress other races than their own.'[30] The irony did not escape Robert Lansing either, and he shared such concerns. He noted in his diary on 22 January 1919 that 'all the races of Central Europe and the Balkans in fact, are actually fighting or about to fight with one another ... the Great War seems to have split up into a lot of little wars.'[31] Francis Lindley, high commissioner and later ambassador to Austria, felt that assertiveness was needed, convinced that 'the only way to extricate themselves from their appalling muddle is to take them all in hand and make them do what they are told,' adding that the Allies had to 'make all these people understand that they have got to live together as neighbours whether they like it or not'.[32] On 24 January, they issued an edict warning that 'possession gained by force will seriously prejudice the claims of those who use such means,'[33] but this must have been offered more in hope than expectation. As Colonel House put it:

> ... in the endeavour to be free everything else was overlooked. No tribal entity was too small to have ambitions of self-determination. Social and economic considerations were unreckoned with, and the only thought for the moment was [to become again] masters of their own fortunes and desires...[34]

Inevitably, the various factions took little heed of the warnings issued from Paris, and, just like Pilsudski in Poland, tried to present the Allies with a *fait accompli*. Thereafter, unable to reverse the territorial gains, the Allies would give up and move on. By the time the peace conference opened, therefore, the Czecho-Slovaks had already achieved possession of all the territory they were to claim in the forthcoming negotiations. Seymour soon concluded that 'the heirs of the Habsburg empire would furnish no assistance to the Conference in its task of territorial delimitation by entering into friendly agreements among themselves.'[35] In any case, the Allies had no meaningful resources at hand either to try to restore some semblance of order, or to impose their will, as maintaining garrisons everywhere was clearly impossible.

With the war over, demobilisation was key to maintaining social cohesion at home and keeping down the costs of stationing hundreds of thousands of troops all over the globe. Churchill nevertheless saw the risks involved and warned Lloyd George that if he was to have any chance of enforcing his will, he needed to have 'a great army' at his back.[36] In practice, this was impossible. When Henry Wilson advised that he wanted to withdraw four British battalions stationed in southern Europe and transfer them to Egypt and Turkey, the protests of Eyre Crowe, the head of the political section of the British delegation, fell on deaf ears. Consequently, he had to admit that 'we have by the withdrawal of all our units, lost every chance of promoting a just solution of the conflicts in this important theatre of international conflicts'.[37] Balfour, on the other hand, saw little merit in the Allies enforcing their will, even if they had the means to do so. He cautioned that 'we have to guard against the danger of being supposed to use our principles to further our fancies ... we have to deal with states which are passionately sensitive on these questions of territorial boundaries ... we cannot be popular, our only chance is to be just.'[38]

Despite the expectation that it was going to be a long haul, and that little would be heard except for bickering and claims for territory, the hearings of the various interested parties were scheduled to commence in the office of the French minister for foreign affairs, Stephen Pichon, in the Quai d'Orsay on 5 February 1919. In these opulent surroundings, furnished with an 'old pearly grey carpet marked with red roses ... rich Gobelin tapestries and high French windows',[39] Wilson, Clemenceau and Lloyd George settled down to hear the arguments. Here, Seymour provides us with intriguing pen pictures of the various characters present:

> ... the young and smiling foreign minister of the Czecho-Slovak Republic, Edward Benes, magnetic of manner, frank in discussion. His diplomatic skill had combined with the solid honesty of President Masaryk to win the recognition of the Allies for the infant state...[40]

Other delegates presented less sympathetic pictures. To Queen Marie of Romania, her prime minister, Ion Bratianu, despite his determination to fight her realm's quarter, came across as 'a tiresome, sticky and tedious individual',[41] whose presence she could barely tolerate. Her impression concurred with that of Seymour, who recalled he was 'rather moody, fighting for the treaty of 1916, resentful of opposition'.[42] By contrast, Count Albert Apponyi, the Hungarian delegation's aged chief negotiator, grasped the hopelessness of his country's situation: 'I could not refuse the saddest of duties, though I had no illusions as to there being any possibility of my securing some mitigation of our lot.'[43] He had evidently come to terms with the fact that his country, with Austria and Germany, was to be a net loser in shaping the new European order envisaged by the peacemakers. General Smuts had suggested that the proceedings might benefit from the formation of a sub-conference of all the former Habsburg states. Here they might try to settle their differences amicably, through debate. Under Allied stewardship, he suggested optimistically, they would in the process be tutored in 'the new habits of cooperation, [and this] would help to allay the old historic differences which still remain'.[44] Lord Hardinge believed that a somewhat firmer hand was needed:

The whole question depends on whether the governments decide upon a definite policy to be pursued in connection with the remains of the Habsburg Empire, or whether we continue to follow a policy of drift which is tending towards Bolshevism in German-Austria and Hungary, with the eventual union of German-Austria with Germany.[45]

With this in mind there was certainly an air of immediacy about, but as we have seen with Poland, defining boundaries – assuming the warring parties would allow them the time to do so – was painfully difficult. Centuries of mixing and free movement, particularly along what were to become the new borders, would at best leave large pockets, at worst substantial communities of minorities in one or other of the new states. It soon became clear that another commission would have to be established to properly investigate, analyse and adjudicate upon the eyewatering complexities inherent in properly deciding their structures. Although faced with an almost insurmountable task, Seymour was convinced that, all things considered, 'their decisions resulted from honest study and were only slightly affected by selfish political considerations.'[46] Perhaps so, but as future events were to show, they often got it wrong.

The well-established yardstick by which decisions ought to have been made – the alignment of borders according to their ethnic make-up, thus minimising as much as possible the creation of 'discontented groups of irredentists'[47] – would be sorely tested as the construction of the new states was debated and negotiated.

It soon became evident that if the countries were to enjoy any economic future, suitable infrastructures and communications systems had to be allocated to each. Therein lay the paradox, however, because several new states were going to have to try and secure a share of infrastructures originally evolved for one single political and economic entity. This was the reason for the arguments between Poland and the Czechs over Teschen, and Germany and Poland over Danzig. Ultimately, their feelings would have to be made secondary to other factors such as 'physiographic features, the disturbance of normal economic life, and all too frequently the logical route of established railway systems'.[48] Seymour summarised thus:

Bohemia was looked upon as a bulwark against a resuscitated Germany which might sometime in the future plan a new drive to the east. They also desired adequate railway connections between the Czechs and the Romanians, an ideal which compelled the extension of Romanian boundaries beyond the limit that strict justice might have required ...
If the linguistic lines were crossed or recrossed by a railway or canal, it would be questionable policy not to arrange the political frontier in

such a way as to leave the railway or canal entirely within one state or the other, so as to avoid troublesome customs interference with trade.[49]

This made practical sense but did not resolve some matters. For instance, how could a state ensure its economic success if it had been deprived of the communications facilities that its neighbour had been granted? Equally, how could it be determined whether one state or another was in greater need of the available industrial, agricultural or mineral resources, which could be awarded only to one? After all, it was Wilson himself who insisted that every state 'should have a right to conditions that will assure its economic life'.[50] For Nicolson, this meant excruciating choices and many sleepless nights: 'Even the puddles in the pavements assume for me the shapes of frontiers, salients, corridors, neutralised channels, demilitarised zones, islands.'[51]

It is clear that such considerations were not decided upon lightly or by the swift scrawl of a pen. They were frequently taken to the Council of Four so that they could adjudicate, and this was invariably undertaken in the drawing room of President Wilson's home in Paris. The American president appears to have treated these far-reaching and vital issues with somewhat more scrutiny than his colleagues, with Seymour describing how one might open the door of the room to find 'President Wilson himself, on all fours, kneeling on a gigantic map spread upon the floor and tracing with his finger a proposed boundary ... in such matters [he] took a keener interest than either Lloyd George or Clemenceau.'[52] Colonel House was seemingly much less concerned than his boss about the specifics involved in determining justice. He felt that it was more important to get the whole matter cleared up 'than ... haggle over details'.[53]

Nevertheless, when the Four did adjudicate on such matters, and when the choice came between the interests of either Austria/Hungary or one of their former imperial possessions, they invariably came out against the former. There were also egregious examples of double standards when it came to the policy of keeping the nationalities within their political boundaries wherever possible. Professor A. C. Coolidge, chief of the field mission attached to the American delegation to the peace conference, summed up this inconsistency in a memorandum of 10 March 1919:

> ... the clearest case of contradiction between nationality rights and those of history and geography is that involving the boundary desires of the Czechs who – illogically but humanly – base their claims to the two halves of their territory on opposite principles. In Bohemia they demand their 'historic boundaries' without regard to the protests of a large number of Germans who do not wish to be taken over in this way. In Slovakia, on the other hand, they insist on nationality rights and ignore the old and well-marked 'historical boundaries' of Hungary.[54]

The historian Carl L. Becker, wrote furthermore that 'in arranging the boundaries of Czechoslovakia, the conference departed rather from the principle of self-determination in order to gratify the patriotic sentiment of the Czechs, or to safeguard their military and economic interests.'[55] As a result of these blatant double standards, the new Czecho-Slovak state, though landlocked, emerged as well appointed as any of its neighbours, receiving the lion's share of the industry of the old empire such as the Skoda works, along with access to coal and lignite, and a rich agricultural sector. As we shall see later, it was to all intents and purposes 'economically independent', taking possession of resources eyed with considerable envy by its neighbours.[56] Again, as in Poland, this had come at the expense of homogeneity. As a result of such compromises, what resulted from the deliberations of the conference was 'a polyglot, for of its 14 million inhabitants there were more than a third belonging to other nationalities, chiefly Magyars, Germans and Ruthenes'.[57]

The leader of the Austrian Socialists was quite scathing in his evaluation of what had been produced: a state comprising people 'all filled with hate one against the other, arrested in the progress of their whole economic and social development and in the progress of their civilisation, by hate and national strife, nourished by tyranny and poisoning their whole public life'.[58] He could of course have been speaking of the same conditions that prevailed under the Habsburgs, but at least the peoples of the Dual Monarchy had their beloved monarch to look to as a unifying figure. In 1939, Lloyd George wrote retrospectively that the peace had instead simply produced 'recognition of a polyglot and incoherent state … and the incorporation of thousands of protesting Magyars and some millions of angry Germans'.[59] He went even further:

> I cannot imagine any more likely provocation for a future war than to have the German people surrounded by small states, of which many have never had their own governments, all containing large numbers of Germans clamouring for reunion with their native land.[60]

France was nevertheless prepared to overlook these realities in order to forge alliances with this and that new state, particularly Poland, to ensure its security. Reconciliation with Germany still looked decades away, so it was essential to form close ties with young and reliable nations to serve in any future war with Germany. A simple calculation demonstrated that France's population of 40 million, added to Poland's 30 million and Czechoslovakia's 14 million, gave them a huge potential manpower advantage over Germany's 65 million.[61] Such a combination could form a new European political alliance. Should Germany resume its place as the dominant state on the continent, confronting it would potentially be at least three militarily and economically strong powers. These, alongside

France's other gains from the Treaty, provided the illusion of a series of interlocking arrangements which together guaranteed security for some time to come.

Italy had also expected to gain from the peace. The Italians attended the negotiations to collect on the promises made to them by Britain and France in 1915 in the Treaty of London. Indeed, Balfour assured them as late as January 1918 that 'we – I mean Britain and France ... are bound to uphold the treaty in letter and spirit,'[62] but in making such promises he was counting without the American president and his Fourteen Points. This clash of ideologies came especially to the fore in the debates and discussions over the creation of a Southern Slav state in the Balkans. According to Nicolson, the Italians were wholly opposed to such a move, because they wanted an arrangement which created a 'chain of weak and separated states upon their northern and eastern borders'[63] which they could dominate and exploit for their own ends. What they saw instead was a strong and resilient Germany to the north and the formation of a potentially formidable nation of 13 million Slavs to the east when the Kingdom of Serbs, Croats and Slovenes – later Yugoslavia – was created in December 1918.

Of Yugoslavia, Orlando complained that it 'will have taken the place of Austria, and everything will be as unsatisfactory as before'.[64] This fear would bring Italy into frequent conflict with its neighbours, especially with respect to the control of the Adriatic. Furthermore, although it had its biggest threat removed through the defeat of Austria-Hungary, that was probably all the Italians could hope for. If they had to bargain for more, they had very little with which to barter. Exhausted by the war, Italy had no world role to play, and in the negotiations the whip hand was always held by the United States, Britain and France. According to Nicolson, therefore, the Italians were entitled to 'scant esteem'.[65] Nevertheless, the Italians were determined to recover the Tyrol as they had long coveted it and it was among the promises made to them to encourage them to join the Allies. It would also be the final piece of the reunification jigsaw started by Garibaldi and Cavour, and perhaps for this reason if no other, this was a definite red line.

There was another aspect to Italy's wish to gain control of the territory, and one which might have resonated with the French: security. Italy had fought long and costly campaigns against the Austrians and the Germans along its northern border, proving the need for a strong Alpine frontier. This was something the Italians were determined to secure, regardless of ethnic or linguistic considerations.[66] Italy therefore demanded the Trentino and Tyrol as far as the Brenner Pass, which meant that 250,000 Austrians would be left on the Italian side of the new border, as well as a similar number of Slovenes and Croatians to the north-east. The Trentino was overwhelmingly Italian-speaking, so this caused little concern, at least to the Allies, and the Italians insisted that they could only be safe if they held the territory sloping up to the Brenner Pass to serve as a natural barrier. In Poland and Czechoslovakia, when such issues arose, it had become the practice to find in favour of the successor or victor state, and its future viability when adjudicating on frontiers. Wilson was expected to take a different position with the Tyrol because of the minority issue, so it came as something of a shock to all concerned when the president found in their favour.

Prior to the conference, Wilson is said to have assured the Italians that he would not try to block their demands. Critics of the president had already been somewhat scathing about his judgement, and Nicolson explained that he seemed to be 'quite unaware of what this concession really implied ... Professor Coolidge later admitted that Wilson gave his consent without due consideration and frankly regretted it afterwards but felt bound by his word.'[67] Wilson had second thoughts once he realised a quarter of a million Austro-Germans and Slavs would be trapped inside Italy, but by then it was too late. Instead, to satisfy any qualms with respect to the large German population, some provisions were to be made to protect their interests. Indeed, endless assurances had been made as to the protection of their language, customs and autonomy, but as tenuous as these were from the beginning, when Benito Mussolini came to power in 1922 they were dispensed with entirely. He toyed with the prospect of solving the problem by removing the Austrians, but when this proved impractical he embarked upon a programme of Italianisation. German-language schools were closed down, the German and Slav languages were suppressed, and local government abolished. People were even forced to change their names to something more Italian-sounding.[68]

Yet the Tyrol was not Italy's only concern. The acquisition of this territory may have gone some way to meeting its security concerns to the north, but it still viewed the prospect of a powerful Yugoslav state on its flank with trepidation. Serbia and Italy had originally been quite close allies, and with the latter sponsoring the prospect of a Southern Slav state, the two nations' relations appeared to bode well for the future. As time went on, however, and Serbia realised it did not need Italian help, its role as a potential protégé changed to one of rival, and the relationship soured. By the end of the war the Italians saw Serbia and its aspirations as more likely to lead to war than guarantee peace.[69] Perhaps out of bitterness at having been denied the spoils they felt they had been promised, the Italians chose to stand their ground over the question of the port of Fiume. This key asset lay on the Adriatic coast on the other side of the Istrian Peninsula from the equally strategic Trieste, which Italy had also seized at the end of the war. Fiume, however, would prove more contentious. It had been Hungary's chief port, with a mixed population of Hungarians, Italians and Croatians, but if every Italian in the city and its outer suburbs was taken into account it could just about be claimed that they represented a slim majority. Thus, the ownership of Fiume began to take on the character of a cause celebre, with gangs of Italian youths roaming the city and intimidating non-Italians while poets and politicians at home extolled the natural justice of Fiume regaining its rightful place within the bosom of the motherland.

In Paris, one delegate also tried to explain Fiume's commercial importance by claiming that 'it will be very difficult for us to keep up the commerce of Trieste unless we control Fiume.'[70] Therefore, Italy's claim fulfilled two principles: ethnic predominance and importance to the country's future prosperity. As these terms had been argued successfully by the French with regards to Kehl, and also by Czechs, Poles and Slovaks, to deny the same rights to Italy would be, as Eyre Crowe insisted, 'contrary to all justice ... [and] must lead to perpetual discord'.[71] To make matters worse, Italy was becoming increasingly angry with the reticence of the Allies to honour other wartime promises, such as its territorial expectations along the Dalmatian coast, and official recognition of its sovereignty over the Dodecanese Islands in the Aegean. Nevertheless, President Wilson could not be persuaded and referred repeatedly to 'self-determination'. Nicolson observed how 'it drove them [the Italians] mad to feel the Fourteen Points were being relaxed in favour of France and Great Britain, while being rigidly enforced as against Italy.'[72] Furthermore, he insisted:

> The most ardent British advocate of the principle of self-determination found himself, sooner or later, in a false position. However fervid might be our indignation over Italian claims to Dalmatia and the Dodecanese it could be cooled by a reference, not to Cyprus only but to Ireland, Egypt and India. We had accepted a system for others which, when it came to practice, we should refuse to apply to ourselves.[73]

Wilson again tried to act as interlocutor, and proposed that Fiume, like Danzig, become a free port, and that Istria be shared between Italy and Yugoslavia, with Italy receiving some of the islands and the seaport of Valona in Albania. Italy was not satisfied with this compromise, so Lloyd George tried to strike a deal whereby Italy received East Istria with Fiume placed under League of Nations protection. With no agreement in sight, it appeared that this issue might rumble on indefinitely. Then, on 24 April, Wilson somewhat impetuously issued an appeal directly to the Italian people over the heads of their government. A disgusted Orlando stormed out of the conference, only returning in May for yet more inconclusive talks. The French tried to break the impasse by suggesting that Fiume become independent, demilitarised and administered by the League of Nations for fifteen years. At the end of this period, a referendum could be held on its future, like the solution found for the Saar.

Then, on 12 September, an Italian patriot called Gabrielle d'Annunzio took the law into his own hands. With a small band of likeminded comrades, he marched on and seized the city on behalf of Italy. This kind of brigandage inevitably failed to solve anything, and some form of compromise was inevitable. In November 1920, Rome came to an agreement as part of the Treaty of Rapallo whereby the city would, after all, be afforded the status of a free state. Subsequently, d'Annunzio and his fellow adventurers were ordered to leave, but this only proved to be a stop-gap solution and when the ultranationalist fascists came to power under Mussolini they renewed their agitation. In January 1924 it was annexed after Rome and Belgrade conspired through the Treaty of Rome, in which the Yugoslavs were compensated with territory elsewhere. The Free State government was then exiled and proceeded to appeal against the action.

Another disgruntled former ally was Romania. Its delegates brought to Paris a list of demands based upon promises which had been made in the Treaty of Bucharest, signed in August 1916, to tempt them into the war on the Allied side. However, as Romania's critics would be quick to point out, its contribution had fallen far short of expectations, both in the letter and the spirit of the agreement. Soon after entering the war Romania was soundly thrashed and occupied by the Central Powers, playing no further role in the conflict. Having signed a separate peace treaty with Germany in May 1918, it then opportunistically re-joined the fray in November once it was evident the Allies were on the verge of victory.

Like Italy, but perhaps with far more justification considering its duplicity, Romania was believed to have forsaken any of the victors' spoils. Prime minister Ion Bratianu nevertheless stuck to his guns, marching into the conference and demanding the Allies live up to their original treaty promises. The only thing in his favour was that his country's reputation, however damaged, was at least in better shape than that of the Hungarians, at whose expense his demands would be made. It had come down to the question of who had most earned the Allies' contempt. As Nicolson succinctly explained, 'for centuries Magyars had oppressed their subject nationalities ... the hour of liberation and retribution was at hand,'[74] and the Romanians were not about to let this opportunity slip through their fingers.

One of the choicest dishes on the menu was the district in southern Hungary at the confluence of the Danube, the Theiss and the Maras, known as the Banat of Temesvar. As usual it was something of an ethnic stew, and Serbia also had designs on the territory. The Banat was roughly divided between a predominantly Serb east and a largely Romanian west, but it also contained smaller pockets of Germans, Greeks and Bulgarians. Clearly, whichever way the Banat was allocated, there would be minorities to consider. The peacemakers were also left with the quandary of how to allocate the railways, navigable rivers and canals, 'through which no frontier could be drawn without injury to the economic interests of the inhabitants'.[75] The railways and canals had been routed in the interests of serving a unitary economy, but like such other imponderables as Teschen,

Danzig, Kehl and Fiume, a way would have to be found so that they could serve the needs of two or more masters. The commission created to adjudicate this quandary came to the only decision that they could under the circumstances – they awarded the western third to the Serbs and the remaining two-thirds to Romania. The compromise so enraged both claimants that they temporarily suspended their mutual dislike 'in their common disgust with the peace conference',[76] as Seymour recounted.

Another of Romania's claims was for the annexation of Transylvania. A popular uprising of the Romanian population there at the end of the war had successfully supplanted the Magyar rulers. A government was established which immediately declared union with Romania, and its delegates needed this to be validated by the peace conference in the face of vehement opposition from the Hungarians. Transylvania was also extremely ethnically diverse and, as Seymour explained, 'large colonies of Magyars and Germans are to be found ... [but] without the railways running north and south, communication between northern and southern Transylvania would be costly or impossible.' He lamented that the new Romania included 'a notable Magyar fringe'.[77] It was in fact something more than a fringe, as Hungarians constituted approximately 23 per cent of the population. Nicolson confided in his diary with surprising sympathy for the Magyars:

> Hungary is partitioned ... irresponsibly partitioned. They begin with Transylvania... Hungary loses her south. Then ... while the flies drone in and out of the open windows, Hungary loses her north and east. Then the frontier with Austria.[78]

General Smuts also believed the treatment of Hungary had been reprehensible, and Nicolson wrote that it 'feels that all we have done here [in Paris] is worse, far worse than the Congress of Vienna. The statesmen of 1815 at least knew what they were about.'[79] Nevertheless, Nicolson's sense of injustice was not widely shared. The Magyars' reputation as oppressive and exploitative overlords was widely held, and the ruthless suppression of their subject nationalities under the Habsburgs common knowledge. Public sentiment was reflected by English humourist and poet Alan Patrick Herbert. He crafted an unlikely ditty which called upon 'the Hairy Magyar' to 'stew in his horrid juice'.[80] Thus, in the minds of many, particularly those subject races that had for so long suffered under their Magyar masters, this was no more than poetic justice, and there was scant sympathy for the 3 million Magyars left as minorities within the borders of the new countries: 1 million in Transylvania, 700,000 in southern Slovakia and the remainder in the Banat and Vojvodina.

Although approximately 330,000 Hungarians chose to return to Hungary rather than live under foreign rule, their experience served to ingrain a sense of injustice and feed the resentment and bitterness which would come home to roost twenty years later. The Hungarians eventually signed, under protest, the Treaty of Trianon on 4 June 1920, a document which divested them of the majority of their former territory and reduced the country to a shadow of its former glory. Territorial emasculation was not Hungary's only fate. It also had to accept war guilt, the trial of war criminals, and exclusion from the League of Nations until it had passed a probationary period. In addition, its army had to be cut to 35,000 men and conscription was abolished.

Although Romania had been an unreliable and feckless ally, the conference held to its generally accepted principle of rewarding the victors rather than the vanquished. One delegate explained that 'the balance must naturally be inclined towards our ally Romania than towards our enemy Hungary.'[81] However, one Hungarian delegate put the severe outcome down to the simple fact that the Allies were 'frightfully bored by the whole peace conference ... [it was] a labyrinth from which they cannot find a way out ... they have created in the peace treaties a great number of international problems which they will not know how to solve.'[82]

Another reason for the conference being so accommodating to the Romanians was the Communist coup that had been carried out in Hungary by the revolutionary Bela Kun. A left-leaning journalist before the war, Kun was indoctrinated in Russian captivity. He became dedicated to the unlikely idea of a Soviet-style republic in his homeland, linked in a union with Austria, with both as satellites of Russia. Instead, upon staging a revolution and declaring the Soviet Republic on 21 March 1919, measures were taken which immediately plunged the country into chaos. The regime shut down all private shops and commercial enterprises and abolished private property, which at a stroke alienated the very middle class the country needed to try to get back on its feet. For some reason only grocery stores, tobacconists and pharmacies were exempted from the measures. Nor did the new government endear itself to the working class that it claimed to be serving, forbidding them to run expropriated factories for themselves. The regime then proceeded to terrorise the population as it sought to root out counter-revolutionaries and suppress the slightest sign of opposition to its rule. The instability this heralded, in addition to the potential for a Communist government on the Allies' doorsteps, presented another problem. The Hungarians were deeply unpopular – indeed, Lloyd George was of the opinion that 'there are few countries which need a revolution so much'[83] – but by the same token there was no appetite to see the revolution succeed or spread. Lord Hardinge voiced the fears of many among his contemporaries when he warned that 'the situation everywhere is deteriorating rapidly and in favour of the Bolsheviks ... it is difficult to know what measures can now be taken to relieve the situation.'[84]

As we have seen, there were very few British or French troops available to despatch, so the Foreign Office and Paris had to accommodate

Romania's territorial demands in part at least to elicit its help in suppressing the uprising, or at the very least containing it. Despite their concerns, the Allies still dithered and prevaricated instead of taking decisive action. They simply imposed a futile blockade, which did little to deter the rebels, and the lack of any response encouraged Kun to push his luck further. In June the Hungarian army attacked the Czechs to regain territory lost in Slovakia and then mounted an offensive against Romania on 23 July. They soon found out that they had bitten off more than they could chew. The Romanians encircled and crushed the Hungarians, and then, supported by the Czechs, proceeded to press against Kun's forces, delivering the *coup de grâce* at the end of the month.

On 31 July, Kun had to concede that his short-lived workers' paradise was finished. The following day the Revolutionary Council resigned, and on 3 August Romanian troops occupied Budapest and proceeded to ransack the capital. They removed anything of value, including railway locomotives and carriages, industrial machinery, farming implements and anything else they could haul away. This booty was taken back to Romania as what the invaders considered to be legitimate reparations, but it left Hungary in an even more dire state than before. With Bela Kun and his dream of a people's utopia swept away, some attempt had to be made at restoring a modicum of stability. On 1 March 1920, Hungary established a constitutional monarchy with Vice-Admiral Miklos Horthy as regent, and later Pal Teleki as premier.

The Treaty of St Germain-en-Laye, signed on 10 September 1919, left neighbouring Austria as a small, landlocked country of 32,370 square miles and 6.5 million people, a third of whom lived in a capital which was now far too large and grand for its diminished circumstances. It was to be, as James Headlam-Morley called it, a 'ludicrous and stupid' settlement,[85] but as one third of the Central Powers deemed responsible for the war, little more could have been expected. In addition to the dissolution of its monarchy, the loss of its empire and the distribution of its navy among the Allies, Austria's army was limited to 30,000 men, conscription was abolished and union with Germany was forbidden. Like its erstwhile ally, it was also to be subject to reparations. A further bone of contention was the debate over culpability for the war. Austria and Hungary had been the indisputable cores of the old Habsburg empire, but the monarchy entered the conflict severally and separately. If one part was culpable, it could have been argued that all were implicated in the alleged collusion and conspiracy to wage a war of aggression against Serbia; after all, if the empire had emerged victorious, all would have expected a share of the spoils. Nevertheless, the conference decided that only the Austrian-Germans and the Magyar-Hungarians would be held to account, and 'attempted to lay the sins of the Habsburgs' upon the new states of Lesser Austria and Lesser Hungary. They alone were to be punished 'by being forced to assume responsibility for a war debt and reparations ... incurred by the Habsburg government'.[86] The decision to treat all but Austria and Hungary as successor states not responsible for the war was heavily criticised. Nicolson considered it an iniquitous injustice, noting in his diary, 'Lunch with Maynard Keynes. Discuss Reparations of Austrian treaty. We are fully agreed on the absurdity of applying to Austria the German reparations and indemnity clauses.'[87]

The Reparations Commission set up to decide how much Austria would have to pay was due to report back by May 1921. By this time the full extent of Austria's economic collapse had been exposed and it was clear that such was the dire condition of its economy that it was not going to be in any position to pay anything beyond some livestock from its already greatly diminished herds. It was decided that the indignity of having been divested of some 233,000 square miles of its former empire would have to suffice and the question of an additional indemnity was quietly dropped. Nevertheless, Austria did secure one or two minor concessions, one of which concerned a territorial dispute that had emerged with Yugoslavia on the border at Klagenfurt. The Yugoslavs had pre-emptively seized the territory in November 1919, insisting that it was vital for their security and that Austria's counter-claim that its population of 150,000 was predominantly German lacked veracity. Understandably, following generations of co-existence, the German and Slovene communities had become bilingual and intermixed. The heady atmosphere created inevitably led to communal infighting and rising tensions, which threatened to degenerate into open conflict between the two claimants. However, there seemed to be little sympathy in Paris for the Yugoslavs' position, and one member of the British delegation, Seton-Watson, went so far as to accuse them of having lost 'all sense of proportion'[88] with respect to the amount of territory they were attempting to claim. Like the Poles, they seemed to be overstretching themselves, and grasping at whatever spoils they could secure before the clock ran out.

Attempting to arbitrate, the conference suggested partition or a plebiscite to determine the wishes of the population. Initially opposed to either solution, the Yugoslavs were eventually talked round, and the subsequent vote in 1920 came out in favour of remaining with Austria. The outcome was not necessarily the result of any patriotic fervour on the part of the electorate, however; more likely it was due to fear of the economic dislocation which might result from leaving Austria for the dubious benefits of a less well-developed Yugoslavia. A second modest win for Austria followed a further territorial dispute with the Yugoslavs, who wanted to control the strategically important Trieste–Villach–Vienna railway. Again, Italy came to Austria's support and backed its claims, and as with Klagenfurt it was agreed to put the issue to the vote, which found in favour of Austria. Austria also won a territorial dispute with its erstwhile partner in crime Hungary over the fate of Burgenland. It had, according to the 1910 census, a superior claim over the region, with 74 per cent of the population being Germans and only 9 per cent Hungarian, but nonetheless the Hungarians were determined to keep it. The two eventually came to blows, but by 1921 the Austrians won the day and held on to the territory. Otherwise, this 'pathetic relic',[89] as Nicolson called it, seemed condemned to the same fate as other small and unimportant European states.

In the opinion of Austrian foreign minister Otto Bauer, his country's fate represented the most egregious of double standards and application of injustice: 'No less than two-fifths of our people are to be subjected to foreign domination, without any plebiscite and against their indisputable will, thus being deprived of their right to self-determination.'[90] Equally, the French were determined that this should not apply to Austria. The British were more sympathetic to the concerns of France and the successor states than those of a defeated foe. Foreign secretary Lord Curzon insisted that the union of Austria and Germany 'would have a direct and unfortunate effect upon the position of the new states of Czecho-Slovakia and Yugo-Slavia, whom His Majesties Government are morally bound to support'.[91] It therefore appeared that the aspirations of the German Austrians, almost alone among those nationalities who sought unification with another state, were to be denied for the foreseeable future. The Danes were allowed to vote to return to Denmark, and even obscure Marienwerders could decide their future, but the notion of German Austrians uniting with the German Reich was far too dangerous to be contemplated.

Another state to have emerged from the conflict with a tarnished reputation was Bulgaria. Its fate was deliberated upon more out of animosity than any sense of moral justice or even perhaps strategic interest. Like Romania, it was largely detested by the Allies for its deceit and duplicity both before and during the war. Nicolson writes, 'I cherished feelings of contempt ... they had behaved treacherously in 1913 and in the Great War they had repeated this act of perfidy ... and lengthened the war by two years.'[92] Whether or not they quite had that much influence on the outcome of the war, Nicolson shared the widespread belief that Bulgaria had started the Second Balkan War of 1913 for its own ends and joined the Central Powers for entirely mercenary motives when it might have been a greater asset to the Allies. In an unprovoked act of aggression, Bulgaria joined Germany and Austria-Hungary in their combined attack on Serbia solely for the promised spoils. Balfour had said of them in July 1919:

> ... there has been no action more cynical and more disastrous than that undertaken by the Bulgarians. Had the Bulgarians not behaved as they had, Turkey would not have entered the war, the disastrous Gallipoli campaign would not have taken place; the war would have ended years sooner, and needless suffering would have been saved...[93]

Again, Balfour may have been rather overstating Bulgaria's influence, but its decision to throw in its lot with Germany and Austria-Hungary was to many observers perfectly in keeping with the reputation it had earned as 'the spoilt child of the Balkans'.[94] Eleutherios Venizelos, the Greek prime minister, called it 'the Prussia of the Balkans',[95] although his own appetite for territory would prove just as insatiable. The omens were not propitious. Nevertheless, when the Bulgarian delegates arrived at the conference they were determined to brazen it out, and the Allies were equally determined not to accommodate them. Bulgaria had originally demanded all of Thrace, which had provided its only access to the Aegean, but instead lost Western Thrace to Greece. There was no demographic justification for it remaining with Bulgaria; after the Turkish population, the next largest community was indeed Greek. Eastern Thrace, too, would have been taken by Greece had the Turks not later fought a war to retain it. Only Italy saw any merits in the territory remaining under Bulgarian administration, but this support was mainly due to its policy of wanting to do everything it could to undermine the Yugoslavs. Greece was also awarded the part of Macedonia that Bulgaria seized in 1913 following its partition among the Serbs, Greeks and themselves. This particular measure could be attributable not just to the general principle of denying Bulgaria as much as possible in the region, but to a desire by Lloyd George to create a strong Greece to act as his surrogate in the region, much as France was doing in its support for Poland. The bigger and stronger their clients, the better.

Bulgaria had also expected the return of southern Dobruja, which it had lost to Romania after the Second Balkan War of 1913. If that year's census was to be believed, the area contained 112,000 Turks, roughly the same number of Bulgarians, 10,000 Tartars and only 7,000 Romanians.[96] Romania therefore had a weak claim on the territory, but of course neither was there much appetite to return it to treacherous Bulgaria. The US proposed that part of the territory might be repatriated and the rest retained by the Romanians, but this was opposed by both Britain and France. France took the view that a wartime ally, even one as unreliable as Romania, ought not to be forced to return territory to a defeated foe, particularly one as generally reviled as Bulgaria. Nevertheless, the Americans had their way; to rub more salt in the wound, the Yugoslavs were to be awarded another 990 square miles in small pockets along their eastern border. In all, Bulgaria lost about 10 per cent of its territory, an outcome which Balfour conceded afterwards 'might be neither equitable nor conducive to peace in the Balkans'.[97] In the meantime, the country had little option but to sign 'even a bad peace'[98] at Neuilly on 27 November 1919.

Bulgaria's armed forces were to include no air force, no worthwhile navy and an army of just 20,000 in addition to a gendarmerie of no more than 13,000 men and 3,000 border guards, little more than an armed militia. Nor were the Bulgarians permitted to have heavy artillery. Because they were also forbidden to have a conscript army, they would find it difficult in any case to recruit enough volunteers to serve in either organisation. Moreover, their unemployed officers would give vent to their bitterness by becoming active in the right-wing revanchist organisations and various revolutionary groups which would store up trouble for the future. Balfour also insisted that Bulgaria be held liable to pay reparations, a measure opposed both by Eyre Crowe and by Harold Nicolson. They believed that the territorial losses were probably punishment enough, and Crowe minuted that 'Bulgaria should be treated rather tenderly' on this subject.[99] In any case, what could they do if Bulgaria did not pay?

Nevertheless, over the heads of wiser council, it was decided that Bulgaria must pay £90 million over a period of thirty-eight years, in addition to surrendering stocks of coal and cattle. In the end, as Eyre Crowe and others prophesised, the money was never collected, and it was eventually written off as a bad debt. The loss of territory, particularly Thrace, also meant that it would have to accommodate over 250,000 refugees who either fled or were expelled from its ceded lands, an operation that would continue well into the 1920s. This situation was exacerbated after Greece sought to make room for expelled nationals from Turkey following its disastrous war in Anatolia. For all this turmoil, the country at least emerged from the proceedings in Paris relatively homogeneous, with few of the ethnic tensions that would bring so much friction to its neighbours. The census of 1926 revealed that out of a total population of nearly 5.5 million, Bulgarians constituted 83.2 per cent, with 4,557,000 people. The next largest ethnic group was Turkish, with 10.5 per cent, or 577,000 people. The remainder consisted of nearly 70,000 Romanians, plus pockets of Jews and gypsies.[100] In Bulgaria's case it was bitterness at the territorial losses that would lead to conflict, with frequent border disputes with Greece, Romania and Yugoslavia prompting refugee crises and lasting enmity until the opportunity to settle the score presented itself two decades later.

Here, then, was the new Europe, geographically and politically transformed at the whim of a few men in Paris who for the most part believed that what they had decided was based upon fairness and justice and above all was true to the mantra of 'self-determination'. The two great empires were no more, their vassal states free to seek their own way in the post-war world, but Versailles would soon prove to be a settlement which fell far short of what Colonel House, Maynard Keynes and of course Jean Monnet had advocated or envisaged. For all his efforts, Lloyd George would return home to be 'blamed for the failure of the peace conference to restore immediately prosperity in war ravaged Europe... [and] particularly blamed for creating the new national states of Poland, Czechoslovakia and Yugoslavia'.[101]

9

All the Elements of
a National Rising

King Alexander I of Yugoslavia and his queen. (Library of Congress)

The peacemakers may have meant well, but as a result of their decisions a few untested states had been manufactured at the expense of two long-established nations. In the process, integrated economies based upon historic customs unions and single markets had been dissolved with the result that, as Leopold Amery of the War Council put it, 'we shall simply have of the whole of Central Europe a reproduction on a larger scale of what the Balkans were after 1913.'[1] Furthermore, the peacemakers had invested a considerable amount of stock in the goodwill of those who had pressured and lobbied for the establishment of these countries. In return, by nearly every measure from which one might judge open democracy and respect for human rights, their leaders would fall far short, and in the process betray the trust which had been placed in them.

Czechoslovakia had emerged from the peace settlement a potential beacon of freedom after centuries of alien rule. Nonetheless, its many nationalities prompted Italian dictator Benito Mussolini to joke that 'Czecho-slovakia should instead have been named Czecho-Germano-Polano-Magyaro-Rutheno-Rumano-Slovakia.'[2] Ensuring that everyone received equity and fairness in such a complex society would require great commitment and determination. Indeed, Benes and Masaryk had undertaken to form such a free and democratic republic true to the spirit of the League of Nations Covenant. They promised that there would be no favouritism in the appointment of government posts, and strict measures would be put in place to ensure that all minorities were protected. The state's Germans in particular, despite having been relegated in the hierarchy of the country, were promised life on 'an equal footing with Czech',[3] and the new government had willingly signed the Minorities Treaty to that effect. Once the conference had ended, however, and their new state was duly recognised, Masaryk was able to drop all pretences and clamp down on anything that resembled opposition to his newly won domains. As early as March 1919, the signs were not good. The Czech authorities responded ruthlessly to demonstrations and outbreaks of dissent by Germans who were agitating for the right to join either Germany or Austria. Their heavy handedness did not go unnoticed, and provoked the Swiss German-language newspaper *Neue Zuerichter Zeitung* to declare on 7 March that:

> ... the acts of Czech brutality against the German Bohemian demonstrators ... who had assembled ... for entirely peaceful demonstrations for self-determination ... has eradicated any possibility of understanding ... the Czech government is wrong if it thinks it can break the resistance of three and one half million German Bohemians with terrorist methods.[4]

When communists led a national strike in December 1920, it quickly turned to violence and a declaration of martial law, arrests, and show trials. A Law against Terror was then passed,[5] ostensibly in the interests of public order, but which instead was used as an instrument through which to suppress any sign of dissent. Under Masaryk's guidance, the Czechs began almost immediately to adopt measures that would incrementally ensure their in-built domination of the country, essentially replicating what the Magyars had done in the former Hungarian half of the old monarchy. The ultimate goal was to guarantee that, despite Mussolini's wry observation, the country would present to the world an exclusively Czech character.

Arguably the most egregious example of the manner in which the Czechs attempted to do this was manipulating the national census. To this end the Czechs and Slovaks were counted as a single nationality or 'state forming people' and thus could claim to constitute 65 per cent of the total population. Because the Czechs, as we shall see, had no intention of giving the Slovaks genuine equal footing, this sleight of hand was employed solely to ensure Czech domination over everybody else. It also conveniently ignored the fact that the country contained more Germans than Slovaks, and in doing so further emphasised their alienation. Language, too, was to play a significant role in reinforcing Czech dominance. Under the Habsburgs, many people spoke in three tongues – their own plus whatever they needed to communicate for business and to chat with their neighbours.[6] By asking the respondents only for their 'mother tongue' rather than the language 'of daily use', as was done in 1911, the number of 'Germans' recorded dropped significantly from 3,750,327 to 3,123,568, and Magyars from 1,070,854 to 745,451,[7] further bolstering the illusion of a 'Czech' majority. It was also hoped that by creating a hostile environment, 'natural wastage' among Germans and Magyars, including migration, would in any case facilitate the eventual decline in their percentage of the population and proportionately increase that of the Czechs. This would clearly be a slow process, however. Even by 1930, although there were 7,447,000 Czechs and 2,309,000 Slovaks, they still faced a sizeable 3,218,000 Germans, 720,000 Magyars, 569,000 Ruthenes, 100,000 Poles and 266,000 others (including 100,000 Jews and 100,000 gypsies).

In the meantime, another way of achieving hegemony was to ensure that both the executive and its civil servants were overwhelmingly Czech, and the foreign ministry would ultimately include few if any ethnic Germans or Hungarians.[8] Germans were also kept out of public services through a combination of forced retirement and intimidation. Thousands more, because they could not hope to pass impossibly rigid language tests, lost their positions to Czechs who subsequently moved into German areas and took over their posts.[9] Increasingly oppressive laws were passed to prevent free movement, and German Austrians were forbidden to visit relatives in Czecho-Slovak villages without permission. From March 1921 the authorities could alter German and Hungarian town, regional and street names to Czech or Slovak ones.[10]

It was therefore inevitable that when the new country designed its state symbols and emblems, those relating to its historically Czech Bohemian and Moravian heritage overshadowed those of any of the other communities. Czech imagery dominated the national flag, state crest, national anthem, postage stamps, and the country's new coinage. Passports, too, were only issued in Czech and French. Little if anything could be found to reflect German, Magyar or even Slovak themes, and only some legacy laws and administrative practices survived to remind people of former German influences. Five of the country's Czech political parties further entrenched Czech dominance by conspiring to form a bloc in parliament which they hoped would enable them to veto any proposed legislation which was contrary to their interests.[11] As their domination of government took hold, the Hungarians, Poles and German parties sought to defend their communities by grouping under nationalistic banners rather than presenting policies based upon more traditional platforms.[12] Nevertheless, with the Czechs firmly in control of the state apparatus, they would be facing an uphill struggle if they attempted to pursue aims that did not chime with their vested interests.

One early challenge facing the country was land reform, which was perfectly legitimate to address, but also threatened the position of both the Magyars and Germans. In 1919, fully a third of all agricultural land and forests was still owned by Germans or Germanised Czechs and Magyars, just a couple of hundred families at most. Two out of three peasants in Slovakia had no land of their own at all, an imbalance which was soon exacerbated by the demands of returning soldiers and the strains of the post-war economy. Increasingly vociferous demands for change resulted in the controversial and divisive Land Control Act of April 1919, which limited arable holdings to no more than 150 hectares. The excess would be expropriated, with compensation applied incrementally, in what Masaryk hailed as 'the greatest act of the new republic'.[13] By implication as well as by implementation, it was soon evident that the biggest losers of any redistribution would be the two formerly dominant nationalities. The first estates to be seized and redistributed were those owned by German and Magyar landowners, and the net beneficiaries were their former Czech and Slovak peasants.

Nor were the Germans and the Magyars the only ones to feel the material consequences of Czech muscle flexing. Although a decree had been issued enabling Slovaks to supplant Magyars,[14] it did not help the Slovaks themselves very much in the long run. Moreover, the cynical motives behind combining Czechs and Slovaks in the census was underlined by the realisation that this was never going to be translated into actual parity in the administration or civil service. Popular Slovak Catholic cleric and politician Father Andrej Hlinka claimed that despite constituting 17 per cent of the population, ethnic Slovaks held less than 2 per cent of the posts in central government.[15] Moreover, Slovaks complained that they were short-changed by the effects of the land redistribution which was being undertaken. Such was the dire condition of his people within the new country that Hlinka would later claim that 'in their brief association with the Czechs' the Slovaks had 'suffered more than from the Magyars in a thousand years'.[16] Although this was a dramatic claim to make so early in the life of the new country, many Slovaks realised that they were, like the Germans and Magyars, second-class citizens. Many would feel compelled to emigrate and seek a better life as minorities in other countries, and those who chose to remain would increasingly seek redress through agitation and confrontation.

To be fair, some of the disparity between Czech and Slovak was due to legacy social issues. The traditional imbalances which existed between the largely urban and industrial Bohemian Crown Lands and the poorer Hungarian highlands and Ruthenia were pronounced, and did not appear to have been greatly ameliorated by Masaryk's land reforms. Perhaps such contrasts were understandable insofar as those living in Bohemia, Moravia or Silesia were closer to Prague and more familiar with a system of government inherited from Austria; but those in the former Hungarian regions of Slovakia and sub Carpathian Ruthenia were geographically and culturally remote and naturally more familiar with the heritage and practices of the Hungarian half of the old empire.[17] Czechs also considered themselves to be somewhat more urbane and sophisticated than their compatriots further east, who were inclined to hang on to old traditions and a culture of deference towards their 'betters'. The historic link between Magyar aristocrat and Slav peasant would not be easily broken, despite the best efforts of the government in Prague. Consequently, on the abolition of aristocratic titles, which were largely held by Germans and Magyars, there was widespread disquiet. Moreover, many Czechs did not necessarily share their Slovakian compatriots' religious allegiances. There was a growing anti-clerical mood, with many resenting the power and influence exercised by the Church over the lives of so much of the population. In a country which was 80 per cent Catholic, this would prove another bone of contention. It did, however, offer one of the few opportunities for the Czechs to defer to Slovak sensitivities. At Hlinka's urging, the Vatican was granted permission to nominate bishops to Czech sees, although the government did reserve the right to veto their decisions.

Even the fact that Czechoslovakia had been endowed with the overwhelming majority of the former empire's industry would prove to be a double-edged sword. Having inherited 70–80 per cent of manufacturing, including the Skoda works and its vast capacity in arms and motor car manufacturing, plus porcelain and glass industries, sugar refineries, and 40 per cent of the empire's distilleries and breweries, no other successor state was better placed to succeed. Had the country been more socially cohesive, this should have proved a boon. However, in inheriting all this wealth, the new state also inherited its owners, as most light and heavy industry was located in the Sudetenland, belonging to Germans and run by German-controlled banks. Czechs ran just 30–40 per cent of industry, and in Slovakia the situation was even worse, with only 5 per cent in Slovak hands. In line with Prague's pursuit of Czech interests, measures were soon taken to repatriate ownership of industry. All companies and financial institutions operating within the country were required to register as Czech and to include Czechs on their boards. These measures were understandably met with hostility by the Germans and Magyars, especially in the Sudetenland. Here the earliest seeds of discontent were being sown alongside the skewing of census statistics and inequality in government employment. Furthermore, during the war, retreating Hungarian troops ruthlessly dismantled and stole what little industrial material existed in Slovakia. Not only did the serious imbalance between the industries of the two ends of the country exacerbate their differences, but Slovak salaries were lower even though their inherited tax system meant that they had to pay more than their Czech counterparts.[18]

This is not to say that Prague was entirely hostile to its non-Czech citizens. Evidence that the government had other issues to address can be seen by the raft of social legislation that was being enacted. There were over 150 nationwide reforms between 1918 and 1923, introducing an eight-hour day, sickness and unemployment insurance and limits to the employment of women and children. Legally, of course, these new rights applied to all citizens, and if done so equitably and fairly ought to help to draw its various ethnic groups closer together and help to create a more equal and cohesive society.

Financial reforms were also introduced, intended to adjust the economy for the realities of a post-war world. The Czech crown was introduced in April 1919 to replace the old Habsburg currency and all of the others in circulation. This measure helped the country avoid much of the inflation which dogged its neighbours and served to attract capital for investment, so that by the end of the decade the crown was one of the strongest currencies on the continent. Moreover, as a result of its underlying economic strength, Czechoslovakia saw considerable growth and prosperity. Per capita gross domestic product put it among the top ten economies by 1929, above Germany, France, Italy and the UK. All this was fine, but then came the Great Depression, which even Czechoslovakia could not escape. Between 1928 and 1934 the price of agricultural produce plummeted by a third and the nation's debt doubled. The crisis also served to expose the consequences of breaking up Austria-Hungary. For example, the sudden appearance of an international border to separate Felwiclek/Slovakia from what remained in Hungary prevented agricultural labourers from travelling freely to the Hungarian Plain for seasonal work.[19] Consequently, agricultural products such as sugar beet were left to rot because there weren't enough labourers to harvest them. Furthermore, the new national border cut off Slovakia from its traditional markets in Hungary, and its coal mines and refineries lay idle for want of customers.[20] As Father Hlinka explained, all the Slovak rivers 'flow towards the Hungarian Plain, and all our roads lead to Budapest ... from Prague we are separated by the barrier of the Carpathians.'[21]

Lack of demand for Czech exports saw industrial production fall by 40 per cent, and during the same period exports fell by 70 per cent. The balance of trade was 500 million crowns in credit in 1928, but 200 million in debit by 1933. Furthermore, unemployment increased to 750,000, or 16.6 per cent of the working population.[22] Matters were looking bleak, but the government was energetic in attempting to find solutions. State subsidies, devaluation of the crown and trade agreements with Britain, the US and South Africa revived key companies such as Skoda, the shoe manufacturer Bata, and the car manufacturer Tatra, so much so that by 1936 productivity was back to 96 per cent of 1929 levels.[23] By 1936, industrial workers made up 44.6 per cent of the working population, and the country had returned to being one of Europe's top ten producers of industrial manufactures.

Seen in the round, the Czechs' combination of political, social and economic reforms came at a cost and served to further highlight racial tensions within the state. German industrialists and owners were bitter at their losses due to the reforms, and then due to the economic depression; nor did the economic recovery do much to address the traditional imbalance between Czechs and Slovaks. By 1939, most of the same causes for disunity and mutual animosity would exist as had been in play twenty years before. Furthermore, when Hitler came to power in January 1933, he proceeded to ratchet up hostility towards the Czechs and encouraged Czechoslovakia's German population to agitate for more autonomy and self-government. This was a red rag to a bull for the Czech government, which retaliated in October 1933 by outlawing the local Nazi Party and the Sudeten German Party. This proved just the first of several fractures within the uneasy structure of the country, as the Sudeten Germans were joined by the Magyars and Slovenes, who were also becoming increasingly restless.

This growing disaffection was not helped by the fact that, on 18 December 1935, Benes was appointed the country's president in succession to Masaryk, confirming the widespread suspicion that 'the same old gang would remain in charge' regardless of how people voted.[24] Czech dominance, entrenched and reinforced by a state structure designed specifically to promote their own interests, was fuelling the fires of discontent. Father Hlinka was also becoming increasingly radical in his outlook, in August 1933 making an incendiary speech in which he announced, 'There are no Czechoslovaks. We want to remain just Slovaks – out with the Czechs!'[25] Seeing no sign of improvement in their status or any change coming from Prague, the Slovak population became more strident. In September 1936, at the Slovak People's Seventh Congress, Hlinka read out a declaration asserting Slovakia's right to autonomy within a federal Czechoslovakia, and in November 1937 students in Bratislava took to the streets waving banners and demanding protection for the Slovak culture and its language. There were also claims that the Pittsburg Agreement, issued in the war and in the white heat of enthusiasm for a free state, had been violated and that Slovaks need no longer feel bound by it.

While the young Czechoslovak state began to experience its inevitable decline, it could have done worse than to take as an object lesson the fate of its neighbour Austria. Adolf Hitler, picking up where the Weimar Republic left off, had commenced the pursuit of his long-held dream of dismantling the Versailles Treaty. In *Mein Kampf*, he stated that 'German-Austria must return to the great German motherland,' and of particular relevance to the Germans of the Sudetenland was his assertion that 'German blood belongs in a common Reich.'[26] The Czechs therefore observed with understandable trepidation the slow drip of German infiltration into Austrian political life, something which its chancellor, Engelbert Dollfuss, tried to resist. Austria had itself followed a route of increasingly right-wing politics and was far from being democratic, but its president nevertheless resisted the overtures of the country's powerful, overbearing neighbour, especially as it enjoyed the protection of fascist Italy at this time.

Hitler knew he could not yet risk alienating Mussolini, and so was forced to stay his hand. He instead persisted through vicarious means, instructing his agents and Nazi plants to cause as much agitation and disruption as they could to destabilise the state and create the circumstances in which union with Germany became inevitable. When a coup was staged in July 1934, a combination of Italian posturing and the loyalty of the Austrian army thwarted the attempt. However, Dollfuss was assassinated in the brutal fighting which accompanied the coup. Undeterred, Hitler continued to bide his time. The new chancellor, Kurt Schuschnigg, tried to appease Hitler, hoping to fend him off with the signing of a friendship pact in 1936. This was supposed to guarantee Austrian independence, but instead compelled the Austrians to follow a foreign policy sympathetic to Germany and to accept Austrian Nazis in the government.

In the meantime, Hitler had been cultivating closer ties with Mussolini for many reasons, not least of which was to weaken the relationship between Italy and Austria. This culminated in Hitler and Mussolini signing a treaty in October 1936 which stripped Austria of its guarantee of independence and left it helpless in the face of further Nazi agitation.

The next two years witnessed a slow-burn of gradual Nazi infiltration and undermining of the state, which was a necessary precondition to concocting some justification for usurping the government. On 12 February 1938, Schuschnigg found himself ordered to Germany and pressured into accepting more Nazis into his administration. Most significant was Arthur Seyss-Inquart, whom Schuschnigg was forced to appoint to the key post of minister of the interior, and Hans Fishbock, who became minister of finance. This was swiftly followed by an intensification of pro-Nazi agitation, as Hitler issued instructions for the country to be so undermined that an excuse could be given that German troops had to intervene to restore order. In the hope of pre-empting the

Germans, Schuschnigg announced on 24 February that a referendum would be held on 9 March to settle the issue once and for all, asking the Austrian people whether or not they wished to remain a sovereign state. Schuschnigg's weak position was underlined by the fact that all Hitler really had to do was demand the referendum be scrapped and that he resign in favour of Seyss-Inquart. This exposed Austria to the tender mercies of both the Austrian Nazis and those waiting across the border in Germany. The hapless and friendless chancellor duly resigned on 11 March, and Seyss-Inquart was appointed in his place. The Nazi stooge promptly invited Germany to enter the country in order to ensure 'order' was maintained.

On 15 March, Hitler embarked upon a triumphal procession into the country of his birth. He was so overwhelmed by his delirious welcome that he abandoned plans to make Austria a mere satellite of Germany and announced to the crowd of thousands that the two countries would be united, and the *Anschluss* was completed. For the first time since their estrangement under Bismarck in 1866 and final divorce in 1871, Hitler was reuniting these German-speakers, adding 6.5 million to the growing population of the Reich. The very thing that France had plotted and connived to prevent, and upon which much of its defence planning was based, had occurred, and there was nothing it or its allies could do to stop it. Nor were the implications of this momentous event lost on the wider world. The Sudeten Germans, again with the encouragement of the Nazis, ratcheted up their own demands. On 24 April their leader, Konrad Henlein, issued his Karlsbad Programme, in which he insisted upon full administrative and legal autonomy for the region. Benes, both fearful of and enraged by this brazen challenge to his authority, ordered partial mobilisation of the army, prepared to crush any sign of an insurrection.

This escalation understandably antagonised Germany, but it also wrong-footed Britain and France, who at this time were still counting on their policy of appeasement to keep Hitler in check. The last thing they needed was a provocation which gave Hitler an excuse to build upon the *Anschluss* to make similar moves elsewhere. Instead of supporting the Czech government, France and Britain made it clear that if the Czechs precipitated open warfare they could not expect support. Meanwhile, the 'plight' of the Sudeten Germans was receiving widespread publicity throughout Germany, which in turn was using its propaganda value to actually elicit world sympathy. Consequently, although it was arguably the Berlin-backed Sudeten Nazis who were provoking the Prague government, Benes' response was interpreted as the cause of the emerging crisis. Britain and France, looking to avoid war at all costs, increased the pressure on Prague to accommodate Henlein. A now harassed and cornered Benes announced on 5 September 1938 that almost all the points put forward by Henlein had been accepted, but the Sudeten leader, possibly well tutored by the Nazis in the art of brinkmanship, responded by announcing that his party was breaking off negotiations. Hitler cynically added to the tension by making a provocative speech at the Nuremberg Rally of 12 September in which he declared his support for the Sudeten Germans and emphasised their plight as an abused minority.

After the failure of an attempted coup, Henlein fled to Germany to receive further instructions. In the meantime, Hitler had been upping the tempo and his threats and cajoling had achieved their goal. Benes' stance had won him few friends, and the general consensus was that the Sudeten Germans should get what they wanted. Neville Chamberlain, the British prime minister, flew to Hitler's alpine retreat at Berchtesgarden on 15 September. Without even notifying the Czechs of his intentions, he agreed in principle to the transfer of the Sudetenland to Germany.

These concessions were broadly met with approval, and on 16 September Lord Runciman, who had headed the abortive British mission to try and resolve the crisis, concurred that those areas which were predominantly and undeniably German should be given the self-determination denied to them in 1918. Against this backdrop of rising tensions and provocations, the French also agreed to the solution on 18 September. The Czechoslovak government, with no friends and only hostility from its neighbours, reluctantly and bitterly accepted the plan too. The Munich Agreement followed, which was signed on 30 September 1938 – without a Czech representative even being present – by Britain, France and Germany and with the Italian dictator Mussolini acting as guarantor. On 1 October the evacuation of the Sudetenland began and the first step in the dissolution of the Czechoslovak state had been taken. Poland, too, seized its chance to recover the territory surrounding Teschen which it had been denied in 1920. The Poles proceeded to annex its 419 square miles and 242,000 people, and between 2 and 12 October the region was absorbed into the Polish state.[27] On 5 October, Benes, his dream in shreds, resigned as president and was replaced by Dr Emil Hacha, an equally hapless figure.

On 6 October, Slovakia seized its chance and declared itself 'a sovereign and independent nation', autonomous within the Czecho-Slovak Republic,[28] with Father Gaspar Tiso as its premier. Shortly afterwards, the non-Czech inhabitants of Carpathian Ruthenia demanded autonomy too. President Hacha belatedly tried to reassert some semblance of authority by dismissing the Ruthene government on 6 March. This act pushed Tiso into the arms of Hitler. Tiso was convinced that his only option to protect his country was not by autonomy but outright independence. Needing little persuasion, and now with what he thought of as a powerful sponsor behind him, he proceeded to act on 14 March. The Ruthenes swiftly followed suit, declaring themselves the Republic of Carpatho-Ukraine. It was to be a very brief independence, and on 15 March 1939 Hungarian troops marched in and annexed the territory.[29] German troops occupied the rest of Bohemia and Moravia the same day, and the Republic of Czechoslovakia, not quite twenty years old, disappeared. Benes left the country to brood in exile for the next seven years, while Hacha remained as Hitler's temporary satrap. Thus were extinguished the lofty dreams of Wilson and the other peacemakers. Their well-meaning but flawed decision-making had condemned the state to failure almost from its inception. Even more tragically, the same motives and the same fatally flawed implementation were to bring down the rest of the successor states. The great new sovereign Polish Republic, which had also joined the comity of nations with high hopes and lofty expectations, was destined to disappoint too.

Poland enjoyed few of the economic endowments bestowed upon Czechoslovakia and faced a raft of challenges. Not least of these was the harmonisation of three different economies, laws and bureaucracies, nine separate legislative systems and five currencies. It also inherited an incompatible railway system, consisting of different gauges and networks, even operating on both the right- and left-hand sides.[30] All three empires had naturally developed their respective railways to promote internal communications, trade, free movement and military efficiency.[31] They provided links to Vienna, Berlin and St Petersburg and their markets to the west, south and east, in the process observing the protocols, rules and regulations that applied within their particular borders. With these dissolved, they were now seriously out of kilter with the geography of their new state. As a railway specialist at the time explained, 'A train from Warsaw to Zebryzdowice ran for the first 300 km under the Napoleon's Code and the Russian Law, in Silesia, for the first 60 km under the German legislation, and finally for the last 40 km, it found itself under the domain of the Austrian law.'[32]

The war had wrought its own havoc, destroying infrastructure, railway stations, points, signalling systems and all the other paraphernalia of a functioning rail system. Sir William Goode, British director of relief missions and a member of the British delegation to the peace conference, had embarked upon a fact-finding tour of the whole of central Europe early in 1919, where he found 'chaos ... in countries where I found wagons ... I found ... a shortage of locomotives, where there were locomotives there was a shortage of wagons.'[33] Those wagons which could be found were so dilapidated that according to Ethel Snowden their passengers 'travelled in an ice-cold train, with broken windows and tattered upholstery, and with no opportunity of eating warm food'.[34] It was hardly surprising, therefore, that one of the first steps the government in Warsaw decided upon was to initiate a ten-year plan of reconstruction for these vital arteries. New rolling stock, engines, and lines would need to be built and all the different gauges and locomotive types in the three zones integrated and harmonised. Once achieved, they would satisfy one of the most important physical elements constituting a unitary state.

An early start was made with the purchase of 150 locomotives from the US in 1919, followed by an order for a further twenty-five in 1920.

Another 3,000 were seized from German stocks under the terms of the reparation clauses of the Versailles Treaty. The construction of new lines was begun in 1920, filling in gaps and replacing those lines destroyed during the war. In 1923 an engine factory was opened, and in 1927 the first experiments in electrification were undertaken. Inevitably, the economic depression of the 1930s had a negative impact, and in fact caused a considerable contraction, with a huge drop in revenue and the loss of thousands of jobs. These lean years led to better times, and by 1939 a network existed which was not only the equal of many but would prove of considerable benefit to friend and foe alike.

A modernised railway system alone would not resolve all the embryonic state's issues with harmonisation and integration, not to mention the almost insurmountable matter of reconstruction. Much of Poland's most productive land, agricultural and industrial, had existed on some of the most fought over and devastated territory after Belgium and France. One district in particular, that of Dzikow near the town of Tarnobrzeg, close to the Austrian–Russian border, suffered five offensives by the Austro-Hungarian army and four by the Russians plus three major battles. The area had been occupied twice by Russian forces, resulting in the destruction of 3,000 farms and homes and the devastation of 35,000 acres of forests and woodland.[35] In total, one contemporary observer estimated that throughout the territories most affected by the fighting, 1.8 million buildings had been destroyed, 11 million acres of agricultural land had been rendered unusable, and 2 million head of cattle, 1 million horses and 1.5 million sheep had been slaughtered. Furthermore, 7,500 bridges would need to be rebuilt. They would also have to survive without the 15 million acres of forests that had been destroyed.[36]

The new country not only had to restore its agricultural base, but also develop its economy into one which might match those of its bigger neighbours. This would have to be undertaken by diversifying and embracing further industrialisation. Here, too, Poland faced almost insurmountable challenges. Lacking the windfall enjoyed by Czechoslovakia, the Poles had to begin more or less from scratch. In what had been Congress Poland, some 4,000 electrical motors and engines and almost 4,000 tooling machines had to be replaced, most of which had been stolen by one or other of the enemy combatants in the ebb and flow of the conflict.[37] With the help of loans, increasing quantities of industrial apparatus were imported between 1927 and 1928,[38] and by 1938 Poland could boast some 225,000 industrial operations. But even so, with most only employing between one to four people,[39] these were far too small to pose a serious economic challenge to competitors such as Krupp in Germany or the massive expansion being planned in Soviet Russia.

Despite Poland's best efforts, it would therefore prove difficult to move away from a dependency on agriculture. So much so that the percentage of the population engaged in this sector would only drop from 70 per cent in 1921 to 61 per cent in 1939. It did not help that Poland was sandwiched between two unfriendly states which would do all that they could to undermine its efforts. Germany in particular was presented with a golden opportunity to frustrate Polish economic growth when in 1924 the government in Berlin decided to introduce import duties. These were scheduled to come into effect when the clause in the Versailles Treaty requiring Germany to grant favoured trading status to the victors and successor states expired in June 1925. The Germans almost immediately imposed damaging tariffs on coal imported from Polish Upper Silesia, a much-needed source of foreign exchange for the Warsaw government, because over half its coal production was exported. Poland sought to retaliate in kind by matching the German tariffs, but this tit for tat hurt the Poles far more because Poland accounted for only 5 per cent of Germany's overall trade. This so-called Tariff War would persist for nine more years, although the Poles would prove far more resilient than the Germans anticipated.

Meanwhile, the Polish government pursued other avenues by which to grow its economy. One was the financial reforms that were introduced under the premiership of Wladysaw Grabski. A start had actually been made during the German occupation, when in 1917 the marka was introduced. This was intended to become the currency of the puppet state they planned to establish, and the new Polish government opted to retain it after they had taken control. It was decided that the old German notes should be replaced with truly Polish ones bearing the symbols and motifs of the new state on them, and to this end 8 tons of newly printed Polish banknotes were ordered from Waterlow and Sons of London in 1919.[40] Nevertheless, there were still millions of notes and coins from the old empires still in circulation, making the setting of exchange rates very challenging. To try and address this situation, the government issued a complete ban on the importation of money from Germany, Austria and Russia on 11 March 1919,[41] but the problem of fiscal consolidation proved a far harder nut to crack and would require more than simply printing more or indeed banning different types of banknotes. The Polish marka started to lose its value as the inherent shortcomings of the economy as a whole began to be felt. To increase the money supply and stimulate growth the government proceeded to print more and more notes, today known euphemistically as quantitative easing. Instead of resolving the situation, this tactic simply resulted in a continuous downward spiral and ultimately hyperinflation, the shock of which Poland was in no position to absorb. The consequences for the ordinary people were dire. One contemporary observer recalled how:

> ... if anyone sold anything and did not at once buy something else with the money, he would lose heavily. There were many who sold house or field, or part of their cattle, only to keep their money either at home

or in some bank. These lost all they had and became beggars ... there were heaps of money. One had to carry it in briefcases or baskets ... for things for the house one paid in thousands, then millions, and finally in billions...[42]

The clawing misery and suffering endured by the majority of the population can well be imagined, but the government did work hard to alleviate the situation and the economy finally started to stabilise with the introduction of the new uniform Polish currency, the zloty, in 1924, and the establishment of the Bank of Poland. Government revenues were further improved through other measures such as more efficient tax collection, especially from the monied higher classes, who, as we shall see, enjoyed a privileged status in the new republic. These measures made a balanced budget possible for the first time in 1926, and this improving situation was maintained until 1930/31. Indeed, in 1929 there was a modest budget surplus, assisted in part by the securing of a 'Stabilisation Loan' from the US in 1927.[43] Such was the improvement in the country that by 1928 unemployment was practically nil,[44] while living standards in some sectors also rose thanks to investment in infrastructure. One of the most impressive examples was the decision to build a port at Gydnia, 22 kilometres north of Danzig on the Baltic Sea, giving the Poles their own autonomous facility outside of the Free City. Work began in 1921 and three years later a 550-metre pier, a 175-metre wooden tidal boom and a nascent harbour had been constructed. It received its first major ship in August 1923, and an improving economy allowed further investment and expansion throughout the 1920s and 1930s. A consequential growth in demand for skilled labour saw some wages increase by as much as 40 per cent.[45]

The booming economy also saw recovery begin in Eastern Galicia, for so long the orphan of both Austria and now Polish planning, with the construction of distilleries, breweries, brick and tile factories and sawmills.[46] The government even found sufficient revenue to fund some social and welfare programmes, including the introduction of the eight-hour working day and a new Catholic university in Lublin. Of course, such investment in the arts and social improvements could only last while the economy grew. This fact was brought brutally home when the Great Depression started to bite. By 1933, gross national income had declined by a quarter and nearly wiped out the gains of the previous decade. The social consequences were terrible, and again it was the ordinary people who suffered most. Despite the country having mountains of it, people were reduced to stealing coal in order to heat their homes because they could no longer afford to buy it. The health of the population nosedived, with 3,500 cases of typhus recorded in 1934, and suicide rates increased as people lost hope and despaired of their situation. By 1935, in the words of one witness, 'life [has become] wretched for us'.[47]

The economy was not the only problem the Polish state was facing. As we have seen, there was a broad church of opinion among politicians and others regarding the constitution of the new state. Not only were there different schools of thought as to the political system to be adopted, there were substantial minorities who would have preferred not to be part of the country in the first place. They nonetheless found themselves caught inside a state for which they felt little or no sense of affinity. At best they were indifferent; at worst they openly hostile to the country in which they had been unceremoniously planted. This was in no small part due to Poland having expanded its borders far beyond what could be justified on ethnographic grounds. Now, some 30–40 per cent of the population was non-Polish, and for the most part these people were seen as a huge inconvenience.

The peacemakers were aware of this. They had received reports of the inter-communal violence that accompanied the formation of the new states, and this is why they required founders to sign treaties protecting the rights of minorities. Such guarantees from Poland were endorsed by Paderewski and Dmowski on 28 June 1919, ostensibly to 'assure full and complete protection of life and liberty to all inhabitants of Poland without distinction of birth, nationality, language, race or religion ... [and confirm that] all inhabitants of Poland shall be entitled to the free exercise, whether public or private, of any creed, religion or belief'. The fact that the text referred to 'inhabitants' underlined the fact that these protections must apply to anyone who found themselves within the borders of the new state, irrespective of whether they were, or would later become, fully fledged citizens. Like Benes and Masaryk, the Polish delegates in Paris had been prepared to make whatever concessions necessary to secure their objectives[48] but proved less inclined to honour them once they had been granted the keys to their new country. In theory, the Minorities Treaty was not the only supposed check on the government. Undertakings had been made in Article Seven of the 1921 Treaty of Riga, signed with Russia, in which both parties had agreed to accord mutual and reciprocal rights to one another's minorities. Even Poland's own constitution of 1921 had enshrined within it, among other undertakings, the promise that 'all citizens are equal before the law', with no impediments to free and equal access to public office.

Arguably the single group who would be least tolerated of all were the country's Jews. During the war they had been considered by many to be the enemy within, accused of disloyalty by other communities. It was claimed that the Jews saw an independent Poland as a threat to the status some had enjoyed within the three former empires. Even more damning, the pro-Russian National Democratic Party accused the Jews of outright support for Germany,[49] and of helping to foment an atmosphere of mutual distrust and hostility.[50] Therefore, almost from its inception, Poland saw the Jewish community, especially its peasants, as a threatening 'other', and the Christian parties were happy to exploit these fears for political advantage. Such was the suspicion and distrust in which Jews were held that some extremists were already demanding their expulsion or at the very least that strict limits be placed upon their influence in education, culture and politics.[51] Even before the country had been properly constituted, pogroms had broken out in which Jews in Ukraine and Eastern Galicia were targeted. It became so serious that the US delegation to the peace conference sent respected lawyer and diplomat Henry Morgenthau Senior on a fact-finding mission to the country, following which he confirmed that violence against Jews had broken out in many cities. Over 280 people had perished and many hundreds more had been injured.

The Jewish community was scattered throughout the country and itself divided by social, cultural and religious differences. By no means were all Jews wealthy, or even well-to-do. In eastern Poland they were generally poorer and more Orthodox, with only 8 per cent speaking Polish or identifying as Polish,[52] although in the towns and in the countryside they could often form 80 per cent of the population.[53] Urban professional Jews tended to be better educated, constituting 25–40 per cent of the population of Warsaw, Lvov, Lodz and Krakow.[54] These Jews also tended to be better integrated, spoke Polish rather than Hebrew and generally identified as Poles. Making up 47 per cent of the skilled workforce, many were quite prosperous tradesmen or artisans, working as tailors or shoemakers, and owned or managed half of the country's commercial enterprises. Some 50 per cent of Poland's lawyers were Jewish, making them natural targets for their less successful and often resentful neighbours.

The fears of extreme nationalists about Jewish influence were irrational. While the Polish population as a whole would increase by 40 per cent between 1900 and 1936, that of the Jews would grow by less than 7 per cent.[55] This could largely be attributed to the hostility they were to experience by the 1930s, as half of all those Jews who left Europe for the US and Palestine came from Poland.[56] But these statistics did little to assuage the suspicion in Poland that Jews enjoyed a disproportionate dominance in many key aspects of commercial life, and the new state did all it could to alienate and marginalise them.

Although anti-Semitism was largely kept at bay into the mid-1920s, it spiked after the death of Pilsudski in 1935. The right-leaning government was also minded to take its lead from the Nazis in Germany, whose economic boycotts of Jewish businesses and professionals escalated in the hope of forcing more of them to emigrate, surrendering their businesses and much of their wealth in the process. Warsaw thus passed statutes by which Jews were denied the right to buy or own land, to employ gentiles, or to be employed by gentiles.[57] Steps to bar them from newly nationalised industries, such as tobacco in 1937, threw 30,000 out of work while bans on religious practices such as the kosher butchering of meat led to further business closures. Universities joined in the campaign of intimidation, imposing segregation and deterring Jews from enrolling. By 1938 Jews constituted only 10 per cent of Poland's student rolls compared to over 20 per cent in 1929,[58] and with the government and the Catholic Church tacitly tolerating and encouraging these measures, they had nowhere to turn for justice or redress. Little did they know that within a couple of years they would endure a form of victimisation which few in Europe could have imagined.

The Jews were not the only ones to suffer in the cause of Polonisation. The country had inherited, or rather netted, other malcontents whose dedication to the great project was less than enthusiastic. White Russians, or Byelorussians, concentrated in the north-east found that independence did not bring equality or greater freedom to them either. Backward and economically deprived under Russian rule, they had anxiously awaited land reforms they had been promised as a means of alleviating their poverty. However, when it transpired that yet again their Polish neighbours were to enjoy the fruits of the resulting bounty, bitter resentment and anger exploded into violence. The army was mobilised in response and proceeded to deepen the rift with its uncompromising reaction. Relations inevitably deteriorated. Nonetheless, demands for radical solutions like a split were not unanimous. Many sought an accommodation with the new state through assimilation by serving in the army, improving their educational opportunities and accepting the influence of the Catholic Church.[59] Still, relations would remain tense, and most looked to the day when they could secure their freedom, just as in their turn Pilsudski and Dmowski had yearned to escape from Habsburg rule.

Poland's Ukrainians were another substantial minority, with around 3.5 million in Eastern Galicia and another 1.5 million in the territory ceded by Russia under the Treaty of Riga. Largely poor peasants, they still harboured generations-old resentments towards the Polish landowning aristocracy that prospered under the Habsburgs and continued to do so in the new republic.[60]

Here, too, anticipated land reforms did not materialise, at least not for their benefit. Instead a combination of harassment and Polish settlement was used to wear down resistance. Radicalism threatened complete upheaval, and matters came to a head when a young Ukrainian nationalist tried to assassinate Pilsudski in 1921.[61] In the spring of 1922, an underground movement, the Ukrainian Military Organisation, began a campaign of violence, sabotaging grain stores, railways and bridges, and ambushing members of the police. Further assassination attempts were made against high-ranking government figures and administrators. More peaceful activists organised the boycotting of both the 1921 census and the elections of 1922.

Again eschewing conciliation, the government instead responded by imposing an anti-Ukrainian School Law in 1924. This act of vindictiveness replaced the previous dual system with mixed schools whose teachers were almost exclusively Polish. They would now teach only in their own language, hoping in the process to supplant Ukrainian entirely.[62] This heavy-handed approach also applied to higher education, and by 1938 all courses at Lvov University were taught in Polish. Faced with such discrimination, many scholars were compelled to move to Russia, Czechoslovakia and even Germany to study instead. Warsaw's implacably ill-disposed attitude also resulted in the suppression of the Ukrainian-language press, the closing down of cooperatives and even the banning of the boy scout movement.[63]

Although the situation became so severe that the League of Nations voiced its concerns and an uneasy peace was restored, it failed to lead to a meeting of minds. The government had undertaken to put in place reforms and pull back on their more oppressive policies, but they did little to assuage Ukrainian estrangement. The Ukrainians instead joined many Byelorussians in seeking more drastic solutions to their problems, and in 1938 submitted demands for a devolved parliament of their own. The government refused to consider such a proposal, so tensions and sporadic violence continued until the country itself was again partitioned in 1939.

Arguably the most serious hurdle to unifying all its minorities around a Polish core was the presence of 800,000 largely angry, embittered and resentful Germans. Unlike the Jews, Ruthenes and Ukrainians, they were not exposed, weak or easily intimidated by discriminatory statutes and laws. From the earliest days of the Weimar Republic they had a powerful sponsor encouraging separatism and funding movements dedicated to maintaining a culture of grievance. Germany also pursued its own policy of agitation and revanchism from the other side of the border, never reconciled to the theft of its eastern lands and doing all in its power to maintain a perpetual sense of burning injustice at the loss. However, Germany was still nowhere near strong enough to recover the territory by force, so had to rely upon constant niggling and nit-picking.

For its part, the Polish government in Warsaw sought to put the issue to bed through diplomacy. To this end the two governments signed an accord in Geneva on 15 May 1922 which formalised the division of the still disputed area of Upper Silesia. The economically unimportant western Upper Silesia remained German, but the eastern portion, which containing the rich coal seams and iron ore deposits, was reluctantly confirmed as Polish. The agreement was also supposed to guarantee the rights of their respective minorities for a period of up to fifteen years under the supervision of the League.[64] This did not satisfy either party, so soon afterwards, in August 1924, the two countries met again. One partial solution was simply to allow individuals to undertake an orderly departure from one side of the border to the other to join their respective communities. This produced the Vienna Convention, by which it was agreed to exchange the 30,000 Germans and approximately 5,000 Poles who had declined to accept the nationality of their parent state.

The programme was due to be carried out in three phases, with the first tranche on 1 August 1925, the second by 1 November 1925, and the last by 1 July 1926. The Poles, however, eager to expel their Germans, proved far more zealous in adhering to the letter of the agreement, and on 1 August 1925 proceeded on schedule with the first tranche. It soon became clear that the transfer would not be the orderly undertaking envisioned. Within the space of a week nearly 20,000 Germans – two-thirds of the total – had been uprooted. They found themselves streaming into the small German town of Schneidemuhl, only 3 kilometres from the border. Its infrastructure and services were overwhelmed when the town's population of 10,000 tripled almost overnight.

The ruthless attitude of the Poles caused outrage in Germany. The German government offered to cancel further expulsions, but they were rebuffed, and the situation continued to deteriorate. Only the intervention of the British succeeded in finally persuading the Poles to see reason and cancel the second tranche.[65]

Although passions were cooled somewhat, the animosity remained, and the entire episode had clearly done little to improve German–Polish relations. Nor had the accord helped to weaken Germany's determination to recover its eastern territories. On 7 September 1925, President Stresemann assured former Crown Prince William that Weimar Germany remained unalterably committed to 'the recovery of Danzig, the Polish Corridor, and a correction of the frontier in Upper Silesia'.[66] This is why, when Stresemann signed the Treaty of Locarno the following month, its clauses pointedly omitted to offer the same assurances to Germany's eastern neighbours as to its western ones. His sentiments were widely shared by his compatriots, who almost unanimously awaited the restitution of the 'bleeding frontier',[67] just as the French had constantly looked to recover the lost provinces of Alsace-Lorraine.

As soon as Germany was admitted to the League of Nations in 1926, it proceeded to bring human rights cases against the Polish government. Berlin even tried to defend ethnic Germans who lived in areas which had never been Reich territory. To a certain extent the German policy achieved its aim, provoking a reaction from the Polish government which would only exacerbate the situation. After all, it had already shown how it dealt with malcontents among its other minorities. The appointment of Adolf Hitler in 1933 understandably inflamed matters, especially as his policy was even more uncompromising than that of his Weimar predecessors. It was not just the Polish border he wanted to see dissolved but ultimately the entire Polish state. As the threat materialised, Poland's concerns for its security began to grow. In some quarters, it was even being suggested that it might be wise for a pre-emptive strike to be launched against Germany before it had a chance to rearm and use its industrial superiority to outnumber and outgun its neighbour.

In the hope of provoking a reaction which might elicit an attack in the name of self-defence, 80 per cent of the Polish army was stationed on the border with Germany, but the latter failed to take the bait and an uneasy calm returned. In the hope of strengthening its position, the Polish government sent representatives to France with a proposal for some sort of joint action, but Paris was now increasingly basing its defence strategy on the construction of the Maginot Line, and this realisation forced another rethink. Perhaps after all, diplomacy ought to be given a chance. This produced the unlikely Polish-German Non-Aggression Pact of 26 January 1934, which, in the words of its preamble, was to herald 'a new phase in the political relations between Germany and Poland'. Both countries undertook not to resort to war against one another for a period of at least ten years, during which time Germany would respect Poland's borders and bring the longstanding tariff war to a conclusion. This could only ever serve as a sticking plaster, however, and mainly benefited the Nazis insofar as it put their eastern ambitions on hold while they consolidated their power and pursued their schemes for dismantling Versailles in the west. Nor did it resolve the minorities issue. Thus, the outstanding problems of the two countries' respective nationalities were condemned to fester until Hitler became increasingly vocal and aggressive as he prepared to resolve the problem by force.

The difficulties Poland faced in resolving its economic, religious and ethnic challenges were compounded by the very structure of the state, in which social inequality was so entrenched. Some 93 per cent of the population had to manage with a share of just 25 per cent of national wealth while the remaining 7 per cent, notably the descendants of the former ruling elite, enjoyed the remaining three-quarters.[68] This situation served to perpetuate both the social divisions and class distinctions which had governed the former empires, and in turn fuelled the religious and racial intolerance endemic in the new state. This situation was unlikely to be redressed as long as most politicians were part of or descended from this very aristocracy, despite the fact that the constitution had ended entitlements or privileges enjoyed as a birth right. Indeed, although Article 96 abolished aristocratic titles as a step towards a more egalitarian society, the practice persisted, especially in the countryside, where, as in equally conservative Hungary and Slovakia, the pervasive sense of master and serf persisted. In this respect as in others, old habits died hard despite the growing sense of injustice felt by more radical minorities for whom of course race and class were ultimately difficult to separate.

The old landed aristocracy's enjoyment of this disproportionate share of political power was perpetuated by a plethora of political parties, each representing vested or minority interests, and vying for domination in right-wing coalitions. This self-serving arrangement encouraged greed and corruption and produced a succession of unstable and short-lived governments. The parliament, or *Sejm*, frequently resembled the old Habsburg parliament in Vienna, where chaotic scenes disrupted meaningful debate and descended into free-for-alls that made it impossible to enact legislation. As the leader of the Radical Peasant Party, Stanislaw Thugett, explained, 'in Poland everyone desires to be in the opposition, but nobody is willing to take the responsibility. Poland cannot prosper by criticism alone.'[69] It was a situation which led to the work of parliament being frequently frustrated by filibusters and behind-the-scenes shenanigans. Finally, on 12 May 1926, an exasperated General Pilsudski staged a coup promising better government and a more efficient legislature.

The coup succeeded, and the government fell. Fresh presidential elections were promised, but despite his popularity Pilsudski declined to assume the post of president. He instead nominated a close colleague, who was armed with the remit to sweep away the endemic corruption and herald an 'act of moral renewal'.[70] Pilsudski was appointed to the post of minister of defence instead, one that he held until his death in 1935. However, the high expectations following the coup failed to produce the fresh start everyone had hoped for. Another eleven governments would come and go before Pilsudski's death, and he would head two himself. The inability to reform was in large part to be blamed on the essentially paternalistic and aristocratic ruling class, which was resistant to change or any meaningful reform challenging its vested interests, and consequently the hoped-for clearing out of the Augean stables never materialised. By the time Pilsudski died, the military regime over which he had presided was the same corrupt old boys' network of self-serving politicians and unelected bureaucrats.

Corruption and graft were not the only dark features of the Polish state. Gradually it assumed those of an authoritarian regime, and the effects of these developments were not confined to its minorities. In July 1935, reforms were implemented which halved the size of the *Sejm* and placed limits on the right to vote in the Senate. Furthermore, the nomination of candidates was taken away from individual parties entirely and entrusted instead to unaccountable electoral colleges. By exploiting growing tensions with neighbours and apprehension over internal cohesion, the powers invested in the president were also gradually increased, giving him the right to rule by decree in a range of circumstances. In addition, a Council of Ministers could declare a state of emergency and suspend civil liberties without the approval of the *Sejm*.[71] The Communist party was banned in 1934, followed by a decree that gave the authorities the power to 'detain without a court order, any person who menaces peace and public order'.[72] These measures could partly be justified as a response to the rhetoric emanating out of Nazi Germany, intended to foment dissent and threaten its borders, but like all such 'emergency' legislation, they could all too easily be employed to stifle opposition and silence criticism.

A façade of democracy was nevertheless maintained, with opposition parties and the press given the appearance of freedom to criticise and oppose. However, newspaper editors could suffer severe sanctions and risked being closed down for printing anything of which the government disapproved. These measures created increasing anger and resentment among the public, and even greater polarisation within parliament. In a demonstration of public disgust, there was a mass boycott by the electorate of the elections of September 1935, with a turnout as low as 35 per cent. Polish expats and political exiles had started to agitate against the regime, hoping to form a united front led by disenchanted former politicians such as Paderewski, but the western powers were reluctant to provide any meaningful support so long as Poland continued its role as an anti-Soviet barrier. The initiative failed to gain any momentum, and the unfortunate country continued its slow descent towards authoritarianism and dictatorship. Worse still, it was starting to run out of friends.

French politicians were becoming increasingly disillusioned with the potential of the Polish army to make any significant contribution to France's planned defence, and the General Staff was losing confidence in Poland's abilities. Although the Poles had fought successful wars to expand their country, and equally victorious ones defending those gains, they were heavily reliant on the French for equipment, tactics and many of the other fundamentals of a modern army. Poland was a poor country and lacked the resources for wholesale modernisation despite having a huge proportion of its GDP lavished upon it. Although on paper the Polish army looked formidable, counting 1.7 million soldiers, more than 4,000 field guns, 1,200 tanks and 745 aircraft by 1939, it would prove a disappointment. French despondency added to Poland's growing sense of isolation, in turn worsened by the German reoccupation of the Rhineland in 1936 and the continued construction of the Maginot Line. This also made the non-aggression pact with Germany increasingly meaningless, especially as their hostile attitude was adding to European tensions. The Munich Crisis of 1938, which resulted in the demise of the Czech state, further underlined Poland's own exposure to revanchism, its lack of allies and the foolishness of having made so many enemies.

Feeling increasingly isolated, Polish foreign minister Joseph Lipski travelled to Paris in January 1939 to sound out the French government's intentions with regards to guaranteeing Poland's independence. Similar covert approaches were made to London, resulting in the welcome public undertakings made in March 1939 by Neville Chamberlain that further acts of aggression by Germany would not be tolerated, especially following the takeover of Czechoslovakia. These brought some reassurance, but it was also clear that undertakings were one thing and the ability to back them up was another. Russia was sounded out to determine its position, but despite their pact of 1932 there was scant sympathy for a country which had seized so much Russian territory. Ironically, their treaty had been extended in May 1934 to remain in force until 1945, but Stalin, like Hitler, had only agreed to the pact as a gesture, mainly to conceal his long-term ambitions. Relations with Russia had been severely tested already when Poland became an accomplice to the partition of Czechoslovakia, prompting Moscow to threaten unilateral revocation of their non-aggression pact. It was therefore evident that Poland was going to get short shrift if it were to seek help from that quarter. In any case, even if help was provided and Russian troops took up position inside the country, who could say if they would leave once any emergency had passed?

Poland's fate was essentially sealed when Hitler sent foreign secretary Joachim von Ribbentrop to Moscow to sound out the Soviet government for what was to prove one of the most craven undertakings in modern history. In the meantime, twenty years of agitation and demonstration against the territorial decisions taken at Versailles, and the constant appeals and complaints against the alleged ill treatment suffered by its German minorities, now reached a crescendo. In the midst of Berlin's feverish propaganda war against Warsaw, the secret negotiations in Moscow concluded on 23 August 1939 with the signing of the Molotov–Ribbentrop Pact. The two states were at last to realise their determination to recover the territory they had lost and divide Poland between them. Hitler proceeded to further pressure the Warsaw government, which resisted while it hoped for some miracle. Finally, on 1 September 1939, the *Wehrmacht* crossed the border. Two weeks later, in accordance with the terms of the pact, the Soviet army crossed from the east and Poland ceased to exist. The second of the key achievements of Versailles had thus disappeared into the shadows, a fate aggravated by internal ethnic tensions and failure to embrace the democracy their leaders had promised the peacemakers, but above all caused by vehemently hostile outside forces beyond their control.

The third successor state, the Kingdom of Serbs, Croats and Slovenes, was another newborn which might have prospered had there been the will to cooperate and work for the common good. Instead, just as in Czechoslovakia and Poland, poor decision-making had created a hybrid state within restive borders. Furthermore, there was yet again one group determined to dominate the others, and this time the ethnic mix was potentially the most explosive of all. In addition to the Serbs, Macedonians, Montenegrins, Croats and Slovenes, who together constituted nearly 80 per cent of the population, there were Bosnians, Germans, Hungarians, Albanians, Romanians, Turks, Czechs and Slovaks, Ruthenes, and Greeks. There was also a huge diversity of religions, with more than 6 million Eastern Orthodox adherents, nearly 5 million Roman Catholics, at least a million Muslims and over

200,000 Protestants. All these people were expected to somehow coalesce and form a political and cultural whole, a prospect at which perhaps even the Habsburgs would have balked. As the majority nationalities could not even reach a consensus as to what form of government the new country should have, this factor alone opened up furious debate and provided the basis for bitter infighting and internal conflict.

Most Croatians, mindful of their hard-won status under the Habsburgs, wanted the federal system of government promised by Emperor Karl. Surrendering this to become just a part of a larger unitary state, with decisions made in a distant capital, was not an appealing prospect. The model many Croatians favoured contained a devolved parliament in Zagreb, which would also represent the other former Austro-Hungarian provinces, and another for the Serbians in Belgrade. Matters of mutual interest such as foreign affairs and defence would be administered by joint ministries. Although there were some who favoured outright independence, it was generally agreed that they would be better placed within a federalised structure, especially with Italy harbouring designs upon Croatian territory.[73] The founder and leader of the Croat Peasant Party, Stjepan Radic, was nevertheless hostile to such an arrangement. He was scathing of those who he claimed were 'scaring our people like little children [with the Italian threat] ... and think that in this way you will be able to win over the people to your policy'.[74] Radic believed that the overwhelming mass of Croatia's largely peasant population shared his position. He insisted that they did not want to live under another monarchy, but instead were demanding an agrarian 'peasant republic'.[75] The Slovenes, too, had enjoyed a measure of self-government under the Habsburgs and did not want to lose their separate cultural identity either. They, like their Croat brothers, viewed virtual annexation into a Greater Serbia with a great deal of trepidation, although again there were fears of being left out in the cold and at the mercy of Italian encroachment in their affairs.

Most Serbians had assumed that essentially the same political system that governed them before the war would prevail within the new wider state. This was especially so since, having been a unitary, independent, sovereign nation for over a century, they had no experience of any other system. The initial plan had been to create an expanded Serbia, ruled from Belgrade and embracing all those who had previously lived under the Dual Monarchy. Having been the original victim of Austrian aggression and instrumental in the Balkans' liberation from Austro-Hungarian occupation, they saw this as no more than their due. Half of the male population between the ages of eighteen and fifty-five had perished in the war,[76] many fighting the same Croatian forces serving the Central Powers, while many Slovenes fought for the monarchy on the Italian front. Serbians considered that their sacrifice gave them at the very least the moral authority to take a leading role in the formation of the new country, and their king held much the same point of view.

Being fellow Slavs, many – particularly the peacemakers in Paris – assumed that the Croats, Slovenes and Serbs ought to have been natural bedfellows. It was the generally held view that they would welcome their new free future and willingly meld within a single national framework. Nevertheless, as Pasic pointed out so vocally, 'just because [they all] speak one language'[77] did not justify placing them all under one government. In fact, their historic and cultural bona fides could not have been more different. Croats were the product of the Western Roman Empire, followed Roman Catholicism and used the Roman alphabet. Their culture and outlook were naturally influenced by those traditions. The Serbs were of the Byzantine Empire, Orthodox Greek and using the Russian alphabet. Despite a lengthy period of independence, they remained strongly influenced by centuries of Ottoman rule. Inevitably, these somewhat more down-to-earth but tougher Serbs looked upon the Croat as effete and morally undermined by what was perceived to have been a more comfortable life under the Habsburgs.

There was a further complication: the Macedonians. They remained resentful of their annexation to Serbia during the Balkan Wars of 1912–13. Despite their hopes of establishing a state of their own after the end of the war, the peace conference instead confirmed Serbian sovereignty, giving little hope for a change in their fortunes. They were therefore antipathetic to being incorporated into the new state and if given a choice would have much preferred to be part of Bulgaria, a country with which they felt they had far more in common culturally and linguistically. An ostracised Bulgaria was, however, as we have seen, unlikely to be allocated more territory at the expense of a former ally. Instead, the government in Belgrade responded to this discontent in what they referred to as 'Southern Serbia' with punitive and oppressive measures, the garrisoning of 50,000 troops in the territory, the banning of the Macedonian language and the imposition of lengthy prison terms for any dissenters. As a result, it was highly unlikely that their voice would be heard in any conversations which might affect their future.

The tough people of mountainous Montenegro were also in a unique position. Theirs had been a small and little-known independent kingdom in its own right prior to the war, but in November 1918, with its government and king exiled, a provisional administration unilaterally declared its intention to unite with Serbia, despite the opposition of many of its inhabitants. There were thus already deep divisions between those seeking integration and those who wanted to re-establish an independent monarchy.[78]

If these were the conflicting and contradictory views of the larger nationalities, what consideration would be given to those numerous minorities whose voices would be drowned out by their bigger brothers? Such divisions, with an unfriendly Italy eagerly awaiting an opportunity to exploit them, made for challenging negotiations over the future shape of the country. They were further complicated by the usual wartime undertakings and various promises that had been made, and which their beneficiaries now expected to see honoured.

Undaunted by such obstacles, the Yugoslav Committee that had been established in London in 1915 under the auspices of the British government sought to guide the shape of the new country. Considering the widely differing and contradictory views with which they would be confronted, this proved no easy task. These lengthy deliberations culminated in the Corfu declaration of 7 July 1917, in which Croatian president Dr Ante Trumbic and Serbian prime minister Nikola Pasic announced that the Serbs, Croats and Slovenes should indeed unite as a constitutional monarchy under the Serbian king. In October of that year, the Slovene National Council, led by Monsignor Anton Korlec, finally confirmed that they would also join, followed by a divided Montenegro. However, the proviso was that the future constitution of the new state must enjoy a democratic mandate, being valid only if it was endorsed by a majority vote. The two proposed systems also had their unofficial sponsors. The French saw a centralised unitary state as the basis for a strong Yugoslavia, which of course they viewed as essential to their plans for reliable regional partners. The Italians, on the other hand, as we have seen, favoured a weaker federal structure.[79] In their minds, this would have made it easier to exploit Montenegrin disaffection, encourage Bulgarian irredentism and provide for their own minorities in the lands of the former empire.

On 9 November 1918, representatives of Croatia and the southern Slav countries met in Geneva with the Serbs as the Yugoslav National Council. Serb representatives recognised the National Council as the legitimate government of the South Slavs of the former Habsburg monarchy, and it was agreed that a twelve-member joint ministry would be established, six from the Council and six from Belgrade, and that a Constituent Assembly would be created to work out the constitution of the new state. Nevertheless, this solution was rejected by both Belgrade and Zagreb. It was soon evident that, as in Czechoslovakia and Poland, the most forceful nationality within the country would begin to impose its will upon the others. The government in Belgrade insisted that their constitution of 1903 should be used as the template of the constitution for a unitary state, at least until one for the new kingdom could be agreed, which for many meant the same thing. In the event, although the Interim National Parliament would be in place by March 1919 to prepare for elections to the Constituent Assembly, these were to be delayed until November 1920.[80]

One understanding at Corfu was honoured, however, and on 1 December 1918 this was formalised by a proclamation in Belgrade which declared that 'the whole inseparable ethnographical territory of the South Slavs'[81] was now a monarchy under Serbia's ailing King Peter I.

As he had not yet returned to his realm, having spent much of the war in exile with his government on Corfu, his son Prince Alexander responded on his behalf:

> ... in the name of His Majesty King Peter the First, I now declare the union of Serbia with the provinces of the Slovenes, Croats and Serbs in an indivisible Kingdom. This great moment should be a reward for the efforts of yourselves and your brothers, whereby you have cast off the alien yoke. This celebration should form a wreath for the officers and men who have fallen in the name of freedom...[82]

These words were heavy with portent. To many they implied that Serbians, whose blood it was that had been spilled to realise this arrangement, would sit at the pinnacle of the future kingdom. It was looking bleak for those like Stjepan Pasic and his Croatian peasants, or the Montenegrin monarchists, who lived in fear of being ultimately subsumed into a Greater Serbia. King Peter would actually only enjoy his new status for a brief period. He would soon be dead, and his ambitious successor would take his place as Alexander I.

On the face of it, Alexander appeared eminently qualified to assume the mantle. Born in Montenegro in 1888, the second son of King Peter and godson of Czar Alexander of Russia, he received a traditional first-class education in Geneva and at the age of seventeen was enrolled in the Imperial Russian Military School at St Petersburg. Here he learnt the art of command but also the rudiments of despotism, and when his elder brother renounced the throne in 1909, he became the heir apparent. The Balkan Wars gave him the opportunity to prove his mettle, taking command of the Serbian Army and showing himself to be a good soldier and effective leader.

He repeated this performance in the First World War, saving his army from destruction when he led it to safety in Corfu following the offensive led by Austria, and, after it was reinforced and re-equipped, to victories on the Salonika Front. A strong relationship of mutual respect with the army, and especially its officer corps, developed a bond which would stand Alexander in good stead later. He thus emerged from the war with his reputation enhanced, having earnt the right to succeed as the ruler of Serbia and of the Croats and Slovenes.

As in Czechoslovakia and Poland, however, the minorities and other subjects he had inherited were largely considered unwelcome appendages. Like many Serb nationalists, he saw himself not as king of a Yugoslav polyglot state but of a Greater Serbia, and this fervent belief would serve as his guiding principle for the rest of his life. Indeed, the US ambassador to Yugoslavia, John Dyneley Prince, would later report that Alexander admitted to being 'opposed to all this Yugoslav nonsense. The country must be Greater Serbia and the Serb alone must dominate.'[83]

Furthermore, the successive administrations over which Alexander presided would be Serb-centric and prove equally intolerant towards any dissident voices or threats to the status quo, reacting ruthlessly to any manifestations of opposition. When fervent anti-communist Milorad Draskovic was appointed minister of internal affairs, one of the first measures he took was to annul the election results for Belgrade because the communists had emerged with the largest share. This was followed by similar arbitrary measures in Croatia, where the communists had also been victorious in a number of district administrations. Such early signs for the democratic process did not make for healthy political debate.

When the promised elections to the National Assembly were finally held on 28 November 1920, they did nothing to assuage fears of Serb domination. A total of sixteen parties contested the 416 seats with a voter turnout of 64 per cent, and hopes of a free and fair process were dashed. The results appeared to justify accusations that the vote was rigged, and in the following months the parliament was boycotted by all fifty-eight communists, fifty-two members of the Croatian (Republican) Peasant Party, eleven from the People's Club, twenty-seven from the Yugoslav Club and five from the Agrarian Union as well as minor party deputies. This protest, however, left only thirty-five deputies to oppose the bill adopting the new constitution, opening the way for the 223 dedicated centrists of the Democratic, Radical Peasant, JMO, Dzemijet, Bandsman and Agrarian Union parties to debate one of the first orders of business: the country's constitutional framework. Passed on 28 June 1921, the Vivovdan Constitution delivered almost exactly what the Serbians wanted, which was a monarch at the head of a centralised unitary state with its capital in Belgrade. As the king was also to have a raft of reserve powers, he could exploit the lack of consensus in parliament, which would often descend into the same kind of mayhem and Spanish practices that hamstrung the Polish parliament.

The sheer number of parties and subsequent lack of order put further hurdles in the way of progress. Legislation could be filibustered and blocked, while attempts at forming coalitions again, as in Warsaw, resulted in self-interested administrations. Even then, bartering and concessions aimed at one group would frequently provoke the resentment of another, and the process would have to start all over again.[84] On one occasion, four members who had been suspended for unacceptable behaviour returned to their seats the following day and refused to leave. The police had to be called to throw them out, leading to howls of protest that yet again paralysed the session.[85] In the face of such anarchy, the government issued decrees, or *obznana*, which could circumvent normal channels. These would be used widely as a means of quashing opposition generally, and most particularly in the pursuit of anti-communist legislation. Memories of the communist uprising in Hungary by Bela Kun, however abortive it proved to be, were never far from the Serbs' minds, and their overriding priority was the protection of the status quo.

When opposition to the new regime led to extreme acts of resistance, the government seized its chance. While he was still heir, Alexander almost fell victim to a bungled attempt on his life by an embittered communist. This was followed by the assassination of Draskovic, which enraged the Serbs but played into the hands of those determined to see the communists eradicated entirely. The subsequent trial of suspects proved to be little more than an exercise in totalitarian propaganda. The entire leadership of the Communist Party was accused of being complicit in the crime, and on 1 August 1921 its virtual exile from national life was guaranteed by the 'Law on the Protection of Public Order and the State'. This legislation stripped the communist deputies of their parliamentary immunity and meant that they could now be prosecuted on any contrived charge the government might bring against them. Furthermore, its far-reaching Articles prohibited any form of aid or assistance to anarchists, communists or foreign terrorist groups, and threatened punishments ranging from twenty years' hard labour to death. Further provision was made for the suppression of communist-inspired strikes, and the law even forbade the wearing or displaying of any symbols, flags or insignia which might be interpreted as attempting to inspire the overthrow of the monarchy.

Effectively, then, any dissent or opposition from whatever quarter could now be labelled communist and mercilessly repressed. Furthermore, the government in Belgrade had already decided upon a particularly radical solution to the persistently hostile Macedonians. On 24 September 1920, the 'Regulation for the Settlement of the New Southern Regions' had been enacted to colonise the region with Serbians. The intention was to overwhelm the indigenous population with interlopers and ultimately outnumber them, much as the English had attempted to 'plant' Scottish Protestants in Catholic Ireland during the reigns of Elizabeth I and James I. Although by 1928 nearly 70,000 hectares of land had been allocated to 6,377 Serb families,[86] the programme did little to solve the issue of Macedonian separatism, instead sowing greater discord.

Aside from this excessive implementation of policy, the government did have some legitimate motives for pursuing wider land reform across the country. The new state was another in which agriculture dominated the economy and way of life of its inhabitants. It provided a living for 75 per cent of the population, most of whom lived on estates in Slovenia, Croatia and the Vojvodina and which before the war were mainly owned or managed by German, Austrian and Hungarian landlords. Remnants of ancient Turkish feudalism still persisted in Kosovo and Macedonia, and there were even Muslim landlords in Bosnia who owned farms worked on by Christian sharecroppers. Some Dalmatians still lived as tenant farmers under a system dating from the Romans, and Serbia itself was still a patchwork of widely scattered small farmsteads.

This eclectic mixture of traditions and inefficient, hopelessly outdated processes was compounded by the presence of the former gentry and ruling classes, who, as in Poland and Slovakia, expected to retain their ancestral privileges. The destruction wrought upon the land by conflict and peasant uprisings at the end of the war had gone some way to purging the farms of their former owners, but returning soldiers and embittered peasants, particularly in Slavonia, had ransacked the farms and left them devastated and unproductive.[87] From 1919, efforts had been made under the provisional government to implement a programme of land redistribution which led to 10 per cent of agricultural and 20 per cent of arable land being allocated to peasant families. This gave land once owned by only 12,000 people to around 2 million.[88] Montenegrin and Serb families originating in Croatia and Herzegovina had been relocated to Kosovo to farm land that had been 'vacated' by its 40,000 to 80,000 Turkish and Albanian owners,[89] but these plots proved too small to be viable. Subsequently, although the reforms promised to herald an era of egalitarianism they did little for productivity, with yields falling and efficiency declining.

Similarly, industrial distribution was largely a lottery, dependent upon which legacy empire the respective regions had evolved from. For example, some areas possessed mines and textile factories, if these had not been destroyed in the war, whereas others were entirely reliant upon the land. Such regional variations proved to be a further source of communal resentment, as Croatian and Slovenian lands had been better developed under the Habsburgs than the more southern regions, and this produced a certain amount of jealousy, especially among the Serbs who resented the fact that their former enemy had emerged from the war apparently better-off than they had. Subsequent efforts to expand into light industry and to invest in infrastructure projects such as the railways were therefore severely undermined by the financial situation, and with a shortage of capital the government was compelled to seek foreign loans and sell off mining rights in order to raise revenue.

They would also remain highly dependent upon the erratic income from the sale of agricultural produce, a market sector subject to fluctuating prices, competition and unpredictable harvests. This was particularly irksome because the kingdom contained considerable reserves of valuable minerals such as aluminium, chromium, cobalt, copper, iron, lead, magnesium, nickel and zinc. In spite of having sold off the mining rights to foreign companies, until the 1930s they remained disappointing sources of revenue. There was also the requirement to invest large sums in the 140,000-strong army, upon which the state was dependent both to protect the regime from frequent external threats and to maintain order internally. Despite these shortcomings, there were a few signs of improvement and the kingdom saw modest growth during the later 1920s before the Great Depression struck.[90] Regardless of these efforts, Yugoslavia nonetheless remained rather backward compared to its richer neighbours, a situation which would exacerbate other factors troubling the country. Perhaps better central government coordination and control of the economy might have stimulated greater economic development, but this was hampered by an administration which was frequently trapped in legislative cul-de-sacs.

Much of the blame for this could be laid at the feet of Serbian Nicola Pasic, leader of the Serbian People's Radical Party and the kingdom's prime minister until he died of a heart attack aged eighty-one in 1926. He was a seasoned politician, having previously held the portfolio of Serbian prime minister before the creation of the Serb, Croat and Slovene state, and had shared his monarch's anti-communism and determination that Serbia dominate the new country. He pursued this aim by paying for Slovene and Muslim votes and ensuring Serbians occupied practically every key civil service post and the ranks the army's officer corps. He also presided over a culture of corruption and graft. Top ministers were eligible for a full pension after only a year, and after two their family also qualified; dread of losing such lucrative sinecures helped to keep them in line. In return for this self-imposed largesse, barely one truly meaningful and far-reaching programme of legislation had emerged from the ten cabinets headed by Pasic during his tenure,[91] and there was no obvious sign that any positive change was forthcoming.

As a result, few if any of the laws, taxes and other reforms essential to effective government could be enacted to reconcile the country's five railway networks, five currencies, six customs areas and legal systems and three separate banking systems.[92] These needed standardisation and root-and-branch reform, but muddle and mayhem plagued progress. For example, the Austrian crown, Croatia's currency under the Habsburgs, had seriously declined in value during and after the war. Despite the government in Belgrade undertaking to redeem them at a rate of four to the Serbian dinar, the Croatians were faced with the brutal realisation that they had effectively lost three-quarters of their wealth.[93] These and other legacy issues added to discontent and plagued hopes of unifying the various nationalities. Punitive laws could only go so far in addressing them, and the conviction grew that the leadership of a determined strongman was required to resolve them. The situation was so dire that ambassador Dyneley Prince felt that only fear of the army and Italian intrigue was keeping the country from dissolving entirely. He held to the conviction that the 'salvation of the country must come from a military fascism, strictly but benevolently applied ... [which would be] ... welcomed by the majority of the Yugoslavian people'.[94]

By 1928, with parliament in stalemate, it was inevitable that physical violence would break out at some point. In a typically chaotic session on 20 June, Radical deputy Punisha Ratchitch became increasingly frustrated as he tried to make himself heard above the din. Exasperated, he shouted obliquely, 'Serbian interests have never been in such grave danger save when guns and rifles have been firing. If I see my people in danger I openly state that I shall use other weapons if necessary, to protect their interests.'[95] This outburst was met with ill-concealed derision by his Croatian opponents, one of whom yelled what was interpreted as an insult, and an apology was demanded. When none was forthcoming, Ratchitch brandished a revolver. Incensed, he opened fire; in the ensuing fusillade two Croats were killed and the Croatian People's Peasant Party leader, Radic, was shot in the stomach. It was a wound from which he would die a few weeks later.

When the news got out, the Croat public was in uproar. Hundreds of thousands attended the funerals, while the grievously wounded Radic tried to calm them down by assuring them that he was confident the king would broker a solution to this tragic turn of events. When Radic himself succumbed to his wounds, one of the few moderating voices within the Croat camp had been lost. Instead of seeking conciliation, his comrades demanded retribution, and all of the Croatian deputies walked out of parliament. They returned to Zagreb and defiantly established a separatist parliament in direct competition to Belgrade. King Alexander tried to resolve the dilemma constitutionally, and attempted to form administrations on non-partisan lines, but the same disruption and chaos accompanied any attempts to legislate, and the entire machinery of government looked close to staggering to a halt. Alexander had by now become utterly exasperated. Used to obedience and instant results, he was driven to distraction by reports of constant stalemate and anarchy in his parliament. A hardworking man, he expected the same of his subordinates but felt they were feckless, idle and self-serving.

Having tolerated the situation for nearly ten years, Alexander resolved to take the drastic action needed before the situation became irretrievable.[96] On 6 January 1929, he made his move and issued a royal proclamation in which he decreed the proroguing of the constitution and parliament, and his decision to exercise his right to rule directly.[97] As he explained to his subjects, he had come to this decision because 'the parliamentary system and our whole political life are taking on an increasingly negative character, from which the nation and the state have hitherto only suffered harm ... we must seek new methods, and strike out new paths.'[98] He further cited the corruption of the politicians, their constant placing of self-interest above that of the country, and the abject failure of parliament to govern effectively in all the ten years of its existence. To assuage any concerns, he assured his people that his only motive was 'in the shortest possible time to realise the establishment of such institutions, such state government and such form of constitution as shall best answer to the general needs of the nation and the interests of the state'.[99]

Alexander proceeded to nominate a cabinet headed by General Peter Zhivkovitch, the commandant of his Royal Guard, supplemented by experts on various key subjects, such as economics and law, to fill the necessary ministerial portfolios. Almost immediately several new statutes were passed, the first of which was the far-reaching 'Law Respecting the Powers of the King and the Administration of the Serb-Croat-Slovene Kingdom', which legitimised the pseudo-dictatorship and consolidated his right to rule by decree. He also banned all parties of a religious or ethnic nature and introduced press censorship.[100] To a divided public tired of squabbling and stalemate, these drastic steps initially met with a positive response, especially as it was made clear that they were only to be imposed until common sense and order had been restored. Most people inferred from this that parliamentary democracy, once reformed, would return.[101]

The king and his new administration certainly acted promptly, and like a new broom swept right through the administration, overhauling the ministries, cutting public spending and addressing the endemic corruption in the administration. It was also found that an army of 140,000 did not require so many full generals on its payroll, and thirty-two were unceremoniously forced to retire. Criminal law was finally codified and rationalised to apply to one country rather than several, and much of the other legislation stuck in parliament for ten years was rushed through in ten weeks.[102] Such was his determination to act that he introduced 163 new laws – unimpeded by democracy – in the first year alone.[103]

The king was not slow to take advantage of the new regime to pursue measures aimed at further entrenching Serbian domination of the state. Later that year, on 3 October, the 'Law Altering the Appellation and Administrative Divisions of the Serbs Croats and Slovenes' was passed. This wordy statute abolished the existing thirty-three provinces and replaced them with nine larger ones.[104] It also gave Serbs a majority in six of them. By shamelessly reassigning pieces of territory as necessary, the king was able to create the required population ratios most conducive to a Serb-dominated government.[105] One of the more pragmatic measures, though again taken without much thought for the diverse make-up of the nation, was the creation of a common education system with standardised textbooks and curricula.[106] On the same day, he decreed that the name of the country was now officially Yugoslavia, removing at the stroke of a pen the old title that specified its separate entities, and which had for so long underlined its divisions. Regardless of this draconian and sweeping decision, it was evident that it would take more than a change of name to alter the people's perceptions of themselves. Neville Henderson made his thoughts clear when, as British ambassador in later years, he rather cynically referred to the country as 'a crossword puzzle', adding that 'it is easier to say Yugoslavia than to make it.'[107]

The natural resentment which followed the unpopular reorganisation of the boundaries soon manifested in protests. In 1930, Bosnian Muslims took to the streets angry at the loss of their religious community's longstanding Autonomous Statute of 1909, while Slovenes balked at the loss of their sports clubs and political organisations.[108] Nor were they alone in their outrage, for groups in Croatia, Macedonia and Montenegro added to the sense of indignation at the king's high-handed approach to such sensitive issues. The French government was particularly disquieted by this turn of events, and urged the king to loosen his personal hold on the country, using the possibility of economic and military aid to sugar the pill. Subsequently, in 1931, Alexander reluctantly agreed to reconstitute a slightly revised form of the constitution, although this appears to have been more in deference to etiquette than out of any true conversion to the concept of parliamentary democracy.

The reworked constitution was clearly more form than substance when it was officially unveiled, again by royal decree, on 3 September 1931. Its articles expounded the constitutional nature of the new monarchy, assuring subjects that they were all 'equal before the law' and enjoyed 'personal liberty', with the right to freedom of religion and conscience. There were to be no restrictions on freedom of expression or association, and 'all offices in all branches of the civil service are open on equal terms to all citizens'. It also insisted that the courts and their judges were independent and free from interference from the executive. An upper house, the Senate, was also to be established, but half of its members were to be his personal appointees. Alexander also maintained for himself extensive rights and liberties. Firstly, he and his heirs and successors were guaranteed under Article 35 to be 'inviolable'. Moreover, the king could not 'be held responsible for anything whatever … nor can he be sued'. Having rendered himself immune to any consequences for his actions, he enshrined within Article 116 powers which any potentate might have dreamed of exercising:

> In case of war, mobilisation, disorder or disturbances endangering public order and the security of the state, or in general if public interests are endangered, the King may, in such extraordinary case, decree all absolutely necessary measures to be taken throughout the entire Kingdom or in any part thereof, irrespective of constitutional and legal prescriptions. All exceptional measures taken shall subsequently be submitted to Parliament for approval.

Effectively this gave him very much the same powers he assumed when he suspended the previous constitution, now with the added guarantee that he wouldn't be held responsible for anything. Furthermore, with parliament heavily weighted in his favour, he was unlikely to come under particularly close scrutiny. The system for nominating candidates for election to the new parliament was also naturally biased strongly in favour of the government and made it excruciatingly difficult for anyone other than a Serb to run. As a result, the new elections produced 145 members of the former Radical Party, fifty-seven former Democrats and twenty-eight of the old Croatian Peasant Party,[109] essentially the status quo ante in all but name. In 1932 Alexander appointed Serbian centralist and Radical Party leader Nikola Uzonovitch as prime minister, but, as he was determined to keep real power for himself, the man would act as little more than his mouthpiece. The Croatians were understandably far from satisfied, and their new leader, Dr Matchek, persisted with demands for a more democratic, federal form of government.[110] Alexander used his new powers to have Matchek arrested, convicted of treason and sentenced to three years' imprisonment. There was widespread indignation at the king's treatment of this popular figure, and relations deteriorated still further, with demonstrations and protests accompanying futile petitions for Matchek's release. Alexander was unmoved, responding that he would maintain his position until all such malcontents 'had died out'.[111]

Realising that they would get no justice in Yugoslavia, desperate Croat deputations travelled to western Europe to plead their case. An appeal was submitted to the League of Nations, claiming that the legislation being enacted was in breach of the Minorities Treaty. The response was disheartening. They were reminded that they were not a minority but a national group within a state, and that therefore the provisions of the treaty did not apply to them. Their only option was to approach a member state to act on their behalf, claiming that the constitution breached the terms of the Treaty of St Germain. Only then might the League be able to adjudicate. In the interim such international luminaries as Albert Einstein took their case to the Human Rights League, but this august body lacked the power to do anything. The Croat plight had now reached British ears, and Ben Riley and Rhys Davies, Labour members of the House of Commons Balkans Committee, decided to see for themselves. They travelled to the country, and their subsequent report, 'Croats Under Yugoslavian Rule – A Visit of Investigation', was subsequently published in October 1932. It made for sombre reading, and completely vindicated Croatian claims.

Riley and Davies witnessed the blatant manipulation of electoral constituencies and the fixing of the parliamentary system so that Serbs, despite constituting just 35 per cent of the population, consistently returned 65 per cent of the parliament's deputies. They also identified systemic attempts to eradicate the Croat identity through the guise of eliminating divisive influences. Wherever the two investigators travelled they could sense that they were under surveillance, and when they endeavoured to gauge public opinion their respondents 'had to tell us everything almost in whispers' rather than freely express themselves as guaranteed in the constitution. They were in little doubt that the country was effectively a police state, run by an absolute monarch and with a parliament that did little more than rubber-stamp his decrees. Furthermore, its judges and magistrates were far from independent and faced dismissal if their decisions did not chime with the expectations of the king. Their suspicions were indeed borne out by a remark made by Mirco Komnenovic, minister for social politics and public health, to the effect that when a 'suspect is brought in [to custody in] a state of psychosis',[112] he or she is too intimidated and disorientated to do any more than confess guilt and face the consequences. In other words, the policy was to keep the people cowed and in a perpetual state of fear.

The two visitors were even minded to question whether the decision to create the state in its present form was a wise one. It appeared to them that the Allies had simply thrown 'all these people into one camp … and expected them to work harmoniously together forever again', a damning indictment of the misjudged and ill-considered decisions made in Paris in the name of self-determination. Indeed, the situation they found in the country was so dire that 'all the elements of a national rising are innate in the Croatian peasantry'. If such an outcome was to be avoided, they concluded, 'the spirit of the Treaty granted by the Allied Powers must be adhered to'. Unfortunately, Davies and Riley were just two among many voices crying in the wilderness.

Where Alexander had made some tangible progress, and largely with the approval of his subjects, was in the area of foreign relations. He had been prescient enough to appreciate that his kingdom could not survive without friends and allies, and so embarked upon a series of diplomatic efforts. These included promotion of the Little Entente with Czechoslovakia and Romania – a strategy that was initially popular with France, too. He also concluded a pact with Turkey and sought friendlier relations with neighbouring Greece. What little freedom of action Italy had left to Albania was also exploited to the full in the hope of securing a treaty of commerce. In 1934, Yugoslavia, Romania, Greece and Turkey signed a further treaty known as the Balkan Pact, providing for mutual defence in the event of attack by a third party – a wise move with the Nazi hold on Germany tightening and the threat from Italy.

Alexander's attempts to reach an understanding with Rome were far more important but proved contentious. A start had been made before he became king, when the two countries had signed the Treaty of Rapallo in November 1920. It was an attempt to settle outstanding border differences and address Italy's sense of being short-changed by the peace treaty. It was also received with some relief by large elements of the French and British press as a sign of an easing of tensions. As well as the short-lived agreement over Fiume, the accord gave Italy some of the territory denied to it by President Wilson, including the western parts of Cariola, around half of Inner Cariola, almost all of the former Austrian Littoral and some territory in Dalmatia. In this eagerness to placate the Italians, however, more than half a million Croats and Slovenes found themselves under alien rule, provoking yet more animosity among Alexander's already discontented subjects. This was bad enough, but the notorious Nettuno Conventions, thirty-two clauses involving economic, social, religious and cultural understandings signed with Italy on 25 July 1925, provoked even more anger. Although this document safeguarded the rights of Italians living in Croatia, it proved totally unacceptable to the Croatians themselves. The rancour and protracted debate this provoked went on for four years, at which point the king had to intervene and enact the Nettuno Conventions by decree.

Despite Alexander's best endeavours to secure a lasting peace with Italy, their subsequent activities became a growing source of anxiety. In 1932 they began to construct intimidating naval installations on the coast of Albania, followed by fortifications and new roads that led ominously to the Greek and Yugoslav borders. Following Mussolini's seizure of power it was also widely suspected that he was conniving to revive some form of Austro-Hungarian state which would be under his influence and could be exploited in order to extend Italian control over the wider Balkans.[113] Despite growing reservations over his pro-Italian policies, seen as appeasement by many, Alexander justified his actions by insisting that above all else 'we have to settle important and difficult questions with Italy ... we must reduce all causes of friction to a minimum.'[114] Perhaps, but it was at the cost of creating greater friction within his own realm.

In being so personally identified with statutes, legislation and treaties which were responsible for so much discontent, Alexander inevitably made himself a target for violence. In 1934, while on a state visit to Paris in the pursuit of a treaty with the French government, he was assassinated by a Macedonian separatist. The shock and genuine grief at the news of his murder temporarily united the stunned country under their new king, Peter, and his regent, Prince Paul. It was also hoped that a new king would herald an era of genuine democracy, and the early signs were promising. Paul ignored his more hawkish ministers, who were urging him to declare martial law and carry out wholesale round-ups of suspected conspirators. Instead, as a token of goodwill, he granted amnesty to political prisoners and indicated that he may even pursue a policy of decentralisation once fresh elections were held.

The people grew optimistic, feeling that their fortunes were about to change, but the election that followed on 5 May 1935 proved to be far from free and fair. The government's control over the press and distribution of election material gave them an in-built advantage. By contrast, the opposition parties were heavily restricted, and their meetings were actually broken up by the authorities.[115] Faced with such oppressive measures, the people rioted – most inevitably the Croats and the Slovenes. The socialists were seen as a particular threat to the status quo and singled out for attention. Subsequently, the *ancien regime* consolidated rather than loosened its hold on power, and because of such skulduggery it won the vast majority of the seats again. The new government made vague assurances of a better, more democratic future and managed to bring most of the warring parties together temporarily, but still the promised reforms did not materialise. The old schisms soon resurfaced.

Sensibilities were further compromised when a proposed concordat with Rome, intended to clarify the rights of the Catholic Church in the country, proved highly unpopular among the Orthodox Church. Its negotiation provoked further demonstrations when students and peasants alike united in voicing their opposition. Violence erupted, and the police responded with further repression. Regardless, the concordat was pushed through parliament in 1936 despite the Orthodox Church threatening to excommunicate any deputies brave enough to vote for it.[116] News that the law had been passed was met with rioting, and tensions ran high for weeks. Police were bussed in from Croatia and Slovenia to deal with the demonstrators, and in one incident they fought a pitched battle in which hand-grenades were thrown.

Ironically, despite this uproar, the hated concordat was not even ratified by the Senate and so did not pass into law. Prince Paul nonetheless allowed himself to be persuaded that the accompanying agitation was a communist-inspired plot to undermine the kingdom, but the intemperate atmosphere was also spilling over to other parties with their own axes to grind. Leading politicians issued a joint declaration demanding that the constitution be suspended, a caretaker government installed, fresh elections held and a new government of national unity formed. This should then work to draft a new constitution guaranteeing the monarchy, democratic parliamentarianism, the unity of the state and the liberties of the individual.[117] Despite the pressure, Prince Paul resisted, claiming rather disingenuously that because he was merely regent for Peter and holding the constitution in trust, it was his duty to pass it on intact. None the more for his reluctance, the writing was on the wall. Unless serious and meaningful concessions were made, the kingdom would disintegrate entirely and he would have nothing to pass on to the young king when the time came.

Key among the issues facing Yugoslavia was the rift with Croatia, which was too urgent an issue to ignore. Despite a succession of proposals being put forward, all were vetoed for one reason or another; it appeared that this open sore would fester for years, if the country could survive that long. The growing popularity of the Croatian Peasant Party under its new leader, Vladko Macek, demonstrated that the momentum for change was becoming unstoppable, even to arch-centralists. When the Croatian Peasant Party won 80 per cent of the franchise in Croatia and Dalmatia in the elections of 1938, the urgency of entering into meaningful negotiations became irresistible. On 26 August 1939, a surprisingly generous 'compromise', or *Sporazum*, more wide-ranging than the *Nagodba* of 1868, was finally agreed. A separate Croatian *Banovina* would be created comprising almost 30 per cent of the state territory, with a population of 4.5 million including 168,000 Muslims and nearly 900,000 Serbs. It was to have its own elected assembly, with budgetary and internal matters devolved to it, while Belgrade would retain control of foreign affairs, trade and defence.[118]

Not surprisingly, the solution was welcomed by the Croats but repudiated by others, primarily the Serbs and Bosnian Muslims. Macek was understandably delighted, as to him national territory was 'the most important marker of every nation's existence'.[119] Even the organ of Serb nationalists, *The Serbian Voice*, or *Srpski glas*, gave the agreement its guarded approval so long as it did not compromise the integrity of the rest of Yugoslavia. One spokesman for the Serbian community condemned it, however, insisting that 'the ancestors of today's Serbs successfully defended [the land] from foreign occupiers in the course of centuries'.[120] Essentially, the Serbs thought that too much was being conceded to the Croats while Macek interpreted the agreement as a first step towards even greater autonomy. Unfortunately, while these strides in constitutional reform were finally being made, events elsewhere meant that they were going to be tragically short-lived.

Three days before the *Sporazum* was signed, the Molotov–Ribbentrop Pact had sealed the fate of Poland and indirectly that of the entire Balkan region. Whatever agreements had been made between Croat and Serb was fast becoming an academic exercise. With Nazi policy becoming more and more strident, Yugoslavia's prime minister, Milan Stoyadinovich, sought to find some middle ground with the Germans while maintaining the integrity of the kingdom. However, this policy was to have profound consequences for Yugoslavia's allies, and prove the utter worthlessness of the treaties so blithely signed during the course of the past twenty years. Self-interest proved a greater pull than mutual support, and this was brought home during the Munich Crisis of 1938. Just when the Czechs were at their most vulnerable, the Yugoslav government made it clear they would not, after all, honour their treaty obligations under the Little Entente for fear of provoking Germany. Nevertheless, despite the perfidy of their government, some 100,000 sympathetic Yugoslavs volunteered to fight, and thousands more demonstrated in support, once again risking ruthless suppression at the hands of their own police.[121]

In taking this action the Yugoslav government had proven itself to be seriously out of step with large swathes of public opinion, but the Balkan region was becoming more tense and Yugoslavia was confronted with very difficult choices. Italy had annexed Albania completely in April 1939, and the true motives behind its road-building activities became evident in October 1940 when it invaded Greece. By this time France, too, had been defeated by Germany, leaving Britain as the only significant ally in the region. Hitler was becoming increasingly agitated and insisted that Yugoslavia decide with whom it was going to throw in its lot, and the British felt the same, having gone to the aid of the Greeks after they successfully repulsed the Italians. However, the Germans were nearer and more intimidating.

In 1941, having secured Bulgarian membership of the Tripartite Pact and support for a renewed attack on the Greeks, Hitler put even more pressure on Belgrade. Prince Paul was summoned to Germany for a secret meeting on 4 March, at which he was subjected to the usual round of threats and browbeating designed to get him to agree to what the Führer wanted. Suitably harangued, the Yugoslav regent and his foreign ministers returned home to consider their limited options. Having decided to sup with the devil, they sneaked out of Belgrade on 25 March and proceeded to Vienna, where Hitler and von Ribbentrop were waiting for them. Here they signed away their country's brief twenty years of independence and appended their signatures to the pact. Ribbentrop made the usual empty assurances that Germany would respect 'the sovereignty and territorial integrity of Yugoslavia at all times',[122] but such gestures did nothing to allay the fears of the general public who were stunned by the decision taken by their perfidious government.

The day after the agreement was signed, a coup was staged by the Air Force which ousted Paul and installed Prince Peter on the throne as King Peter II. When Winston Churchill heard of the dramatic turn of events in Belgrade he was delighted, expressing his joy in a speech soon after when he told his audience, 'I have great news for you and the whole country. Early this morning Yugoslavia found its soul.'[123] It may well have found its soul, but it was soon to lose something perhaps even more precious. Hitler flew into a fury and ordered that the country be punished 'with merciless brutality ... in a lightning operation'. His War Directive No. 25 stated that 'efforts will be made to induce Hungary and Bulgaria to take part in operations by offering them the prospect of regaining the Banat and Macedonia.'[124] On 6 April, the country was invaded by Germany and its allies, and Belgrade was subjected to bombing by the *Luftwaffe*.

Yugoslavia had now joined Czechoslovakia, Poland and the rest of Europe as members of what would ultimately become one of the continent's most brutal experiments in economic and political union. Ahead of them lay years of German domination that would see them ravaged and mercilessly exploited in the interests of a regime whose evil knew no bounds.

10

Accept German Prices and Adjust to German Measures

Hjalmar Schacht, Hitler's economic guru and one of the architects of *Grossraumwirtschaft*. (Library of Congress)

Even as the successor states were embarking upon their doomed efforts at nation-building, critics and outside observers remained convinced that salvation lay in closer cooperation. Indeed, soon after the First World War ended this was still seen as a feasible aim. To the earnest urgings of Colonel House and Maynard Keynes were added those of Headlam-Morley, who felt that it was 'quite probable, and I think quite desirable, that some economic union should in the future be established between the Danubian states'.[1] Others were more considered in their evaluations, particularly considering the circumstances prevailing at the time. Sir William Goode conceded:

> ... as a profession of policy there is probably no one of these governments [Czechoslovakia, Poland, Yugoslavia, Hungary and Austria] that will not adhere to the policy that it is to their own interest to trade freely amongst themselves, but there is a natural disinclination to put such a policy into execution when it involves taking bad money in exchange for good food or coal.[2]

This statement goes some way to underlining how important it was for the successor states to reform their old miscellany of currencies into stable national ones, for without such basic reforms the implementation of productive trade between them was seriously compromised. In the meantime, some efforts were being made to smooth and facilitate this commerce, underscored by a series of largely fruitless conferences convened in the 1920s and even into the 1930s. One, held at Porto Rosa in October 1921, had among its hugely optimistic objectives the lifting of all import and export restrictions, the negotiation of trade treaties between successor states on an equal basis, and the application of a more liberal trade regime with third party states. The conference failed, largely because, as Sir William Goode had predicted, no real consensus could be found. The Czech delegation in particular had insisted upon the maintenance of current tariffs and import-export restrictions,[3] and without movement on this there was little prospect of a solution. Such an impasse, compounded by the generally held conviction that sovereignty meant the right to exercise control over tariffs and negotiate bilaterally rather than as part of a customs union, was perhaps most deeply felt by the two countries which had found readjusting to the new political landscape almost impossible: Austria and Hungary.

Where once Austria, as the linchpin of the old monarchy, had enjoyed free and easy access to its own lands and those of its partner Hungary, these former vassals had suddenly and unceremoniously cut it off. Now, instead of open borders inside a customs union and a free market, it was confronted by hard borders and high tariffs. The capital, Vienna, was now faced with the problem of finding almost a million litres of milk a day, much of which had come from Hungary, Bohemia and Moravia.[4] As it could supply at best only 70,000 litres a day from its own resources, this dire situation led to terrible conditions for the population and was especially damaging to the health and wellbeing of its children. Ethel Snowden witnessed 'mothers ... tearful about the lack of milk, which their plentiful paper money could not buy because there was none to sell', and 'pitiful babes, small, misshapen or idiotic through the lack of proper food', their plight made even worse by the shortage of 'medicines ... soap ... disinfectants'.[5] Subsequent medical examinations carried out by foreign organisations revealed that nearly a quarter of the city's children were severely malnourished, 56 per cent undernourished and only 21 per cent classed as properly fed. Snowden was convinced that 'but for the magnificent work of the American Relief Commission, the Society of Friends, and the Save the Children Fund, the coming generation would have dwindled out of existence'.[6]

The country's vital supplies of sugar beet were down from 1 million tons to just 8,500 tons a year, the new state possessing only four of the 200 sugar refineries which once served its needs.[7] Shortages led to the hoarding of what little food and fuel was available, and it was common to see desperate Viennese hiking out into the countryside to collect firewood. Efforts to overcome this crisis and become more self-sufficient would be further hampered by the unproductive mountainous terrain which covered much of the country, with only 21 per cent of the land tilled compared with Germany's 48 per cent.[8] Seymour noted that this lack of natural resources and control of navigable waterways, railways or other communications meant that 'the new Austria lacks many of the conditions conducive to economic prosperity',[9] a situation quite at odds with the high-minded pronouncements of his bosses.

The Social Democrat government had tried to alleviate the suffering by introducing price controls on food, and even requisitioned stocks to ensure fairer distribution, but the financial strain this imposed on the national budget was proving unsustainable. Even increasing taxation on an already hard-pressed public could not make up for the shortfall between revenue and expenditure. Unfortunately, the desperate government attempted to print its way out of trouble, thus producing the 'bad money' mentioned by Sir William Goode and exacerbating an already dire situation.

The favoured stand-by of quantitative easing was introduced in 1919 to stimulate the economy and improve the money supply but resulted in the circulation of crowns rising from 831 million in 1919 to 7 trillion before the experiment was finally abandoned in 1923. This disaster inevitably resulted in rampant inflation, with the value of the currency dropping from 16.1 to the dollar in 1919 to 70,800 a couple of years later. This unsustainable situation led in 1922 to the Austrian government appealing to the League of Nations for help. After the League stepped in, a protocol was negotiated and signed at Geneva on 4 October 1922, under which Britain, France, Italy and – perhaps surprisingly – Czechoslovakia agreed to provide a loan of £30 million.[10] Strict conditions were attached.

As part of the rebalancing of the economy, food subsidies had to end, the civil service had to be reduced by 70,000 and the Central Bank had to accept large-scale restructuring under a commissioner general appointed by the League. His task was to work with the Austrian government to implement these reforms and he had been given wide-ranging powers to ensure they were put into effect. As a result, the country returned to the gold standard, and a new currency, the Austrian shilling, was created to replace the now worthless crown. Furthermore, to ensure the integrity of the new currency, the government was placed under strict limits as to the amount it could print.

Rather than express gratitude for this apparent salvation, however, most Austrians felt totally humiliated by the conditions to which their once proud imperial nation had been reduced. This capitulation to the power of the League, or the 'Slavery of Geneva' as some described it,[11] simply engendered bitterness and resentment. As the director of the Finance Ministry, David Fischer, conceded, the acceptance of the loan and its conditions meant that Austrians were now 'bound hand and foot and must accept every kind of influence on their domestic legislation, on their taxation, [and] on their trade policy'.[12] It is partly due to this dire situation that many Austrians sought to revive the idea of union with Germany. Karl Renner, Austria's chancellor during this period, commented how 'the fear of famine and unemployment and the sudden contraction of the field for enterprise, made nearly everyone think of *Anschluss* as the only possible solution.'[13] As we have seen, however, the achievement of this aim had to wait for a whole new set of circumstances to change the country's fortunes.

Austria's dilemma was shared by its former 'partner in crime', Hungary. The Hungarians, too, faced a dire future unless something could be pulled out of the hat. The challenges they faced must have felt almost insurmountable, the country having lost 84 per cent of its forests, 43 per cent of its arable land and 83 per cent of its iron ore deposits. In addition, 62 per cent of its railways, 63 per cent of its roads and all of its gold, silver and copper deposits now resided in other countries. The agricultural economy was around half of pre-war levels, and industrial capacity between 60 and 65 per cent. The resulting lack of tax receipts meant that the government would have to dip into valuable gold and foreign currency reserves to meet up to half of its expenditure in 1921–22 and as much as 80 per cent in 1922–23.

Faced with such insuperable challenges, Hungary's options were very limited. A sensible option might have been to make approaches to neighbouring states and attempt to negotiate reciprocal trade or customs arrangements, along the lines that were being proposed at the various economic forums. Hungary however, had lost little of its former chauvinism and arrogance, and defeat in the war had not caused it to re-evaluate its own status or those of its former subjects. Ultranationalist Count Isthvan Bethlen, who became the country's prime minister in 1921, shared his fellow Magyars' disdain for their new neighbours. He was loath to embark upon any kind of economic customs or tariff arrangement or have any truck with a Danubian Federation. Indeed, even if Hungary would have been admitted into such an arrangement, he considered the prospect demeaning to Magyar pride. Bethlen also feared that it would eventually lead to Hungary being subsumed into some kind of Slav-dominated economic and political union and losing what little sovereignty – and self-respect – it had left.[14]

Bethlen instead favoured the country seeking recovery through its own efforts, and in 1924 succeeded in negotiating a 250 million gold crown loan through the League of Nations, half of which came from Britain. Inevitably it came with conditions, key among them that the government establish a National Bank, which started operating in June of that year. The nation's finances also needed a complete overhaul and by January 1927 a new currency, with the rather uninspiring name of pengo, had been introduced. These reforms helped investment in both the agricultural and industrial sectors, and by 1929 they would almost be back to pre-war levels. Nevertheless, Hungary's problems were far from over.

For many thinkers, bilateral, multilateral and especially unilateral responses to Europe's post-war challenges fell woefully short of what was really needed – bold, daring and audacious solutions. These convictions were held by men such as maverick visionary Count Richard Coudenhove-Kalergi. Born in 1894 to an Austro-Hungarian diplomat and the daughter of a Japanese landowning oil merchant, he led a peripatetic life during which he served as a politician and more latterly as a self-styled philosophising guru. His travels and his heritage had imbued him with an irrevocable conviction that the only way to secure peace and preserve European pre-eminence was to form a deep political union in addition to economic ties. As early as 1921, the count warned darkly that if they did not, then 'while Europe is breaking up, it must sink to complete loss of political influence, until one day, after losing its colonies, in debt, bankrupt and impoverished, it will succumb to invasion.'[15]

Coudenhove-Kalergi also articulated such dire prophesies in a book, *Pan Europa*, published in 1923. In this book he proposed a new world order limited to five mega-states: a United States of Europe, a Pan American Union, the British Empire, the USSR and a Pan Asian Union. He even suggested in 1929 what he thought should become the national anthem of his United States of Europe, Beethoven's 'Ode to Joy'. In 1926, a Pan European League was formed which held its first congress in Vienna. It also established branches in Paris and Berlin to spread the gospel of unification and the evils of nationalism and drew the support of luminaries such as Albert Einstein, Thomas Mann and Sigmund Freud.

One elder statesman persuaded by this new doctrine was Aristide Briand. He was elected honorary president of the Pan Europa Movement in 1927 and spoke in favour of a European Union in a speech given at the League of Nations in September 1929. On 1 May 1930 he wrote the 'Memorandum on the Organisation of a Regime of European Federal Union', which he sent to the governments of twenty-six countries. The proposal was for the League members who were European countries to form an economic and political union along the lines of the League itself. Unfortunately, their responses were lukewarm, couched in evasive terms, giving various reasons why such an idea was not yet feasible.[16] Nonetheless, the League took his proposals seriously enough to set up a committee of enquiry, but this too concluded that the most practical outcome for Briand's ideas would be the creation of a European Federal Union, which would link states loosely so as not to compromise their sovereignty.

Such reticence echoed the reservations expressed by those sceptical about the potential reach of the League itself and minded some observers to doubt it would ever come to pass. Francis Deak of Columbia University, writing in *Political Science Quarterly* in 1931, wrote that 'unless they realise that our completely changed civilisation requires a completely different method of dealing with the relations between nations ... there can be little doubt that this European Union will bring just as much disappointment as did the League of Nations.'[17] On a peaceful and stable continent a persuasive argument could perhaps have been made for deeper integration, but most countries were still guarded and preferred to advance incrementally. The Ouchy Convention of 1932, which was signed between Belgium, Luxembourg and the Netherlands, provided for eventual economic union, but slowly; in the meantime, it limited its aspirations to annual 10 per cent reductions on tariffs levied upon one another's exports and the mutual granting of 'most favoured nation' status. This half-hearted approach was just the kind of thing that Coudenhove-Kalergi railed against, but unless circumstances changed it was probably the best that could be hoped for.

That change came with the re-emergence of an aggressive, chauvinistic and disruptive Germany. The bleak forecasts that men such as Maynard Keynes made in 1919, warning that the punitive peace would result in Germany's terminal decline, had proven premature. Despite occupation, hyper-inflation, economic depression and mass unemployment, it remained a force to be reckoned with. Where Keynes had perhaps been vindicated was in his grim predictions for the rest of Europe. Much of the pain suffered could have been put down to the absence of Germany as an economic driver, but under both the Weimar and Nazi regimes this situation changed in their determination to see a rejuvenated and stronger Germany emerge from the calamity of 1918. This was not being undertaken out of any sense of altruism, however, and German motives had not gone unnoticed. On 11 February 1930, the chief of the Imperial General Staff, General George Milne, sent the British government a memorandum in which he outlined his analysis of German intentions, explaining it was

... laying the foundation for a large [economic] expansion at some future date. Their immediate problem ... [is] to organise the nation as a whole and industry in particular, so it may be ready once more to convert itself into a war machine should the necessity arise, and in the meantime to prevent the military spirit from dying out in Germany.[18]

In fact, as Milne rightly suggested, since the start of the 1920s successive German governments had striven to restore the country's position in Europe, a strategy which had assumed a renewed significance with the coming to power of Hitler in 1933. The incremental undermining of the Versailles peace was symptomatic of this, wearing down the former Allies and causing division and disagreement among them. The negotiation of Locarno in 1925, the constant agitation over Germany's lost Polish lands, the destabilising of neighbours such as Austria, and the promotion of Sudeten separatism all played a role. The endgame would be to replace the existing European order with *Großraumwirtschaft* (literally 'large-area economy') a German-dominated self-sufficient Greater Economic Area designed to serve the needs of the Reich.

Hjalmar Schacht, who had long advocated the revival of a customs union,[19] found himself embroiled in this much more ambitious project. President of the Reichsbank from 1924 to 1930, and again from 1933 to 1939, he was also appointed minister of economics in 1934, and plenipotentiary general for war economy in 1935. In this capacity he sought to achieve German economic recovery in part by duplicating the strategy employed by US president F. D. Roosevelt with his New Deal and by adopting some of the theories espoused by Maynard Keynes. These and other initiatives would together create the environment around which German rearmament was made possible. Schacht was not the only proponent of such policies, and the concept was eagerly embraced by other leading Nazis. One, Hans Ernst Passe, a deputy minister in the Hitler cabinet in 1934, stated that 'the time has come for [the] attainment of *Großraumwirtschaft* to become our most important economic policy goal.'[20] He confirmed that under German control the sole aim of this 'organised economic space'[21] would be the exploitation of Europe for the exclusive benefit of Germany.[22] As an economic illiterate, Hitler did not understand – and cared even less – that the measures he employed would ultimately prove inflationary and unsustainable, and as the ends justified the means he would come to ignore Schacht's increasingly shrill warnings and ultimately force him to resign. Before this parting of the ways, however, Schacht would prove instrumental in creating the economic 'miracle' which would pave the way for German rearmament.

As General Milne predicted, before Germany could recreate the war machine dismantled in 1919, it had to lay the groundwork through peaceful means. This it hoped to achieve through a series of ostensibly innocuous trade agreements, largely negotiated through the 1930s. Firstly it needed to address two fundamental problems: worsening cash reserves, and a shortage of raw materials such as rubber, cotton and, perhaps most significant of all, oil. To resolve this twofold crisis, something very audacious would be required. Schacht provided the solution when he was charged with drafting the ambitious and far-ranging Neuer Plan[23] in September 1934. As he explained, this New Plan was designed to ensure Germany 'purchased solely from her own customers' and 'only if they could pay'.[24] The scheme meant that the allocation of money became subject to control by a central government office, while imports were managed by Control Offices.

Efforts would also be made to promote exports through subsidies, by demanding reciprocal trade from Germany's trading partners, and extremely clever currency manipulation through the employment of so-called 'clearing accounts'. In addition, multiple currency manoeuvres and foreign exchange discrimination were to be exploited as part of a deliberate system designed to compel trading partners to buy from Germany. If they resisted, the Germans could simply raise the prospect of the recalcitrant nation being unable to export to the Reich. As Schacht remarked in 1935, their suppliers were selling their produce to them because they 'have to, therefore they have to accept German prices and adjust to German measures'.[25] Consideration would soon turn to the creation of a single currency for the whole of the continent, which would naturally be dominated by the Reichsmark, and which was being referred to in some circles as the Euromark.[26]

One by one, Germany's neighbours would find themselves ever more closely aligned to the demands of the German economy, which, as General Milne predicted, and politicians such as Winston Churchill warned, had just one ultimate objective. For example, in 1934 a trade agreement was signed with Hungary in which Germany would accept large deliveries of grain, livestock and pork products. As a result, agricultural exports to Germany doubled in a single year – butter threefold, cattle sevenfold, lard and bacon twentyfold – leading to Germany's share of Hungarian exports increasing from 11 per cent to 22 per cent.[27] These agreements certainly boosted the Hungarian economy, but at a cost. Payment for these products was not straightforward, for 90 per cent of Germany's imports from Hungary were paid for not in hard currency but in kind, in the form of industrial products, as was Schacht's intention. This arrangement would increasingly deprive Hungary of the means to purchase goods and services from other countries, and thus bind it ever closer to the Reich.

In the meantime, Germany was amassing almost 500 million Reichsmarks in German clearing debts and proving tardy in the delivery of goods in kind.[28] Yugoslavia found itself in a similar predicament to that negotiated with Hungary. Its economic circumstances improved considerably when Germany began importing much more in the way of agricultural products and timber, as well as the zinc, chromium, copper, bauxite and other key minerals lying otherwise unexploited in the ground.[29] Yugoslavia also found a ready market for its vegetable oil and other agricultural produce, so that by 1937 Germany accounted for a third of its exports. By the time Hitler had begun to threaten the country physically in 1940, this would have risen to 90 per cent of Yugoslav trade, reducing it to little more than an economic vassal of the Reich. To the Nazis, invasion and occupation would simply be a logical extension of this arrangement.

When the Austrian Nazis finally achieved their dream of union with Germany, their country became a further economic, political and military asset, expanding the borders of the Reich and emboldening Berlin to extend its growing dominance over its neighbours. Finland was drawn in as the growing menace of Soviet designs became increasingly apparent, and by the end of the 1930s, in exchange for credits to buy armaments, it helped to meet Hitler's requirements for nickel, molybdenum and platinum.[30]

The unequal nature of these treaties did not go unnoticed, however. The Finnish government would eventually express its concerns that the economic alliance with Germany might result in the terminal decline of its own manufacturing industry, and Sweden increasingly saw in German economic policy a threat to its own sovereignty.[31] Even Italy, a close friend, ally and eventual dependent of the Reich, would become uneasy at the scale and scope of Germany's ambitions, fearing its comparatively modest sphere of economic interest in the Mediterranean would be placed at a serious disadvantage by Germany's aggressive economic policies.[32]

Germany was nevertheless doing too well out of its tactics to loosen the reins, and in March 1939 Romania effectively became another German satellite, concluding arrangements which would result in it supplying Germany with wheat and, far more significantly, energy from its oilfields at Ploesti.

By the time countries such as Romania had been drawn into Hitler's web, the Second World War had broken out and the Germans no longer had to hide behind the veil of legality and negotiation to exploit their neighbours. Denmark, for example, could be forced to sign an unequal trade agreement in November 1940, by which it would undertake to send fixed quotas of pork and butter to Germany.[33] With German troops by now ensconced in the country, there was little that could be done to resist. Much worse was to follow.

Winston Churchill appreciated the horrific implications for the United Kingdom if it too succumbed to the Nazis. Perhaps even more importantly, he knew what a German-dominated Europe could mean for the United States. Consequently, five days after the Nazi *blitzkrieg* of 10 May 1940, which saw the invasion of France and the Low Countries, he warned President Roosevelt that 'if we go down you may well have a

United States of Europe under Nazi command far more murderous, far stronger, far better armed than the New World.'[34]

Churchill had good reason for such alarmism, as the betrayal of Czechoslovakia had provided a case study in German intentions. The Munich Agreement had specified that British and French approval had to be given before Sudeten could be incorporated into the German economic sphere,[35] but the Germans treated this undertaking with the same contempt as any other and proceeded to implement their plans almost before the ink was dry. The subsequent partition was also seen to be a further element in Germany's longer-term strategy. Hermann Göring made clear in July 1939 what was proposed for their new conquest when he stated that it 'has taken place ... in order to increase German war potential by the exploitation of [its] industry'.[36] To this end, Bohemia and Moravia's substantial industrial complexes, mines, steelworks and factories, were 'sold' to German industrialists, reversing the measures undertaken by Masaryk in the 1920s, while Czech assets in Germany were confiscated and Czech banks liquidated. The lignite mines owned by Prague-based Jewish owners such as Ignac Petschek were likewise appropriated by the Germans,[37] and their owners reduced to penury.[38] The Germans also dismantled several steel and chemical factories and reassembled them in Austria.

Such was the value of Czech military assets in particular, and so skilful were the Germans in exploiting them, that the arms production centres of Skoda and the factories in Brno which produced light artillery, small arms and military vehicles would account for around 10 per cent of German arms requirements by the end of the war.[39] Because the thirty-five army divisions which had been prepared to defend the country in 1938 surrendered without firing a shot, sufficient artillery, small arms ammunition, tanks, armoured vehicles and other equipment had fallen into German hands to equip half the *Wehrmacht*. Much of this was eventually used to supplement the invasion of Poland, and then France and the Low Countries, and later still many obsolete tank models became strongpoints along the Atlantic Wall, which the Allies would confront in June 1944.

The Nazi authorities even imposed a 'protection' fee, a tax designed as a contribution towards the financing of the German war effort and occupation.[40] As Germany increasingly tightened the screws, the Czechs found themselves with little choice but to accede to German demands. Not only were they helpless militarily and politically, but the Nazis controlled access to their coal, electricity supplies and transport links.[41] Failure to cooperate would have led to these essential commodities being cut off until the population complied, froze or starved. Slovakia, nominally independent but under German 'protection', was similarly exploited. In 1939, its government tried to slow down the rate of German activity in the country by reducing imports from the Reich to the level of exports, but it was too late. Among the other measures that had been taken to ensure Germany benefited from trade with both the Protectorate and Slovakia was a disadvantageous exchange rate between the Reichsmark and the crown to make German imports unfairly cheap.[42] Consequently, Germans benefited from cheap consumer goods which became too expensive and too scarce for Czechs and Slovaks. However, neither were seen as long-term economic partners. As Reich Protector of Bohemia and Moravia Reinhard Heydrich explained in October 1941:

> The future of the Reich depends after the end of this war on the ability of the Reich and its people to hold on to, to dominate and, when necessary to absorb into the Reich these … [territories which would provide] … raw materials and food … [provided by] a workforce of 'helots'.[43]

In the long term, Germany clearly saw such territories as sources of cheap labour. To this end, more than 150,000 Slovaks, willing and unwilling, would be sent to work in Germany, and Czechs and Slovaks together would account for 13 per cent of all the foreign labourers working there.[44] Moreover, to achieve German targets for aircraft production, the number of Czechs in the industry would rise to twenty-five times the number at the beginning of the war, with 141,000 workers scattered across 135 different plants.[45] Nevertheless, despite Heydrich's claims, the country had much more than just human resources. The indictment read out at the Nuremberg Trials after the war explained how:

> … the defendants seized and stole large stocks of raw materials, copper, tin, iron, cotton, and food; caused to be taken to Germany large amounts of railway rolling stock, and many engines, carriages, steam vessels, and trolley buses; plundered libraries, laboratories, and art museums of books, pictures, objects of art, scientific apparatus, and furniture; stole all gold reserves and foreign exchange of Czechoslovakia, including 23,000 kilograms of gold of nominal value of 5,265,000 … The total sum of defendants' economic spoliation of Czechoslovakia from 1938 to 1945 is estimated at 2 trillion Czechoslovak Crowns.

In the face of such rapine, Czech patriots fought back as best they could. Resistance group Defence of the Nation passed news of enemy activity to the London-based Czech government in exile, including intelligence gleaned by Czech policemen while serving a interpreters for the Nazis. Widespread sabotage was also carried out, from workers in factories undermining machinery to armed activists causing damage both inside the protectorate and also within Germany itself. One of the most audacious acts of resistance was the assassination of Heydrich in June 1942, but this resulted in brutal reprisals in which hundreds of innocent Czechs were killed.

Of course, Hitler had never made any secret of his plans to extend German hegemony eastwards, where German dreams of *Ober Ost* had come tantalisingly close to being realised a quarter of a century before. The Treaty of Versailles had crushed those ambitions but, as we have seen, neither the Weimar nor the Nazi regimes had been reconciled to the loss of so much land to Poland. The subsequent systematic campaign of agitation and undermining of the new state, culminating in its invasion and partition twenty years later, had reopened its potential for exploitation. A month after Heydrich gave his revealing speech, Göring chaired a meeting on Poland's future, in which he confirmed that these new lands must also be exploited, 'from colonial viewpoints and with colonial methods'.[46]

In the autumn of that year, Göring also issued instructions for the officials in the east to place emphasis upon 'the formation of priority areas in those economic branches which are decisive for the German war economy'.[47] Poland, containing many of the essential raw materials lost by Germany through the Treaty of Versailles, was to be a prime prospect for the predatory application of *Großraumwirtschaft*. Upper Silesia and all the other lands ceded to Poland in 1919 were almost immediately reintegrated into Greater Germany with the establishment of a 'new unitary industrial area' and its coal mines, steelworks and other industrial concerns were restored to German ownership. Racial theories were ruthlessly implemented, with the Germanisation of management and administration.[48] German penetration of capital into businesses previously owned by the Polish state or foreign investors reached 100 per cent, once major heavy industrial firms were bought up or taken into trusteeship by German companies.[49] Inevitably, all Polish banks were expropriated, liquidated or simply absorbed into German institutions, while the occupiers imposed an exchange rate of two zloty to the Reichsmark. In order to guarantee the penury of the occupied population, Poles were only permitted to exchange a maximum of 250 Reichsmarks, and the remainder, much of which sat in bank accounts, was seized along with the institutions themselves.

As the north-eastern Polish territories (Danzig-West Prussia and the *Wartheland*) were designated for the earliest settlement of *Volkdeutsch* colonists, they received substantial support in the form of finance, infrastructure, fertilisers, farm machinery and seed. The building of warehouses and silos was also undertaken, in addition to the construction of farm schools and food processing factories.[50] These provinces would then join other territories as suppliers of cereals to the Reich, which in return would export all the necessary impedimenta for further exploiting the land for farming. By contrast, the central region encompassing Krakow and Warsaw, known as the General Government, was to become a vast dumping ground for those people not wanted in the annexed areas. Its grain-producing capacity was reduced by 750,000 hectares, and subsequently its yield fell from a pre-war average of 4.5 million tons to 3.9 million in 1943; the potato crop also plunged from more than 14 million tons before the war to less than 9 million in 1941.[51] By the end of 1940, approximately 325,000 Poles, mainly those displaced from the annexed territories, had been moved to the General Government and a further 45,000 were sent there in 1941. This was only intended as a temporary measure, however, with a further evacuation planned to make space for the proposed German colonists. To this end, in late 1942 and into 1943, 110,000 Poles were again expelled. The long-term plan was to settle 12.5 million Germans over a period of thirty years, replacing and eradicating all evidence of the land's previous inhabitants, leaving perhaps 4 million Poles for whom they might find a use as slave labour or servants.

Many of those who had survived Habsburg and Hohenzollern rule and gone on to serve as the elites within the new Polish Republic were to be liquidated as part of the Nazis' new plan for Europe. There was clearly no room in either the annexed territories or the General Government for Poles to act as anything other than peasant labour. Therefore, the Germans had no use for intellectuals, clergymen, teachers, journalists, politicians, doctors, landowners or businesspeople. These people were rounded up and either shot or imprisoned. Place names were to be systematically Germanised; Lodz, for example, was renamed Litzmannstadt.[52] Children whose physical characteristics met the demanding requirements of the ideal 'German' were the only individuals spared, seized from their families to be re-educated and Germanised. Otherwise, every conceivable measure was taken to eradicate Poland's cultural and social existence. Poles kept on to work in factories were permitted some semblance of a human existence but faced shifts of ten to twelve hours and had little or no food. Prices and wages were also fixed,[53] never providing enough to spend on the open market. The food ration in 1941, a barely tolerable 700 calories, was only 25 per cent of the proposed minimum, but within a few years had dropped even further to 15 per cent.[54]

For a young state which had only recently emerged from the shadow of previous invasions and partitions, being reduced once again to the status of a vassal was intolerable. Its armies had fought bravely and put up a stubborn but fruitless resistance in the face of first the Germans and then the Russians, and the humiliation of defeat left the population helpless but defiant. In retaliation, a few surviving elements of Poland's army fought on as the Polish Home Army, resisting the Nazis and doing their best to upset Nazi plans through sabotage and guerrilla warfare, diverting valuable resources. At its height the Home Army numbered about 200,000, its activities culminating in the brave but hopeless Warsaw Uprising of August 1944. This gallant attempt to preserve the nation's independence and self-respect was brutally suppressed and caused the deaths of approximately 200,000 fighters and civilians, all while Stalin's armies of 'liberation' waited a few miles away, looking on and doing nothing to help. Still more suffering was to be endured, first inflicted by vengeful Germans and then by the Soviet Army as it reclaimed the territories regained in 1939 and lost in 1941. Before that could occur, however, Russia would have to endure its own nightmare.

As in Poland, the almost limitless opportunities offered by the exploitation of Russia had always been a key motivation for its invasion. Here, too, the vast gains achieved through the clauses of the Treaty of Brest-Litovsk had been snatched away in Paris in 1919. The potential offered by Russia's natural wealth had never been forsaken, and though relations were amicable under the Weimar Republic, they naturally cooled with the coming to power of the overtly anti-Soviet Nazis, and trade between the two had contracted from 223 million Reichsmarks in 1934 to 53 million Reichsmarks in 1938. Hitler had never made any secret of his plans for the Soviet Union, so frankly and candidly described in his polemic *Mein Kampf*. Nevertheless, pragmatism had to overcome ideology, at least in the short term, hence the Molotov–Ribbentrop Pact, which led to the invasion and partition of Poland. Accompanying commercial agreements would also yield a mutually beneficial bounty for both parties, and prior to June 1941 Germany received vast quantities of produce and raw materials, making a substantial contribution to *Großraumwirtschaft*. Moscow undertook to deliver 180 million Reichsmarks in raw materials in exchange for 120 million Reichsmarks' worth of finished manufactures. The Germans also cynically granted credits to the value of 200 million Reichsmarks over seven years at highly favourable rates.

On 11 February 1940, an agreement had been signed under which the Russians were to send, among other commodities, 1 million tons of grain, 500,000 tons of metal ore, 139,500 tons of cotton and 900,000 tons of oil to Germany in exchange for finished goods, synthetic material plants and naval vessels. The Russians would also undertake purchases on behalf of Germany through third parties, in order to circumvent the Allied blockade. An agreement was also signed in early 1941 by which the Russians undertook to supply 2.5 million tons of grain and 1 million tons of oil by May 1942, in exchange for which Germany would provide them with more capital goods.[55] There was therefore little to suggest that Germany would not receive all the resources it required without recourse to war. Indeed, in the course of the first six months leading up to the invasion of Russia, Moscow had dutifully honoured, and even exceeded its quotas and sent 254,000 tons of oil, 547,000 tons of grain, 75,000 tons of manganese, 56,000 tons of phosphates and 7,000 tons of nickel.

Then relations began to deteriorate, and serious cracks appeared as Hitler began to lay down the usual preliminaries to invasion – negative comments, barbed threats and claims of aggressive behaviour on the part of his intended victim. Indeed, both countries had been breaching the terms of the 1939 pact for some time, with Russia's hostile actions against Finland and the Baltic states threatening to cut off vital sources of raw material to Germany, which it still needed in spite of Russian largesse. Of course, the agreement that had been made with the Soviets was only intended to facilitate the conquest of Poland, and long before a German signature had been placed on it, Hitler had planned Operation Barbarossa. Hitler did want Russia's material wealth, but he also wanted more land. If he took the land, he reasoned, the raw materials would come with it. In War Directive No.25, he made clear what German policy was to be:

> The newly conquered territories in the East must be organised, made secure and, in full cooperation with the armed forces, exploited economically.[56]

As early as October 1940, *Ministerialdirektor* Gustav Schotterer, head of the Eastern Section of the Economics Ministry, mirrored Hitler's sentiments when he spoke of the need for 'a sensible division of labour between the agrarian and industrial areas of Europe',[57] and this would mean the complete de-industrialisation of the USSR and its relegation to the role of supplier of raw materials, food and manpower. On 13 March 1941, the *Oberkommando der Wehrmacht*, or OKW, produced 'Guidelines for Special Fields', stating that the primary objective of the occupation of the Soviet Union was 'the exploitation of the land and the securing of its economic value'.[58] Behind this lay the rationale of other well-known directives such as those which ordered the immediate execution of all communists and Jews, and the insistence that the war against the Soviet Union was to be fought on ideological grounds as much as military or economic. Its inhabitants were entirely expendable, and the more who died through combat, de-housing, exposure to the elements and starvation the better. They had no future in the new order.

On 19 March 1941, in line with the Nazi state's predilection for duplication of effort, proposals for the military-economic exploitation of the east were approved by Göring, under the auspices of the 'Economic Staff East', which met for the first time on 9 June 1941. Its priority was to be the 'easing of the German food situation through comprehensive provisioning of the troops from the land, and evacuation of all surpluses to the Reich for the sustenance of the German population'.[59] In other words, there would be no food for the local population save for those who were to be exploited as slave labour. The masterplan included the wholesale expulsion of upwards of 31 million native Russians and their replacement by colonists from Germany and other parts of Europe.[60] Schlotterer had confidently predicted in October 1941 that

4 million Germans would have been resettled in this way within ten years.[61] Of those Russians not dispensed with, over 600,000 would find themselves conscripted by the *Reichsbahn Ost* to build Road No. 4, which was to facilitate the smooth flow of goods and people to and from the newly conquered territories and the Reich.

When the *Wehrmacht* entered Ukraine, many peasants had naively hoped that one consequence of the German 'liberation' from Soviet rule would be a restoration of their individual rights. They welcomed the end of Soviet domination, having believed Nazi propaganda and promises of the establishment of an independent government. In the short term they were rewarded with the reopening of their churches, the release of Ukrainian prisoners of war and a relaxation of the rules governing the hated collective farms. Even an administration established by separatists was tolerated. Many were more than willing to participate in the mass murders of Jews in the darkest aspect of the planned new order. Coming to an arrangement with the Ukrainians could have reaped dividends for the invaders, then. Certainly, for some in the Nazi hierarchy, this was the best means by which to ensure the smooth functioning of the German war economy. Germany's last ambassador to Moscow before the invasion, Count Werner von der Schulenberg, went so far as to advocate that 'the definitive status of the Ukraine can only be settled after the conclusion of the war. As [a] possible solution [I] envisage a strong autonomy of the Ukraine within a Russian confederation, or under certain circumstances an independent Ukraine within a confederation of European states.'[62]

Nonetheless, it did not take long for the Ukrainians to be disabused of any notions of a partnership. When the *SS* arrived to take over from the army, the separatist leadership was dissolved and its supporters were promptly rounded up and shipped off to camps. Ukraine was then partitioned, with the south going to Romania, the west being annexed to Poland, the centre being allocated to a civil administration known as *Reichskommissariat Ukraine*, and the remainder coming under military control. The brutally efficient Erich Koch was appointed *Reichskommissar*, and he proceeded to implement plans to prepare the territory for German settlement. He certainly made no secret of his attitude to his new subjects, telling *SS* chief Heinrich Himmler that 'the best thing would be to kill all men in the Ukraine over fifteen years of age'.[63] As in Poland, Himmler certainly intended to see any potential figureheads exterminated:

> Like the skimmed fat at the top of a pot of bouillon, there is a thin intellectual layer on the surface of the Ukrainian people; do away with it and the leaderless mass will become an obedient and helpless herd…[64]

True to his word, Koch directed his men to embark upon a merciless pogrom, killing Ukrainians for the mildest transgressions, deliberately spreading disease and holding back food supplies. Some 38,000 people from the capital, Kiev, were shipped off to serve as slave labour in Germany almost immediately, and the remainder found themselves worked to death on farms and in factories. The only recourse open to most of the victims was to undermine the regime as best they could. One worker later explained how they would attempt sabotage by interfering with 'all sorts of junk, mending some things, breaking others. Everybody was working for himself and went away with cigarette lighters, buckets and pans to use in barter.'[65]

These pin pricks were as nothing next to two factors which seem to have caught the Germans unawares. First, in anticipation of the inevitable war between Nazi Germany and Soviet Russia, Stalin had approved the wholesale dismantling and transfer of entire factories and other material to the east of the Urals. Also, as the Soviet Army retreated they enacted a scorched earth policy following the invasion, which was designed to render useless anything that could not be moved. Both measures would severely stymie the Reich's presumptions about how much of the resources of the conquered territories they could exploit and how quickly. Soon after the invasion began, an 'Evacuation Soviet' was formed to mastermind the transfer of factories across the Urals. Perhaps a quarter of the entire Soviet industrial capacity is estimated to have been moved in this way.[66] Subsequently, although Soviet tank production totalled just 6,274 in 1941, once the new factories were up and running this number exceeded 24,000 in 1942.

The scorched earth policy also proved highly effective. Of 189 sugar beet processing factories in the Soviet Union before the war, 147 were situated in Ukraine; however, only around thirty-five or forty were operational in time for the 1941–42 harvest. The region's potential wheat yield was similarly compromised by the fighting, and here too it had to be conceded that it would be some time before production was up to the limits demanded by Göring and the ambitious plans drafted by the various ministries. The same disappointments applied to the windfall of natural resources the invaders expected to scoop up. The precious manganese mines of Nikopol had been captured in 1941, but due to their condition they were not operational until the summer of 1942. Ironically, this vital commodity had been in ample supply prior to Germany's attack on the Soviet Union, and although it was eventually to supply nearly 89 per cent of its needs it was lost again following the Russian counteroffensives of 1943. Rather more prompt were the dividends to be reaped from the capture of Mariupol in eastern Ukraine in October 1942. This industrial centre contained metallurgical plants, chemical and coke works, mills and a power station, but again they could only be of use to the Germans for as long as the Russian forces could be kept at bay.

Of course, one of Hitler's key objectives was the oil-rich Caucasus. Romania had, as we have seen, been providing most of Germany's needs, but Hitler was afraid that reliance on this one source of supply was unwise. This convinced him of the need to push south to the Caucasus, where the oilfields provided 90 per cent of Russia's output. Indeed, before the offensive began he admitted to General von Paulus, commander of the ill-fated Sixth Army, which would be sent to Stalingrad, that 'if I do not get the oil of Maikop and Grozny, then I must end this war.'[67] Thus *Fall Blau*, or Case Blue, was implemented, involving a drive south and the capture of Stalingrad in order to block supplies from being sent up the River Don. Although on 25 July 1942 German troops did manage to capture Rostov-on-Don, which offered access to these vital supplies, subsequent Soviet counteroffensives led to successive withdrawals, forcing the *Wehrmacht* back to its starting point, scuppering any hopes of exploiting the fields and hammering one of the first nails in the coffin of *Großraumwirtschaft*.

Ultimately the opportunities offered by the Soviet Union would be shattered just as those of *Ober Ost* had disintegrated. Hitler's arrogant boast that the German army had only to kick in the door of Soviet Russia and the whole edifice would come crashing down proved disastrously ill-judged. Despite its shattering early losses, the Russian army recovered and reorganised enough to consolidate and hold its fronts before recovering its losses. Tragically, it would take millions of lives and the destruction of whole towns, cities and villages for Russia's final victory to come to pass.

The early promise of great profits from the Balkans similarly failed to materialise. Serbia was placed under direct German military rule after the invasion of Yugoslavia, but in August 1941 a puppet government under General Milan Nedic was established. It also included members of the country's fascist-leaning United Militant Labour Organisation, the Zbor, several of whom were appointed to its administration. The Germans also occupied the Banat, while the Hungarians took Vojvodina, Bacha and Baranya, and Bulgaria took Macedonia east of the Vardar River along with small areas of southern Serbia.[68] Slovenia was divided between Germany and Italy,[69] the former planning merciless Italianisation and the latter the deportation of the population to make room for German colonists. The Italians also installed a puppet regime in Montenegro, parts of which, as well as Kosovo and western Macedonia, were ceded to Albania. This had been an 'independent' province of Italy since April 1940,[70] and the tariff and customs union which Italy had imposed was now extended to include the expanded territory. Only Rome was allowed to negotiate treaties with third-party states, and the government also assigned sole rights to Italian companies to extract its natural resources, especially its considerable offshore oil reserves. Mussolini's attempt to emulate Hitler's more ambitious and successful economic exploitation had nevertheless backfired somewhat. Despite the oil, subsidies to the tune of some 15 million leks had to be provided annually. Italy also took Dalmatia, the Adriatic Islands and a significant part of Istria for themselves,[71] further serving to right the perceived wrongs it had been forced to accept after 1919. An 'Independent' State of Croatia was also created, absorbing Slavonia and Bosnia-Herzegovina, but it was a distorted parody of the *Sporazum* of 1939.

A capacity for cruelty and barbarism that had not been seen before was also revealed. Antagonisms and antipathies which had to an extent been held in check under the monarchy now exploded into an orgy of recrimination and the settling of old scores. The governing ultranationalist Ustase embarked upon an uncompromising campaign of ethnic cleansing which they pursued until the end of the war. On 17 April 1941, the Legal Decree for the Defence of the People and State declared:

> Whosoever and in whatever manner offends or has offended against the honour and vital interests of the Croat nation, or in whatever manner threatens the existence of the Independent State of Croatia or the state authorities, whether in deed or whether in mere intent, this person had committed the crime of high treason.[72]

Using this warped legal document as justification, the Ustase proceeded to murder all those Serbs and their clergy they could find, burning their villages and destroying their places of worship. In Bosnia-Herzegovina they favoured the Muslims in a policy of divide and rule, deriding their Serb neighbours while lauding the Muslims as the 'flower of the Croatian people'. For their part the Hungarians embarked upon a genocidal campaign against the Serbs, measures duplicated by the Germans in the Banat. Not to be outdone, the Bulgarians and Albanians embarked upon similar reigns of terror. Caught in the middle was the small Jewish population of 36,000, who were hated by the Catholics and vilified by the Ustase. Subjected to all kinds of abuse, many were sent to the death camp at Auschwitz in Poland, where between 20,000 and 31,000 of them were to perish.

While the Nazi overlords were far from averse to this orgy of rabid nationalism and anti-Semitism, it was also proving inconvenient, interfering in the primary German aim of maximising the economic exploitation of the territories. There were deposits of coal, iron ore, silver, zinc, manganese, nickel, chromite and copper sitting in Serbia and Macedonia, and reserves of bauxite in Croatia. In the latter, all three branches of the armed forces had contracts worth 22 million Reichsmarks by June 1942, spread around twenty-one companies. By July 1943 there were orders worth 109 million Reichsmarks across sixty-three firms,[73] but the economic incompetence of the Ustase effectively scuppered any chance that Croatia would be a key element of *Großraumwirtschaft*. Unable to deliver the agreed quantities of Bauxite and other metals, or the grain that had been promised, the balance of payments deficit worsened. The kuna – the currency adopted upon the 'independence' of Croatia – was subsequently to lose 90 per cent of its value by 1943. Industrial production was also 10 per cent lower than before the war, and few of the 250,000 Croatians sent to work in Germany made a positive impact.[74]

Serbia, too, had large expectations to satisfy. By 1942 it had orders to the value of 13 million Reichsmarks to meet for parachute silk, aircraft components and other commodities. As elsewhere, the general productivity of its textile mills and other factories was disappointing, and even with forced labour only half the pre-war level of copper was extracted. Ultimately, Serbia's most significant contribution would be the 100,000 labourers sent to work in Germany.[75] The Nazis' failure to fully utilise the resources of the country could not be laid solely at the door of incompetent collaborators, however. After its invasion, Yugoslavia became embroiled in a bitter and ruthless civil war while simultaneously fighting Axis forces. The two main rival resistance armies – one comprising the long-outlawed communists under the leadership of Josip Broz, better known as Tito, and the other fighting for the return of the monarchy – were of particular concern. Between them they fought hard and bitter guerrilla campaigns, hampering Axis efforts to exploit the country, and compelling them to transfer much-needed forces from other fronts. The occupation of the country had at least imbued a sense of national purpose and a grudging acceptance of the need to work together to defeat the common foe.

Mitteleuropa had been another dream that defeat in 1919 had expunged. Then, following the breath-taking success of the German campaign in the west in the summer of 1940, it again became a reality. Soon after establishing themselves in Belgium, the occupiers re-annexed Eupen and Malmedy and directed that the commerce of Antwerp be suppressed for the benefit of German North Sea ports.[76] Although such small countries offered few of the potential riches promised by the exploitation of the Soviet Union, Belgium's administration, headed by Alexander von Falkenhayn as military governor of Belgium and Northern France, was determined to tap its resources to the utmost. Relations initially bore a veneer of respectability to ensure the population was kept compliant and passive. Consistent with practice in most countries occupied in the west, the German authorities left the government and administration in Belgian hands as long as they cooperated in the pursuit of *Großraumwirtschaft*. As in 1914, one way this could be undertaken was through the drafting of young Belgians to work in Germany. Although there was not yet any compulsion to do so, they had little option as their immediate prospects for employment at home were bleak, and there would also be no unemployment benefit for those who declined.

One measure taken to try to ameliorate the plight of the workforce was initiated by the Galopin Committee. Named after Alexandre Galopin, the governor of the main Belgian holding company, the *Société Générale*, it represented over 40 per cent of the country's industry, and it was hoped that by keeping factories open and employment high they might be able to ensure few people were sent to Germany.[77] This strategy inevitably threw up its own issues, as the committee naively thought it could refuse any contracts seen to be in the interests of the German war effort by blocking orders which might have a military dimension and delaying wherever possible the delivery of those it did fulfil. This policy was not entirely successful as it required unanimity, and there were several companies prepared to accept profitable contracts irrespective of their purpose.

Members therefore fulfilled orders for such undertakings as barrack and airport construction and the supply of materials for the Atlantic Wall. As a result of such collusion, industrial profits and dividends grew respectively to 3 billion and 2 billion Belgian francs in 1942, but there was no hiding the fact that this work was not for the benefit of the occupied.

Whatever the morals of such a policy, it did keep unemployment low and made the country important to the Reich economy. It meant that Belgium was also supplied with 596,000 tons of agricultural products in recognition of its usefulness, which contrasted favourably with those occupied territories deemed of negligible value to the war effort such as Greece, which was plundered mercilessly.[78]

Even so, such steps could not cushion the population entirely from its share of problems. The pressures of war and German expropriations saw rationing imposed and taxation become increasingly burdensome. Even before the war Belgium imported 1.2 million tons of cereals from Canada, the United States and Argentina, and once the blockade started to bite this accounted for a shortfall of some 17 per cent.[79] German largesse could only do so much to offset these shortfalls, and Belgium's agricultural production continued to decline. Nor could the best efforts of the committee spare the people from the Germans' insatiable demand for workers. Though trying to appear fully employed in work of vital importance to the Reich, the Belgians had compulsory labour imposed in October 1942, leading to nearly 150,000 more workers being sent to Germany, exacerbating the country's own problems but never proving enough to solve Germany's.[80]

These measures also stiffened resistance to the occupation, and in response to industrial action Belgians suffered a ban on trade unions, a clampdown on free speech and an administration increasingly staffed with yes-men willing to do the Nazis' bidding. As the oppression worsened and the bitter realities of collaboration with a criminal regime dawned on people, resistance intensified. It took a variety of forms, from passive to highly active and dangerous. Everything possible was done to undermine *Großraumwirtschaft* and render assistance to the Allies. Complex networks of escape channels for Allied airmen were formed, and resistance fighters carried out acts of sabotage. The German reaction was predictable, and brutal repression followed any acts of resistance. Before liberation came, 17,000 of those brave enough to challenge German hegemony had been murdered.

The Dutch nightmare echoed Belgium's, beginning with the destruction of the vital port of Rotterdam on 14 May 1940, which prompted the capitulation and subsequent occupation of the Netherlands. Unlike in the First World War, when its neutrality saw it spared the excesses of *Mitteleuropa*, the Netherlands was now deemed to be an integral element of *Großraumwirtschaft*. Newly installed governor Arthur Seyss-Inquart proceeded to extract all he could from the country to feed and supply the Reich. Soon after the Germans arrived in May 1940, vast quantities of oil, coal, textiles and cocoa beans were stolen, and from 1942 onwards Dutch workers were forced to work in Germany. Other arrangements were entered into more willingly, however. Dutch capital found its way into various Reich enterprises, and 12 million guilders was invested in economic initiatives via the Reich Ministry for the Occupied Eastern Territories, or *Besetzten Ostgebiete*, in the Baltic States, Belarus and Ukraine. Dutch businessmen offered their skills in managerial posts, while Dutch companies, rendered idle by the German occupation, also expanded eastwards. As the Dutch were categorised as Aryans, their farmers were invited to participate in the colonisation of the east, and on 22 November 1941 the first trainload of Dutch farmers set off by train to the vast steppes of the Soviet Union. By the time the territory was being recovered by the Russian army some 6,000 hapless would-be eastern European Boers had made their way there.

Such collaboration, willing or otherwise, was by no means emblematic of the Dutch people as a whole. Many clandestine organisations sought to undermine the occupation through a variety of means, increasing in sophistication as the war progressed. Some hid Jews while others created complex escape networks to help downed Allied aircrew escape capture and return to the UK. Strikes were quickly organised, and every means by which to disrupt the smooth running of the country were carried out.

Luxembourg, like Belgium occupied for the second time in a generation, was to be exploited in a similar fashion. The duchy originally came under the administration of von Falkenhayn, but in July 1940 one of his deputies, Gustav Simon, was appointed to the civil administration of the territory. In August its occupation status ended, and Simon's task was to prepare for its full integration into the Reich. His job was first to 'Germanise' the population by expunging all domestic and foreign cultural influences, and to this end German laws were enshrined in

Luxembourgish statutes, non-Nazis removed from their posts, labour unions abolished and political parties disbanded. The German authorities sought to remove any who refused to accept their fate, even passively. In all, around 1,500 families would be uprooted and deported to the east, and their places taken by Germans.

The country's most significant industry was steel production. However, things looked bleak when German supplies of coke were cut off before the invasion in May 1940 and were further depressed by the loss of the French markets. If Luxembourg was to recover, the value of its steel industry had to be made demonstrable to the occupiers, who of course saw themselves as the industrial core of the new order. Instead of investing in these furnaces, the Germans called up 1,200 foundry workers for army service and replaced them with workers from the east, demonstrating that this tiny outpost of the new Reich would not figure much in German plans for the foreseeable future. Despite the inevitability of the privations which were to be endured by all countries under German occupation, few among the tiny civilian population saw any merit in overt resistance. Remembering the brutal treatment of their compatriots during the First World War, most resigned themselves to their fate. Instead, as in Belgium, they mainly worked on escape lines for prisoners, downed Allied aircrew and those avoiding conscription for forced labour or the German army.

Denmark found itself in a similar situation to the Netherlands and Luxembourg, being of limited value to the Reich unless it could make some demonstrable contribution to *Großraumwirtschaft*. The country had been left isolated by the war, losing the UK as a major trading partner and with few natural resources of its own with which to barter apart from the pork and butter it would agree to send to Germany. Of more immediate importance was the fact that Denmark was dependent now upon Germany for its coal and oil supplies. Although the Danes had anticipated this and stockpiled before the war, these reserves could only last so long, and the government would need to ensure it could maintain supplies. To this end, in the spring of 1940 an agreement was negotiated with Berlin whereby workers would be provided for German mines in exchange for supplies of coal and oil. Although many such workers were to find themselves forced to work wherever they were needed, by 1941 this arrangement saw a total of 41,000 Danes working in Germany, or at home in Denmark for Germans.[81]

Resigned to being a German vassal for the foreseeable future, the Danish government also tried to seek a more advantageous arrangement and discussed deeper economic cooperation. These proposals included customs and monetary unions, but Germany's counterproposals, including a demand that Denmark abandon the krona, were strongly opposed by the Danish parliament, royalty and trade unions, and subsequently came to nothing. The stain of such potentially deep collaboration was eventually rescued by the coming of peace, although some firms did consider establishing branches in the east, and contracts were offered for the construction of industrial plants and other infrastructure projects. As in most of the other western European countries the Germans occupied, they also refrained at first from controlling the government and civil administration too overtly. Then, as Danish resistance to their rule intensified, the authorities responded with increasingly punitive measures, such as restrictions on freedom of assembly, stricter censorship and arbitrary arrests. When a military administration took total control in 1943, the move prompted strikes and threatened to paralyse the country. Nevertheless, well aware of the potential for brutal reprisals, the small kingdom mostly opted to sit out the war, limiting itself to the most discrete and clandestine means of undermining the occupation.

Thus Belgium, the Netherlands, Luxembourg and Denmark all had their respective roles to play in the grand Nazi scheme, but it was France, one of Europe's richest countries and the owner of a large overseas empire, that was the real cherry on the *Großraumwirtschaft* cake. It would also prove surprisingly easy to manipulate into contributing to the new order. A significant factor in this was that French society was bitterly divided, and it was this very division which many blamed for the ease with which its army was defeated on the field of battle, having collapsed in just six weeks. France had just emerged from a turbulent decade of extremist politics, in which the 1930s witnessed often violent confrontation. In 1935, a coalition of leftist parties came to power as the Popular Front, and introduced a raft of reforms, including the forty-hour week, paid holidays, the nationalisation of the arms industry and greater control of the country's financial institutions. These steps provoked rancour among capitalists and industrialists and led to inflation and capital flight. They also resulted in the return of a right-wing government which attempted to reverse some of the Popular Front's policies. By the time the Germans swept through the Ardennes in May 1940, these wounds were far from healed, handing Hitler an economy which, though bruised, was far from battered and offered huge prospects for the extension of *Großraumwirtschaft*.

After the capitulation, France was partitioned into five regions: Occupied, Vichy, the *Zone Interdit*, the north-eastern departments under the jurisdiction of Falkenhayn, and the annexed departments of Alsace-Moselle. Most people resigned themselves to their fate and hoped things would not be too bad. They rationalised their attitude by adopting the philosophy of *Collaboration a raison*,[82] an acceptance of their lot and of the fact that, as in 1871, Germany had won, and that they just had to make the best of it. It was now considered everyone's patriotic duty to pull together to help the country recover, and initially occupation brought an unexpected windfall. As in Belgium, defeat had created massive unemployment, with some 1.5 million made jobless by the sudden brake put on industrial activity. Then, as the Germans embarked upon their exploitation of the country, it enjoyed something of a mini-boom. Consumer demand was stimulated by the presence of 100,000 German occupation troops, 40 per cent of whom were stationed in Paris. Here they indulged in luxury items such as perfume and wine, and enjoyed all that the restaurants, bars, hotels and theatres had to offer. Although much of this spending power had originated in the 400 million francs a day that the Treasury had to find for the cost of the occupation, at least some of it was being recycled on the streets of Paris and other French towns and cities.[83]

Industry's order books also filled, with 70–90 per cent of the work coming from Germany. Contracts were signed in September 1940 between Aluminium Francais and two companies in Berlin and Dessau for the sale of aluminium and aluminium oxide. Also, late in 1940, contracts were signed between German firms and the Comptoir de Phosphates and the Mines de l'Ouenza for the delivery of raw materials such as iron ore. Both the occupied and unoccupied zones would export considerable amounts of food and raw material to the Reich before the liberation, the occupied zone in particular containing 76 per cent of the country's coal, 95 per cent of its steel production capacity, and half of its textile and metallurgical production.[84] In all, 63 million tons of coal, 1.9 million tons of petrol and fuel, 4.8 million tons of iron ore and 1.2 million tons of bauxite would be exported to Germany. By 1943 France would be supplying 2,887 tonnes of crude steel, amounting to 31.5 per cent of Germany's total monthly consumption.

Soon after the occupation, the Germans performed an audit of the country's assets, weeding out those deemed surplus to the requirements of the Reich. By 1942, 1,500 factories had been closed, mainly around Paris and producing luxuries such as ceramics, fabrics and furniture. Others which the authorities considered crucial to Germany's needs included the Renault motor car plant, and representatives of Daimler-Benz and the German military authorities arrived at the site of the factory in the Paris suburb of Billancourt to conduct a survey. In line with Nazi policy, they had been instructed to assess the plant and determine its suitability for wholesale removal to Germany along with its workforce, where it would be converted from motor car production to military vehicles. Instead, its owner, Louis Renault, offered to cooperate with the Germans in turning the factory over to war production so long as they undertook to leave it in situ. This made sense to the Germans, as they would be spared the time and trouble of having to break it down and reassemble it. For its employees, this meant being able to remain in their homes and work in familiar surroundings. Although at the time this appealed to everyone concerned as a logical compromise, Renault was arrested after the war. Although never charged with any crime, he died in custody and his business was confiscated by the state.

Renault's apparent altruism may well have been misplaced, but fellow industrialists, smarting from the endemic labour problems of the 1930s, quickly appreciated the opportunities presented by German victory. Eager to offload their burdensome factories, they also hoped in the process to divest themselves of troublesome employees and shop stewards by reporting them to the authorities as hostile to the new Franco-German understanding.[85] The Vichy regime of General Pétain and Pierre Laval proved equally keen to abet their new masters. As early as 16 August 1940, they set up the Comites d'Organisation to run the industries in their zone and manage the process of cartelisation designed to benefit big business and, of course, the Reich itself.[86]

The Nazis were not only concerned with France's considerable industrial potential; demands for cereals and other foodstuffs were also insatiable, with 2.9 million tons of wheat, 2.3 million tons of oats and 725,975 tons of potatoes being exported to the Reich. Nevertheless, such vast quantities could not be maintained without consequences, and shortages in fertiliser eventually affected yields. By 1943, land cultivated with grain dropped by 1.4 million hectares compared to before the war,[87] with a huge impact upon the economy and France's ability to meet both German and domestic needs. Edible oils and fats also became scarce, and commodities such as eggs, butter, cheese, meat and other basics were almost impossible to secure in towns and cities. The average daily intake of bread in 1940, 350 grams, had dropped to 180 grams by 1943, and children were developing symptoms typical of malnutrition, being more stunted than their pre-war counterparts. Adults found it harder to recover from ailments as their immune systems struggled to cope. People with relatives in the countryside started to beg for food parcels, and it was estimated that by 1943 some 13.5 million such packages had found their way into the postal system. Prices inevitably rose, but rather than impose controls the Vichy Government, in one of its rare examples of resistance, allowed a black market to flourish for as long as there were surpluses to sell. They reasoned that at least they could sell to French customers, whereas if legitimate channels were used the goods would probably be snapped up by the Germans.[88]

Inevitably, the German authorities embarked upon a drive to find recruits to work in Germany. By the beginning of 1941, a year after the campaign for volunteers to work in the Reich had begun, just 48,500 men and women had responded. In Vichy the government and the Germans reached an agreement whereby one prisoner of war would be released for every three people who volunteered to work in Germany. That would mean finding 4.5 million volunteers, if all French prisoners of war were to be returned. With the necessary quotas unmet, on 16 February 1943 Laval introduced the *Service de Travail Obligatoire* (STO) or Compulsory Labour Scheme. It meant that men aged twenty or twenty-one were to register for two years of service in Germany, although many also found themselves co-opted into the Organisation Todt to work on the Atlantic Wall.[89] Circumstance also played a role in helping to resolve some of the endemic labour shortages. The occupation had shut off a traditional destination for seasonal migrant labourers from Italy who went to northern Europe to work in the fields or in the mines of Lorraine. In 1931 over 29,000 had worked in the Longwy steel basin alone, and of these 18,500 were from Italy. As the Germans could use this manpower every bit as much as the French, an agreement was signed in February 1942 for the redeployment of 60,000 Italians to work on German farms. Such was the need for labour in the Reich that another 204,000 were sent to work in the factories.[90] Despite even these figures, German demand remained unsatisfied.

In his book *Inside the Third Reich*, Albert Speer, the minister of armaments and war production, described perpetual battles for manpower between Nazi ministries assigned similar objectives. On more than one occasion Speer found himself in competition with Fritz Sauckel, who in early 1942 had been appointed general plenipotentiary for labour deployment in the Office of the Four-Year Plan. Speer proposed to utilise factories in France to manufacture clothing, shoes and textiles, so that industrial capacity in Germany could concentrate upon armaments production. This involved keeping sufficient manpower in country to perform these tasks. Sauckel, on the other hand, was under intense pressure to meet his own demanding quotas and was trying to secure the same French workers as labourers in Germany. He needed 500,000, of whom half had to be found by March and of which 150,000 must be skilled workmen.[91] This tug-of-war persisted until mid-1943, when Speer complained to Sauckel and asked that the French staff working on behalf of the Nazis be exempt from conscription.[92] Speer suggested that these workers could be counted against Sauckel's quota as 'assignments to German armaments production' and thus satisfy his requirements.[93] Sauckel, fearful for his own position, did not go along with this proposal, so Speer went over both his and his boss Göring's head and appealed directly to Hitler. The Führer agreed with Speer – one of the few acolytes he respected – and Sauckel was told not to seek any further conscript labour from Occupied France. The same arrangements were to apply to factories in Holland, Belgium and Italy. Despite this decision, a constant interdepartmental struggle would plague the supply and allocation of manpower.

A crucial factor aggravating the constant shortage of labour was that Hitler, for reasons of morale, had always been reluctant to impose the same pressures upon his own people as he was prepared to inflict on those outside of the Reich. Despite the despotic and callous nature of the Nazi regime, Hitler remained conscious of the need to keep the people as quiescent as possible, effectively bribing them into collaboration with his plans. This reluctance to expose Germans to the realities of total war meant that as late as October 1943 some 6 million German civilians were still employed in the manufacture of unnecessary consumer goods,[94] with hundreds of thousands employed in the postal services and in other so-called reserved occupations. Therefore, while millions of Germans were employed producing items such as refrigerators or in roles designed to maintain morale, many of those foreigners pressed into service in Germany worked on weapons of war and in associated industries, often in appalling conditions.

Furthermore, many did so in enterprises which are still popular household names today. By the end of 1944, technology giant Siemens, a mainstay of the German economy since its foundation in 1847, had a total workforce of 244,000 which included 50,000 slaves. Even before the war started, the company gladly accepted 3,600 Jewish labourers to compensate for personnel called up to the armed forces. Advantage was taken of the free labour available at the female concentration camp at Ravensbruck to operate a factory nearby. Women's generally smaller, more slender hands and fingers were ideal for the intricate work involved in producing electrical switches and other fine components, and by 1944 2,300 were being used for such work. Hungarian prisoner Tikma Slomavic wrote:

> My two sisters and I built electrical switches for airplanes ... two shifts worked around the clock ... we worked at least six days a week for twelve and fourteen hours a day.[95]

Tikma and thousands of others may have been underfed, overworked and brutally treated, but the war was a boon for Siemens. A post-war analysis compiled in 1950 by the Office of Military Government for Germany concluded that 'the effect of the war was to make Siemens even more of a monopoly than it was before.'[96] It was not alone. Another mainstay of Germany's industrial hegemony was the Ruhr-based steel giant Krupp, founded in 1812. Key to Germany's preparation for war in the 1930s, the company produced everything from synthetic fuels and chemicals to warships, field guns and torpedo tubes. In all, the company exploited the availability of approximately 70,000 labourers and 23,000 prisoners of war in eighty plants around Europe, including Essen, Bremen, Breslau and Kiel.

Volkswagen, company of the eponymous car designed by Ferdinand Porsche and supposedly inspired by Adolf Hitler, had spread its commercial tentacles less widely than industrial behemoths such as Siemens and Krupp. Its factory at Wolfsburg in Lower Saxony only opened in 1939 but was soon commissioned to construct military variants of the VW, the Kubelwagen and the amphibious Schwimmwagen. A shortage of workers in 1940 was met by Italian labour, but as war demands grew the management sought additional – and cheaper –

manpower from more nefarious sources. Eventually 70 per cent of the workforce comprised Polish and Russian women, whose presence also created another problem for the management. When women fell pregnant, the factory offered them the services of an on-site creche which they were assured would care for their infants while they were on their shifts. Instead, such was the neglect and indifference shown to the children that 350 to 400 of them perished in miserable, insanitary and inhumane conditions while their mothers laboured in the car plant. Of far greater importance to the managers were the production quotas, and their exploitative and inhumane practices enabled them to produce an estimated 50,000 Kubelwagens and 14,000 Schwimmwagens during the course of the war.

The abuse and exploitation of Europe's labour force involved still more iconic car manufacturers. By 1944, almost half of Daimler-Benz's 63,610 workers were civilian forced labourers, prisoners of war or concentration camp inmates, and so too was much of the BMW workforce, with perhaps as many as 50,000 forced labourers, which also included concentration camp prisoners. Audi meanwhile had 20,000 slaves at its disposal, of whom 4,500 died at Flossenburg. Chemical companies, steel manufacturers and high-end motor manufacturers were not alone in this conspiracy of exploitation and brigandage. Fashion designer Hugo Boss also had its quota of skilled slave labourers working in sweatshops turning out uniforms for the Hitler Youth and the SS.

Nevertheless, as dystopian as the experiences of those tragic individuals were, there was another category of human suffering even more debased. Hitler's diabolical plan to consolidate *Großraumwirtschaft* by destroying all those states which still opposed him led to the development of weapons both ingenious and fiendish. These were the V1 flying bomb and the V2 rocket, weapons which if developed earlier in the war and in sufficient quantities may have turned the tide in Germany's favour. Fortunately for the Allies, interdiction raids and the advance of their armies had compelled the Germans to move their production facilities out of range and out of sight. This tactic, however, would prove the harbinger of even greater human suffering. The final destination for Polish and French coal and bauxite, Krupp steel and the other raw materials supplied through *Großraumwirtschaft* were these weapons, which in turn were tested and manufactured under the most inhumane and sadistic working conditions.

The manufacturing site was an underground complex of mines near Nordhausen in central Germany, originally worked for gypsum in the 1930s but deemed ideal for building and testing weapons. The site was expanded into a huge 1 million square foot complex of tunnels, using a total of 60,000 slave labourers from the nearby Dora concentration camp, mainly French and Russian prisoners of war. These men worked twelve-hour shifts, sleeping and eating where they laboured in filthy conditions, working assembly lines and unloading trains. Even Speer's own largely self-justifying book concedes to the utter barbarism of their working environment:

> ... the sanitary conditions were inadequate, disease rampant; the prisoners were quartered right there in the damp caves, and as a result, the mortality among them was extraordinarily high...[97]

Those who finally gave up, collapsed and died, 20,000 in all, were thrown onto the backs of lorries and transported to the crematoria at Buchenwald. Before their nightmare at the factory finally ended in March 1945, it had manufactured some 4,575 rockets which together killed fewer people than life in the factory did. After the war, some of those responsible were tried, but only a handful of the SS guards and officers ever received justice. The scientists involved were captured by the Americans and after a cursory interrogation departed for the USA to live comfortably while developing the plans they had nurtured serving the Nazis. Among them was the later famous Wernher von Braun, one of the geniuses who masterminded the V2 and whose skills would produce the rockets which eventually took man to the moon in 1969. Like Speer, he would later disavow any knowledge of, let alone responsibility for, the miserable suffering of those who served him in those fetid mines.

Few could have imagined the suffering that awaited one community. The Jews of Europe, since the days of their migration to the imperial centres of Germany and Austria, had been marginalised, shunned and then persecuted. For these benighted souls Hitler and his acolytes had in mind a particularly gruesome end. The tragic story of the 'Final Solution' is widely known for its wanton cruelty and the barbaric nature in which the victims' lives were destroyed at Auschwitz, Chelmo, Sobibor among other sites, and their remains disposed of in crematoria and on funeral pyres. It has been estimated that between 4 million and 6 million of Europe's 11 million Jews were slaughtered. What has been less widely appreciated is the manner in which this industrialised murder was gradually refined and perfected so that the programme could be incorporated into the economic pursuit of *Großraumwirtschaft* itself. Many scholars agree that when the Nazis embarked upon their programme of expansion and exploitation, they might have been largely content with the expulsion of the Jews and the expropriation of their property. Initially, the so-called *Einsatzgruppen* which accompanied the *Wehrmacht*, along with the regular forces themselves, engaged in large-scale massacres of Jews, and the shooting of entire communities by murder squads became common practice to expedite the disposal of those communities they encountered.

One example of many thousands was witnessed in the Polish village of Jedwabne near the border with East Prussia, its population of 3,200 divided more or less evenly between Poles and Jews. When the Nazis arrived in July 1941, the gentiles suddenly gave vent to pent-up jealousies and resentments which, as we have seen, went back generations. One villager later recalled that:

> ... my wife came and told me to get up and said that bad things were going on. Near our house people were beating Jews with clubs ... many tried to escape into neighbouring fields, but only a few succeeded ... a small vigilante group of peasants were milling around and trying to ferret out and catch hiding and fleeing Jews...[98]

Hunted like animals, the desperate Jews had nowhere to go. Others faced even worse fates than beatings; one witness recalls Jews herded into a barn which was then 'doused with gasoline and lit, and in this manner fifteen hundred Jewish people perished'.[99] Encouraged tacitly and then openly by the Nazis, and increasing in scale and scope as they extended their reach throughout Poland, the Baltic States and Russia, such acts saw the beating, burning and shooting to death of tens of thousands of completely innocent people. The policy lacked proper direction and focus, however; the objective was to kill people and then seize their property and assets. Beyond that, no firm plans existed to maximise the benefits from exploiting entire communities.

There was a sea change in policy and planning following the invasion of the Soviet Union when the Nazis realised that the victimisation of the Jews of Russia, in addition to those of Poland and the rest of eastern Europe, presented a huge logistical and organisational challenge. The Nazis had been experimenting with gas vans, in which Jews were packed and then killed by the vehicle's exhaust fumes, but this was just as slow as mass shooting. Then a subsidiary of IG Farben, Degesch, solved the problem with a product it had been manufacturing since the early 1920s: Zyklon, a widely used pesticide. The soon-to-be infamous brand was manufactured in crystal form, creating blue pellets which produced a lethal hydrocyanic or prussic acid gas when exposed to the air, and which due to its highly toxic nature was stored and transported in airtight circular metal tins. This 'B' variant had caught the eye of those charged with effecting the 'Final Solution', and negotiations were soon underway to work out how to apply the product to the perpetration of genocide. Experiments were undertaken in the cellars of the infamous 'Death Block II' in Auschwitz in September 1941 using hundreds of Russian and Polish prisoners. Having calculated how to perfect the poison for its new application, lucrative contracts were signed by both the *Wehrmacht* and the *SS* to produce millions of the tiny pellets. Degesch used the firms Tesch and Stabenow of Hamburg and Heerdt-Linger to distribute the poison to murder camps scattered all over Nazi-occupied Europe.

This solution came in time to meet an almost commercial approach to the issue of removing the continent's Jewish population. The newly established 'independent' Slovak state had at its head an ultra-right-wing government of rabidly anti-Semitic Catholic zealots. They were desperate to rid themselves and their society of their Jews. When the Germans asked for forced labour early in 1942, they eagerly offered 20,000 of their Jewish workers on condition they also took their elderly, sick and very young dependents, totalling about 90,000. In exchange for divesting them of their unwelcome Jews, the Slovaks would pay compensation of 500 Reichsmarks for each deportee. Having arrived at an agreement, deportations began in April 1942, in time for the subjects to fall victim to the most efficient means ever conceived for mass murder. However, not all those destined for the gas chambers went straight to their deaths. For some there was a brief reprieve.

The fate of millions more had also been decided, but before they were ready to travel they needed to be held somewhere in readiness. To this end, hundreds of thousands were packed into ghettos in cities such as Warsaw, Krakow, Lublin, Minsk and Smolensk. One was at Lodz in the General Government of Poland, which had long been the centre of the country's textile, shoemaking and tailoring trades, and contained tens of thousands of skilled artisans. It was in the interests of the commercially minded occupiers to maximise the profit to be made from those held captive, and was equally seen as a means for the victims to prolong their lives for as long as they could prove useful. Thus, by 1943, nearly 100 factories, employing 70,000 people – some 85 per cent of the ghetto's total population – were working ten- to fifteen-hour shifts producing items such as uniforms, accoutrements and boots for the Germans. This mutually beneficial arrangement continued for some time, but eventually the ghetto's inhabitants were herded onto cattle trucks headed for Auschwitz. Before they were shipped off, those who had any property left were told they should pack everything they would need for their new life in the east – pots, pans, bedding and such. Before they boarded the transports, they were told to label these items carefully, because they would follow later. Instead they were looted and sent to German cities, allocated to those whose property had been lost in air raids.

The railways were originally developed as part of the unification of the peoples of the German and Austrian empires and to stimulate commerce and trade. The coming of the Nazis, however, meant that like so many other aspects of European society they were to be put to far more malign uses. The cattle trucks and engines which once transported food, fodder and livestock from one corner of the continent to another instead carried people. The criminal most associated with 'keeping the trains running' was Adolf Eichmann. He had attended the notorious Wannsee Conference in January 1942, which decided upon the manner and means of the exterminations, and his role was to be considerable. He was responsible for the identification, assembly and, perhaps most infamous of all, transportation of the Jews from all over occupied Europe to their ultimate destinations in the death camps. He achieved this with the use of only 2,000 trains, provided primarily by the Deutsche Reichsbahn (DRB), the Polish Ostbahn and other national carriers.[100] The management of the railways also meant that although each trainload contained space for an average of 1,000 transportees, as many as two or even five times as many could be crammed into each shipment, giving each person just 2 square feet of space for an excruciating journey lasting days or weeks.[101]

Once they had arrived at the extermination camps, the cursory selection process separated those to be worked to death and those to be despatched immediately to the gas chambers – those too old, too young or too infirm to perform labour. They were told they were going to take a shower and their clothing was to be deloused, so they stripped naked in the huge changing room. Thus relieved of their shoes and spectacles, plus any prosthetic limbs and long hair, they were herded into the gas chamber where the door was shut behind them and it went dark. Then they stood waiting, before the sound of the Zyklon B pellets being sprinkled above their heads could be heard. An *SS* guard on the roof in a gas mask had opened a vent and proceeded to pour the poison down the shaft, where it reacted with the air to create the lethal gas. Those inside immediately began to gasp for air, panicking and struggling to escape, but all would be dead within fifteen to twenty minutes. The poison air was then pumped out, and another fifteen minutes later the *Sonderkommando*, or prisoner orderlies, began to drag the bodies out.

Before they were disposed of, gold fillings would be removed, and women's intimate parts examined for any other valuables they had managed to conceal. What did not find its way into the pockets of the guards, usually cash and jewellery, would be sent back to Germany and reused, including the prosthetic limbs, spectacles and shoes. In the meantime, the bodies of the dead were sent to the crematoria, and their ashes scattered around the grounds of the camp. Still their use to the economy of the Reich was not over. In January 1943, the commandants of eleven camps received orders from the *SS* to ship the hair from the women victims to three processing plants in the Reich. It was first 'cured' in the lofts over the crematoria and then gathered in 20-kilogram bales before being shipped off for use in the manufacture of such things as thread, rope, cloth, carpets, mattress stuffing and the lining of U-boat crew's boots. It was also used in the manufacture of delayed-action bombs. At twenty pfennigs a kilogram, it proved an extremely lucrative contribution to the profit-and-loss sheet of *Großraumwirtschaft*.

Those Jews spared selection for the gas chambers, and for whom there were still uses, were brutally exploited as free labour in nearby factories. These factories were established specifically for this purpose, so that the evil cycle of death and misery could further profit the persecutors. Perhaps one of the most infamous belonged to IG Farben, parent company of the patent-holder for Zyklon. One of the other enterprises which the company was hoping to exploit was the production of synthetic rubber, and Auschwitz was selected as the site for its manufacture. It was chosen primarily because it was on level ground, close to sources of water, coal and other raw materials and could use the excellent rail links established to bring the prisoners destined to be murdered in the gas chambers. To this end, those selected from the death transports that arrived at Auschwitz were initially put to work constructing the factory, which was finished in October 1942. Named Auschwitz III, 'Monowitz', up to 11,000 prisoners were there at any one time, many worked to death or sent to the gas chambers once they proved incapable of labouring any longer. Thus even the 'Final Solution', the plan to eradicate all Jews from German-occupied Europe, proved a highly efficient and profitable enterprise, contributing to the Nazi war chest.

Few if any of these components of *Großraumwirtschaft* could have been implemented as efficiently if the Nazis had relied entirely upon coercion and compulsion. In every allied territory, and every land they occupied, the Germans found willing collaborators ready to participate in the creation of the new European order. It has never been easy to put an accurate figure on the number of collaborators the Nazis were able to recruit, but in France at the beginning of 1941, the Parti Populaire Francais (PPF) is believed to have contained 6,000 members, and the Rassemblement Nationale Populaire (RNP) had an estimated 20,000. In Belgium there were perhaps 20,000 in the Rex Party, which closely aligned itself to the ambitions of the Germans for a greater Europe, and there were also some 50,000 people in the Vlaans Nationaal Verbond (VNV). In the Netherlands the Nationaal Socialistiche Beweging (NSB) had something in the region of 100,000 adherents in total by 1945.

Many may have been attracted by the potential perks rather than ideology, but there were others who made a more philosophical contribution to the cause of uniting Europe behind the Nazis. Men such as the Belgian Pierre Daye, who published a book in 1942 entitled *L'Europe aux Européens*, in which he argued for pan-Europeanism as a defence against both the communists and the dominance of Anglo-Saxon capitalism. In Norway, the infamous Vidkun Quisling took power in 1942 and proceeded to try to shape Norwegian society to meet the demands of *Großraumwirtschaft* by introducing the corporate state and indoctrinating the population through education and the Church. His efforts were vigorously resisted by the majority of the population, however, who rejected all such efforts to integrate their nation into the greater Reich. Quisling, whose very name, despite his failure, became synonymous with treachery and collaboration, was tried after the war for treason and subsequently executed. In the Netherlands, Anton Mussert shared the aspirations of his Norwegian counterpart, but he too lacked the common touch, the charisma or the authority to carry his people. His writ never extended beyond his NSB membership, and despite his verbosity and grandstanding, his enthusiasm for *Großraumwirtschaft* never translated into results. France too had to face the post-war world as a net collaborator with the German occupiers. The humiliation of defeat was translated into that of partition, giving many Frenchmen the awful choice of sullen acquiescence, resistance or collaboration. As we have seen, many politicians, such as Pierre Laval and General Pétain, eagerly snatched at the chance of more power, and keenly cooperated with German plans. Although such widespread collusion helped the Nazis fully execute their policies, Hitler's worldview, and that of the Nazis more generally, meant that another potential opportunity was slow to be exploited.

Unlike so many of his predecessors – Napoleon, Bismarck and the Habsburgs among them – who saw integrated militaries as integral to their vision of a unified European super-state, Hitler initially did not appear to subscribe to this philosophy. In fact, he had insisted on 23 March 1939 that 'the populations of the non-German territories will not be called upon for military service but will be available [instead] for labour service.' He certainly adhered to the latter half of this edict, but the exigencies of war meant that he would promptly have to re-evaluate the former. The execution of his plan for the invasion of the Soviet Union could not have been possible on the colossal scale envisaged had it not been for the inclusion of many non-German contingents.

On 22 June 1941, in addition to German troops the invasion force consisted of a Hungarian Army Corps, an Italian Army Corps and two Romanian Army Corps, in addition to Czechs, Ruthenes and Serbs, Austrians and Finns. This immense undertaking, involving 3.5 million men, delivered the first multinational European army under a single command since 1914. The other arm of the Nazi war machine, the *Waffen SS*, grew tenfold during the war to nearly a million men, thanks at least in part to recruits from Norway, Holland, Latvia, Estonia, Bosnia and France. Its ranks even grew to include captured Russians, employed to garrison the Atlantic Wall and serve in anti-insurgency roles. Nevertheless, this dilution of the organisation was not universally welcomed by its existing members. *SS Brigadeführer* Theodor Eicke was scathing about the quality of these additions, considering them to be 'intellectually substandard ... they do not understand the words of command and are inclined to insubordination and malingering.'[102]

Nevertheless, collaborationist groups saw advantages to associating with the *SS* beyond simply ingratiating themselves with the Nazi leadership. Mussert offered 300,000 men, and Léon Degrelle, the leader of the Rex Party, demonstrated his loyalty to the greater German idea by commanding a unit of volunteers to fight in Russia alongside the Germans. Degrelle's *SS Wallonia* fought with particular determination, perhaps because they felt they had little to lose; of 2,000 men, only 632 survived. The Legion des Volontaires Francais contre le Bolshevisme (LVF) was formed as a stand-alone unit of the *Wehrmacht* by former communist Jacques Doriot, who was awarded the Iron Cross in recognition of his contribution to the Reich's war effort.

One significant exception to this apparent enthusiasm was tiny Luxembourg. As we have seen, the German occupation authorities saw it now as a *Gau*, an integral part of the Reich, and as such its qualifying males were eligible for service just like any other German. The Luxembourgers, however, did not see it that way. They had almost unanimously declined to become German, and when orders for obligatory military service were issued in August 1942, the people responded with strikes and other expressions of resistance. The Germans reacted with their characteristic brutality, beginning with the shooting of twenty-one hostages and the transportation of hundreds more to concentration camps. Despite virulent opposition, 11,168 men were conscripted, of whom 2,848 would be killed or reported missing in combat on the Eastern Front. Many were shot for desertion.

Superficially, the European crusade against Bolshevism enjoyed widespread support and embraced determined participants from across the continent. At one stage the ranks of the *Wehrmacht* included 3,000,000 foreigners or 18 per cent of its total number. Had they succeeded in extending and consolidating *Großraumwirtschaft* across the Russian steppes and on to the Urals, they would have been guaranteed a place in the pantheon of Nazi lore. Instead, the drawbacks far outweighed the advantages. Research revealed very similar problems with cohesion and discipline as that which existed within the multinational Austro-Hungarian army in the First World War:

> Army units with a high degree of primary group integrity suffered little from desertions or from individually contrived surrenders. In the *Wehrmacht* desertions and surrenders were more frequent in groups of heterogeneous ethnic composition in which Austrians, Czechs and Poles were randomly intermixed with one another. In such groups the difficulties of linguistic communication and the large amount of individual resentment and aggressiveness about coercion into German service, the weakened support of leadership due to their inability to identify with German officers ... hampered the formation of cohesive groups.[103]

Racial attitudes soon relegated any non-Germans to second-class status and exposed them to discrimination when it came to the allocation of rations, shelter, equipment, weapons and ammunition. Instead of camaraderie and *esprit de corps*, all that was fostered was division, so rather than help to sustain and preserve the German Reich the *Wehrmacht*'s new patchwork hastened its downfall.

The effect of the war on Germany's allies could be gauged from entries found in the diary of a Hungarian soldier killed at Stalingrad. One entry records his distrust of both his allies and the minorities in his own army: 'How can we possibly trust those who are not Hungarian?' Another reflects the utter misery of the fighting: 'Oh God, stop this terrible war. If we are to take part in it for much longer our nerves will break.'[104] The ultimate failure of the *Wehrmacht* was due to its military collapse rather than animosity within its ranks, but this was symptomatic of the general failure of the Nazis to foster the conditions necessary to impose *Großraumwirtschaft*. The incoherent, overlapping structure of the Nazi state prevented effective coordination of effort and the prioritisation of objectives. As we have seen from Speer's account, different departments often pursued similar aims but lacked any motivation to cooperate. Although a limited policy of collaboration in the west did, to a certain extent, facilitate improved outcomes for the Nazis, in the east, as seen in Ukraine, the local populace was alienated even though their active participation could have proved invaluable. Expecting to win, and therefore never having to atone for their excesses, the Germans saw no need to work with those they conquered and oppressed. To them, the ends justified the means.

As the Nazis finally confronted defeat, their propaganda machine cynically sought to promote the prospect of a European Economic Community based upon mutuality instead of exploitation and enslavement,[105] but it was too late. The end came as the result of the combined military might of the Allies – the vast Russian armies moving inexorably from the east and, from 6 June 1944, the British and American armies pushing from the west until the Reich consisted of little more than the immediate confines of the *Führerbunker*. Here Hitler's warped dream finally ended on the late afternoon of 30 April 1945, when he put a gun to his head and simultaneously bit down on a cyanide capsule, essentially the same compound which had been used to despatch millions of Europeans in his name. The charge sheet the Nazis left behind was used as the basis for Europe's next show of unity, the Nuremberg War Crimes trials, which saw many of Hitler's co-conspirators condemned to death. Count 3 of the indictments summarised the accusations:

Systematically terrorising the inhabitants [of occupied territories] ...

[The] policy of the German government and High Command to deport able-bodied citizens from such occupied countries to Germany and other Occupied Countries...

Ruthlessly exploited the people and the material resources of the countries they occupied, in order to strengthen the Nazi War Machine, to depopulate and impoverish the rest of Europe, to enrich themselves and their adherents, and to promote German economic supremacy over Europe.

Conscripted and forced the inhabitants to labour and requisitioned their services for purposes other than meeting the needs of the armies of occupation and to an extent far out of proportion to the resources of the countries involved. All the civilians so conscripted were forced to work for the German war effort ...

Section J stated:

In certain occupied territories, purportedly annexed to Germany, the defendants methodically and pursuant to plan endeavoured to assimilate these territories politically, culturally, socially and economically into the German Reich, and the defendants endeavoured to obliterate the former national character of these territories. In pursuance of these plans and endeavours, the defendants forcibly deported inhabitants who were predominantly non-German and introduced thousands of German colonists.

The defeat of the Nazis had been made possible by the harnessing of a shared determination among the nations of Europe, those defeated and occupied as well as those able to resist invasion or occupation. It was not only the superhuman efforts of the Soviet Union in resisting and then repelling the *Wehrmacht*, the gallant efforts of the British people, supported by thousands of men and women from throughout their Commonwealth and Empire, or the significant contribution of the American forces. The three great powers were also assisted and supported by thousands of Europeans who had fled occupation to fight as Free French, Free Czech, Free Poles and those who remained behind to resist the occupiers in many other ways. It was an unprecedented joint effort which together won over the dark forces of evil and returned the continent to a sort of peace. Hitler, Goebbels and Himmler were dead, and others such as Göring, Sauckel and Speer were awaiting trial. They had all abandoned their evil work, leaving millions of victims to pick up the shattered remnants.

Throughout the continent the living symbols of Nazism's perverted version of freedom of movement survived in the form of some 60 million displaced persons (DPs). These former slave workers, conscript workers and prisoners of war from every former occupied territory sought a way home or turned to criminal activity to survive. In May 1945 the number of DPs in the western zones of occupation alone stood at 4 million.

There were 1.5 million Russians, 1.2 million French, 600,000 Poles, 350,000 Italians, 200,000 Dutch, 200,000 Belgians, 100,000 Yugoslavs, 60,000 Czechs, and 10,000 Danes, Norwegians, Greeks and

Luxembourgers.[106] Many were placed in special camps to await repatriation. Some used their new-found liberty as an opportunity to exact revenge upon their former torturers. In Munich, DPs made up just 4 per cent of the population but records claimed that they were responsible for 75 per cent of the city's crime. In November 1945, a mob of DPs killed thirteen Germans in a single night; orders were subsequently issued for anyone caught participating in such lawlessness to be shot out of hand. As long as DPs remained on German soil the problem persisted, and even in 1947 there were still half a million in the country.[107] The scale of the task was described in a letter written by Major General Gerald Templer, deputy chief of staff for the British element of the Allied Control Commission in Germany, to Margot, Lady Reading in October 1945:

> It is obviously hard for you in England to realise the immense difficulties which have confronted us in our task of repatriation and bringing relief to the 2.5 million displaced persons we found in this zone at the beginning of our occupation. They are completely disorganised, in need of food, clothing, accommodation, fuel and medical treatment, and require repatriation at the earliest possible moment...[108]

Nonetheless, for many the prospect of return to their home countries was not welcomed. This applied in particular to those Soviet citizens who for one reason or another had ended up in Germany. Many were 'volunteers' who had agreed to serve the Reich rather than perish in a camp, while others were among the 2 million who had been pressed into service but for whom the thought of return was an unimaginable horror. Lieutenant Michael Bayley, of Princess Louise's Kensington Regiment, was serving in Hagen-Haspe in the Ruhr and was charged with collecting those to be returned to the Soviet Union. He recalled '[Russian] people who had literally been slaves on German farms, falling on their knees in front of you and begging to be allowed to stay'.[109] Nor was Lieutenant Bayley's experience an isolated case. Captain Anthony Smith, on secondment from the Royal Artillery to help in a similar role in an areas around Winsen, south-east of Hamburg, reported how 'it quickly became apparent that 99 per cent of these people did not wish to return to the motherland, because ... life as slave labourers in Nazi Germany had been better than life in Russia.'[110]

In the American zone, too, problems of unwilling returnees arose, as an official review covering the period 1 October 1946 to 30 September 1947 explained. As of that date there were 328,000 DPs being held in 393 assembly centres, and during 1945 an average of 332,000 had been repatriated every month. This plunged to just 4,150 a month in the first nine months of 1947, and was at 2,427 in September of that year.[111] The reason for this, the review admitted, was quite simply that they did not want to go:

> The United Nations DPs now remaining in the US occupied area are essentially those for whom a return to their homeland offers no attraction as long as the present political and economic uncertainty continues to exist in Eastern Europe.[112]

This is even more shocking when one considers what most of these people would face if they remained. Nearly every significant European city was either badly damaged or completely destroyed due to shelling, bombing, street fighting or deliberate acts of destruction by the retreating Germans. Widespread famines had broken out as a result of agricultural production plummeting by up to 20 per cent compared to pre-war levels, and there was little or no fertiliser, seeds or working farm machinery to be found with which to improve the situation.[113] Compounding the loss of agricultural productivity was the fact that livestock levels had also plunged by 44 per cent.[114] Industrial production had dropped by two-thirds,[115] and the only functioning seaports were at Antwerp and Bordeaux. Damage to Dutch infrastructure and its means of production amounted to some 7.7 million guilders, double its GNP.[116] Only three of twenty-six major railway bridges were still usable, and nine out of fifty-nine of its most important road bridges. Some 85 per cent of its docks for handling bulk goods had been wrecked, and half of its Rhine Fleet shattered. During the fighting and particularly during their retreat, the Germans deliberately flooded 200,000 hectares of the country, equal to 8.5 per cent of its cultivated surface area, leaving part of Zeeland useless until 1953.[117]

The war had seen half of Poland's industry destroyed with as much as 80 per cent of its 30,000 factories, 75 per cent of its bridges and 84 per cent of its rail infrastructure destroyed, along with 30 per cent of the housing stock, totalling a 70 per cent loss in productive capacity.[118] It was estimated that damage to the tune of US$50 billion in 1939 values had been inflicted on the country and its population, amounting to US$626 per head of population.[119] Nearly 85 per cent of Warsaw had been levelled by the Germans as the result of bombing and systematic demolition following the Polish uprising. Of the 25,000 buildings standing in the pre-war city, hardly any survived. It had a thriving population of 1.5 million in 1939, but by 1945 only a few thousand remained,[120] eking out a feral existence amid the bombed-out houses and shattered streets. Captain Klochov of the Soviet 3rd Shock Army later recorded that he and his troops 'saw the destruction of Warsaw when we entered its empty streets … nothing was left but ruins and ashes covered by the snow. Badly starved and exhausted residents were making their way home.'[121] In all, Germany's policies in Poland saw the destruction of some 6 million Polish lives, over 21 per cent of the country's pre-war population.

Vienna, once Emperor Francis-Joseph's pride and joy, had also been bombed and fought over. The city so adored by its citizens as a quiet oasis of calm amid the hustle and bustle of the empire had become a monument to hubris. Whereas Francis-Joseph's legacy as emperor lay in its magnificent buildings, Hitler as its latter-day overlord had marred the skyline with three huge flak towers with walls 11 feet thick, not that they proved entirely effective. Fifty-two air raids resulted in nearly 37,000 houses being rendered uninhabitable. St Stephen's Cathedral, to which the emperor had processed with such solemnity and pomp in the old empire's heyday, had suffered grievous damage. Most of the roof, the north tower, the gothic windows and the choir had been destroyed. The Vienna State Opera House, much admired by Hitler, had been another sorry victim. Although the façade, frescoes, the main stairway vestibule and the tearoom had survived, the auditorium and the stage had been destroyed, along with the props and 150,000 costumes for many of the operas young Hitler had admired. Another casualty was Hitler's nemesis, the Academy of Fine Arts, which had twice rejected his application to enrol as a student. Spared the destruction wrought upon its neighbours by the bombing, it would nevertheless forever sport the bullet marks etched into the walls of its storehouse. Street battles fought between advancing Russian troops and defending Germans had also reduced countless roads and streets to rubble-strewn thoroughfares, and shops and houses into strongpoints. In this devastated city, the population now struggled to survive.

Beyond the capital, cities spared for much of the war found themselves targets as the conflict progressed and became increasingly bitter. The town of Graz suffered fifty-six air raids, Linz forty-eight, Wiener-Neustadt twenty-nine. In all, between 13 August 1943 and the end of the war, 120,000 tons of bombs were dropped on Austria, killing 30,000 Viennese and 1,980 in Graz. Only eighteen houses in Wiener-Neustadt were left intact, and the population dropped from 45,000 to 860.[122]

On 11 February 1945, Prague, a hotbed of Czech-German nationalist street-fights in the days of the monarchy and latterly capital of the tragically short-lived Czechoslovak state, was also bombed. Widespread damage was inflicted by the 150 tons of ordnance that was dropped, and 2,000 people were killed or wounded. Ninety-three buildings were destroyed. A month later the industrial north-east was targeted, with another 370 people killed. The Skoda factory was hit, as well as the Faust House, the Emmaus Monastery and the Vinohrady Synagogue.

Of Budapest, once the capital of the proudly independent-minded Magyar half of the Dual Monarchy, only 20 per cent survived. All of its bridges and 32,000 of its homes were destroyed or damaged; the

Hungarian parliament was gone, as well as the great castle and the old palace. Those fortunate enough to survive were to be found huddled petrified in cellars and tunnels, hiding from the Russians when the vengeful behemoth entered the city. Poet and novelist Sandor Marai, was moved to describe how 'your feet will sink in blood ... the scattered dead gaze at the heavens. Smoke signals swirl up from the depths of the firmament ... side by side in the castle church lie corpses of dead princes and slaughtered horses.'[123]

Across those parts of the Soviet Union occupied by the Germans, more than 3,000 towns and cities had been destroyed and 17,000 villages wiped off the map. 427 of its museums were plundered, and 1,670 Russian Orthodox churches, 532 synagogues and 237 Catholic churches were destroyed or damaged, including the cathedrals at Kiev, Chernigov and Vitebsk. The human cost the Russian people paid has been calculated at 10 million soldiers, over a third of whom were deliberately starved to death in captivity, and between 10 million and 15 million civilians – one fourth of its population. Furthermore, in addition to the massive expropriations of natural resources and theft of property, the Germans stole 180 million books and 500,000 works of art.

In Leningrad alone, the Germans had destroyed 15 million square feet of housing, depriving 716,000 people of their homes. In addition, 526 of the city's schools and other places of learning had been destroyed, along with twenty-one scientific institutions, 101 museums and similar buildings, 840 factories and seventy-one bridges. Of the Hermitage Museum, founded by Catherine the Great, 300,000 square feet of rooms and 60,000 square feet of glass and windows had been damaged. The financial toll of the 900-day siege the city endured was estimated at 45 billion roubles.[124] The city of Stalingrad, also subject to a disastrously counter-productive campaign by the Germans which has been identified by many as the beginning of the end for the German army, had been so mercilessly bombed and shelled at the very outset of the campaign that only 20 per cent of its structures survived the opening of the battle. Furthermore, in addition to the military losses, some 40,000 civilians trapped inside were killed during the six months of fighting there.

As for Germany, the country responsible for all this misery and destruction, it had sown the wind and unsurprisingly had reaped the whirlwind. As the *Times* editorial of 8 May 1945 put it, 'In a score of great cities of Germany barely a building stands intact; the Russian armies have swept like an avenging hurricane over the shattered avenues and palaces of Berlin.'[125] It had lost 10 per cent of its pre-war population, or 7 million people, and of all Germans born in 1924, 25 per cent had been killed and 31 per cent wounded by 1945. The *London Evening News* of 8 May 1945 described 'more than sixty million Germans cooped up in compounds, waiting in bread queues, wandering about aimlessly'.[126]

Hamburg, once christened the Venice of the north for its network of canals, had reportedly sustained more damage in the war than all the bombed cities of Britain combined. RAF Bomber Command had done its utmost to put it out of commission, and by the war's end its port was blocked by fifty sunken ships and nineteen floating docks.[127] 76 per cent of Frankfurt's houses were uninhabitable; in Cologne it was 66 per cent, and in Hanover 99 per cent. Of 16 million houses in Germany some 2,340,000 were completely ruined, and 4 million sustained at least 25 per cent damage, leaving 20 million people homeless in western Germany alone.[128] It was calculated that the total area of the rubble across the entire Reich ran to 400 million cubic metres, equal to the entirety of Great Britain.[129] Across the British zone of Germany, only 1,000 of 13,000 kilometres of railway was working, and only half of Germany's locomotives and a third of its coaches were serviceable.[130] The sights which met the members of the Allied forces of occupation shocked even war-hardened veterans. Second Lieutenant Phil May of the Green Howards wrote home in April 1946, 'The Ruhr towns are really in the most terrible state ... you could not realise how shocking it really is. Mile after mile of absolute ruin and destruction.'[131]

The capital of the Third Reich was arguably the most shattered city of them all. Reuters correspondent Harold King sent a report on 10 May 1945:

> Berlin is a city of the dead. As a metropolis it has simply ceased to exist ... Among hundreds of well-known landmarks which have disappeared or been irreparably damaged are the former Palace, the Opera House, the French, British, American and Japanese Embassies, Goering's Air Ministry, Goebbel's Propaganda Ministry, and the Bristol and Adlon hotels... [132]

King's account told only half the story. Bombing and shelling had laid waste to more than 10 square miles of Berlin's built-up area, leaving 3 billion cubic feet of debris to clear up. After the British and Americans between them had dropped 75,000 tons of bombs,[133] around 1.5 million homes had been damaged in one way or another, and every third house was either completely destroyed or uninhabitable. Of 33,000 hospital beds, only 8,500 were usable, and 95 per cent of the city's tram system had been destroyed.[134] Amid all of this, the authorities had to try to find accommodation for the almost 30,000 refugees flooding into the city and its 53,000 orphans.[135]

At the top of the ruined *Kurfürstendamm* stood what remained of the Kaiser Wilhelm Memorial Church. The hands on the clock were fixed at 7.30 p.m., the moment that a bomb from a morning air raid in November 1943 led to its destruction. The 630-acre Tiergarten looked like a First World War battlefield, filled with bomb craters, shattered stumps of trees and rubble-filled lakes overlooked by the gutted embassies.[136] The Reichstag, once home of the German Empire but left empty by Hitler's

Reich, was now a gutted, bullet-ridden shell covered in graffiti, with the streets around it barricaded with furniture and other items plundered from the surrounding ruins. The Kroll Opera House, where Hitler's dictatorship was sanctioned, was now a rubble-laden skeleton, and the apartment blocks put up during Berlin's heyday had been turned into strongpoints, their cellars packed with cowering refugees and homeless Berliners. It was calculated that it would require ten trains of fifty wagons working non-stop every single day of the year for sixteen years to remove all of the rubble.[137] US Army Colonel Joe Stevens, who was despatched on a fact-finding mission by the Supreme Headquarters of the Allied Expeditionary Force, surveyed the devastation and reported solemnly that Germany's 'ability to wage war in this generation has been destroyed'.[138]

Such was the legacy bequeathed to Europe by *Großraumwirtschaft*: a continent united in misery, suffering and destruction, its victims looking not for reconciliation and rapprochement but justice and revenge.

11

The End of This War
Will Be Written in Blood

Edward Benes, co-founder of Czechoslovakia and author of the infamous Benes
Decrees. (Library of Congress)

Even as the attempt to enslave the continent was being implemented, Italian
anti-fascists Altiero Spinelli and Ernesto Rossi were optimistically looking
forward to the new Europe which could emerge from an Allied victory. In
June 1941, from their prison cell on the island of Ventotene in the Tyrrhenian
Sea off the southern coast of Italy, they urged their fellow Europeans to
embrace the idea of a new post-war settlement. They blamed the present
catastrophe on the very nature of the continent's pre-war structure and the
territorial jealousies it had stoked and were convinced that the vicious cycle

261

of war punctuated by uneasy peace had to end. The so-called Ventotene Manifesto which emerged from their deliberations roundly condemned the outcome of the 1919 peace settlement for 'creating boundaries through areas inhabited by mixed populations' and 'providing seaports for landlocked countries', insisting that such problems could have been avoided entirely if the continent had existed as a socialist 'European Federation'.

The authors also believed that the Europe they now envisaged would 'have at its disposal a European armed service instead of national armies', thus hopefully eliminating the means by which the continent might go to war with itself again. The two expressed their conviction that 'a free and united Europe is the necessary premise to the strengthening of modern civilisation' and called for 'the definitive abolition of the division of Europe into national sovereign states'.[1] Considering the fact that they were then incarcerated in a prison cell on an island overseen by German guards, they did not advocate a punishing peace with Germany, and warned that it should not be 'broken into pieces or held on a chain once it is conquered', thus repeating the mistakes of Versailles. It was hardly surprising, however, that such magnanimity would receive at best a lukewarm reception and at worst cynicism and hostility when the war finally ended and the true extent of Nazi crimes became evident.

Equally optimistically, Winston Churchill and President Roosevelt signed the Atlantic Charter in August 1941, which echoed President Wilson's overly ambitious vision of a new world order following the First World War. Self-determination, equal access to trade and raw materials, economic progress and peace were all avowed sentiments which would be incorporated into the Declaration of the United Nations on 1 January 1942. The United Nations Organisation, which followed on 24 October 1945, finally consigned the defunct and discredited League of Nations to the dustbin, its headquarters shifted from Geneva to New York as befitted the United States' new pivotal role among the arbiters of international affairs, assuming the mantle so unceremoniously rejected in 1919. Its mission statement, by repeating the sentiments of the Atlantic Charter, promised the dawning of an era of peace and reconciliation.

These fine words, however, were the high-minded aspirations of those who had themselves been spared the most terrible consequences of the war. Germany's immediate victims were less magnanimous and instead looked to the end of the war as the day of reckoning for the suffering which had been inflicted upon them. The day after VE Day, Captain Saul Padover, a historian and political scientist serving as an officer in the Psychological Warfare Division of the United States Army, reflected the general mood when he wrote that

> ... by this act of defeat, the Germans were more cut off from the rest of the world than ever before. They were no longer members of the community of peoples but a race apart, cursed and feared as no race has

ever been in recorded history. Only the coming generation of Germans can redeem their country...[2]

These thoughts were shared by the editorial of the British newspaper *News Chronicle* on 9 May 1945:

> [Hitler's] people have been given such an object lesson as no nation, lusting after power, has ever had before. If the Germans are not at this time well and truly convinced of the folly of their ways, their minds are indeed impermeable.[3]

Conservative MP Mavis Tate had campaigned against the Nazi persecution of the Jews in the late 1930s. Having visited the concentration camp at Buchenwald, she returned incensed by the horrors she had witnessed:

> ... the Hun ambition may be foiled, but the Hun spirit still lives... There is a deep streak of evil and sadism in the German race ... only with extreme firmness will we eliminate the beat from the German heart...[4]

Thus it would not be enough to expunge every vestige of the Nazi ideology that had brought Germany and its neighbours to their knees. Many were convinced that Germany had to be prevented from ever again visiting such an apocalyptic experience upon Europe.

Despite the noble sentiments expressed in the Atlantic Charter, Germany's fate was far from decided, and in 1944 President Roosevelt asked Henry Morgenthau Jr, secretary to the Treasury, to prepare a draft paper for him to take to the Second Quebec Conference. He wanted something he could discuss with the Allies to determine the fate of post-war Germany, and the conclusions were utterly uncompromising. Morgenthau not only advised that Germany be demilitarised but also proposed its almost complete de-industrialisation. Divested of the means to wage war, it would become a semi-pastoral society, like Switzerland, content to pass its days tilling the fields and milking its cows. The industrial might of firms such as Krupp and the rich deposits of raw materials which had fuelled Germany's growth into a world power would be allocated to its neighbours. Poland would be awarded those parts of East Prussia which had not been occupied by the Soviet Union, plus the southern portion of Silesia. France would take the Saar and the Ruhr, and the surrounding area would be internationalised. Much of the Ruhr would also be stripped of its industrial infrastructure and these assets distributed as reparations in lieu of cash. The rest of the country would be divided into two autonomous and sovereign states, North and South Germany, isolated from politically but linked in a customs union with neighbouring Austria.

This revolutionary solution was presented at the conference when it convened between 12 and 16 September 1944. It understandably met with a positive response from General de Gaulle and Jean Monnet, whose Five-Year Plan had also envisaged the internationalising of the Ruhr and the Rhineland and the imposition of a protectorate over the Saar. President Roosevelt, too, was initially favourable, finding in the proposal the means by which to remove the need for America's sons to have to intervene militarily on the continent again. He also assumed that Churchill would be amenable to a solution that would render Germany harmless and make the British the dominant state in Europe. Instead, the astonished British leader likened such an outcome to being 'chained to a dead body',[5] while foreign secretary Anthony Eden explained that such an outcome would ultimately leave Germany unable to feed its population and simply make it an economic liability not only to the UK but to the rest of Europe.

Furthermore, Churchill insisted that the undoubted crimes of the Nazis should not be used as an excuse to 'indict a whole nation',[6] and he was not alone. There were other moderate voices who believed a peaceful and prosperous future for the continent rested upon a de-Nazified and rehabilitated Germany. This approach reflected Rossi and Spinelli's position, at least with regards to the post-war treatment of Germany, and as events would prove, harshly punitive measures were not among the options adopted by the victorious powers. Moreover, events in the west were to show that a lenient peace was in the interests of Europe as a whole.

Subsequently, while demilitarisation was accepted as essential, complete de-industrialisation was seen as counterproductive. Instead, the Yalta Conference of February 1945 agreed that Germany should be divided into zones of occupation and pay reparations of 20 billion Reichsmarks, largely through the dismantling and redistribution of a proportion of its industry as well as the labour of its people. Furthermore, it was to be agreed that German industrial production once back up and running must not exceed 75 per cent of its 1936 level. This was when the Four-Year Plan to prepare for a war economy had begun, and the country ought not profit from any of the schemes and plots hatched by the Nazi regime. The policy of extracting reparations in kind proved to be a wise one. Its cities may have been laid waste, but Germany's physical industrial infrastructure had again survived, battered and bruised but remarkably intact. Thanks in large part to the efforts of men such as Albert Speer, Germany ended the war with 75–80 per cent of its plant and 90 per cent of its mining and steel industry still functioning. Even in the Ruhr, only 30 per cent of plant and machinery had been destroyed.[7]

Indeed, such had been the resilience of the German war economy despite years of bombing by the RAF and the USAAF that even in December 1944, 218,000 rifles had been manufactured (twice as many as in 1941), and an astonishing 1,840 armoured vehicles had been built (twice as many as in the whole of 1941). Four times as many automatic weapons and five times as many tanks had also been produced at the war's end than at the beginning.[8] Krupp, even at the height of the bombing campaign, was able to produce 520,000 tons of steel in 1942/43 and another 475,000 tons in 1943/44.[9] Of course it must also be remembered that much of the vital raw material needed to facilitate this remarkable resilience was provided at the expense of the countries Germany had occupied, but nevertheless, when the Allies entered Germany's industrial heartland they encountered substantial resources and assets, which, despite their best efforts, had survived to be exploited to their advantage now that peace had been achieved.

Clearly, the conversion of so much of Germany's industrial potential under the Nazi Four-Year Plan had to be reversed, but the assets to be allocated between the Allies still left a healthy industrial base upon which to draw. The Allies later insisted that despite the largescale removal of industrial plant, the loss to the German economy amounted to no more than 3 per cent of the total, or 700 million Reichsmarks. The Germans' own audit produced a much higher calculation of 5.3 per cent, but even this figure meant that nearly 95 per cent of Germany's industrial potential had been left intact, and this, as we have seen, was not much worse than it had been in 1939. Therefore, Germany likely retained sufficient economic slack to recover once its reparations obligations had been met.

Unfortunately, now that Nazism's defeat had been secured, relations between the Western Allies and the Soviet Union were beginning to sour, and one of the earliest signs of friction came over the division of the spoils. Although much of this had been agreed at Yalta, with 75,000 tons of steelmaking equipment already shipped to Russia by February 1946,[10] the Soviets were exhibiting undue haste in the removal of anything and everything that could be taken from Germany and be put to use in Russia. This enthusiasm for exacting the maximum in reparations was also contrasting poorly with Moscow's reluctance to adhere to other undertakings made with its allies. While the German civilians in their care were receiving scant attention with regards to food, medicines and the other necessities of survival, the British and American zones were costing their respective taxpayers nearly US$600 million a year, of which US$64 million was spent on Germany in 1945 and US$468 million in 1946.[11] The fact that the Russians were doing next to nothing by comparison was starting to cause considerable unease, compounded by the fact that they were lax in supplying the western zone with the quotas of cereals that had been agreed in exchange for coal and dismantled plant. The food aspect of the agreement was particularly problematic because the Soviet zone contained most of the the country's agricultural and pastoral land. The Western Allies badly needed its produce; as General Lucius Clay, military governor of the US zone, explained:

… we have to have food. West Germany had never been self-supporting. Even Germany as a whole could not raise enough to sustain its people

... Moreover, the produce was not available to the western zones. Yet the population in these zones had increased by about 4 million and was to increase still more...[12]

By May 1946, the situation had become so acute and relations so bad that the shipment of reparations to the Soviet zone was halted in the hope that the Russians would decide to be more accommodating.[13] This was not done on a whim. The Soviets were also acting in bad faith in eastern Europe, and generally failed to meet their obligations and honour the undertakings which had been made during the war. Alarm bells rang in the British and American camps, and discussions were held to consider the best response to Moscow's growing estrangement. Churchill had warned Roosevelt of such an outcome during the war, but his caution was overruled by the US president, who naively thought that the Russian dictator was a man of his word. Now the chickens were coming home to roost, and the Soviet Union's plans for their zone were clearly diverging from the more liberal regimes favoured by their former allies.

It was also evident that treatment of Germany on anything like the lines of the Morgenthau Plan would have been disastrous and entirely self-defeating, and even the compromise of using German industrial capacity as reparations might wreck its economy if the Russians continued with their rapacious policy. Recognising this, on 5 September 1946 the British and Americans decided to shield their western zones as best they could by agreeing to merge them, creating a combined so-called Bizone, to be officially established the following year. The French, for their part, no doubt in their desire to turn the tables on their erstwhile occupiers, preferred to continue with their mandate. Unlike their allies, they even managed to make a profit of US$2 million on their occupation costs by imposing similar charges upon the Germans as had been extorted out of them during four years of German occupation.

Leaving France to plough its own furrow, the British and the Americans proceeded to consolidate their positions, and in Stuttgart on 6 September US secretary of state George Byrnes gave a speech in which he clarified US policy. He left no one in his audience in any doubt that he envisaged no de-industrialised wasteland dependent upon western aid. He confirmed that 'Germany should be administered as an economic unit' and insisted that the zones of occupation should not be treated as 'self-contained economic or political' entities. Essentially, he said, 'we favour the economic unification of Germany' and a 'central German administrative agency [for] industry and foreign trade' so that the country could in time stand on its own two feet. Byrnes did assuage French concerns to some extent by confirming that 'Germany must be prepared to share its coal and steel with the liberated countries of Europe,' but at the same time he added that it 'must be given the chance to export goods in order to import enough to make [its] economy self-sustaining'. His French audience would also have been glad to hear him concede that 'the United States does not feel that it can deny to France ... its claim on the Saar territory ... [but] ... she should readjust her reparation claims against Germany' in return.

This concession however, was more than offset by Byrnes' insistence that 'the United States will not support any encroachment on territory which is indisputably German ... the people of the Ruhr and the Rhineland desire to remain united with the rest of Germany. And the United States is not going to oppose the desire.' As French foreign minister Léon Blum later admitted, the Morgenthau Plan was now a dead letter and France had no choice but to toe the line. 'In the matter of Germany,' that is the imposition of anything like a vengeful peace, 'France was now a voice crying in the wilderness.'[14] It would not be de-industrialised or pastoralised, partitioned or relegated to the status of a vassal, but encouraged to thrive and make a positive contribution to the recovery of the continent. In time, the Bizone would be enlarged to include the French zone and encouraged to evolve into a self-sustaining political and economic unit under German administration and Allied support. Nevertheless, Germany would have to accept some sanctions.

The French protectorate over the Saar would last for ten years, during which time France would be allowed, as after 1918, to exploit its huge coal reserves, and by 1949 it would account for a quarter of all French output. Other than that, there were to be few if any of the territorial gains achieved at the end of many of the preceding wars, and particularly those seen at the end of the First World War. Alsace-Lorraine of course, re-annexed in 1940, was once again returned to France, and the other territorial adjustments made by the Nazis in the west were also revoked. The Dutch, who had shared the French appetite to expand their borders at Germany's expense, hoping to enlarge the country by as much as 50 per cent, did not see their aspirations met. The Americans vetoed the idea and the Dutch had to be content with just 69 square kilometres of the German Reich. Even this would eventually be repatriated in 1963, in exchange for 280 million Reichsmarks.

Like the French, the Netherlands had endured a long occupation as the Germans spent four years extracting every ounce of profit from the country. The end of the war understandably saw their former subjects in little mood to be magnanimous towards their conquerors as well as those fellow Dutchmen who collaborated with them. Dutch minister of justice Hans Kolfschoten was particularly uncompromising and composed a plan to expel the German population, codenamed Operation Black Tulip. Replicating the frequent experience of Dutch men and women during the occupation, those earmarked for deportation, now designated 'hostile subjects', would be woken up in the middle of the night and given an hour to collect their belongings before being taken to a transit camp, from which they were subsequently returned across the border. Nevertheless, the ejections did not commence until 1946, and when this project ended with the signing of peace between the two countries in 1951, only 3,691 Germans had been deported. This was just 15 per cent of what had been the country's German community, so it could have been much worse.

The British, true to their seemingly limitless capacity for extracting humour out of misfortune, were urged by the popular raconteur, dramatist and satirist Noel Coward to take pity on their defeated foe. During the war he penned a light-hearted ditty in which he implored his compatriots not to 'be beastly to the Germans', not to 'be beastly to the Hun', which inevitably met with a mixed reception, although Churchill was said to have been rather amused. It seemed to fairly reflect the general feeling of relief that victory had been achieved and that most people simply wanted to pick up their lives where they left off and move on. Many German and Italian prisoners of war who had been incarcerated around Britain decided to remain, and such was the warm reception they received from the British that many married and built families and careers in the UK. A well-known example was Bert Trautmann, a paratrooper who was captured and found himself a prisoner in Lancashire. Declining repatriation, he went on to become goalkeeper for Manchester City Football Club. Although far from unanimously welcomed at first, he soon gained the fans' respect and would become immensely popular.

In the west, then, Germany and its population had escaped much more lightly than might well have been the case had the situation with Russia been different. It was to be in the south and the east that Germany would suffer the greatest losses, both territorially and ethnically as those Germans who had settled and lived alongside their neighbours for generations paid the price for the failure of *Großraumwirtschaft*.

As we have seen, from Czechoslovakia to Russia, German minorities had coexisted for generations, frequently in a privileged position over their neighbours, and when the two great European empires dominated the continent they had often been skilled artisans, engineers, landowners or government officials. After the collapse of the empires they were resented as unwanted reminders of the past, or as disruptive minorities agitating against their new governments. After 1919, they were often used as pawns for German propaganda, and following the German conquests had re-established themselves as advantaged minorities. In Romania, for example, the Germans in Transylvania enjoyed privileges following a statute guaranteeing them the right to make their own laws, and in Croatia and Slovakia the *Volkdeutsche* were practically self-governing. In Bratislava they were represented in the ministry by their own secretary of state, and the taxes they paid were used exclusively for their own benefit. They enjoyed the fruits of the Nazi conquests in Poland and the Czech lands, profiting from the discrimination practised upon those regarded as racially inferior.

These same people were now isolated and exposed, at the mercy of the people whose enmity they had engendered for so many years.

The resentment and animosity felt against them had now reached the point where the only practical solution was their wholesale removal. At Potsdam, the 'Big Three' agreed with the application of ethnic cleansing and issued a decree to the effect that 'the transfer to Germany of German populations or elements thereof, remaining in Poland, Czechoslovakia and Hungary, will have to be undertaken.'[15] Article XII specified that the expulsions should be done in an 'orderly and humane manner',[16] although, as would be demonstrated before too long, the expulsions and population exchanges that followed would be far from that.

In any event, the victorious Allies were really only validating decisions which had been taken years before by governments exiled in consequence of Nazi aggression. Czechoslovakia's Edward Benes had fought to create a free Czech state only to see it betrayed and dismembered in 1938. He and the rest of the government-in-exile had to sit and wait as news of the outrages and indignities inflicted on his people filtered back from his country. He remembered the role the Sudeten Germans played in bringing about his nation's downfall and then exploiting and profiting from its annexation to the Reich. He was determined that peace would bring about a final reckoning and reiterated his government's position in a lecture at Manchester University as early as 2 December 1942. He openly and avowedly advocated that as soon as liberation was achieved the government would implement a policy of ethnically cleansing the Sudeten Germans from his country once and for all.[17] As the Nazi reign of terror proceeded, Benes became more strident and uncompromising, and on 27 October 1943, he gave a speech on the radio:

In our country the end of this war will be written in blood. The Germans will be given back mercilessly and manifold everything they have committed in our lands since 1938 ... there will be no Czecho-Slovak who does not take part in this task and there will be no patriot who does not take just retribution for the suffering the nation has experienced.[18]

His government proceeded to lay the groundwork for their return to the country, when they would be able to put his threats into practice. These measures were to become known as the infamous 'Benes Decrees', steps that were deemed perfectly valid at the time but which, over fifty years later, would prove highly controversial. On 8 May 1944, Benes decreed that any crimes committed against Sudeten Germans and Magyars by Czechs between September 1938 and 28 October 1945 were to be defined as legal acts.[19] This gave virtual immunity to any Czech who conspired to perform, participate in, or abet the killing of anyone even suspected of being a collaborator. It also exposed any Sudeten German or Magyar to intimidation, arbitrary arrest or even execution, leaving them with no recourse to the law. When Benes met with his Communist counterpart Klement Gottwald in Kosice in April 1945, his decrees were not only sanctioned but legitimised within the newly formed National Government Programme. Having agreed the reconstitution of the Czechoslovak state, the document approved the wholesale expulsion of those Germans and Hungarians who had been complicit in the occupation of Czechoslovakia and who actively collaborated in and profited from the suffering inflicted upon the Czech and Slovak populations. In the meantime, Benes proceeded to issue a raft of further decrees designed to prepare the ground through a process of coercion and intimidation.

On 19 May 1945, Benes legitimised the confiscation of any property owned by 'unreliable persons' – namely Germans and Magyars – who 'had served the war effort for Fascist or Nazi purposes'.[20] This was followed on 19 June 1945 by the aptly named 'Retribution Decree', authorising trial in 'Special Peoples Courts' of anyone suspected of supporting the Slovak Republic, the Protectorate or German rule in the Sudetenland.[21] Those found guilty faced imprisonment or death. On 28 March 1946, the provisional Czech government passed a law stating that all Germans were jointly and severally guilty of any crime committed against the Czechoslovak state and would therefore be punished collectively. They were stripped of their citizenship and property rights and their expulsions began, with 1.3 million destined for the US zone and 800,000 for the Russian. Only those considered useful for post-war reconstruction would be allowed to remain after being recategorized as 'anti-fascists'.

Thousands more were sent to concentration camps, where many died due to maltreatment and disease, and still more suffered in forced labour camps. It has been alleged that, in all, some 10,000 died in Bohemia and Moravia between 1945 and 1948. Carpathian Germans also fled or perished in camps such Svaijava, and others were sent to Siberia to work in labour camps. Of the Slovakian Germans, just 24,000 remained after the expulsion, and according to figures compiled by the German Federal Ministry for Expellees in Bonn, a total of 267,000 Germans died at the hands of the Czechs during the expulsions from the Sudetenland.[22] In order to ensure every last vestige of their presence was expunged, the towns and villages where they had lived and worked for centuries suffered the traditional ignominy of having their German names erased and replaced with Czech ones.

The Slovaks were also determined to be rid of their Magyars. Benes, however, having obtained the agreement of the Allies for his plan to expel all Germans and Magyars in 1943, found the British and Americans less enthusiastic when at the end of the war they realised the scale of the project. The Russians saw things differently, and particularly approved of removing minorities judged to be a potential threat to Stalin's new eastern European order. In January 1945, Soviet foreign minister Molotov suggested Slovakia and Hungary undertake a straight population exchange, an idea which did not appeal to the Hungarians but which the Slovaks understandably welcomed.[23] In the interim, and irrespective of Hungarian sensibilities, the Slovaks embarked upon a programme of Slovakisation whereby those Magyars who did not chose to leave of their own volition were left in no doubt about the future they faced in a hostile new state.

As early as 25 May 1945, all state employees of Hungarian nationality were dismissed without compensation, and those who had already retired had their pensions stopped. The Hungarian language was banned, and telegrams and letters written in Hungarian were left undelivered.[24] A further decree of 22 June confiscated all Hungarian-owned real estate of more than 50 hectares and another of 22 July seized all the cash and valuables deposited by Hungarians in the country's banks. In addition, a programme of Slovak colonisation of Hungarian areas was started, and 40,000 Magyars were resettled nearer to the border. So swift and uncompromising were these measures that they alarmed the Western Allies, but the Czechs and Slovaks had friends in high places. It might have been assumed that the US ambassador to the newly reunited Czech and Slovak state, Laurence Steinhardt, would provide a balanced account of what was happening. Instead he preferred to gloss any concerns over: 'Reports of persecutions and expulsions ... have been grossly exaggerated and have been designed to operate as a spearhead [for Hungarians] to win the peace after having lost the war.'[25]

Despite the treatment being meted out to the Magyars in Slovakia, or perhaps because of it, the prospect of a population exchange was seen by many observers as the best solution. The problem for the Hungarians was that 75 per cent of the Magyars in Slovakia were dependent upon the land for their livelihoods, so uprooting them for a new life in a strange country with few prospects presented a major problem. One suggestion was that they remain in place and get on with their lives but with Slovakia ceding to Hungary the land they occupied. The Slovaks would have got rid of them and the Hungarians would not have to take in landless peasants with no means of making a living. Unsurprisingly, the Czech government dismissed this practical if politically unacceptable idea out of hand.

With an impasse reached, it was proposed to pass the whole problem to the Allied Council of Ministers to adjudicate upon, and an agreement was finally signed on 27 February 1946. It was nevertheless a very one-sided affair. Magyars were to be subjected to compulsory resettlement in Hungary, but ethnic Slovaks had a choice over whether they migrated to Czechoslovakia. In the event, it is estimated that between 45,000 and 120,000 Hungarians were expelled and their property seized, while approximately 72,000 Slovaks emigrated in the other direction. Although the worst excesses experienced by the Sudeten Germans were for the most part avoided in Slovakia, the conditions of departure were equally severe and the transport similarly spartan. Deportees were allowed to carry a total of 100 kilograms of food, clothing and other luggage, and would travel by rail in tightly packed trains.[26] It was all reminiscent of the traumas recently endured by the victims of German spite and callousness, and perhaps that was the intention (though none of those was allowed to carry and keep 100 kg of belongings).

In the meantime, the fate of Hungary's Germans was being decided. On 20 November 1945, the Allied Control Council approved a plan for their expulsion, by which time tens of thousands had already left the country alongside the German army as it fled from the Russians.[27] The Soviets understandably saw this measure as a logical corollary of the need to accommodate expelled Magyars. As Soviet delegate Andry Vyshinsky stated dryly on 20 September 1946 at a session of the Political and Territorial Commission for Hungary:

> 500,000 Germans from Hungary must be transferred to the American zone in Germany ... the second question is this: if these 500,000 people are transferred from Hungary to Germany, will there be room enough left in Hungary for 200,000 Hungarians transferred from Czechoslovakia? I think ... there should be no objection therefore on the part of the Hungarian government to receiving Hungarians in place of Germans.[28]

Germans in the east faced equally dire experiences. Initially over half a million fled in the face of the invading Russian armies in January 1944 and a further 100,000 from Memel and Gumbinnen. Their suffering might have been less severe had their officials not delayed issuing orders to evacuate. Many officials shared the Nazis' ideological refusal to accept defeat, while others feared the reaction should they be seen to have invoked evacuation plans prematurely. Consequently, it was not until the end of October 1944 that instructions were received to evacuate the civilian population from a zone about 25 miles behind the fighting front, with over 600,000 people relocated to Saxony, Thuringia and Pomerania.[29] Many evacuees harboured hopes that their removal was only a temporary measure, believing in the ultimate German victory that would allow them to return home, unaware of the decisions being made by the Allied powers and bilaterally between the Poles and Russians. A few thousand determined individuals did manage to return clandestinely, only to be expelled again when the official programme began.

In scenes reminiscent of the tactics employed by the Nazis, the Polish authorities carried out early-morning raids, giving Germans only minutes to pack belongings before they were despatched across the River Neisse in massed groups. Anyone who tried to re-cross, or simply looked as if they were thinking of it, was fired upon by Polish and Soviet troops.[30] Those not destined for removal westwards faced a possibly even worse fate:

transportation to Russia for forced labour. As in Czechoslovakia, only those who had skills the Poles needed to assist in the economic recovery of the country remained, and thousands of miners and industrial workers between the ages of seventeen and fifty were spared the round-ups and the treacherous marches east and west.[31] Those despatched to the industrial districts of the Urals, the Donetsk Basin and the Don, or the collective farms of Russia, faced terrible conditions which did not improve until 1948, when the health conditions of many workers reduced productivity so much that the decision had to be taken to close the camps. In all, it was calculated that 100,000 to 125,000 of those transported to the east perished there.[32]

Poland had also realised significant territorial advantages at Germany's expense, the Allies having agreed that 'Poland should receive a considerable increase in territory in the north and the west'[33] in addition to the territory it would recover and which it had owned in 1939. This concession was largely academic, as Poland and the Soviet Union had already undertaken to move their respective borders, with the former being compensated in the west for her concessions in the east. This step returned to the Russians much of the territory ceded at the Treaty of Riga, which it had seized in 1939 and lost again in 1941. Starting in March 1945, once the land had been liberated, and in accordance with the bilateral agreements made with the Russians, the first Poles from the territories ceded to the Soviet Union were being resettled. They would need somewhere to live, so more Germans would be victimised by a decree which declared that 'all property which had been given up and abandoned' would forthwith be forfeited to the Polish state, regardless of the circumstances.[34] Those not yet expelled were subject to arrest and summary justice in 'Extraordinary Criminal Courts', a policy of collective punishment that led to thousands being sent to work in terrible labour camps such as that at Katowice in Upper Silesia.

Once Danzig was designated a 'Regained Territory' and came under Polish law, a provisional authority for its administration was established in May. Its task was to expedite its resettlement by Poles and an extensive publicity campaign was mounted in order to attract those with the skills needed to work in the mines and factories. Attempts were even made to lure those miners of Polish origin from as far afield as the Ruhr and France, who along with their forbears had many years before sought work and a better life.[35] Poles began to move into East Prussia, East Pomerania and Silesia, seizing property and occupying farms. In echoes of what was taking place in Czechoslovakia, German mayors were dismissed, and civil servants and other professionals were replaced by Poles. The zloty was introduced throughout the Regained Territories, and German place and street names substituted with Polish ones. Polish was declared the official language and the use of German severely suppressed. Ethnic Germans were also ordered to distinguish themselves by wearing distinctive armbands. The human cost of the deportations was frequently overlooked as the desire for vengeance concentrated the minds of the Poles, who were motivated primarily by the need to establish a homogeneous nation no longer encumbered by ethnic tensions and the need to take account of the interests of this or another minority group.

Alarmed by reports emerging from the east of such developments, the US expressed its concerns. Representations were made to the Polish and Soviet governments, but they met with little sympathy. Both had suffered so much under Nazi rule that they had no pity for those Germans left to face the music. Nevertheless, mindful that US cooperation was still desirable, they eventually agreed to meet and discuss the situation. On 17 November 1945, an arrangement was reached whereby 3.5 million Germans still located in the east would be shared between the British and Russian zones. Once again, things would not be quite what they seemed. The Soviets undertook to accept 2 million and the British the balance.[36] In fact, according to figures compiled by the Polish authorities, 1,178,872 deportees had left between 25 February and 1 September 1946, but the British zone had already taken 956,654 up to August. Another 183,196 had made their way on their own.[37] Official British figures showed that their zone had received 1,360,821, or 83.4 per cent of the 1,632,562 deportees expelled during 1946 alone. Clearly, the Russians were deftly endeavouring to divert the elderly, sick and underage from their zone to the British while withholding the fittest and the youngest for use as forced labour. Such were the pressures being placed upon the British that a unilateral decision had to be taken to drastically reduce the number of transports accepted in their zone. The episode also served to further underline the deteriorating relationship between east and west, and to justify the decisions being taken by the British and Americans.

In the meantime, the Poles were proceeding with their own programme of resettlement, keen to replace those expelled Germans with their own people. The massive undertaking reached its peak in 1946, with Polish government figures indicating that between 14 February 1946 and 2 January 1947 the population had increased by nearly 2.5 million to 4,584,000. These included 1.4 million Poles resettled from areas ceded to Russia, 237,000 displaced persons who had been repatriated from central and western Europe, and just shy of 2 million from elsewhere in Poland. The total population by the end of 1948 was just over 5 million, and numbers continued to rise until 1952, when it peaked at 6 million.[38] In addition, approximately a million ethnic Germans remained and adopted Polish citizenship; many of them had Polish names, spoke Polish and had lived among their fellow countrymen for generations. In an attempt to regularise their status, a decree of April 1946 restricted the granting of Polish nationality to those Germans who could prove their lineage and who were prepared to pledge an oath of loyalty to the state. In a further decree of January 1951, all remaining Germans who were still in the country were required to adopt Polish citizenship.[39]

Treating Germans in this arbitrary manner may have fulfilled its primary purpose, but as a consequence it split families from their loved ones. Perhaps understandably, there was little sympathy for those who had suffered in this way, and little or nothing was done in the short term to address the issue. Eventually, though, consciences were pricked. From March 1950 until the end of 1952, a programme codenamed 'Link Action' was operated to reunite families separated and estranged by the expulsions. By the time it ended, 44,000 more Germans had been transferred to Germany – mainly the old, infirm and sick.

Poland's desire to be a unitary homogeneous state also extended to the Jews who remained, having escaped the persecution of the Nazis. Approximately 200,000 had survived the war as refugees in Russia, and their repatriation began in 1946. By June, a total of about 140,000 had returned. However, for these people there was no warm welcome, for they found their properties taken over by strangers who resented their return, especially when they asked awkward questions. The war and their shared suffering had not diminished the longstanding suspicion and resentment which their fellow Poles had for them, and there had been little sympathy for those sent to be gassed in the extermination camps. Once these people had been loaded onto lorries, and then packed into the cattle trucks that took them off to be murdered, that was supposed to have been the last anyone heard of them. Thus, tragically and perversely, many of those who had survived the discrimination of the 1930s and the mass slaughter of the 1940s fell victim to the brutal reception that awaited them upon their return when peace came.

The hostility and suspicion directed at those who dared to show their faces again was such that the animosity spilled over into random violence and then pogroms, which were carried out as part of a policy to intimidate them and force them to move away again. One particularly tragic affair took place at Kielce in July 1946 when forty-one Jews were killed and sixty injured by bitter Poles desperate to be rid of them. As a consequence, more than 64,000 Jews had fled by September 1946, and by November a total of 120,000 had left for Germany, Austria and Italy. By the summer of 1947, 247,000 Jews had been given sanctuary in reception centres in the western zones of Germany, in Austria and in Italy. Some 73 per cent were from Poland; the remainder were Romanian, Hungarian, Czechoslovakian or German.[40] Finding no peace or security in post-war Europe, the lure of Palestine as a haven from persecution became irresistible to many, and between 1947 and 1951 approximately 387,000 European Jews fled to the fledgling state to begin new lives free from persecution.[41]

There were old scores to settle in Yugoslavia as well. The internecine hatred and tribal animosities brought to the surface by the German and Italian occupations had not been assuaged by their defeat or the coming of the Soviets. As the German army made good its escape from Yugoslavia, the Croatians saw that their only hope was to flee the country and try to secure safe passage to the Allied lines. Their leader, Ante Pavelic, led 100,000-200,000 Ustase troops and their terrified families towards the Austrian border in May 1945, pursued all the way by vengeful partisans of various persuasions. They managed to get as far as Bleiburg on the Yugoslav–Austrian border, but here they encountered British troops who cut off their escape, holding them between a rock and a hard place. Between 30,000 and 40,000 managed to escape, but the rest were captured, and 30,000 died on a forced march back into Yugoslavia. Then, near the village of Tezno, the partisans proceeded to exact their revenge. Commencing on 20 May, a five-day orgy of bloodletting resulted in the deaths of a further 50,000 Ustase soldiers and 30,000 civilians, though the figures are estimates.[42]

The Germans who had been unable to flee when their army retreated were even more exposed to Yugoslav revenge, but the plan to evacuate all 500,000 occupants of the Vojvodina failed due to poor organisation, incompetence and a lack of time. Consequently, around 150,000 still remained when the partisans liberated the region during September and October 1944.[43] Many of these had their property – including their factories and businesses – confiscated and redistributed among their former Serb, Croat, Montenegrin and Greek subjects. Farmland totalling 1,647,000 hectares, 38 per cent of which had been owned by German families, was also sequestrated and handed over to Yugoslavians. Furthermore, to ensure their existence was completely erased, the use of the German language was forbidden either in public or in private.[44] Here, too, familiar German place names were erased in a campaign designed to expunge any indication that Germans had once called such places home. Numerous towns and villages in which they were once part of thriving communities were left desolate by their departure. By May 1945, 80–90 per cent of the German population was spread across forty camps, enduring maltreatment and conditions so severe that around 46,000 of them perished.[45] By 1991, when Yugoslavia broke up, there were hardly any Germans left of the 500,000 who lived there in 1945. A census taken in 2001 showed that there were around 3,000 ethnic Germans in Croatia, 500 in Slovenia, and just over 3,000 in Serbia.

The Italians, too, knew their fates were sealed if they remained. They had lived in the region for generations, and proceeded to colonise and exploit the territories they seized alongside the Germans in 1941. Their subsequent departure, however, was more protracted. The exodus started as early as 1943, when the country surrendered to the Allies, and even when they declared war on Germany their safety was not guaranteed. Some sources claim that between 6,000 and 11,000 Italians were executed or subsequently perished in camps at the hands of partisan groups, while the remainder fled, mainly from Istria, Zadar and Fiume. By 1950, up to 250,000 Italians in all had left although repatriation did not end completely until 1960. By the time the first official census was taken, there were just 36,000 respondents remaining who identified themselves as Italian.[46]

Nor were the Hungarians left in Yugoslavia entirely safe. While a small number managed to make good their escape in the autumn of 1944, the majority remained in the Vojvodina. Here they faced the wrath of Tito's partisans, and as many as 40,000 were said to have been killed between 1944 and 1945. Thousands of others were incarcerated, although they were dealt with far less harshly than the Germans because, fortunately for them, with Yugoslavia now a communist ally of Hungary, an amnesty had been granted and most were soon released.[47] Furthermore, many Hungarians had been loyal to Yugoslavia following the invasion in 1941, and this knowledge spared them a far worse fate. The fact that they fared far better than their Axis partners is demonstrated by the results of a census which was held as recently as 2011, in which over 250,000 respondents identifying as ethnic Hungarian still resided in the Vojvodina.

The Russians also had their German minorities, and they too were condemned to suffer the consequences of Nazi invasion and exploitation. The largest group had been known as the Volga Germans, farmers who had settled in the region generations before and who enjoyed prosperous lives until the Russian Revolution collectivised their holdings. Then, in 1940, a suspicious Stalin ordered that the 380,000 or so inhabitants be removed to Kazakhstan and Siberia, an operation accelerated after the German invasion of June 1941. As many as 30,000 died on the cruel forced march east, and they were later joined by Crimean, Black Sea, Caucasus and Bessarabian Germans, all of whom were identified as hostile despite being part of their communities for many years. At the end of the war, any remaining ethnic Germans were similarly uprooted and exiled.

Nearly every European country had been purged of its unwanted minorities. This was done in part so that the peoples of new, homogenised states should not face the issues that had dogged the progress of their predecessors. National rights, ethnicity and territorial disputes ought never again frustrate the progress of communities which now largely shared common values and goals. Sanctioned by the Allies, these policies had also been pursued as a form of collective punishment, but this strategy had not resolved the underlying challenges which now confronted a Europe shattered and dislocated by war. A long-lasting fix to this matter would require the vision and ingenuity of those charged with shaping post-war Europe.

12

Something to Astonish You

Winston Churchill. He called for a United States of Europe, so long as Britain was not a member. (Library of Congress)

While the Czech government-in-exile was plotting revenge, and Britain, Russia and the US were deciding Germany's fate, other Europeans were contemplating the future in different terms. A Belgian delegate to the League of Nations, Frans van Cauwelaert, was writing in the *Washington Post* in May 1942 that he looked forward to a 'moral and material renaissance … after the war',[1] one which would herald a new era of peace and prosperity. Such laudable aspirations, however, could only be achieved once Europe had recovered psychologically from the trauma of war, and as we have seen there was first to be a reckoning on such a scale that it left little scope for a renaissance of any kind. Until that moment arrived, it seemed that the continent's politicians would only be prepared to return to the same laissez-faire approach and piece-meal solutions which followed the victory of 1918.

Belgium and Luxembourg, as we have seen, had negotiated a modest arrangement in 1921, and with the signing of the Ouchy Convention in 1932, it was extended to include the Netherlands, subsequently acquiring the epithet Benelux. As a route to recovery from the Second World War, it was proposed to resurrect this union and extend it further by including France. Negotiations were undertaken to this end, and an agreement was signed on 21 October 1943 for a transitional customs convention, although France declined at this stage to participate. In the meantime, a conference in Geneva in May 1944 was attended by socialist delegates from Italy, France, Germany, Holland, Czechoslovakia, Yugoslavia, Poland, Norway and Denmark. They were looking beyond such modest bilateral arrangements, and their discussions resulted in a declaration in favour of building a much more integrated federal Europe.[2] When the Benelux countries attended the London Customs Convention in September 1944, the outcome of their negotiations suggested a significant shift in that direction. They agreed to work towards a union which would establish free movement of people, goods, capital and services, and a common policy with regards to trade with third parties, to come into operation by 1948 and be fully operative by 1956. This solution, of course, only addressed the problems of three states.

The relationship between Britain and France during this period was different from those of the Benelux countries. It served to underline the scale of the challenges that the continent as a whole faced. Towards the end of the war they had entered into a financial arrangement through which Britain advanced a credit of £100 million to France, later increased to £150 million so that it could make purchases in the sterling area and help to stimulate its recovery. When these funds were exhausted, France had to ask for more, but Britain was itself penniless, and in turn largely dependent upon the US for its economic survival. The war had cost Britain a quarter of its total wealth; its overseas investments were nearly gone, and it had only been kept afloat through the Lend-Lease Programme – and this lifeline was abruptly cut as soon as Japan surrendered in August 1945. This necessitated the urgent despatch to the US in December 1945 of a delegation led by Maynard Keynes, which secured a loan of $3.75 billion from the Americans and a further $1.25 billion from the Canadians.[3] Even these vast sums did not solve Britain's woes, and in response to calls from the French for food and coal to feed and keep their civilian population warm during the first post-war winter, the British were compelled to be less than accommodating. They not only had the needs of their own population to consider, but those in their zone of occupation in Germany. As we have seen, Russian sleight of hand meant that these burdens were growing weekly with the influx of refugees and expellees from the east.

Consequently, these were testing times for the two Allies, and bitterness in some French circles over the perceived British betrayal of 1940 was now compounded by an apparent unwillingness to help France get back on its feet. It appeared that the continent was diverging, with each country choosing to seek its own way. The signs were therefore not immediately propitious, but fortunately more pragmatic minds were contemplating the bigger picture. One of these was General Charles de Gaulle, who in 1940 saved French honour by refusing to accept defeat, and led his Free French alliance to ultimate victory. His intense patriotism and singlemindedness did not immediately lend itself to contemplating the need for Europe to pool its efforts and work for the common good. However, when he revisited his birthplace of Lille in September 1944 shortly after its liberation, he was appalled by what he found.

Four years of occupation, rationing, black marketeering and general neglect had ruined the city. It was evident that it would take years to recover, and this would apply to scores of other towns and cities fought over and shattered in the war. Even this arch-conservative accepted that a 'profound social change' had to come over the country if France was not to lose 'what remained of her substance'.[4] It could not depend simply upon British generosity, and certainly could not pursue its own path to recovery without seeking the cooperation of its neighbours. What de Gaulle had in mind was revealed in an interview for *The Times* which he gave on 10 November 1945. He insisted that despite the legacy of the war, there was a 'community of interest' between Britain and France that made it essential for them to collaborate closely in the common interest. He went so far as to propose that the two nations work together in forming the core of a western European economic grouping.[5] However, and understandably considering the open wounds which still festered since the war, de Gaulle did not express much enthusiasm for Germany in such an arrangement.

De Gaulle's proposition was music to the ears of men such as Belgian lawyer and economist Paul van Zeeland, who used his good offices to establish the European League for Economic Cooperation the following year. It was founded by Belgium, Poland and the Netherlands, and later France, the UK and Germany joined. It proved to be a modest affair, lacking the weight to act as much more than an advocacy group, which is probably why France was prepared to participate alongside Germany. Nonetheless, this would prove to be the first of many such bodies to emerge from the growing realisation among Europeans that closer integration was the answer to the continent's problems.

If de Gaulle anticipated the full and active participation of the UK in his brainchild, however, he was met by a largely unenthusiastic British government. Although the Labour Party swept to power in a landslide victory in 1945, offering radical reforms such as the National Health Service and largescale nationalisation, its foreign policy was perhaps surprisingly conservative. British socialists had received overtures from Europe for closer integration with scepticism when they were made before the war, and they showed scant enthusiasm now. Much of British foreign policy still rested upon the nation's status as a great *world* power, not a European one, and this would only change with the independence of the Indian empire, Burma and Ceylon.[6]

Then came something of a bolt from the blue from former British leader Winston Churchill, who was engaged in his own European tour, revelling in the shower of accolades and honours recognising his role in defeating Nazi Germany. It came as a surprise to many, therefore, that as an arch-imperialist he proved to be one of the more vocal British exponents of the sort of ideas being articulated by de Gaulle and put into practice by Paul Van Zeeland.

The acceptance speech he gave upon receiving an honorary degree from the University of Zurich on 19 September 1946 was entitled 'Something to Astonish you', and certainly lived up to its name. He praised the work of Aristide Briand and Count Coudenhove-Kalergi, who – along with the League of Nations, he conceded – had laid much of the groundwork for greater European cooperation and mutual support. Then, after recounting the consequences of division and conflict which had left in their wake 'a vast quivering mass of tormented, hungry, care-worn and bewildered human beings', he called for 'a kind of United States of Europe'. However, in adding that 'the first step in the recreation of the European family must be partnership between France and Germany' and that Europe could not recover 'without a spiritually great France and a spiritually great Germany', he broke radically with de Gaulle's vision of something in which France and Britain were joint leaders.

Perplexed by the reaction his speech had received, Churchill sought clarification, and sent his son-in-law Duncan Sandys to gauge de Gaulle's reaction. The response he received on 26 November was not very encouraging:

... [de Gaulle] said the reference in Mr Churchill's speech to Franco-German partnership had been badly received in France. Germany, as a state, no longer existed. All Frenchmen were violently opposed to recreating any kind of unified, centralised Reich, and were gravely suspicious of the policy of the American and the British governments. Unless steps were taken to prevent a resuscitation of German power, there was a danger that a United Europe would become nothing else than an enlarged Germany. He stressed that if French support was to be won for the idea of a European union, France must come in as a founder partner with Britain. Moreover, the two countries must reach a precise understanding with one another upon the attitude to be adopted towards Germany before any approaches were to be made to the latter...[7]

On receipt of this disappointing missive, Churchill took it upon himself to appeal directly to de Gaulle on the necessity of Franco-German rapprochement:

> ... it is my conviction that if France could take Western Germany by the hand and, with full English cooperation rally her to the West and to European civilisation, this would indeed be a glorious victory and make amends for all we have gone through, and perhaps save us having to go through a lot more...[8]

The former French general was not in power, however. It was the incumbent government which decided policy. He would therefore have taken comfort from the knowledge that his fears were not mere cries from the wilderness and had currency both in his own country and the UK. Since the end of the war, discussions had been progressing between Whitehall and the Quai d'Orsay towards an Anglo-French Treaty, much along the lines of the abortive undertaking broached by the British and the Americans after the First World War, promising assistance in the event of renewed German aggression. On 4 March 1947, the Treaty of Dunkirk was signed, by which Britain and France agreed on joint action should the Germans again become a threat, while other clauses also opened the way for deeper economic cooperation. This, of course, was in spite of the US and UK beginning to actively protect their occupation zones from what were interpreted as malign Soviet intentions, and the Byrnes Stuttgart speech of the year before, which laid out his plans for the country.

Beyond Europe, too, thinking was not exercised by the threat posed by a renascent Germany. Instead, politicians and academics in the United States were keen to see European prosperity restored to stimulate trade, but also to forestall the spread of communism. George Keenan, a close adviser to the US government, was among those anxious to encourage a European economic revival. Like Churchill, he saw a reformed Germany as pivotal to this objective: 'It is imperatively urgent today that the improvement of economic conditions and the revival of productive capacity in the west of Germany be made the priority object of our policy.'[9]

It was also evident that the dire state in which Europe was left at the end of the war would require more than its own best efforts to stimulate a revival. Even de Gaulle's admirable efforts to urge an Anglo-French axis would not match up to the urgency of the situation without assistance. Fortunately, the US, uniquely among the victors, had emerged from the war richer and more powerful than when it entered it, with tens of billions of dollars in surplus cash to invest. Just as it was evident to men like Edward House in 1919 that continued US prosperity depended upon trading with a Europe able to buy its goods, US secretary of state George C. Marshall gave a momentous speech on 5 June 1947 in which the same methodology was articulated. He proposed a programme of massive American economic and financial aid to western and eastern Europe and the Soviet Union, in exchange for which its recipients would come together, cooperate and provide plans for how they proposed to invest the money for the benefit of the continent as a whole.

The British and French governments were among the first to respond favourably to the US proposals, and on 17 June 1947 Britain's Ernest Bevin and France's Georges Bidault met to coordinate a joint response. By contrast, it soon became obvious that a secretive and paranoid Stalin wanted nothing to do with it. To accede to the conditions for aid, the Soviet Union would have to expose its dire economic condition to public scrutiny, and in the emerging climate of power politics this was not on the cards. Furthermore, the Kremlin saw the American proposal more as a ruse to undermine Soviet influence and draw away the countries it was in the process of occupying. If they accepted the plan, then the allure of communism could be supplanted by that of a market economy, and Soviet expansion might be considerably impeded. Rather than risk this, the Kremlin made it clear that neither the Soviets nor any of their satellites would avail themselves of the American offer. Marshal Tito, too, the legendary partisan leader who had been credited with the singlehanded liberation of Yugoslavia, was also wary of the American offer. He insisted that it was not declined out of fear of reprisals from the Kremlin; instead, he insisted that

> ... our rejection of the Marshall Plan was our own idea, and we were right ... in this way we kept ourselves free from American influence ... we did not accept Russian influence or direction ... the policy was taken on our own initiative and no one forced us into it...[10]

Such reservations were clearly not shared by his western counterparts. Two days after the conference, former foreign secretary Anthony Eden spoke in the House of Commons, describing the plan as

> ... not only important in so far as it affects the economies of both Europe and the United States ... it can mean that European countries are going to be stimulated to agree upon common economic measures for their joint salvation. Such indeed, is the first step towards the United Europe to which my Right Honourable friend the Leader of the Opposition has so much at heart...[11]

Those who welcomed American largesse convened again in Paris in July where the confidently named Committee, later Organisation, for

European Economic Cooperation, or OEEC was established. With its head office in Paris, the ubiquitous Jean Monnet promptly re-emerged as one of its guiding lights and the following September the comprehensive joint plan was submitted to the US. Soviet rejection was accompanied by the announcement of Moscow's own version, COMECON, a very poor relation and something condemned to fall far short of what the American offer would deliver. The Soviet reaction in any case might very well have been predicted, as Churchill had already warned in his Iron Curtain speech at Fulton, Missouri, on 5 March 1946 that from Stettin in the Baltic, to Trieste in the Adriatic, a definitive line had been drawn between the iron grip of communism and the laissez-faire ideology of free market capitalism.

Churchill's predictions, as we have seen, were more than borne out by events, and two months later the diplomat and ardent anti-communist William C. Bullitt endorsed such views at the National War College in Washington. Here he emphasised the threat that an aggressively expansionist Soviet Union posed and underlined the need for a 'European Federation of Democratic states' which could 'face up' to Moscow.[12]

Compelling evidence of Russian bad faith had been emerging for some time, of course, starting with the Soviet Union's behaviour around reparations, its failure to provide the food for the western zones and its cunning in lumbering its allies with as many Germans as possible. Nor had it wasted any time in realigning its borders with Poland, while in 1945 the German zone of occupation plus Romania and Albania were almost immediately brought under the Soviet umbrella. The following year the Bulgarian monarchy was abolished and replaced by a communist regime, which then proceeded to follow the pattern introduced by its neighbours. Any opposition was incrementally suppressed, either by arrests or liquidations, and followed by the imposition of an authoritarian system sympathetic to Moscow. While the west looked on helplessly, the same well-tried tactics were employed in Poland, where the Soviets had also been busy consolidating power. Having been physically realigned in compliance with Stalin's wishes and its population homogenised, Poland's politics faced relentless and uncompromising sovietisation. A combination of intimidation and rigged elections followed and saw the imposition of communist power in 1947.

Then it was Czechoslovakia's turn. The elections of 1946 found Edward Benes heading a broad and somewhat uneasy coalition of left and centre-left parties, but here too the shadow of Moscow loomed over the corridors of power in Prague. A deteriorating economy worsened by an inability to accept American aid gave increasing leverage to the communists in Benes' government. As he found himself overwhelmed by one insurmountable problem after another, Soviet influence grew, until in February 1948 a Soviet-style takeover was engineered. Hungary would follow the next year, but it was the fate of the Czechs which prompted a chastened de Gaulle to remark that 'since Prague has followed the others into outer darkness, the west must join in economic and military cooperation'.[13] Britain, France, the US and the Benelux countries convened urgently in London between 23 February and 6 March 1948, and again in June, to discuss what they should do.

Their deliberations produced the 'London Recommendations'. Key among these was the acceptance that German rehabilitation needed to be stepped up so that it could play an active role in the defence of the west. To this end the French zone was to be incorporated into the Bizone as a first step to merging them into a unitary German state, followed in due course by a measured rearmament. It would not have nuclear weapons or any offensive capability, but the writing was clearly on the wall. The French reluctantly agreed following assurances that nothing would compromise their control of the Saar and that the Ruhr would also remain under international administration for the foreseeable future.

In the midst of the London Conferences, the Treaty of Brussels was also signed on 17 March 1948. Its intention was to expand the remit of the Treaty of Dunkirk, by which Britain, France, Belgium, the Netherlands and Luxembourg agreed on mutual assistance in the event that any one of them was attacked by a third party, which by this time pointedly meant the Soviet Union.[14] Yet another body, this time the Western Union Defence Organisation, under a committee chaired by Second World War hero Field Marshal Montgomery, would be responsible for its operation and direction. Although it was still seen as early days for Germany to play a full part militarily, it was clearly only a matter of time. In line with the London Recommendations, which anticipated her speedy rehabilitation, one key measure towards this objective came in June, when the Allies introduced currency reform to their zone through the replacement of the Reichsmark with the Deutsche Mark. The immediate effect of this was the almost complete eradication of the barter system that had endured in some fashion since the end of the war. This had been seriously impeding the country's economic recovery, which nearly everyone was keen to see begin in earnest.

A paranoid Stalin, naturally as nervous as the French about the implications of a reconstituted Germany, reacted angrily and ordered an immediate but ultimately futile retaliation. He severed all rail and road links into Berlin, hoping to cut it off from West Germany and somehow force an Allied climbdown. Instead his actions produced the Berlin Blockade, as the west came together to mount a massive airlift to fly in food and supplies to the beleaguered city. It was eventually ended in May 1949, after 318 days of international tension, during which 275,000 sorties carried 1.5 million tons of supplies into the city. The episode simply entrenched mutual hostility and made inevitable the establishment of the North Atlantic Treaty Organisation, which extended the remit of the treaties of Dunkirk and Brussels to include North America.

NATO came into existence on 4 April 1949 and was intended to demonstrate to Moscow the west's unwavering solidarity and willingness to defend its way of life at all costs, with an attack on one member being interpreted as an attack on all. Its formation was the first in a sequence of fast-moving events, and the planned merger of the French zone of Germany with the Bizone came into force, creating Trizonia, while negotiations resulted in the Federal Republic of Germany coming into existence on 23 May. A new constitution known as the Basic Law was adopted, and although it was a milestone on the road to complete sovereignty it nevertheless came with caveats. One condition was that the government of the new state would have to accept the creation of the International Ruhr Authority which would continue management of the country's coal and steel output and provide oversight of its economy. In addition, France would continue its protectorate over the Saar, and German rearmament would be strictly monitored. However, as the country achieved its incremental steps towards full sovereignty, it would be allowed to become a member of the Authority and then to participate in its decision-making processes. It would also be allowed to join and play an active role in such bodies as the Council of Europe, the International Monetary Fund and the General Agreement on Tariffs and Trade.

German readmission to the European family had to be a gradual and incremental process because the creation of the republic still had enormous potential implications for French security. Although its creation raised again the spectre of an economically strong Germany and all that it implied, a positive result was that France now had a potential ally of 50 million people. Many Germans were now firmly ensconced on the other side of the Iron Curtain, and although they posed a threat as part of the Soviet Bloc, the existence of NATO gave France much stronger guarantees for its security than any of the bilateral treaties signed since the end of the war. With both the UK and America as members, and with considerable garrisons stationed on the continent, France would have good reason to feel that its security interests had been more than adequately catered for.

Meanwhile, Churchill had been ploughing ahead with his own advocacy for the wider European project. One outcome of this was the convening of the Congress of Europe in the Hague between 7 and 10 May 1948. Here the formation of the Council of Europe would be further debated and a resolution agreeing its basic structure would be passed. He used his influence to make sure that Léon Blum, Jean Monnet, Paul Reynaud and other keen Europeans attended while he led a delegation of 140, which included twenty-two sceptical Labour MPs. The Congress of Europe subsequently passed a series of further resolutions covering the abolition of trade barriers, mobility of labour, coordination of economic policies, promotion of full employment and, perhaps most significant of all, the pooling of sovereignty and economic resources to open the way for the unification of the continent. The speed of change in the two short years since he made his speech in Zurich in 1946 was also emphasised. Hopes that the Soviet Union might also become a member, and that if it did join 'then indeed, all would be well',[15] must have felt a lifetime away.

It was all well and good for Churchill to exploit his gravitas to get endorsement from the Congress for such far-reaching policies, but the government of his own country remained to be convinced. Nor were dubious British politicians' reservations allayed by the ill-advised remarks made by Euro enthusiast Georges Bidault on 11 June in a speech to the French Assembly. Here, his personal ambitions for France within a united Europe were let slip when he announced that 'when I speak of Europe, I mean Europe, capital Paris, for it is in Paris that the sixteen [Marshall Plan] members, have their capital.'[16] Such sentiments disturbed the British above all, as they echoed de Gaulle's and smacked of a resurgence of the country's Napoleonic ambitions. This was reflected in London's attitude to the Council of Europe and British reticence to be embroiled too deeply in the organisation. When meetings took place between 27 and 29 January 1949, the British began to have cold feet about the entire enterprise. Whereas the French and Belgians were altogether more enthusiastic, the British delegates submitted proposals and counter-proposals for a much looser arrangement. These discussions inevitably resulted in a compromise, which was finally signed and agreed upon on the last day of the conference. Due to come into force on 3 August, Article 1(a) of the statute read:

> The aim of the Council of Europe is to achieve greater unity between its members for the purpose of safeguarding and realising the ideas and principles which are their common heritage and facilitating their economic and social progress.[17]

Consequently, all Brussels Treaty countries approved the text and invited Ireland, Italy, Norway, Denmark and Sweden to attend the conference on the establishment of the Council in London, scheduled for 3 to 5 May 1949. The Federal Republic of Germany became an associate member in 1950 and a full member in 1951. The Saar Protectorate, too, became an associate member in 1950 as an indication of French intentions to relax their grip over the territory gradually. The Council's aims, therefore, were not so different to those of van Zeeland's League or even the OEEC created to manage the Marshall Plan, and served to illustrate the propensity for duplication and overlap. Such an approach might risk diluting them all, but in its determination to maintain a hands-off approach, this probably suited British policy. Bevin, for one, was still determined that Britain avoid being drawn into any commitments from which it could not easily extricate itself. This position was clearly articulated in an internal cabinet briefing paper of 27 October 1949:

> ... we should not run risks which would jeopardise our own chances of survival if the attempt to restore Western Europe should fail and we should not involve ourselves in the economic affairs of Europe beyond the point at which we could if we wished, disengage ourselves ... we must remain, as we have always been in the past, different in character from other European nations and fundamentally incapable of whole-hearted integration with them...[18]

De Gaulle, meanwhile, seeing the prospect of deeper British involvement ebbing away, was gradually coming around to the idea that deeper cooperation with Germany was inevitable. Hopes of a rapprochement coming sooner rather than later were raised by the arrival on the scene of Robert Schuman, whose German-sounding name belied his internationalist credentials. Born in Luxembourg in 1886 to a German father and Luxembourger mother, he later assumed French nationality following the return of Alsace-Lorraine to France, qualifying as a lawyer and being appointed to the French Assembly in 1919. Arrested by the Gestapo in 1940, he escaped in 1942 and after the Second World War proceeded to participate in a number of French governments. His most recent post saw him serving as foreign minister, and in that capacity he travelled to Germany in January 1950 to engage in discussions over the future status of the Saar. He was naturally hoping for the Saar to remain closely aligned with France, but the German government countered with proposals of its own. The spectre of a referendum was raised once more, and this did not chime with French plans.

Undeterred by the subsequent deadlock, German Chancellor Konrad Adenauer decided that further discussions might bring France and Germany together and hasten their reconciliation now that the ice had been broken. His unimpeachable credentials would, it was hoped, facilitate any meeting of minds. Born in Cologne in 1876, he too had entered the legal profession and then went into politics, being appointed president of the Prussian state council in 1920. He was imprisoned as early as 1934 for his unwelcome anti-Nazi views but was released shortly after and remained at large for another ten years. Towards the end of the war he was implicated in the July plot against Hitler in 1944 and again found himself behind bars. Following the Allied victory his reputation as a staunch democrat earnt him the appointment as mayor of his home town of Cologne. He then established the Christian Democrat Union and dedicated his political career to bringing about Germany's rehabilitation with her neighbours.

Elected chancellor in 1949, Adenauer continued with his quest, and began to formulate some quite radical plans. In an interview with an

American journalist two months after Schuman's visit, he even raised the quite extraordinary proposal of a political and economic Franco-German union. He told the interviewer that he envisaged a single parliament and shared nationality and insisted that this arrangement would form the nucleus of a far wider European formulation, and ultimately a United States of Europe. Such an outrageously ambitious concept was dismissed almost out of hand by most politicians and much of the press in France, and it might have been supposed that France's own elder statesman too would deride such an idea. However, on 16 March 1950, de Gaulle shocked his audience when he actually welcomed the idea as 'dazzling':

> ... I am convinced that if France, once she is well on her feet and properly governed, called on Europe to reorganise itself, particularly with the help of the Germans, the whole European atmosphere would be changed, all the way from the Atlantic to the Urals, and even the leaders of the Iron Curtain countries would feel the consequences. The key to the liberation of Europe is Europe...[19]

For someone of de Gaulle's stature to endorse such a prospect was one thing, but the Adenauer scheme also had three significant consequences. As we have seen, it caused a shock among most French people, but it was broadly welcomed insofar as it suggested that the two countries were now on the cusp of a genuine understanding. It also served to persuade Schuman that if there was little appetite for political union, a more modest scheme might prove an acceptable alternative. The one fly in the ointment preventing Franco-German rapprochement, as Schuman discovered when he visited Germany, was the Saar. The return of the Saar and the Ruhr to German control was obviously only a matter of time, but the French economy remained reliant on both. Therefore, if an alternative plan could be conceived, one which drew both nations closer together without an overtly political dimension, it might yet secure continued access to this resource.

After the meeting in Germany and Adenauer's interview, it did not take very long for Schuman to devise a compromise plan. Following intensive debate within the French government, and after consulting both Germany and other European states, the outline of a wide-ranging project was sketched out. It was then revealed to the world on 9 May 1950, when Schuman announced:

> ... the French government proposes to place the whole Franco-German production of coal and steel under a common High Authority, in an organisation open to the participants of other European countries. The pooling of coal and steel production will immediately ensure the establishment of common bases for economic development...[20]

The plan, which was the brainchild of a team led by Jean Monnet but came to be called the Schuman Plan, envisaged a common market for coal and steel, with its members delegating sovereignty of these sectors of their economy to an independent authority, the somewhat Orwellian-sounding 'High Authority'. It would invest in modernisation, remove all customs on coal and steel between its members, harmonise costs and seek to create a level playing field regarding workers' rights and conditions across the industry. Most ominously for those concerned about individual national sovereignty, its decisions would be binding on all members and there would be no right of appeal or reference to national governments. Ernst Haas, a US scholar and political scientist, immediately saw the potential for 'spill over' into other industrial sectors, inevitably extending the High Authority's remit ever wider. This was precisely what arch Europhiles wanted, and this was acknowledged by Walter Hallstein, head of the German delegation to the negotiations, when he called it a 'founding charter for the European Union'.[21]

Typically, reaction from across the Channel was mixed. Publicly Churchill was very positive, but the concept was not unanimously welcomed. Any British involvement would have to take account of domestic considerations, namely the predisposition of British miners to such an arrangement. On 9 June 1950, Sir William Lawther, president of the National Union of Miners, representing nearly 500,000 members, gave his opinion:

> ... we want to know what we are signing our hands to. British miners enjoy the highest standard of living in Europe. We do not want to jeopardise this achievement by joining the Schuman Plan before knowing what it is all about... If M. Schuman or anyone else can prove that this plan will not push us back, then it is all right, but we want proof...[22]

Predictably, the very idea of the High Authority exercising supranational powers over the ECSC's members was anathema to the British. Clement Attlee felt it represented a massive departure from other international agreements to which Britain had signed up, explaining that while 'in every instance that surrender is made to a responsible body, a body of people responsible to parliaments, not to an irresponsible body appointed by no one and responsible to no one.'[23] To Jean Monnet's mind this was the whole point of the scheme. Ever since the First World War, when he and Arthur Salter had formulated their earliest collaborations and he saw the benefits of closer Allied partnerships, he had thought in terms of deep integration. He saw this authority acquiring the attributes of a law-making body and assuming the roles, duties and responsibilities of a national parliament – 'the first concrete foundations' for a federation, as he put it.[24] When Monnet visited London to discuss the High Authority with the British government. they naturally suggested that if members had the right of appeal against its decisions then they might be persuaded to accept its adjudications in that spirit. However, Monnet's response to such a heresy was uncompromising:

> ... it would violate the whole purpose of the Authority if a court of Appeal were to be set up which merely re-established the right of national sovereignty over the field which had been allocated by the Treaty to the Authority...[25]

On 8 August, Harold Macmillan nonetheless submitted a counter-proposal, suggesting the High Authority might be required to defer to the Council of Europe in the case of disputes or challenges to its decisions, and that it could then have the final say. Monnet could not be moved. There was no way he could agree to such a dilution of its powers, and likewise the British smarted at the prospect of such a surrender of sovereignty. Subsequent negotiations dragged on until the treaty was signed on 18 April 1951, and came into force on 23 July 1952, without the UK.

Europe clearly needed such an initiative, because for all its promise the Marshall Plan had failed to live up to expectations. Despite providing aid to the tune of US$12 billion, the material benefits had not been as great as might have been hoped, but neither would the ECSC prove to be a magic bullet. Rather than adhere to the edicts of the High Authority, its signatories would continue to exercise a considerable amount of elasticity when it came to their observance of its rules. Freight charges and tariffs remained inconsistent, and when the price of coal was threatened by the emergence of oil as a viable alternative, each of the signatories looked to national solutions to face the challenge while paying lip service to the principle of collective bargaining. Monnet would have to bide his time, for now something of even greater significance to the future of the continent had been unfolding.

The communist North's invasion of South Korea on 25 June 1950 had concentrated minds and reminded Europeans of the possibility of a similar sudden attack upon the west by the Soviet bloc. Churchill told the House of Commons the following day that 'the unity of France and Germany' had thus been made more urgent than ever by the Soviet 'menace', and that 'a larger continental grouping was something to aspire to.'[26] On 11 August 1950, with US and South Korean forces forced back into a tiny pocket in the south, Churchill gave a speech to the Consultative Assembly of the Council of Europe urging that a European army was now imperative. He called upon all the countries of Europe to 'bear their share and do their best' towards supporting such a plan. A resolution in favour passed by eighty-nine votes to five with twenty-seven abstentions, mostly from dubious Labour Party delegates.[27] It had struck a chord. De Gaulle endorsed the idea in a speech he gave on 17 August:

> ... there must be a system of common defence, the plans of which should be normally drawn up by France, and whose chief should be

appointed by France, just as in the Pacific the Americans should be predominant, and in the east the British...[28]

In October 1951, while the Korean War raged, the Conservatives had won the general election and Churchill was returned as prime minister, but he seemed to have left his ardently pro-European credentials on the opposition benches. The United Kingdom's key policy areas were the Commonwealth, the Sterling Area and the relationship with the United States – not Europe, and certainly not participation in a French-led army. After all, as a Foreign Office memo circulated in December reiterated, 'the defeat and humiliation suffered by many European countries has stimulated a desire for closer integration in Western Europe,'[29] something which the victorious British did not yet share, even if world events had shown how vulnerable they were. In a Commons debate on 6 December, Churchill reiterated that 'as far as Britain is concerned, we do not propose to merge in the European army'[30] but added that it would be prepared to be involved 'as closely as possible in all stages of its political and military development'.[31]

This was not a reaction welcomed by the Americans. Since the creation of NATO, and especially in light of events in Asia, the United States wanted a greater defensive burden to be borne by the Europeans, and Britain was supposed to play a pivotal role in this plan. However, when secretary of state Dean Acheson brought the subject up, Churchill derided the prospect.

Despite his public declarations supporting and lauding the idea, in private he raised the spectacle of 'a French drill sergeant sweating over a platoon made up of a few ... Italians, Germans, Greeks and Dutchmen, all in utter confusion over the simplest orders'.[32] Certainly, as experience had shown with the Austro-Hungarian army in the First World War, and to a lesser extent the *Wehrmacht* in the Second, the road to a European army was laid with potential potholes. An army comprised of units from different ethnic groups, speaking different languages and with conflicting loyalties, was not a recipe for a successful and coherent military organism. But then Churchill must have appreciated this when he supported the idea originally, and such drawbacks could not have escaped de Gaulle either.

Despite Churchill's reticence, President Truman and his secretary of state, Dean Acheson, had already made their position clear in September 1950 when they called for a European force of sixty divisions, and most strikingly insisted that at least ten of these had to consist of German units.[33] Such a prospect filled most Frenchmen with dread, but it was clear that the Americans were not prepared to see a docile Germany failing to contribute to its defence while hundreds of thousands of Americans were stationed in their country protecting them from Soviet Russia.

To try and placate the US and assuage their own fears, French premier Rene Pleven and Schuman worked together on a compromise solution, which was unveiled on 24 October 1950. It proposed a European force, including Germany, which would have its own European defence minister, responsible to a Council of Ministers. Pleven accepted that Germany would have no army of its own and that its participation would be subject to strict controls such as Allied supervision of the officer corps. Nor would it have a defence ministry, but a 'Federal Ministry' for the coordination of its contribution to the European army, which would be strictly limited in size and in the types of armaments it would be permitted to deploy. Furthermore, the proposed army would include national contingents each no larger than battalion strength from Germany, France, Italy and the Benelux countries 'under a common political authority',[34] as a way of further managing any German contribution. Critics responded by insisting that such small units were militarily ineffective and likely to create all sorts of operational difficulties, particularly those pointed out by Churchill. The plans' authors nevertheless knew that getting the plan through the French National Assembly would require the German element being minimised as much as possible. As one commentator observed wryly, France had tried to 'rearm the Germans without rearming Germany',[35] and, as an official at the French Embassy in London admitted, this produced a plan which was 'militarily nonsense'.[36]

The American response was equally downbeat. Although he stated publicly that the plan was a 'positive step', Dean Acheson conceded privately that it was a 'hopeless' idea which 'would never be accepted by the German people'.[37] He was right, and West German politician Kurt Schumacher condemned the plan as 'the murder of the European idea'.[38] Acheson's views were also shared by the chairman of the Joint Chiefs of Staff, General Omar Bradley. He admitted that he 'couldn't believe [his] ears' when he learnt of the plan, and British war secretary Emmanuel Shinwell joked that the idea 'would only excite laughter and ridicule' in Moscow.[39] The British also opposed the plan on the grounds of its structure, its undermining of NATO, and the 'substantial relinquishment of national sovereignty' it entailed.[40]

For their part, the Germans, fearful both of the Soviet Union and a rearming East Germany, had already formulated their own idea, enshrined in the Himmerod Memorandum, so named after a meeting of senior German officials and military men at a Cistercian Abbey of that name in the Rhineland. The results of their deliberations had been published in a forty-page document, and not surprisingly it came as something of a bombshell. It proposed the creation by 1952 of twelve tank divisions and 250,000 men in six corps, supported by an air force of 831 aircraft[41] – clearly unacceptable to the French, but much closer to American thinking. A force of such size would certainly take some of the pressure off the US commitment to European defence. The subsequent arguments over the two plans opened a whole can of worms, and some kind of compromise had to follow if the entire project was not to flounder. Charles Spofford, deputy US representative on NATO's Atlantic council, then sought to break the impasse by suggesting a backstop. Parallel to the creation of a European army, NATO itself would establish an integrated force in Europe, in which closely monitored and supervised medium-sized German units would serve until a longer-term solution could be agreed. This seemed to meet with general approval, at least for the time being, and following intensive negotiations between Germany, France, Benelux and Italy, a compromise European Defence Community Treaty was signed on 27 May 1952.

Still, this was not the end of the matter. The treaty also had to be ratified in the respective parliaments of its signatories. De Gaulle was violently opposed to a military organisation that was not dominated by France, which he insisted would 'condemn her to decay'.[42] In November 1953, he called the EDC 'monstrous' and said it would rob the French army of its sovereignty. He blamed this and other 'supranational monstrosities' upon the machinations of men such as Jean Monnet, who in 1940 'had tried to integrate King George VI with President Lebrun' and in 1943 'to integrate de Gaulle and Giraud'. He also angrily asserted that this 'stateless army of Germans and Frenchmen' would ultimately be placed at the bidding of the American commander-in-chief',[43] the US president. He was also adamant that any such organisation must have Britain as a member if it was to have any significance at all. With the UK still aloof from such an idea, he claimed that a cynical Britain was instead

> ... demanding that we join the EDC, though nothing in the world would induce her to join it herself. Abandon your soldiers to others, lose your sovereignty, lose your dominions – that's fine for Paris, but not for London ... And why? It's because we are the continent, the 'unhappy continent', as Churchill has already called us ... No doubt there will be a few British soldiers in Germany and a few observers attached to EDC ... very pleasant indeed to be a guest of honour at the banquet of a society to which you pay no dues...[44]

In the event, such vehement arguments proved to be academic, and although the other potential members agreed, in August 1954 the French Assembly rejected the entire concept by a significant margin of 319 votes to 264.[45] Germany, too, rejected the plan, unable to accept the restrictions that membership would place on German sovereignty.

The collapse of the EDC did little to allay the fears of those like Churchill who felt this left Germany effectively friendless and out on a limb. EDC or no EDC, Churchill was still anxious to 'see the German nation take her true place in the European family of free nations',[46] and that included playing a part in its defence. On 18 September, Churchill shared with President Truman his concern that German participation in European defence must remain 'our number one target'[47] and that if a place was not found for them within the western half of Europe then there was every possibility they might look elsewhere.

Fortunately, negotiations over the EDC had not been taking place in isolation, and it had been a long-held ambition of the US and Britain that Germany should become a fully fledged participant in NATO. As we have seen, the Korean War had precipitated a root-and-branch re-evaluation of its organisation and military structures and American determination for Germany to play its role inside it. France was nervous, of course, but following yet more hard bargaining was offered certain guarantees, among which was that Germany would not have nuclear or biological weapons, and that the British Army of the Rhine would be a reminder that any German aggression faced a significant response. In October 1954, France joined the other members in creating the Western Economic Union, and in agreeing unanimously to invite Germany to join NATO and establish an independent military. Subsequently, on 5 May 1955, the British, French and United States formally ended their military occupation of the Federal Republic of Germany, and it took a seat in the NATO council four days later. The Soviet Union predictably retaliated by creating the Warsaw Pact, in which East Germany was to participate fully. The decision by NATO had therefore drawn the continent closer together while also pushing it even further apart.

In the same month that Germany was finally admitted into the European family as an equal member, the Benelux countries proposed that the ECSC fulfil Monnet's original idea for it and encompass closer harmonisation of the member states' economic and social policies. To this end the six foreign ministers of the member countries met in Messina, Italy, from 1 to 3 June 1955 to discuss what steps to take. Some critics were not convinced that yet another European institution was needed. Europe already had so many, including the European League for Economic Cooperation, the European Council, the Organisation for Economic Cooperation (OEEC), the European Payments Union (EPU), and of course the ECSC, and yet another tier of bureaucracy was considered to be entirely superfluous. However, none of these fulfilled the aims of arch federalists. Dutch minister of foreign affairs Johan Willem Beyen, for one, had seen the limitations of the OEEC in particular, and in 1953 had proposed expanding it on a more supranational basis, to comprise a common market with no customs duties or import quotas between its members. French premier Edgar Faure was more cautious, but his foreign minister Antoine Pinay saw it differently. He had attended the Messina conference and agreed to a resolution to consider a variety of options which may or may not ultimately lead to ever closer European cooperation. In the hope of deciding one way or the other, Belgium's

Paul-Henri Spaak was asked to chair an inevitable committee and oversee subcommittees which would be charged with analysing and producing reports on the various options available for an enlarged ECSC.

At the end of this lengthy process a report was presented on 21 April 1956. Primarily the work of Pierre Uri of France and Hans von der Groeben of Germany, it proposed 'the progressive elimination of customs duties among the member countries ... which must lead to the final realisation of a common market'. Furthermore, there would be a 'customs union ... [and] the establishment of a common tariff with respect to third countries'. The Spaak Report, as it became known, also proposed a common market for agriculture, the harmonisation of legislation and commercial policy, and the free movement of labour and capital as a core element.[48] Essentially it defined the planned body as one of overall economic integration rather than a simple expansion of the responsibilities of the OEEC, but it worried senior French officials. Fortunately for the enterprise, a new ministry under Guy Mollet had been formed that February, and he was quick to exercise his pro-European credentials to ensure the plan did not fall on stony ground. His foreign minister, Christian Pineau, and the state secretary for foreign affairs, Maurice Faure, were also mobilised to see it pushed through over the heads of lukewarm senior officials and an unenthusiastic cabinet. At the subsequent Venice Conference of 29–30 May 1956, Pineau ignored his advisers and accepted the report as the basis for formal negotiation, which began soon afterwards, albeit with safeguards for harmonisation and for France's overseas possessions. The meeting agreed to appoint Spaak as chairman of a further intergovernmental conference to be convened at Val Duchesse, Brussels, on 26 June, which would draw up the rules of procedure and draft the treaty which would create the Common Market.

Inevitably, there was continued opposition among sceptics within France, not least among whom was de Gaulle, but at a ministerial meeting on 4 September, Mollet again forced the proposals through. He then had to persuade parliament to accept it. Despite the staunch advocacy of the pro-Europeans, there remained in France serious reservations regarding how membership of the Common Market would affect relations with its still considerable overseas empire. Algeria, despite the war raging there, was still legally part of France, but its African, Indo-Chinese, Caribbean and Pacific territories could be sacrificed if it joined a European single market and customs union that excluded them. The same dilemma vexed Belgium, which still governed territories in central Africa; Italy, with its residual interests in Somalia; and the Netherlands, with the last remaining piece of its former empire in the East Indies being Dutch New Guinea.

The solution was relatively straightforward and pragmatic: make these territories 'associate members', whereby they would enjoy the same benefits as their metropoles and as a quid pro quo afford the same preferential duty-free trading arrangements to all other members of the Common Market. The solution would in fact prove unnecessary because nearly all these colonies would become independent within a few years, but nonetheless it smoothed the way for the short-term needs of achieving unanimity. Similar debate in Germany echoed that in France, with Konrad Adenauer approving but his minister for economic affairs, Ludwig Erhard, preferring a looser relationship and a free trade arrangement as part of the OEEC. Despite the reservations of naysayers in both countries, the one distinct advantage each would derive from being founder members was the power to shape and mould the 'common market' in their own image, particularly as they would be the two strongest economies in the organisation. Furthermore, having secured special arrangements for her empire, France had, in the short term at least, the potential to enjoy the economic best of both worlds. For Germany, there remained the recovery of the Saar, which was still in French hands. It had played a not insignificant part in the wars with Napoleon, proven a bone of contention in the peace negotiations of 1919, a potential stumbling block in the settlement of 1945, and overshadowed the formation of the EDU, the ECSC and German membership of NATO.

Hoping to finally put the issue to bed, France and Germany agreed to hold a referendum on the Saar's future. When the poll was held on 23 October 1955, some 67 per cent, on a turnout of nearly 97 per cent, chose Germany and turned their backs on France. Unlike when Luxembourg chose France over Belgium in 1919, however, this decision was honoured. On 27 October 1956 the Saar Treaty was signed, establishing the protocols by which the territory would return to Germany on 1 January 1957. With this bone of contention now finally settled for the foreseeable future, both countries could concentrate on the arguably more pressing matter of bringing the Common Market to fruition.

On 25 March 1957, after years of debate, negotiation and argument, the leaders of France, Belgium, Luxembourg, West Germany, the Netherlands and Italy met in the Palazzo dei Conservatori on the Capitoline Hill in Rome for the signing of two landmark treaties: Euratom and the Treaty of Rome. Their respective parliaments then legislated for these to come into force on 1 January 1958. The Treaty of Rome's realisation had fulfilled the dreams of visionaries like Colonel House, Maynard Keynes, Coudenhove-Kalergi, Aristide Briand and Jean Monnet by creating the European Economic Community, and its text left few in any doubt as to the long-term ambitions it represented. Signatories were unequivocally called upon to 'lay the foundations of an ever-closer union among the peoples of Europe ... to ensure the economic and social progress of their countries by common action to eliminate the barriers which divide Europe ... strengthen the unity of their economies and to ensure their harmonious development by reducing the differences existing between the various regions ... and to pool ... their resources to preserve and strengthen peace and liberty'.

Subsequent articles called for the incremental abolition of all customs duties and other trade barriers between members and for the introduction of a common tariff on all imports from outside within ten to fifteen years. Furthermore, all members acceded to the principle of the free movement of goods, services, capital and people, and to the harmonisation of social welfare policies and the abolition of any practices that encouraged unfair competition, such as state aid for ailing industries. The EEC alone would negotiate and conclude treaties with other states or international organisations, such as the General Agreement on Tariffs and Trade, and there was to be a European Court to adjudicate upon any challenges and to settle any disagreements between member states. However, although its institutions were based upon those of the ECSC, sharing the same Court of Justice and Parliamentary Assembly, it had a Commission instead of a High Authority to preside over it. It therefore had the scope to far exceed the criteria of a 'common market' and went much further than the imperial German and Austrian models ever had. In advocating ever closer union it would reverse the Austrian policy of devolution, which had been pursued since the *Ausgleich* of 1867 for Hungary and Croatia, and incrementally dilute national decision-making. Such implications were not lost on those who saw in the signing of the Treaty of Rome the eventual end of the nation state.

Among the doubters was the French president elect, Charles de Gaulle. Ever since visiting his home town of Lille just after the war he had sponsored a form of European unification, but this was not what he had in mind. His vision had been for a union centred around Paris, an intergovernmental organisation in which French foreign and defence policy would not be compromised, as he also felt it was by participation in NATO. Nevertheless, having been on the side-lines and out of office since 1946, he could only witness and comment upon the progress that had been made. Then, amid immense constitutional turmoil in the country, with civil war having been threatened, he was elected president on 21 December 1958, armed with a mandate to restore French pride and constitutional stability. Despite the fact that it had been done and dusted after so much irksome negotiation, he would immediately set about unpicking the Treaty of Rome.

Soon after taking office, de Gaulle embarked on his quest. After a round of bilateral meetings held in France during the summer of 1960, a summit was held on 10–11 February 1961 from which emerged further consultations under the chairmanship of the French ambassador to Denmark, Christian Fouchet. During yet another summit in Bonn on 18 July, Fouchet was asked to draft 'proposals on the means of giving the union of their peoples a statutory character'.[49] Fouchet returned with a plan in which there would be intergovernmental cooperation, not only in culture, education and science but in foreign and defence policy, and with the right to opt in or out of any decisions. The new organisation would comprise a Ministerial Council, a Commission populated by senior foreign ministry officials and a Consultative Assembly of delegated national parliamentarians. De Gaulle thus backed a *Europe des Etats*, as he put it, without a High Authority – especially with regards to foreign affairs and defence.

Apart from de Gaulle, however, only Chancellor Adenauer appeared to be taken with the idea. He saw in the Fouchet Plan a reminder to the members' respective publics that the Treaty of Rome 'was not only economic but political ... something bigger than any of their countries alone'.[50] Because of this it would ease them into the realisation that the competencies and powers their governments planned to cede through ever closer union would inevitably lead to the end of the nation state.

Others, particularly the Dutch, were hostile. They suspected that de Gaulle had an ulterior motive. Instead of rejecting the Fouchet Plan outright, however, the Dutch insisted that it ought only to be adopted if Britain could be persuaded to become involved. De Gaulle was perfectly aware that Britain would not follow French national and defence policy and, faced with the intransigence of the Dutch and a general lack of enthusiasm, his idea fell by the wayside. The bruised French leader felt the Americans had influenced the rejection of the plan, telling a press conference that a 'non-European federator' was behind its failure.[51]

In 1995, de Gaulle's former finance minister, Valerie Giscard d'Estaing, admitted that had the Fouchet Plan been given more serious attention Europe might not have had to 'wait three decades' for the EU to evolve such a strategy with regards to foreign policy and defence,[52] which remains a distant dream for many arch federalists today.

Thus, from its inception, the EU was to consist of a tug of war between the federalists and the bilateralists. But if anyone was under any illusions with respect to the direction of travel, they were enlightened by a landmark test case which was heard in February 1963. A Dutch company, Van gen den Loos, imported a particular type of plastic from West Germany, and the Dutch customs force demanded an import tax to be paid, which the company claimed violated Article 12 of the Treaty of Rome. This stated that signatories should 'refrain from introducing between themselves any new duties on imports or exports or any charges having equivalent effect, and from increasing those which they apply in their trade with each other'. Members were required to reduce tariffs incrementally until they disappeared altogether, not impose new ones. The company therefore interpreted this article as entitling them to reclaim the tax they had paid. Dutch customs officials argued that the company had no right to pursue them as the terms of the Treaty applied to member states, and if a state broke the law only the European Commission had the right to act, not a private business. Having reached an impasse, the European Court of Justice was asked to adjudicate. The Court went away to look into the matter and when they returned from their deliberations decided that in point of fact:

> ... the Community constitutes a new legal order for the benefit of which the states have limited their sovereign rights, albeit within limited fields ... the subjects of which comprise not only the member states but also their nationalities...[53]

The interpretation that was placed on this ruling, therefore, was that if EEC law had 'direct effect' on individual citizens of member states, they had the right to take such complaints directly to the European Court over the heads of their governments. The ECJ could then pass judgment and, if necessary, override the judiciary of the member state. In doing so it had essentially assigned to itself the same role as that of the Supreme Court of the United States, and among Eurosceptics, concerned for their national sovereignty, this ruling brought into sharp relief the meaning of 'ever closer union'. Member states had relinquished their rights and devolved them to the supranational body that was created in 1957, and instead of their own legislatures and courts deciding upon policy, it would increasingly be the sole prerogative of those bodies created by the member states.

This became further evident when in 1965, the European Commission put forward proposals for a raft of reforms. These included changing from unanimity to qualified majority voting in the Council of Ministers, and the strengthening of the budgetary power of the European Assembly (later Parliament). There would also be changes to the way that the Common Agricultural Policy, always intended to benefit France, might be reformed. De Gaulle received these proposals with ill-disguised outrage and insisted that majority voting was axiomatic to retaining the sovereignty of its members. He refused to accept the reforms, and a bitter feud ensued. This led to the 'Empty Chair Crisis', whereby the French boycotted the institutions of the organisation and effectively threw it into a state of paralysis. Finally, in 1966, the so-called Luxembourg Compromise was reached, whereby members could hold their veto and exercise it in cases where issues affected 'very important national interests', whatever such a vague phrase was really intended to convey. This seemed to placate de Gaulle, and the organisation was able to function once more. In any case, the outcome would do very little in practice to hinder further integration. In 1967 the Merger Treaty was approved, uniting the three executive bodies of the European Economic Community, Euratom and the ECSC, followed swiftly in 1968 by the completion of the European Community Customs Union.

One of the major outstanding items on the European agenda was the status of Britain and its relationship with the EEC. Britain's initial response to the Treaty of Rome had been to negotiate the European Free Trade Association, created on 4 January 1960 and signed by Britain, Norway, Sweden, Denmark, Switzerland, Austria and Portugal. It was to be simply what its name implied, with none of the ambitions of its neighbour save common tariffs and duties, but it soon became apparent that it was outgunned and outclassed. By 1961, British prime minister Harold Macmillan grasped what was long self-evident and what had dawned on the French six or seven years before that. The British Empire was finished, the Commonwealth was simply a loose and largely informal affair with little or no economic advantage (at least not to the UK), and if the British were not to be completely isolated they had to consider membership of the bigger European club, with all that entailed. Consequently, on 31 July 1961 a meeting of the Cabinet agreed to open negotiations for membership of the EEC, in the face of vehement opposition from the Labour Party, the trades unions and many of Macmillan's own imperially minded and truly conservative MPs.

The task of negotiating British membership was entrusted to Edward Heath. As an officer in the Royal Artillery in the Second World War, Heath had witnessed for himself the utter devastation wrought upon Europe, and his memories of this carnage coloured his views for the rest of his life. Appointed Lord Privy Seal, he accepted the challenge. He soon realised that the economic and material benefits were the points to emphasise, not the inherent political sacrifices required for membership; the economic implications were little different to EFTA, and had no tangible consequences for national sovereignty. The maxim of 'ever closer union' entrenched in the Treaty of Rome was supplanted by more digestible terms such as 'cooperation' and 'collaboration'. This ploy was one which would come back to haunt pro-European British politicians, and especially Edward Heath, in years to come.

Heath might also have been forgiven for assuming that the process would be completed before anyone could look at the small print of the Treaty of Rome. It was not initially felt that Britain would have any problems in being accepted; in fact, it had been made clear from the EEC's inception that the six would welcome Britain's participation and very soon become seven. Furthermore, on 5 September 1961, de Gaulle gave what ought to have been an encouraging speech, in which he stated that 'the six have always wanted other countries, and particularly Britain, to join the Common Market, accept its obligations and reap its benefits.'[54] Nevertheless, in January 1963, to the astonishment of nearly every pundit and politician in Europe, Britain's application was actually vetoed by the French, or more precisely President de Gaulle himself. His suspicions of British motives had grown, and he now felt that the presence of the United Kingdom at the table would throw into chaos the delicately arrayed checks and balances of the nascent organisation. In January, he articulated his reasons for exercising his veto:

... the Common Market of the Six formed a coherent whole; they had many points in common, while Britain was very different. She was

301

scarcely an agricultural country at all; also unlike the Six, she had 'special political and military relations' with the outside ... following Britain, the other countries of the EFTA will want to join ... we shall have to start building up quite a different Common Market ... the cohesion of all these numerous and very different states would not last long...[55]

De Gaulle was afraid that Britain's membership would see French pre-eminence in the organisation compromised even more than it already was, especially having seen his Fouchet Plan flounder. He also felt that the USA would use British involvement as a 'Trojan Horse' to extend its own influence. De Gaulle wanted to employ the organisation as a version of the Little Entente of the 1930s, using it towards his own ends and as a way of aiding French defence. He did not want Britain rocking the boat. The veto was not well received by many of his fellow countrymen, nor by the other five members. This did not seem to trouble him very much, and, having weighed up the pros and cons, de Gaulle was undeterred: 'They'll scream and kick, and then ... they'll get used to it.'[56]

The veto came as a blow to Ted Heath and the Conservative government, especially when the economic disparities between the EEC and Britain were scrutinised. Between 1958 and 1964, the total income of EEC members had expanded by 68 per cent; the British income had only increased by 36 per cent. European industrial output had also increased in this period by 49 per cent, while Britain's grew by just 31 per cent. The average income of EEC citizens had grown by 51 per cent and the average Briton's by 23 per cent. During these years, Britain's trade with the Commonwealth increased by only 1.6 per cent compared to 98 per cent with the Community.[57] On the other hand, food prices in the UK were lower than in the Common Market as a result of the 1947 Agricultural Act, which had guaranteed British farmers good prices and assured markets in the UK for their products, in exchange for efficient farming practices.[58] Joining would mean accepting the terms of the Common Agricultural Policy, as a result of which prices would go up for British consumers.

Nonetheless, in the round it was considered to be pure statistical common sense for Britain to join; it simply could not afford to take no for an answer. When the Labour government of Harold Wilson came into office in 1966, it decided that it was clearly in Britain's interests to make another application, and one was duly submitted in 1967. Again, it was President de Gaulle who foiled British plans, this time tempering his veto with the reassuring aside that it was close, but not yet quite ready to become a member. Then the entire political landscape suddenly changed when de Gaulle resigned the presidency in 1969 after he lost a referendum on French constitutional reform. When Edward Heath won the 1970 general election at the head of the Conservative Party, one of his first steps was to reopen negotiations. These took a further two years, and Britain was finally accepted in 1972, with Heath signing the Treaty of Accession in Brussels on 22 January. He then had to have the treaty ratified by parliament, and on 17 October the European Communities Act was introduced into the House of Commons. The preamble stated blandly that it was:

> An Act to make provisions in connection with the enlargement of the European Communities to include the United Kingdom together with (for certain purposes) the Channel Islands, the Isle of Man and Gibraltar.[59]

The brief, twelve-clause bill received 200 hours of debate before being passed into law, and Britain was to accede to the organisation with effect from 1 January 1973. It was only then that its true implications were laid bare, for anyone who cared to study the bill. Its passage gave EU law supremacy over UK national law, and some types of EU legislation such as treaty obligations and regulations were given automatic effect in the UK legal system. No additional UK legislation was required. If there was any doubt over the legitimacy of EU law, the European Court of Justice alone would have the power to make a judgment, and UK courts from this time had the obligation to reject any UK legislation which was shown to be in violation of EU law. While the economic benefits of membership were repeated ad nauseum, these consequences were barely even given airtime.

Furthermore, being an advanced industrial economy, the UK automatically had to make higher contributions to the budget, rising to 20 per cent by the 1980s, and VAT had to be imposed on most commodities. Its fishing areas had to be opened up to the other members, and Britain could no longer buy cheaper food from the Commonwealth on mutually favourable terms, while the 1947 Act would also become null and void. Britain's already increasingly tenuous links with countries with which it once had a close affinity were to be become even further stretched, making the former 'mother country' appear more distant than ever. Furthermore, contrary to promises made before joining and due to the inherently protectionist nature of the organisation, membership pushed up most prices, although this fact was probably partly obscured by the short-term confusion created when Britain adopted decimal currency in 1971.

The fact that Heath had acceded to the Treaty of Rome and committed the country to the most fundamental constitutional change since Magna Carta fed rising hostility towards the institution as well as to him personally. Issues of sovereignty took centre stage for those on all sides of the political spectrum. Conservatives and those on the right resented the severing of ties with the Commonwealth, and those of the left derided the organisation as a great capitalist cartel, designed to exploit workers for the benefit of employers and multinationals. The controversy became such that the Labour government of Harold Wilson, which returned to office in 1974, had to promise a referendum on British membership.

Labour, adamantly opposed to the whole project since 1945 and led in this opposition by men such as Ernest Bevin, had now concluded that Britain's future lay in continued membership. It therefore campaigned on that platform. A government-sponsored pamphlet with a foreword by Wilson, 'Britain's New Deal in Europe', promised that a 'Yes' vote would mean Britain remaining a member of the world's most powerful trading bloc, with secure supplies of *cheaper* food, and with access to support grants via the Regional Fund and the European Investment Bank. The new government also claimed that its renegotiation of the terms of Britain's original membership had given it a better deal on imports from the Commonwealth, the right to exempt necessities such as food from VAT, and freedom to pursue its own policies on taxation and industrial relations. Leaving would mean a loss of confidence from outside investors, rising unemployment and inflation, and the loss of the right to influence the decisions made by the remaining members, with no say on the future economic and political direction of the Community. Instead, it insisted, 'we would just be outsiders looking in.' The political, constitutional and sovereignty implications of 'ever closer unity' were played down as meaning that the Common Market was intended to 'bring together the peoples of Europe'. The persuasive arguments of the 'Yes' campaign, despite the opposition of many politicians and the TUC, convinced 67 per cent of a 64 per cent turnout to vote for staying inside the new, reformed organisation.

Britain's decision to stay led to the gradual but inexorable growth of the Community. The same year that Britain joined, so did the Irish Republic, Iceland and Denmark. Greece joined in 1981, then in 1986 Portugal and Spain. The growth of the geographic reach of the organisation was accompanied by constitutional change. In 1985 the Schengen Agreement was signed and scheduled to be put into effect in 1995, abolishing border controls and passport checks within the EU, allowing free and unfettered movement. The Single European Act, signed in Luxembourg in 1986, gave the European Parliament more powers and extended majority voting, the obvious consequence being the diminution of the power of national parliaments, especially the veto secured many years before by de Gaulle. It also committed the member states to complete implementation of the internal market by 1992. In February 1992 the Maastricht Treaty was signed, extending the powers of the Community. It also saw the introduction of the 'Three Pillars' to consolidate the union further: the European Community (replacing the European Economic Community), the Common Foreign and Security Policy, and the Justice and Home Affairs Policy. These would prove harder to implement than to announce, however. Maastricht was finally ratified in 1997, but not without rancour. In addition to the Three Pillars and the rebranding, the Maastricht Treaty would abolish more national vetoes, and implement laws on employment and discrimination. It was thus the political direction of the Community that had been drawing increased criticism and raising concerns.

Twenty-five years of membership had clearly failed to result in the British people coming to terms with their role in the organisation, and this was evident when British prime minister Margaret Thatcher gave a speech in Bruges on 20 September 1988. It was also one of which Lord Castlereagh, Winston Churchill and even Ernest Bevin might have approved. In it, she assured her audience that Britain was committed to 'willing and active cooperation between independent and sovereign states' but added that 'to try and suppress this nationhood and concentrate power at the centre of the European conglomerate would be highly damaging and would jeopardise the objectives we seek to achieve.' She insisted that 'Europe will be stronger precisely because it has France as France, Spain as Spain, Britain as Britain, each with its own customs, traditions and identity. It would be folly to try to fit them into some sort of identikit European personality.' She also rejected one of the Treaty of Rome's basic tenets when she said that 'it is a matter of plain common sense that we cannot totally abolish frontier controls, if we are also to protect our citizens from crime and stop the movement of drugs, of terrorists and illegal immigrants.' On defence, she told her audience that 'Europe must continue to maintain a sure defence of NATO' and that 'we should develop the Western European Union, not as an alternative to NATO, but as a means of strengthening Europe's contribution to the common defence of the West,' pointedly dismissing the idea of anything that resurrected the European Defence Community, which had been defunct since its failure to launch in the 1950s. She concluded her *tour d'horizon* lecture by insisting:

> Let us have a Europe which plays its full part in the wider world, which looks outward not inward, and which preserves the Atlantic Community – that Europe on both sides of the Atlantic – which is our noblest inheritance and our greatest strength.[60]

Hard statistics were hard to dispute, however, and it was these that mattered most. They demonstrated that British membership had paid economic dividends, with British trade increasing from £7bn in 1973 to £278bn ten years after Thatcher's speech. It was evident that Britain and the rest of the member states had benefited from participation. In the meantime, the EFTA countries were becoming resigned to the fact that they could not compete with their bigger, more powerful brother, regardless of the implications for their sovereignty. Consequently, under the terms of the Treaty of Oporto of 1991, which created the European Economic Area, the

EFTA states committed themselves to adopting all EC legislation regarding the internal market, research and development, social policy, education, consumer protection and the environment. They were nonetheless unable to participate in EU policy making despite having to contribute to the EU budget. Austria, Finland, Sweden and Norway decided that they may as well be full members in that case, and except for Norway, whose electorate rejected the move, all joined the EC on 2 January 1995.

Amid these changes and debates over voting rights and sovereignty arose arguably the most serious developments to affect Europe since the end of the Second World War. The 1980s witnessed the terminal decline of the Soviet Union and the emergence among the states of the Eastern Bloc of a renewed spirit of independence which was driving a wedge between Moscow and her erstwhile vassals. This estrangement culminated in Hungary unilaterally dismantling the border fence between itself and Austria in April 1989, leaving the way open for thousands of East Germans to escape to the West. Then, in November of the same year, in what appeared to be a totally spontaneous act of wholesale rejection of their communist leaders, the famous and much vaunted Berlin Wall was breached. Soon afterwards, West German Chancellor Helmut Kohl grasped the nettle and brought up a subject which until then had been thought unimaginable in their lifetimes. At his urging, the prospect of the two Germanies reuniting was raised, reversing the decisions taken in 1919 and 1945 and holding out the prospect, for the first time in over sixty years, of a partial reinstatement of the Germany created by Otto von Bismarck in 1871.

With the East German economy in ruins and its population sick of living under Soviet domination, the elections held in the country in May 1990 produced a coalition sympathetic to the idea of entertaining Kohls' ten-point programme to initiate the steps towards reunification. That same month the two Germanies signed a treaty which proposed monetary, economic and political union, coming into force on 1 July 1990. The Deutsche Mark would replace the near worthless East German Mark, and the East Germans would begin the process of transferring financial sovereignty to West Germany. In return, West Germany would make grants and subsidies available to its eastern neighbour to both shore up its economy and its industries, and to make the task of reunification easier. Understandably, these developments did not go unnoticed by Germany's western neighbours and fellow members of the EU. Margaret Thatcher in particular was somewhat unnerved by the prospect of a new and enlarged Germany, and the French were not enamoured either. All sorts of questions were thrown up regarding security, and in particular the possibility of Germany reinstating its claims upon Poland for the territory lost in 1945. Mikhail Gorbachev's Soviet Union was not keen either, but after the initial shock passed, and it was accepted as inevitable unless they were prepared to go to war to prevent it, all of the key players acquiesced.

Subsequently, in August 1990 East Germany's parliament passed the necessary legislation to provide for the country to be dissolved and join West Germany, while similar steps were taken in Bonn to legalise the accession of the old German Democratic Republic to the Federal Republic. In this way the legal status of West Germany remained unchanged, and its membership of international bodies such as the UN, NATO and of course the EU were unaffected, while East Germany, by ceasing to exist, automatically abandoned membership of such bodies as the Warsaw Pact and COMECON. Both legislatures signed the Reunification Treaty on 20 September 1990, and it entered into force nine days later. The two countries officially became one sovereign nation state again at midnight on 3 October 1990, East Germany having effectively transformed into five new states: Brandenburg, Mecklenburg-Vorpommern, Saxony, Saxony-Anhalt and Thuringia. Almost simultaneously, East and West Berlin disappeared to emerge as the single unified city, destined eventually to serve as the capital of the reconstituted country.

However, the transition did not go quite as smoothly in practice as it had done in theory, with the knock-on effect of prompting tighter fiscal policy from the Bundesbank once the true cost of taking on an economic basket-case became clear. Germany's elite had grasped at reunification for purely ideological and political reasons, albeit understandably, and it had evidently been undertaken without considering the consequences for the rest of Europe.

The repercussions forced the UK to leave the Exchange Rate Mechanism in 1992 after a financial crisis in London that saw interest rates peaking at 15 per cent. ERM membership had been intended to be a step towards adoption of a single currency, but this bitter experience and its crippling effect on Britain's finances put any thought of this out of the question for a generation.

Thus for the British in particular, the repercussions of Germany's decision stoked the fears and scepticism of the Europhobes and added to a growing body of opinion which saw the whole project as malign. If German reunification could have such unexpected side effects, what else was in store? The German people had barely been consulted on such a momentous step, and certainly had not been warned of any possible consequences. The entire episode had stimulated a greater awareness across Europe of how much was being decided in the name of the people without them being informed. It also served to remind them of the fact that in some countries, people had a voice – in theory, anyway. Treaties such as Maastricht had to be a put to referenda, and one or two electorates had the temerity to question the wisdom of their governments.

Unlike in the plebiscites which were held to decide the fate of peoples at the end of the First World War, however, the outcomes of these polls were not as definitive or as readily accepted. In 1992 Denmark voted 51.7 per cent against adopting the Maastricht Treaty, but were persuaded to vote again in 1993 and this time voted yes, albeit with opt-outs. In 2001 the Irish Republic rejected the Nice Treaty by 53.9 per cent and had to vote again. In 2005 both France and the Netherlands voted 54.9 per cent and 64.5 per cent respectively to reject the new EU Constitution, but although it had to be unanimously accepted by all member states, progress towards the constitution proceeded anyway. In 2008 the Irish Republic rejected the Lisbon Treaty but were persuaded to vote again in 2009. In Britain, the Act was ratified in the House of Commons only after long and bitter arguments and debate.

Such pointers of restiveness were mere cries in the dark, and integration proceeded nevertheless. The implementation of the Schengen Agreement proceeded on schedule, although the Republic of Ireland and the UK both retained opt-outs while other members chose to delay adoption. The implementation of the agreement thus handed the EU greater control over immigration and asylum, something that would create huge issues in the late 2000s when wholesale migration from places such as Syria and Africa provoked controversy, with confrontation and physical attempts by member states to keep migrants out of their countries. Clearly such inconvenient truths as national sovereignty were not to stand in the way of the European Project. The EU juggernaut rolled inexorably on, and in January 1999 eleven states adopted the Euro and all the old national currencies were abolished three years later, finally creating the European currency envisaged by the Germans back in the 1930s.

Meanwhile, other Eastern Bloc states and those once part of the German and Austro-Hungarian empires were starting to eye the opportunities offered by this expanding economic and political grouping. Like East Germany, they had long tired of centralised Soviet-era planning and control, one sinister aspect of which had been a plan proposed by Soviet leader Nikita Khrushchev for the future direction of COMECON. Almost mirroring the Nazis' paradigm for *Großraumwirtschaft*, Khrushchev is reported to have envisaged an arrangement whereby members such as Romania, Bulgaria and Albania would confine themselves to producing food for the Soviet Union and the north-eastern states, which for their part would become the industrial powerhouses of the organisation.[61] Such ideas would not have been welcomed by the leaders of these countries, and contributed to the gradual estrangement between Moscow and its satellites. These and Russia's internal problems meant that the breakup of the Soviet Union was only a matter of time.

When they pulled away, the former Soviet states were willingly assisted by Brussels, which in its eagerness to expand eastwards provided grants and other assistance to enable them to meet the required conditions for membership. As a consequence, by 2004, Estonia, Hungary, Latvia, Lithuania, Poland, the Slovak Republic, the Czech Republic and Slovenia had joined, alongside Cyprus and Malta. Three years later, Bulgaria and Romania were admitted. Croatia, another familiar name from a previous customs union, acceded in 2013, having effectively come full circle. The Croats had secured a large measure of self-government from the Habsburgs in 1868, found themselves unwilling members of a Yugoslav union in 1918, achieved a genuine measure of self-rule in 1939 followed by a violent pseudo-independence in 1941, only to become part of Yugoslavia once again. Croatia was finally independent after fifty years of discontented membership of that union, only to surrender its sovereignty again, this time to the EU.

Croatia's experience was not unique. It is therefore an interesting paradox that so many of the more recent members were countries that had escaped decades of oppression behind the Iron Curtain but were prepared to surrender their newly won independence in order to enjoy the economic and financial benefits offered by the EU. Yugoslavia, for example, had never resolved the nationalism of its distinct republics, which were only bound together by the personality of Marshal Tito himself. When he died in 1980, the entire structure creaked under demands for greater autonomy. In 1991, war broke out between Serbs and Croats and continued until 1992, spreading to their neighbours Slovenia and Bosnia, names which are so familiar from the struggles lasting throughout Austro-Hungarian rule. Bosnia experienced the most suffering during 1993 and 1994 before a ceasefire was negotiated. Finally, under extreme pressure, the presidents of Bosnia-Herzegovina, Serbia and Croatia signed the Dayton Accords, which brought the bloody conflict to an end.

Poland, as we have seen, fell under Russian control even before the Second World War had ended, and in 1952 a Soviet-style constitution was forced upon the country. Strikes became the main weapon of opposition to the regime, culminating in the formation of the Solidarity union in the Gdansk shipyard, although the union was immediately banned under a wave of oppression. As the Soviet Union became weaker, so too did its hold on its client states. Reforms were promised in Poland, with decentralisation and the recognition of Solidarity. One of its leaders, Lech Walesa, became president in 1989, but ironically in 1993 the former Communist Party emerged from elections as the strongest group. Nonetheless, the retreat of Russia continued, and the last troops left the country in 1994. A new constitution was adopted in 1997, and the following year Poland was invited to join the EU and become a member of NATO.

Czechoslovakia remained a relatively quiescent member of the Soviet Bloc from the coup of 1948 until an abortive peaceful revolution was staged in 1968. This was brutally crushed by Soviet troops, but communism was finally overthrown in 1989, followed by a raft of much-needed and long-awaited reforms, when Vaclav Havel and Alexander Dubcek assumed power. The longstanding problems of attaching the Czechs to the Slovaks – attempted in 1919 only to be undone by the

Nazis before being reattached at the end of the Second World War – was finally resolved with their separation as individual nation states in 1993.

Two other former Eastern Bloc countries, Romania and Hungary, endured decades of dictatorship and exploitation under distorted versions of communist rule. Romania had communism imposed upon it by 'little Stalin' Gheorghiu-Dej, who ruled with the proverbial iron fist, but the country became increasingly estranged from Moscow until the 1960s when a complete rift was threatened. As matters worsened, Romania's new leader, Nicolae Ceausescu, grew more and more repressive as he tried to maintain his grip on power. Finally, in 1989, his desperate and exhausted people decided they'd had enough. In a spontaneous act of defiance, both he and his reviled wife were assassinated on Christmas Day.

This game-changing realignment of Europe also saw obscure historic baggage suddenly re-emerge with entirely new significance. The bitterness of those individuals who had suffered as a result of the so-called Benes Decrees had not softened over time, despite leaders offering apologies for historic actions. Before the Czech Republic and Slovakia joined the EU in 2004, Hungarian, Austrian and German politicians sought to make the abolition of the Benes Decrees a condition of accession. Such a step was seen by some as an opportunity to right historic wrongs and injustices, a cathartic exercise that might help forge a new relationship on a completely fresh footing. The European Parliament asked Professors Jochen Frowein and Ulf Bernitz and the Rt Hon. Lord Kingsland QC to investigate Germany's demands and report on their findings.

Their conclusions were published in October 2002, and appeared to be a definitive judgement, stating that 'the confiscations on the basis of the Benes Decrees does not raise an issue under EU law, which has no retroactive effect' and that, in any case, 'the decrees on citizenship are outside of the competence of the EU.'[62] Nevertheless, although the panel considered that 'a repeal of Law 115 of 1946 ... does not seem to be mandatory' because 'individuals have relied on these provisions for fifty years ... we find this law repugnant to human Rights [and] are of the opinion that the Czech Republic should formally recognise this.'[63] The German case had foundered on EU legal technicalities. The Czechs and Slovaks would not consider abolishing the Benes Decrees anyway, fearing this would open the floodgates to further property claims by the Germans and Hungarians. Admittedly, the Germans could have vetoed the membership of the Czechs and Slovaks had they felt strongly enough about the issue, but they did not do so, and accession took place on 1 May 2004 without any further serious objections.

Such legacy issues were inevitable in an enlarging Europe. Other than Germany the original six had been allies, and they had largely reconciled their chequered relationships with the former nemesis. Later members, such as the Baltic States, Poland, the states of the former Yugoslavia and of course the Czech Republic and Slovakia, had suffered much in the

Second World War. Only the promised benefits of membership could assuage any fears of involvement in an organisation dominated by their former foe. The overriding motive of applying to become a member of the EU has been national self-interest, and adherence to the aspirations of the so-called founding fathers of the Treaty of Rome has been of secondary consideration. Few signatories have grasped the true implications of assenting to 'ever closer union', but it was considered a price worth paying for EU grants, subsidies and investment, and the opportunities afforded by the free movement of goods, services, capital and people.

The downside has been largely felt by the citizens of the EU but overlooked by the so-called 'Eurocrats' in Brussels, who are considered aloof and far removed from the challenges of day-to-day life. Issues such as migration, competition for employment and the suppression of wages, national identity and even sovereignty are secondary to the bigger picture of building supranational institutions and ultimately a United States of Europe. Public confidence in the entire structure did take an enormous knock in 1999 when revelations of fraud, nepotism and simple incompetence within the Commission reverberated throughout Europe. All twenty members of the Commission were forced to resign before they were sacked wholesale by Parliament. After it was reconstituted under a new president, Romano Prodi, only a handful of the original commissioners were re-appointed. Prodi promised a root-and-branch reform of the way the Commission was run and publicly acknowledged its shortcomings.

Concerns were being raised in other quarters, too. Jacques Derrida, a prominent philosopher, expressed disquiet about the direction of travel of the EU, remarking that 'in trying to redefine itself, Europe is forgetting and ignoring its cultural history.'[64] Author B. Guy Peters also had qualms, writing that 'if the EU is to become a genuine political entity, better mechanisms of popular political accountability need to be articulated for the Commission.'[65] In a speech to the European Parliament, made on 15 February 2000, Prodi referred to 'the paradox of European integration', whereby Europe has achieved a half-century of peace and prosperity but has left its citizens disenchanted and anxious, and its institutions appearing undemocratic, opaque and elitist.[66] Nearly twenty years later, it is almost impossible to know if Prodi's recognition of the organisation's institutionalised corruption has resulted in any meaningful reform. Europe-wide scepticism persisted, and when given the opportunity to do so electorates tried to stem the tide of expansion and integration. Perhaps the most significant example of popular discontent among the ordinary citizens of a member state occurred in the wake of the huge financial crisis that began in 2008.

Arguably the biggest victim of the EU's ambitions was Greece, which proved to be one of the economies least able to withstand the shock that followed the economic crash. After it joined the Euro in 2001 the country enjoyed a boom period, based on borrowing, low interest rates and generous public spending. This created a huge, unsustainable national debt, and when the economy went into freefall unemployment levels soared. By 2013, 28 per cent were out of work, with tax revenues plummeting and public services close to breaking. It has been argued that if the country had kept its own currency, the drachma, the government might have been able to take unilateral steps to assuage the worst effects of the downturn. These could have included quantitative easing, devaluation or lowering interest rates, although as we have seen such steps did not succeed when attempted by the successor states in the wake of the First World War. In any case, such remedies were not possible within the Euro, managed by the German-dominated European Central Bank.

Unable to pay its debts, Athens tried to negotiate loans with the Central Bank, the IMF and the European Commission – the soon to be reviled 'Troika'. These would only be granted if the country, like Austria in the 1920s, accepted the severe austerity measures imposed by the lenders, especially the Germans. Although the referendum held in 2015 to seek public acceptance of this bailout plan saw it rejected by more than 60 per cent of voters, their decision was simply overruled, Greek prime minister Alexis Tspiras lamenting angrily that 'we couldn't overcome the bankers and northern European elites who have absolute power in this continent.'[67] Subsequently, despite the bitter opposition of the people, including demands that Greece should abandon the Euro and go it alone, corporation tax and VAT rates were increased, privatisation was accelerated, public sector pay was cut, funding for public services was slashed and pension ages went up.

The harsh realities of an organisation dominated by rich and powerful states highlighted the implications for the national sovereignties of its smaller members. Because Germany saves much more and spends far less than its partners, particularly on defence, and exports far more than it imports, its robust and vigorous economy is able to withstand the shocks which can topple weaker ones. Unlike many of its neighbours, whose economies are overwhelmingly reliant upon services and consumer spending, Germany still has the enormous manufacturing base established under Bismarck and salvaged from both world wars. Having held the keys to the almost limitless natural resources of the Rhineland, the Ruhr and the Saar, the industries Germany has built and rebuilt have protected its economy from the bitter experiences of countries such as Greece. As the most creditworthy member of the so-called Eurozone, Germany is able to impose austerity on those states which are most impacted by its own fiscal policies. It is disingenuous to compare German motives today with those of the architects of *Mitteleuropa* and *Großraumwirtschaft*, leave alone the *Zollvereins* of Imperial Germany and Austria, but the parallels cannot be overlooked. Nonetheless, when Martin Schultz, a former European Parliament president and leader of the German SDP, admitted in December 2017 that he envisaged a United States of Europe by 2025, the reaction was perhaps to be expected.

Of those who responded to a YouGov survey held to gauge Europe-wide public reaction, 30 per cent of Germans and 28 per cent of French respondents were in favour of a United States of Europe. When the same question was put to the public in other member states, the reaction was even less enthusiastic. Just 13 per cent of Swedes and Finns were for the idea, while approval ratings among the Danes and the British were 12 and 10 per cent respectively. Although by no means the only country to voice such concerns, the people of the United Kingdom are currently alone among member states in having been given the opportunity to exercise the option of resigning and pursuing an independent course. Prior to the referendum on membership of the EU, which was held on 23 June 2016, British prime minister David Cameron embarked upon what he claimed was a crusade to reform the EU and make it more palatable to the British public. His European counterparts remained unmoved, and it became obvious that there would be no modern-day *Ausgleich* to effect the repatriation of national sovereignty demanded by the so-called 'Brexiteers'.

Cameron returned with what one Conservative politician derided as 'thin gruel', but during the subsequent campaign he insisted on lauding the merits of membership and the advantages to be gleaned by remaining in a 'reformed EU'. When compelling arguments for remaining appeared thin on the ground, those urging that the UK stay resorted to warnings of the dire consequences of leaving. The Brexiteers spread equally fallacious claims of the benefits of quitting, promising sunlit uplands and wildly exaggerated assurances of the economic and financial benefits which would accrue. When the poll was held, just over 52 per cent of those who voted elected to leave. Brussels' response was very similar to its reaction after other referenda held by European constituencies: public acceptance of the decision concealing a determination to reverse an outcome which did not meet with its approval. There was further delay before Article 50 was invoked, by which the separation was put in motion, and then nearly two years of obfuscation and delay. Public pronouncements that 'Brexit means Brexit' and intensive negotiations were accompanied by endless debate about the possible outcome.

To many, the deal which British prime minister Theresa May finally presented to the House of Commons reflected the mindset of those determined all along to prevent Brexit. Others derided it as BINO, Brexit In Name Only. Of particular and predictable concern was the arrangement arrived at regarding the future of the border between the Republic of Ireland and the UK, which, as part of the transition deal and along with the rest of the country, would remain within the single market and customs union until December 2022, after which new arrangements are intended to come into effect. If no deal is agreed by the end of the transition period, the UK will enter a single customs territory, the so-called backstop. Northern Ireland, however, would be required to adhere to additional EU single market rules, ostensibly to ensure that the border between north and south remains open.

Unlike the backstops negotiated following the First World War, this one has no fixed end date. The Saar, for example, remained within the League of Nations backstop until 1935, when a referendum on its future was held. The occupation of the Rhineland had an expiry date, although in theory it was not supposed to have been remilitarised. Instead, the agreement arrived at in 2018 reflected Senator Lodge's concerns a century before – that the League of Nations covenants were a ruse through which to lock in its members. Jean Monnet certainly adhered to the philosophy that only compulsion would ensure that the European structures he sought to erect could survive. Under his tutelage the ECSC was specifically designed to dilute its members' rights and limit their freedom of movement, and the Treaty of Rome took this one step further. It was not until the Lisbon Treaty of 2009 that member states were actually given the legal mechanism to withdraw in the form of Article 50. No such understanding applies to the UK backstop. Britain cannot end it without the agreement of the EU, and so could technically be bound to it indefinitely. This has been widely derided as the so-called Hotel California option, whereby Britain is free to check out of the EU but cannot actually leave.

For critics of the EU this state of affairs is symptomatic of an historic mindset, a determination to pursue the project at all costs irrespective of the wishes of its members. This has led to claims that the EU has deliberately constructed a bad deal to discourage other countries from leaving. Indeed, French president Emmanuel Macron admitted as recently as December 2018 that if a poll was held in his country he would expect a similar result to the UK. Furthermore, a nationalist politician's speech in the Walloon parliament which openly berated Brussels simply saw German chancellor Angela Merkel and other luminaries refer again to the need for greater integration. Under these circumstances it is impossible to be sure what the final arrangement for Brexit is likely to be, whether soft, hard or a so-called cliff-edge with no deal at all. Inevitably, so complex has been the internecine wrangling that the prospect of another vote, with a decision to remain, is frequently raised as a possibility.

What is in little doubt is that the present dilemma is but the most recent of many quandaries with which Europe's governing elites have been confronted. Whatever the outcome, it will almost inevitably serve as a stepping stone to the next drama in the continent's long history.

Notes

1 I Find Myself Shoring up Crumbling Edifices

1. Lowe, Norman, Mastering Modern English, p. 38.
2. Anderson, M. S., The Ascendancy of Europe, p. 8.
3. Ibid, p. 8.
4. Taylor, A. J. P., The Habsburg Monarchy, p. 93.
5. Williamson, D. G., Bismarck and Germany, p. 8.
6. Beller, S., Francis-Joseph, p. 88.
7. Williamson, Bismarck and Germany, p. 95.
8. Roberts, J. M., Europe, p. 157.
9. Ibid, p. 159.
10. Hamann, Hitler's Vienna, p. 91.
11. Hastings, Max, Catastrophe, p. 30.
12. Ibid, p. 30.
13. Roberts, Europe, p. 159.
14. Anderson, M. S., The Ascendancy of Europe, p. 336.
15. Ibid, p. 336.
16. Hamann, Hitler's Vienna, p. 393.
17. Ibid, p. 394.
18. Ibid, p. 394.
19. Anderson, The Ascendancy of Europe, p. 336.
20. Ibid, p. 336.
21. Barraclough, Agadir to Armageddon, p. 151.
22. McMeekin, July 1914, p. 40.
23. Anderson, The Ascendancy of Europe, p. 336.
24. Taylor, A. J. P., The Habsburg Monarchy, p. 45.
25. Ellis/Cox, The World War One Databook
26. Herwig, The First World War, p. 239.
27. Clark, The Sleepwalkers, pp. 69-70.
28. Emmerson, The World Before the Great War, p. 95.
29. Barraclough, From Agadir to Armageddon, p. 31.
30. Emmerson, p. 100.
31. Ibid, p. 100.
32. Ibid, p. 104.
33. Hastings, Catastrophe, p. 11.
34. Ibid, p. 10.
35. Hamann, p. 92.
36. Ibid, p. 69.
37. Ibid, p. 70.
38. Ibid, p. 69.
39. Ibid, p. 72.
40. Ibid, p. 69.
41. Emmerson, p. 105.
42. Haumann, p. 326.
43. Ibid, p. 242.
44. Ibid, p. 241.
45. Ibid, p. 329.
46. Ibid, p. 344.
47. Ibid, p. 331.

48. Taylor, The Habsburg Monarchy, p. 163.
49. Roberts, Europe, p. 162.
50. Taylor, The Habsburg Monarchy, p. 159-160.
51. Hastings, Catastrophe, p. 10.
52. Hamann, pp. 123-124.
53. Taylor, The Habsburg Monarchy, pp. 178-179.
54. Roberts, Europe, p. 164.
55. Gilbert, Martin, First World War, p. 4.
56. Hamann, p. 123.
57. Clark, The Sleepwalkers, p. 66.
58. Anderson, The Ascendancy of Europe, p. 231.
59. Laszlo, Peter, Hungary's Long Nineteenth Century, p. 276.
60. Beller, The Habsurg Monarchy, p. 133.
61. Roberts, Europe, p. 161.
62. Ibid, p. 164.
63. Heater, A History of Education for Citizenship, p. 201.
64. Roberts, Europe, p. 164.
65. Taylor, The Habsburg Monarchy, p. 201.
66. Wallis, Central Hungary, p. 433.
67. Roberts, Europe, p. 159.
68. Wallis, Central Hungary, p. 426.
69. Ibid, p. 427.
70. Taylor, The Habsburg Monarchy, p. 81.
71. Clark, The Sleepwalkers, p. 69.
72. Wallis, Central Hungary, p. 426.
73. Ibid, p. 427.
74. Ibid, p. 425.
75. Ibid, p. 425.
76. Ibid, p. 425.
77. Ibid, p. 425.
78. Ibid, p. 430.
79. Hamann, p. 101.
80. Taylor, The Habsburg Monarchy, p. 60.
81. Beller, The Habsburg Monarchy, p. 133.
82. McMeekin, p. 3.
83. Roberts, Europe, p. 165.
84. Gilbert, First World War, p. 6.
85. Hamann, p. 105.
86. Taylor, The Habsburg Monarchy, p. 231.
87. Hamann, p. 95.
88. Ibid, p. 98.
89. Ibid, p. 98.
90. Ibid, p. 98-99.
91. Ibid, p. 102.
92. Ibid, p. 102-103.
93. Ibid, p. 390.
94. Emmerson, p. 94.
95. Ibid, p. 95.
96. Ibid, p. 96.

2. A Sudden, Blessed Opportunity

1. Williamson, Bismarck and Germany, p. 34.
2. Howard, Michael, The Franco-Prussian War, p. 22.
3. Williamson, Bismarck and Germany, p. 54.
4. Howard, The Franco-Prussian War, p. 22.
5. Ibid, p. 55.
6. Whittle, Tyler, The Last Kaiser, p. 35.
7. Ibid, p. 35.
8. Williamson, Bismarck and Germany, p. 42.
9. Ousby, Ian, The Road to Verdun, p. 177.
10. Ibid, p. 178.
11. Ibid, p. 173.
12. Howard, The Franco-Prussian War, p. 448.
13. Ibid, p. 448.
14. Ludwig, Emil, Kaiser Wilhelm II, p. 10.
15. Thompson, David, France, Empire and Republic, p. 333.
16. Williamson, Bismarck and Germany, p. 40.
17. Ibid, p. 40.
18. Whittle, p. 36.
19. Massie, Robert, Dreadnought, p. 65.
20. Roberts, Europe, p. 168.
21. Ousby, The Road to Verdun, p. 177.

22. Masur, Gerhard, Imperial Berlin, p. 88.
23. Roberts, Europe, p. 171.
24. Porter, Ian, Imperial Germany, p. 7.
25. Ibid, p. 6.
26. Whittle, p. 36.
27. Porter, Imperial Germany, p. 7.
28. Williamson, Bismarck and Germany, p. 50.
29. Roberts, Europe, p. 169.
30. Richie, Alexandra, Faust's Metropolis, p. 206.
31. Porter, Imperial Germany, p. 35.
32. Williamson, Bismarck and Germany, p. 51.
33. Masur, p. 72.
34. Roberts, Europe, p. 170.
35. Torpe and Muller, Imperial Germany Revisited, p. 99.
36. Whittle, p. 252.
37. Porter, Imperial Germany, p. 116-119.
38. Richie, Faust's Metropolis, p. 142.
39. Armour, Ian, Porter, Ian, Imperial Germany, p. 22.
40. Roberts, Europe, p. 22.
41. Masur, p. 41.
42. Richie, p. 141.
43. Ibid, p. 142.
44. Roberts, Europe, p. 30.
45. Ibid, p. 167.
46. Porter, Imperial Germany, p. 21.
47. Roberts, Europe, p. 167.
48. Richie, p. 147.
49. Roberts, Europe, p. 28.
50. Ibid, p. 28.
51. Ibid, p. 173.
52. Porter, p. 21.
53. Roberts, p. 167.
54. Williamson, Bismarck and Germany, p. 104.
55. Porter, p. 21.
56. Masur, p. 62.
57. Ibid, p. 133.
58. Ibid, p. 67.
59. Richie, p. 163.
60. Masur, p. 133.
61. Williamson, Bismarck and Germany, p. 107.
62. Richie, p. 160.
63. Ibid, p. 165.
64. Ibid, p. 169.
65. Williamson, Bismarck and Germany, p. 106.
66. Roberts, p. 172.
67. Richie, p. 178.
68. Masur, pp. 104-105.
69. Torp and Muller, p. 100.
70. Richie, p. 207.
71. Ibid, p. 208.
72. Masur, p. 81.
73. Ibid, p. 136.
74. Ibid, p. 136.
75. Ibid, pp. 137-138.
76. Richie, p. 212.
77. Ibid, p. 214.
78. Roberts, p. 176.
79. Armour, Imperial Germany, p. 31.
80. Masur, pp. 111-113.
81. Richie, p. 244.
82. Masur, p. 116.
83. Williamson, p. 51.
84. Ibid, p. 52.
85. Roberts, p. 55.
86. The Ascendancy of Europe, p. 380.
87. Armour, p. 28.
88. Williamson, p. 52.
89. Armour, p. 18.
90. Ibid, p. 29.
91. Ibid, p. 29.
92. Reinkowski and Thum, Helpless Imperialists, p. 154.
93. Ibid, p. 155.
94. Armour, p. 29.
95. Ibid, p. 85.
96. Ibid, pp. 84-85.
97. Ousby, p. 164.
98. Ibid, p. 164.
99. Ibid, p. 166.
100. Williamson, p. 101.
101. Armour, p. 30.
102. Baycroft and Hopkin, Folklore and Nationalism, p. 167.
103. Ibid, p. 168.
104. Armour, p. 86.
105. Holbraad, Danish Reactions to German Occupation, p. 13.

106. Ibid, p. 1.
107. Ibid, p. 13.
108. Armour, p. 30.
109. Ibid, p. 96.
110. Masur, p. 122.

3. A Free Trade Union Should Be Established

1. Fisk, George, Continental Opinion Regarding a Proposed Middle European Tariff Union, p. 7.
2. Ibid, p. 12.
3. Ibid, p. 14.
4. Hayes, Barry, Bismarck and Mitteleuropa, p. 385.
5. Fisk, p. 26.
6. Ibid, p. 36.
7. Ibid, p. 44.
8. Torp and Mueller, Imperial Germany Revisited, p. 100.
9. Whittle, The Last Kaiser, p. 193.
10. Ibid, p. 197.
11. Brechtfeld, Jorg, Mittleeuropa and German Politics, p. 31.
12. Grumbach, Saloman, Germany's Annexationist Aims, p. 74.
13. Bevan, Edwyn, Germany's War Aims, p. 14.
14. Grumbach, p. 20.
15. Ibid, p. 135.
16. Ibid, p. 91.
17. Wheeler-Bennett, John, Brest-Litovsk, the Forgotten Peace, March 1917, p. 345.
18. Szabo and Francis, The Germans and the East, p. 206.
19. Ibid, p. 206.
20. Ludendorff, Erich, My War Memories, p. 521.
21. Ibid, p. 355.
22. Ibid, p. 355.
23. Herwig, The First World War, Germany and Austria-Hungary, p. 293.
24. Ibid, p. 293.
25. Thorsheim, Peter, Waste into Weapons, p. 15.
26. Gilbert, Martin, First World War, p. 247.
27. Ludendorff, p. 342.
28. Ibid, p. 343.
29. Herwig, p. 285.
30. Ibid, p. 286.
31. Snowden, Ethel, A Political Pilgrim in Europe, p. 173.
32. Herwig, p. 291.
33. Ludendorff, p. 354.
34. Rees, Louis, The Czechs during World War One, p. 12.
35. Cornwall, Mark, The Undermining of Austria-Hungary – The Battle for Hearts and Minds, p. 21.
36. Frizzera, Francesco, La Grand Guerra.
37. Dredger, John, Tactics and Procurement in the Habsburg Military, 1866-1918, p. 261.
38. Frizzera.
39. Herwig, p. 346.
40. Ibid, p. 239-240.
41. Ibid, p. 240.
42. Ibid, p. 240.
43. Ibid, p. 347.
44. Thorsheim, p. 15.
45. Herwig, p. 275.
46. Cornwall, p. 29.
47. Snowden, p. 113.
48. Ibid, pp. 113-114.
49. Cornwall, p. 22.
50. Ludendorff, p. 354.
51. Cornwall, p. 281.
52. Ibid, p. 280.
53. Kershaw, Ian To Hell and Back, p. 89.
54. Herwig, p. 354.
55. Ibid, pp. 34-40.
56. Kershaw, p. 88.
57. Tardieu, André, The Truth about the Peace Treaty, p. 257.
58. Barnett, Margaret, British Food Policy During the First World War, p. 29.
59. Hackett, Clifford, Monnet and the Americans, p. 9.
60. Greenhalgh, Elizabeth, Victory Through Coalition, p. 110.
61. Barnett, p. 33.

62. Hansard, 24 February 1915, vol. 70.
63. Rielage, Dale, Russian Supply Efforts in America during the First World War, p. 23.
64. Hardach, Gerd, The First World War, p. 147.
65. Ibid, p. 146.
66. Bell, P. M. H., France and Britain, p. 79.
67. Ibid, p. 80.
68. Barnett, p. 31.
69. Bell, France and Britain, p. 80.
70. Ibid, p. 80.
71. Broehl, Wayne, Cargill: Trading the World's Grain, p. 220.
72. Bell, France and Britain, p. 80.
73. Ibid, p. 81.
74. Greenhalgh, p. 129.
75. Ibid, p. 129.
76. Brinkley, Douglas, Monnet: The Path to European Unity, p. 18.
77. Hogan, Michael, The Ambiguous Legacy, pp. 56-57.
78. Ibid, pp. 56-57.
79. Brinkley, p. 18.
80. Ibid, p. 18.
81. Tardieu, pp. 229-230.
82. Ibid, p. 227.
83. Ibid, p. 217.
84. House/Seymour, What Really Happened at Paris, p. 433.
85. Keynes, John Maynard, The Economic Consequences of the Peace, pp. 127-128.
86. Meyer, Henry and Nijhoff, Martinus, Mitteleuropa in German Thought and Action, p. 340.

4. A General Association of Nations Must Be Formed

1. Millen, Gertrude, General Smuts, p. 85.
2. Sharp, Alan, The Versailles Settlement, p. 49.
3. Ibid, p. 44.
4. Millen, p. 85.
5. CAB 24/2/32.
6. CAB 24/10/85.
7. Ibid.
8. House/Seymour, What Really Happened at Paris, p. 401.
9. Pollock, Sir Frederick, League of Nations, pp. 74-75.
10. Lloyd-George, David, War Memories of David Lloyd George, p. 664.
11. Ibid, p. 1038.
12. Ibid, p. 1039.
13. Ibid, p. 1039.
14. Ibid, p. 1040.
15. Ibid, p. 1040.
16. Millen, p. 86.
17. Ibid, p. 88.
18. Lloyd George, War Memories, p. 1040.
19. Grey, Lord Edward, The League of Nations, p. 3.
20. Ibid, p. 6.
21. Ibid, p. 6.
22. Ibid, p. 7.
23. Ibid, p. 7.
24. Lloyd George, War Memories, p. 1481.
25. Grey, pp. 7-8.
26. Ibid, p. 9.
27. Ibid, p. 9.
28. Ibid, p. 9.
29. Ibid, p. 10.
30. Lows, Roger, Great Britain and Germany's Lost Colonies, p. 129.
31. Ibid, p. 129.
32. Smuts, General Jan, League of Nations – A Practical Suggestion, p. 9.
33. Ibid, p. 12.
34. Ibid, p. 27.
35. Ibid, p. 31.
36. Ibid, p. 32.
37. Ibid, p. 32.
38. Ibid, p. 34.
39. Ibid, p. 35.
40. Ibid, p. 36.
41. Ibid, p. 39.
42. Ibid, p. 39.
43. Ibid, p. 39.
44. Ibid, p. 56.
45. Ibid, p. 70.

46. House/Seymour, p. 399.
47. Ibid, p. 405.
48. Ibid, p. 404.
49. Ibid, p. 404.
50. Nicolson, Harold, Peacemaking, 1919, p. 259.
51. Ibid, p. 146.
52. Ibid, p. 146.
53. Ibid, p. 146.
54. House/Seymour, pp. 414-415.
55. Pollock, p. 90.
56. Ibid, p. 169.
57. The Treaty of Versailles, American Opinion, p. 12.
58. Ibid, pp. 18-19.
59. Ibid, p. 19.
60. Ibid, p. 21.
61. Ibid, pp. 24-25.
62. Ibid, p. 33.
63. Ibid, p. 33.
64. CAB 1/28.
65. The Treaty of Versailles, American Opinion, p. 69.
66. Ibid, p. 70.
67. Ibid, p. 70.
68. Ibid, p. 72.
69. Ibid, p. 73.
70. Ibid, p. 74.
71. Ibid, p. 74.
72. Ibid, p. 77.
73. Ibid, p. 79.
74. Ibid, p. 84.
75. Ibid, p. 80.
76. Ibid, p. 89.
77. Nicolson, p. 315.
78. Hackett, p. 10.

5. Make Germany Pay

1. Melrose, Andrew, The Real Kaiser, p. 220.
2. Grey, Lord Edward, The League, p. 13.
3. CAB 24/2/32.
4. Sharp, Alan, The Versailles Settlement, p. 13.
5. CAB 24/67.
6. CAB 23/8.
7. Lloyd George, David, The Truth About Reparations, p. 15.
8. Maynard Keyes, John, The Economic Consequences of the Peace, p. 68.
9. Ibid, p. 69.
10. Lloyd George, The Truth About Reparations, p. 8.
11. CAB 23/15 (541/A).
12. CAB 23/15/23.
13. Keynes, p. 70.
14. Macmillan, Margaret, Peacemakers – The Paris Conference of 1919 And Its Attempt to End War, p. 202.
15. Lecom, Georges, Georges Clemenceau, Tiger of France, p. 294.
16. Tardieu, André, The Truth about the Treaty, p. 306.
17. Lloyd George, p. 14.
18. Tardieu, p. 400.
19. Sharp, p. 78.
20. House/Seymour, What Really Happened at Paris, p. 425.
21. Nicolson, Harold, Peacemaking 1919, p. 7.
22. Keynes, pp. 20-21.
23. Bakic, Dragan, Britain and Interwar Danubian Europe, p. 7.
24. Macmillan, p. 15.
25. Ibid, p. 18.
26. Ibid, p. 40.
27. Ibid, p. 212.
28. Nicolson, pp. 118-119.
29. Keynes, p. 4.
30. Ducray, Camille, Clemenceau, p. 172.
31. Nicolson, p. 242.
32. Lloyd George, p. 12.
33. Ibid, p. 13.
34. Dockrill, Michael, Goold, J. Douglas, Peace Without Promise, p. 51.
35. Bridge, Makers of the Modern World.
36. Macmillan, p. 201.
37. Markwell, Donald, Hughes and Australia, p. 4.
38. Keynes, p. 62.
39. Tardieu, p. 399.

40. Keynes, p. 71.
41. Tardieu, p. 307.
42. CAB 23/15 (541A).
43. Macmillan, p. 201.
44. Ibid, p. 208.
45. Dockrill/Goold, p. 50.
46. Ibid, p. 51.
47. Macmillan, p. 200.
48. House/Seymour, p. 200.
49. CAB 28.
50. Dockrill/Goold, p. 52.
51. Sharp, p. 89.
52. Tilman, Seth, Anglo-American Relations at the Peace Conference of 1919, p. 425.
53. Keynes.
54. Ibid, p. 9.
55. Ibid, p. 51.
56. Ibid, p. 83.
57. Ibid, p. 86.
58. Ibid, p. 84.
59. Ibid, pp. 48-49.
60. Ibid, p. 70.
61. Nicolson, p. 359.
62. Keynes, p. 71.
63. House/Seymour, p. 427.
64. Taylor, A.J.P., The Origins of the Second World War, p. 52.
65. Ibid, p. 52.
66. FO 374/19.
67. Keynes, p. 70.

6. France Remains in Perpetual Danger of Invasion

1. Sharp, Alan, The Versailles, Settlement, p. 107.
2. Nicolson, Harold, Peacemaking, 1919, p. 320.
3. House/Seymour, What Really Happened at Paris, p. 49.
4. Sharp, p. 106.
5. Ibid, p. 107.
6. House/Seymour, pp. 52-53.
7. Macmillan, Margaret, Peacemakers, p. 182.
8. Dockrill/Goold, Peace with Promise, p. 36.
9. Tardieu, Andrew, The Truth About the Peace Treaty, p. 134.
10. House/Seymour, p. 53.
11. Ibid, p. 52.
12. Schwob, The Ruhr Problem, p. 15.
13. Sharp, p. 108.
14. Ibid, p. 109.
15. Ibid, p. 109.
16. Tardieu, p. 171.
17. Ibid, p. 171.
18. Ibid, p. 172.
19. Ibid, p. 175.
20. Dockrill/Goold, p. 36.
21. Sharp, p. 109.
22. Ibid, p. 110.
23. Tardieu, p. 173.
24. CAB 23/15 (541A).
25. Ibid.
26. Ibid.
27. Ibid.
28. Rose, Inbal, Conservative and Foreign Policy during the Lloyd George Coalition, p. 71.
29. CAB 23/15 (541A).
30. Dockrill/Goold, pp. 35-36.
31. Lentin, A., Lloyd George and the Lost Peace, from Versailles to Hitler, 1919-1940, p. 53.
32. Ibid, p. 53.
33. Macmillan, pp. 184-185.
34. Tardieu, p. 217.
35. Rose, p. 71.
36. Macmillan, p. 211.
37. Sharp, p. 111.
38. Ibid, p. 112.
39. Tardieu, p. 191.
40. Schwob, p. 9.
41. Tardieu, p. 200.
42. Ibid, p. 243.
43. Holt, Charles Downer, Alsace Lorraine Under German Rule, p. 5.
44. Duhem, Jules, The Question of Alsace-Lorraine, p. 5.
45. Holt, p. 86.
46. Ibid, p. 229.
47. Lauzanne, Stephane, Why France wants Alsace-Lorraine, p. 1.
48. House/Seymour, p. 40.
49. Ibid, p. 46.
50. Holt, p. 233.

51. Tardieu, p. 247.
52. House/Seymour, p. 48.
53. Tardieu, p. 258.
54. Ibid, p. 250.
55. Ibid, p. 250.
56. Keynes, John Maynard, The Economic Consequences of the Peace, p. 39.
57. Tardieu, p. 250.
58. House/Seymour, p. 57.
59. Ibid, p. 58.
60. Tardieu, p. 264.
61. Ibid, p. 265.
62. Ibid, p. 266.
63. House/Seymour, p. 60.
64. Sharp, p. 115.
65. House/Seymour, pp. 62-63.
66. Ibid, p. 64.
67. Ibid, p. 65.
68. Ibid, pp. 60-61.
69. Ibid, p. 61.
70. Sinclair, David, Hall of Mirrors, p. 226.
71. CAB 32/2.
72. House/Seymour, pp. 61-62.
73. Lentin, p. 60.
74. Ibid, pp. 54-55.
75. Ibid, p. 58.
76. Hogan, Michael, The Ambiguous Legacy, p. 56.
77. Ibid, p. 56.
78. Meinander/Mangan, The Nordic World: Sport in Society, p. 40.

7.Self-determination May Be a False and Monstrous Idea

1. Lloyd George, David, War Memoirs of David Lloyd George, p. 1517.
2. House/Seymour, What Really Happened at Paris, p. 69.
3. Ibid, p. 71.
4. Prazmowska, Anita, Poland: A Modern History, p. 38.
5. Ibid, pp. 56-57.
6. Ibid, p. 40.
7. Ibid, p. 70.
8. Macmillan, Margaret, Peacemakers, p. 221.
9. Prazmowska, p. 71.
10. Ibid, pp. 82-83.
11. Cab 24/2/32.
12. House/Seymour, p. 71.
13. Ibid, p. 70.
14. Macmillan, p. 222.
15. House/Seymour, p. 71.
16. Macmillan, p. 225.
17. Ibid, p. 229.
18. Ibid, p. 223.
19. House/Seymour, p. 71.
20. Ibid, p. 70.
21. Minute by Hardinge, 12 April 1919, FO608/18.
22. House/Seymour, p. 67.
23. Ibid, p. 67.
24. Buell, Raymond, Poland: Key to Europe, p. 278.
25. House/Seymour, p. 71.
26. Ibid, p. 67.
27. Minute from Drummond to Kerr, 18/1/19, Lothian MSS GD40/17/15.
28. House/Seymour, p. 68.
29. Ibid, p. 73.
30. Ibid, p. 74.
31. Ibid, p. 74.
32. Dockrill/Goold, Peace Without Promise, p. 114.
33. Buell, p. 235.
34. House/Seymour, p. 77.
35. FO 608/141.
36. House/Seymour, p. 78.
37. Dockrill/Gool, p. 116.
38. House/Seymour, p. 80.
39. Ibid, p. 81.
40. Ibid, pp. 67-68.
41. Ibid, p. 82.
42. FO 608/63.
43. House/Seymour, p. 83.
44. Ibid, p. 82.
45. Ibid, p. 3.
46. Macmillan, p. 84.
47. House/Seymour, p. 84.
48. Macmillan, p. 238.
49. Prazmowski, p. 140.
50. Macmillan, p. 238.
51. House/Seymour, p. 86.

8. This Might Be Neither Equitable nor Conducive to Peace

1. House/Seymour, What Really Happened at Paris, p. 87.
2. Ibid, p. 187.
3. Calder, Kenneth, Britain and the Origins of the New Europe, 1914-1918, p. 97.
4. Ibid, p. 118.
5. Ibid, p. 116.
6. Ibid, p. 117.
7. Ibid, p. 115.
8. House, Edward Mandell, The Intimate Papers of Colonel House, p. 337.
9. CAB 24/2/32.
10. House/Seymour, p. 90.
11. CAB 24/2/32.
12. House/Seymour, p. 89.
13. Heimann, Marie, Czechoslovakia: the State that Failed, pp. 25-26.
14. Ibid, pp. 25-26.
15. Ibid, p. 27.
16. Ibid, p. 29.
17. Ibid, p. 32.
18. Ibid, p. 30.
19. Ibid, p. 32.
20. Ibid, p. 32.
21. Ibid, p. 33.
22. Ibid, pp. 33-34.
23. Ibid, p. 33.
24. Ibid, p. 36.
25. Ostereichische Nationbibliotek.
26. Declaration of independence of the Czechoslovak Nation, 18/10/18, pp. 3-4.
27. Heimann, p. 38.
28. House/Seymour, p. 89.
29. Heimann, p. 43.
30. Macmillan, Margaret, Peacemakers, p. 236.
31. Perman, D., The Shaping of the Czechoslovak State, p. 131.
32. Bakic, Dragon, Britain and Interwar Danubian Europe, pp. 12-13.
33. Dockrill/Goold, Peace Without Promise, p. 88.
34. House/Seymoure, p. 431.
35. Ibid, p. 92.
36. Dockrill/Goold, p. 93.
37. FO 608/5.
38. FO 608/5.
39. House/Seymour, p. 93.
40. Ibid, p. 94.
41. Macmillan, p. 135.
42. House/Seymour, p. 94.
43. Macmillan, p. 277.
44. FO 608/16.
45. Ibid.
46. House/Seymour, p. 97.
47. Ibid, p. 97.
48. Ibid, p. 99.
49. Ibid, pp. 97-99.
50. Ibid, p. 105.
51. Nicolson, Harold, Peacemaking 1919, p. 278.
52. House/Seymour, p. 101.
53. Dockrill/Goold, p. 111.
54. App, Austin, The Sudeten German Tragedy, p. 8.
55. Ibid, p. 8.
56. House/Seymour, p. 110.
57. Ibid, p. 105.
58. Macmillan, p. 252.
59. Heimann, p. 47.
60. Sinclair, David, Hall of Mirrors, p. 229.
61. Taylor, A. J. P., The Origins of the Second World War, p. 63.
62. Dockrill/Goold, p. 106.
63. Nicolson, p. 166.
64. Macmillan, p. 120.
65. Nicolson, p. 166.
66. Smith, Denis Mack, Mussolini, p. 37.
67. Nicolson, p. 170.
68. Smith, p. 111.
69. Ibid, p. 37.
70. Macmillan, p. 303.
71. FO 608/15.
72. Nicolson, p. 178.
73. Ibid, p. 193.
74. Ibid, p. 34.
75. House/Seymour, p. 106.

76. Ibid, p. 106.
77. Ibid, p. 105.
78. Nicolson, p. 328.
79. Ibid, p. 335.
80. Gilbert, Martin, The Roots of Appeasement, p. 122.
81. Macmillan, p. 269.
82. Dockrill/Goold, p. 127.
83. Ibid, p. 103.
84. FO 608/11.
85. Bakic, p. 12.
86. House/Seymour, p. 109.
87. Nicolson, p. 349.
88. Macmillan, p. 130.
89. Nicolson, p. 34.
90. Ibid, p. 259.
91. Bakic, p. 11.
92. Nicolson, p. 34.
93. Dockrill/Goold, p. 95.
94. Macmillan, p. 149.
95. Dockrill/Goold, p. 94.
96. Ibid, p. 98.
97. Ibid, p. 98.
98. Macmillan, p. 151.
99. FO 608/225.
100. Ethnic Groups and Population Exchanges in Twentieth Century Eastern Europe, p. 369.
101. Taylor, A. J. P., English History, p. 185.

9. All the Elements of a National Rising

1. Bakic, Dragon, Britain and Interwar Danubian Europe, p. 7.
2. Heimann, Marie, Czechoslovakia: The State that Failed, p. 54.
3. Heimann, p. 59.
4. App, Austin, The Sudeten German Tragedy, p. 6.
5. Heimann, p. 69.
6. Ibid, p. 54.
7. Ibid, p. 64.
8. Ibid, p. 73.
9. App, p. 12.
10. Heimann, p. 69.
11. Ibid, p. 50.
12. Ibid, p. 73.
13. Crampton, R. J., Eastern Europe in the Twentieth Century, p. 66.
14. Heimann, p. 55.
15. Crampton, p. 66.
16. Heimann, p. 62.
17. Ibid, p. 53.
18. Crampton, p. 66.
19. Heimann, p. 62.
20. Macmillan, p. 252.
21. Ibid, pp. 252-253.
22. Crampton, p. 70.
23. Ibid, p. 70.
24. Heimann, p. 77.
25. Crampton, p. 72.
26. Hitler, Adolf, Mein Kampf
27. App, p. 17.
28. Heimann, p. 86.
29. App, p. 17.
30. Latowski, Paul, The Reconstruction of Poland, p. 147.
31. Prazmowska, Anita, Poland: A Modern History, p. 147.
32. Ibid, p. 148.
33. Clough et al., Economic History of Europe, p. 97.
34. Snowden, Ethel, A Political Pilgrim in Europe, p. 25.
35. Kershaw, Ian, To Hell and Back, pp. 70-71.
36. Buell, Raymond, Poland: Key to Europe, pp. 146-147.
37. Ibid, pp. 280-286.
38. Ibid, pp. 129-130.
39. Ibid, p. 144.
40. Latowski, p. xix.
41. Ibid, p. 150.
42. Kershaw, p. 97.
43. Stachura, Peter, Poland in the Twentieth Century, p. 29.
44. Ibid, p. 29.
45. Ibid, p. 30.
46. Ibid, p. 56.
47. Ibid, p. 58.
48. Prazmowska, p. 106.
49. Buell, Poland: Key to Europe, p. 284.

50. Stachura, p. 85.
51. Buell, p. 104.
52. Stachura, p. 84.
53. Ibid, p. 84.
54. Ibid, p. 84.
55. Buell, pp. 298-299.
56. Prazmowska, p. 105.
57. Buell, p. 270.
58. Ibid, p. 292.
59. Stachura, p. 84.
60. Ibid, p. 82.
61. Ibid, p. 82.
62. Buell, p. 270.
63. Ibid, p. 267.
64. Ibid, p. 278.
65. Frentz, Christian Raitz von, A lesson Forgotten, p. 147.
66. Buell, p. 318.
67. Stachura, p. 80.
68. Buell, p. 233.
69. Buell, p. 69.
70. Prazmowska, p. 121.
71. Buell, 101, p. 101.
72. Buell, 106.
73. Serbian, Italian Relations, History of Modern Times, p. 139.
74. Biondich, Mark, Stjepan Radic, the Croat Peasant Party, and the Politics of Mass Mobilisation, 1904-1928, p. 138.
74. Ibid, p. 138.
75. Ibid, p. 138.
76. Lampe, John R., Yugoslavia as History, p. 107.
77. Biondich, p. 138.
78. Harrison, H. D., The Soul of Yugoslavia, p. 170.
79. Ibid, p. 170.
80. Lampe, p. 111.
81. Bayerlein, Henry, The Birth of Yugoslavia, p. 120.
82. Ibid, p. 120.
83. Capo, Hrvoje, Polity of the Kingdom of Serbs Croats and Slovenes, p. 129.
84. Bayerlein, pp. 224-225.
85. Harrison, p. 181.
86. Ramet, Sabrina, The Three Yugoslavias, p. 147.
87. Lampe, p. 116.
88. Ibid, pp. 146-147.
89. Ibid, p. 147.
90. Ibid, pp. 185-186.
91. Ibid, pp. 130-131.
92. Bakic, Britain and the Interwar Danubian Europe, p. 7.
93. Harrison, pp. 179-180.
94. Capo, p. 121.
95. Harrison, p. 182.
96. Ibid, p. 191.
97. Ibid, p. 191.
98. Nijhoff, Martinus, Trifunovska, Snezana, Yugoslavoa Through Documents, pp. 190-191.
99. Ibid, p. 191.
100. Harrison, pp. 192-193.
101. Ibid, p. 193.
102. Ibid, p. 194.
103. Lampe, p. 166.
104. Ibid, p. 162.
105. Croatia Under Yugoslavian Rule.
106. Lampe, p. 162.
107. Ibid, p. 160.
108. Ibid, p. 165.
109. Harrison, p. 196.
110. Ibid, p. 198.
111. Ibid, p. 200.
112. Capo, p. 29.
113. Harrison, p. 234.
114. Bayerlein, p. 234.
115. Harrison, p. 206.
116. Ibid, p. 214.
117. Ibid, p. 217.
118. Lampe, p. 192.
119. Vujacic, Veljo, Nationalism, Myth and the State in Russia, and Serbia, p. 209.
120. Ibid, p. 211.
121. Harrison, p. 253.
122. Shirer, William, The Rise and Fall of the Third Reich, p. 985.
123. Hart, Basil Liddell, History of the Second World War, p. 159.
124. Trevor-Roper, Hugh, Hitler's War Directives, pp. 107, 108.

10. Accept German Prices and Adjust to German Measures

1. Bakic, Dragon, Britain and Interwar Danubian Europe, pp. 12-13.
2. Clough et al, Economic History of Europe, p. 98.
3. Fink, Carole, the Genoa Conference, p. 247.
4. Salzer, Food Supply of the Republic of Austria end of 1919, p. 12.
5. Snowden, Ethel, A Political Pilgrim in Europe, p. 113.
6. Ibid, pp. 113-114.
7. Salzer, p. 13.
8. Ibid, p. 17.
9. House/Seymour, What Really Happened at Paris, p. 108.
10. Macartney, C. A., The Social Revolution in Austria, p. 113.
11. Ibid, p. 116.
12. Feldman, Gerald D., The Great Disorder, Politics, Economics and Society in the German Inflation, 1914-1924, p. 318.
13. Macmillan, Margaret, The Peacemakers, p. 259.
14. Canadian-American Review of Hungarian Studies, vol v, No2 (Autumn 1978), Istvan Bethlen and Hungarian Foreign Policy, 1921-1931, Thomas Sakmyster.
15. Douglas-Scott, Sionadh, Constitutional Law of the European Union, p. 9.
16. Shaim, Hamir, Economic Crisis and French Foreign Policy, pp. 20-21.
17. Douglas-Scott, p. 20.
18. Shamir, p. 20.
19. Nijhoff/Mayer, Mitteleuropa in German Thought and Action, 1815-1945.
20. Berend, Ivan T., Decades of Crisis: Central and Eastern Europe Before World War Two.
21. Walters, William and Haahr, Jens Henrik, Governing Europe: Discourse, Governmentality and European Integration, p. 8.
22. Making the New Europe: European Unity and the Second World War, Edited by M. L. Smith and Peter M. R. Stirk, p. 88.
23. Berend, Ivan T., Decades of Crisis: Central and Eastern Europe Before World War Two, p. 273.
24. Pelt, Morgan, Tobacco, Arms and Politics: Greece and Germany from World Crisis to World War, p. 83.
25. Berend, p. 277.
26. Scherner, Jonas and White, Eugene N., Paying for Hitler's War, The Consequences of Nazi Economic Hegemony in Europe, pp. 10-11.
27. Berend, p. 274.
28. Ibid, p. 277.
29. Harrison, H. D., The Soul of Yugoslavia, p. 243.
30. Scherner/White, p. 335.
31. Smith/Kirk, p. 88-89.
32. Ibid, p. 88.
33. Gildea, Robert, Warring, Annette, Surviving Hitler and Mussolini: Daily Life in Occupied Europe, p. 20.
34. Gilbert, Martin, Churchill, A Life, p. 661.
35. Smith/Stirk, p. 89.
36. James, Harold and Tanner, Jakob, Enterprise in the Period of Fascism in Europe, p. 152.
37. Ibid, p. 163.
38. Ibid, p. 155.
39. Ibid, p. 154.
40. Smith/Stirk, p. 94.
41. Ibid, p. 89.
42. Ibid, p. 93.
43. James/Tanner, p. 151.
44. Smith/Stirk, p. 94.
45. Ibid, p. 94.
46. James/Tanner, pp. 151-152.
47. Ibid, pp. 151-152.
48. Ibid, p. 154.
49. Ibid, p. 154.
50. Gildea/Warring, p. 20.

51. Ibid, p. 21.
52. Scherner, p. 434.
53. Ibid, p. 433.
54. Ibid, p. 437.
55. Kershaw, Ian, Hitler: Nemesis, p. 343.
56. Trevor-Roper, Hugh, Hitler's War Directives, p. 131.
57. Kay, Alex J., Exploitation, Resettlement, Mass Murder, Political and Economic Planning for German Occupation Policy in the Soviet Union, 1940-1941, p. 99.
58. Ibid, p. 71.
59. Ibid, p. 59.
60. Ibid, p. 100.
61. Ibid, p. 99.
62. Clark, Alan, Barbarossa, p. 66.
63. Ibid, p. 65.
64. Ibid, p. 65.
65. Gildea/Warring, p. 52.
66. Clark, p. 130.
67. Shirer, W. L., The Rise and Fall of the Third Reich, p. 1085.
68. Glenny, Misha, The Balkans, p. 485.
69. Ibid, p. 485.
70. Ibid, p. 485.
71. Ibid, p. 485.
72. Ibid, p. 485.
73. James/Tanner, p. 165.
74. Lampe, John R., Yugoslavia as History, Twice there was a Country, pp. 218-219.
75. Ibid, p. 220.
76. Clark, G. N., Belgium and the War, p. 25.
77. Gildea/Warring, p. 45.
78. Ibid, pp. 22-23.
79. Ibid, p. 21.
80. Ibid, p. 65.
81. Holbraad, Carsten, Danish Reactions to German Occupation: History and Historiography, p. 50.
82. Ousby, Ian, Occupation, The Ordeal of France, 1940-1944, p. 141.
83. Farmer, Paul, Vichy Political Dilemma, p. 304.
84. Gildea/Warring, p. 20.
85. Ousby, Collaboration, p. 142.
86. Gildea/Warring, p. 49.
87. Ibid, p. 21.
88. Farmer, p. 305.
89. Ousby, p. 251.
90. Gildea/Warring, p. 56.
91. Ousby, p. 251.
92. Speer, Albert, Inside the Third Reich, p. 422.
93. Ibid, p. 424.
94. Ibid, pp. 425-426.
95. Tung, Rosalie L. (ed.), Learning from World Class Companies, p. 190.
96. Ibid, p. 188.
97. Speer, p. 500.
98. Gross, John T., Neighbours – The Destruction of the Jewish Community in Jedwabne, Poland, 1941, p. 93.
99. Ibid, p. 99.
100. Gigliotti, Simone, The Train Journey: Transit, Captivity and Witnessing the Holocaust, p. 36.
101. Ibid, p. 41.
102. Graber, G.S., History of the SS, p. 154.
103. Karsten, Peter (ed.), Motivating Soldiers: Morale or Mutiny, p. 271.
104. Beevor, Antony, Stalingrad, pp. 181-182.
105. Smith/Stirk, p. 88.
106. Die Fischer Chronik Deutchsland, p. 35.
107. Botting, Douglas, Ruins of the Reich, p. 118.
108. FO 1049/81.
109. Tolstoy, Nikolai, Victims of Yalta, p. 392.
110. Ibid, p. 394.
111. Office of the Military Government for Germany (US), Report of Military Governor, p. 2.
112. Ibid, p. 2.

113. Gildea/Warring, p. 56.
114. Botting, p. 101.
115. Ibid, p. 81.
116. Scherner, Jonas and White, Eugene N., Paying for Hitler's War, The Consequences of Nazi Economic Hegemony in Europe, p. 142.
117. Ibid, pp. 143-145.
118. Ibid, p. 442.
119. Ibid, p. 442.
120. Ibid, p. 442.
121. Beevor, p. 22.
122. Botting, p. 81.
123. Source unknown.
124. Salisbury, Harrison, E., The 900 Days: The Siege of Leningrad, p. 573-574.
125. Gilbert, Martin, The Day the War Ended, p. 243.
126. Ibid, p. 243.
127. Botting, p. 96.
128. Ibid, p. 95.
129. Ibid, p. 95.
130. Ibid, p. 96.
131. Ibid, p. 167.
132. Gilbert, pp. 336-337.
133. Botting, p. 98.
134. Beevor, Antony, Berlin – The Downfall 1945, p. 410.
135. Botting, pp. 98-99.
136. Ryan, Cornelius, The Last Battle, pp. 14-15.
137. Botting, p. 98.
138. Botting, p. 93.

11. The End of This War Will Be Written in Blood

1. Douglas-Scott, Sionaidh, The Constitutional Law of the European Union, p. 78.
2. Botting, Douglas, Ruins of the Reich, p. 78.
3. Gilbert, Martin, The Day the War Ended, p. 267.
4. Dixon, Francis Graham, The Allied Occupation of Germany, The Refugee Crisis, Denazification and the Path to Reconstruction, p. 7.
5. Wheeler-Bennett, John W., and Nicholls, Anthony, The Semblance of Peace, The Political Settlement after the Second World War, p. 179.
6. Ibid, p. 179.
7. Botting, p. 96.
8. Beevor, Antony, Berlin – The Downfall 1945, pp. 9-10.
9. James, Harold, Krupp: A History of the Legendary German Firm, p. 223.
10. Ibid, p. 223.
11. Botting, p. 216.
12. Ibid, p. 101.
13. Ibid, p. 216.
14. Werth, Alexander, de Gaulle, p. 199.
15. App, Austin J., The Sudeten German Tragedy, p. 27.
16. Schieder, Theodor, The Expulsion of the German Population from the Territories East of the Oder-Neisse-Line, p. 82.
17. App, p. 29.
18. Ibid, p. 33.
19. Ibid, p. 44.
20. Ibid, pp. 41-42.
21. Ibid, p. 42.
22. Botting, p. 142.
23. Roman, Eric, Hungary and the Victor Powers, 1945-1950, p. 105.
24. Ibid, p. 104.
25. Ibid, p. 105.
26. Paikert, G. C., The Danube Swabians: German Populations in Hungary, Romania and Yugoslavia and Hitler's Impact on their Patterns, p. 207.
27. Ibid, p. 104.
28. Ibid, p. 105.
29. Schieder, p. 13.
30. Siebel-Achenbach, Sebastian, Lower Silesia, from Nazi Germany to Communist Poland, 1942-1949, p. 122.
31. Schieder, pp. 64-65.
32. Ibid, p. 68.
33. Ibid, p. 82.

34. Ibid, p. 88.
35. Ibid, p. 91.
36. Ibid, p. 113.
37. Siebel-Achenbach, p. 142.
38. Schieder, p. 92.
39. Ibid, p. 121.
40. Botting, p. 131.
41. Ibid, p. 136.
42. Glenny, Misha, The Balkans, p. 530.
43. Portmann, Michael, Retaliation and Persecution on Yugoslav Territory During and after World War Two (1943-1950), p. 63.
44. Ibid, pp. 63-64.
45. Ibid, p. 64.
46. Ibid, p. 59.
47. Ibid, p. 65.

12. Something to Astonish You

1. Ellwood, David W., Rebuilding Europe: Western Europe, America and Postwar Reconstruction, p. 12.
2. Ibid, p. 12.
3. Thorpe, Andrew, A History of the Labour Party, 4th ed., p. 122.
4. Ellwood, p. 17.
5. Bell, P. M. H., France and Britain, p. 74.
6. Thorpe, p. 133.
7. Jenkins, Roy, Churchill, p. 814.
8. Gilbert, Martin, Churchill: A Life, p. 876.
9. Ambrose, Stephen, Rise to Globalism – American Foreign Policy since 1938, p. 135.
10. Auto, Phyllis, Tito, p. 290.
11. House of Commons Parliamentary Debates: 1946-1947, vol.438, p. 2238 (quoted from De Gaulle and the European Union, H. S. Chopra).
12. Ambrose, p. 123.
13. Werth, Alexander, de Gaulle, pp. 211-212.
14. Bell, p. 92.
15. Cannadine, D., Speeches of Winston Churchill, pp. 310-314.

16. Bell, p. 101.
17. From the Statute of the Council of Europe.
18. Bell, p. 103.
19. Werth, pp. 216-217.
20. Bell, p. 108.
21. Douglas-Scott, Sionaidh, Constitutional Law of the European Union, p. 10.
22. Dell, Edmund, The Schuman Plan and the British Abdication of Leadership in Europe, p. 169.
23. Ibid, p. 176.
24. Douglas-Scott, p. 11.
25. Dell, p. 171.
26. Jenkins, pp. 816-817.
27. Gilbert, pp. 891-892.
28. Werth, p. 218.
29. Bell, p. 117.
30. Jenkins, p. 854.
31. Gilbert, p. 900.
32. Jenkins, p. 855.
33. Werth, p. 218.
34. Large, David Clay, Germans to the Front: West German Rearmament in the Adenauer Era, p. 93.
35. Ibid, p. 93.
36. Ibid, p. 94.
37. Ibid, p. 94.
38. Ibid, p. 103.
39. Ibid, p. 94.
40. Ibid, p. 94.
41. Ibid, pp. 98-99.
42. Werth, p. 226.
43. Ibid, p. 226.
44. Ibid, p. 227.
45. Gilbert, p. 932.
46. Ibid, p. 932.
47. Ibid, p. 932.
48. The Spaak Report, 21 April 1956.
49. Dinan, Desmond, Encyclopaedia of the EU.
50. The Fouchet Plan: De Gaulle's Intergovernmental Design for Europe, LSE, LEQS Paper No.117/2016, October 2016.
51. Werth, p. 316.

52. The Fouchet Plan.
53. Douglas-Scott, pp. 225-226.
54. Werth, pp. 323-324.
55. Ibid, pp. 328-329.
56. Ibid, p. 331.
57. Davies, Evan, Aspects of Modern World History, p. 153.
58. Catchpole, Brian, A Map History of the British People since 1700, p. 193.
59. The Legislation website.
60. The Thatcher Foundation.
61. Glenny, Misha, The Balkans, pp. 596-597.
62. Legal Opinion on the Benes Decrees and the accession of the Czech Republic to the European Union.
63. Ibid.
64. Douglas-Scott, p. 43.
65. Ibid, p. 56.
66. Ibid, p. 45.
67. Quoted from a contemporary BBC broadcast.

APPENDIX 1

Peace Treaty of Brest-Litovsk 1918 (Selected Articles)

ARTICLE 1

Germany, Austria-Hungary, Bulgaria and Turkey on the one hand and Russia on the other declare that the condition of war between them has ceased. They have decided to live in peace and accord in the future.

ARTICLE 2

The contracting parties will refrain from all agitation or propaganda against the governments or all state and military institutions of the other side. Inasmuch as this obligation affects Russia, it affects also the territories occupied by the powers of the Quadruple Alliance.

ARTICLE 3

The territories lying to the west of the line determined by the contracting powers and which formerly belonged to Russia will no longer be under her sovereignty. The line determined upon is marked on the appended map (Appendix I), which is an important part of the present treaty of peace.(3) The precise location of this line will be worked out by a German-Russian commission.

In respect to the mentioned territories no obligations towards Russia are to be considered as issuing from their formerly having belonged to that country.

Russia gives up all interference in the internal affairs of the said territories. Germany and Austria-Hungary intend to determine the future fate of the said territories with the consent of their inhabitants.

ARTICLE 4

Russia will do all in her power to have the provinces of eastern Anatolia promptly evacuated and returned to Turkey.

The territories of Ardakhan, Kars and Batum will also be cleared without delay of Russian troops. Russia will not interfere in the new organization of internal juridical and international juridical relations of such territories, but will allow the populations of these territories to establish new governments in agreement with neighbouring states, especially with Turkey.

ARTICLE 5

Russia will, without delay, proceed to demobilize her army, including those army units newly formed by her present government.

Moreover Russia will either bring her warships into Russian ports and keep them there until general peace is concluded or will disarm them at once. The warships of the countries continuing in a state of war with the Quadruple Alliance, in so far as such warships are within the sphere of Russian sovereignty, must be treated as Russian warships.

The prohibition zone of the Arctic Ocean remains in force until the conclusion of general peace In the Baltic Sea and those parts of the Black Sea under Russia's supremacy, the clearing away of mine defense must be begun at once. Merchant navigation in those sea regions is free and is to recommence at once. Mixed commissions are to be formed for the purpose of framing more concise regulations and especially for the purpose of publication of general information as to safe courses of sailing for trading vessels. Such courses must always be free of floating mines.

ARTICLE 6

Russia undertakes to conclude peace at once with the Ukrainian people's republic and to recognize the treaty of peace between the state and the powers of the Quadruple Alliance. The territory of the Ukraine must be, at once, cleared of Russian troops and of the Russian Red Guard. Russia ceases all agitation or propaganda against the government or the public institutions of the Ukrainia people's republic.

Estonia and Livonia must be also immediately cleared of Russian troops and the Russian Red Guard. The eastern boundary of Esthonia passes in general along the River Narova. The eastern boundary of Livonia, in general, crosses the Lakes Chud [Peipus] and Pskov up to the southwestern corner of the latter, thence it runs across Lake Luban in the direction of Lievenhof on the Western Dvina. Esthonia and Livonia will be occupied by German police force until public safety is secured by proper institutions of the country and until governmental order is reestablished. Russia will at once liberate all the inhabitants of Esthonia and Livonia who have been arrested or deported and will secure a safe return of all deported Esthonians and Livonians.

Finland and the Aland Islands will be also, without delay, cleared of Russian troops and the Russian Red Guard and Finnish ports of the Russian fleet and of Russian naval forces. While ice renders impossible the conveying of warships to Russian ports there must remain on board only a limited crew. Russia ceases all agitation or propaganda against the government or public institutions of Finland.

The fortifications constructed on the Aland Islands must be razed at the first opportunity. As regards the prohibition to erect fortifications of these islands in the future, as well as the question of their future in general in a military respect and in respect to the technical side of navigation, a special agreement must be concluded between Germany, Finland, Russia and Sweden; the parties consent that at Germany's desire other countries bordering the Baltic Sea may be called upo to take part in the above agreement.

The prisoners of war of both parties will be allowed to return home. The regulation of questions in connection with the above will be the subject of special treaties mentioned in Article 12.

ARTICLE 9

The contracting parties mutually renounce all indemnifications for their war expenses, that is, for government expenses for conducting the war, as well as all compensation of war losses, that is, such losses as were caused them and their citizens in the zone of war by military operations, including all requisitions made in the enemy's country.

The economic relations between the powers of the Quadruple Alliance and Russia are regulated by decisions contained in Appendices II to V. Appendix II determines the relations between Germany and Russia, Appendix III between Austria-Hungary and Russia, Appendix IV between Bulgaria and Russia and Appendix V between Turkey and Russia.

ARTICLE 12

The reestablishment of public and private legal relations, the exchange of war and civil prisoners, the question of amnesty as well as the question regarding merchant ships which have been seized by one or the other side, will be provided for in separate treaties with Russia, which form an important part of the present peace treaty, and as far as it is possible come into force simultaneously with the latter.

APPENDIX 2

President Woodrow Wilson's Fourteen Points

8 January, 1918:

President Woodrow Wilson's Fourteen Points

It will be our wish and purpose that the processes of peace, when they are begun, shall be absolutely open and that they shall involve and permit henceforth no secret understandings of any kind. The day of conquest and aggrandizement is gone by; so is also the day of secret covenants entered into in the interest of particular governments and likely at some unlooked-for moment to upset the peace of the world. It is this happy fact, now clear to the view of every public man whose thoughts do not still linger in an age that is dead and gone, which makes it possible for every nation whose purposes are consistent with justice and the peace of the world to avow nor or at any other time the objects it has in view.

We entered this war because violations of right had occurred which touched us to the quick and made the life of our own people impossible unless they were corrected and the world secure once for all against their recurrence. What we demand in this war, therefore, is nothing peculiar to ourselves. It is that the world be made fit and safe to live in; and particularly that it be made safe for every peace-loving nation which, like our own, wishes to live its own life, determine its own institutions, be assured of justice and fair dealing by the other peoples of the world as against force and selfish aggression. All the peoples of the world are in effect partners in this interest, and for our own part we see very clearly that unless justice be done to others it will not be done to us. The programme of the world's peace, therefore, is our programme; and that programme, the only possible programme, as we see it, is this:

1. Open covenants of peace, openly arrived at, after which there shall be no private international understandings of any kind but diplomacy shall proceed always frankly and in the public view.

2. Absolute freedom of navigation upon the seas, outside territorial waters, alike in peace and in war, except as the seas may be closed in whole or in part by international action for the enforcement of international covenants.

3. The removal, so far as possible, of all economic barriers and the establishment of an equality of trade conditions among all the nations consenting to the peace and associating themselves for its maintenance.

4. Adequate guarantees given and taken that national armaments will be reduced to the lowest point consistent with domestic safety.

5. A free, open-minded, and absolutely impartial adjustment of all colonial claims, based upon a strict observance of the principle that in determining all such questions of sovereignty the interests of the populations concerned must have equal weight with the equitable claims of the government whose title is to be determined.

6. The evacuation of all Russian territory and such a settlement of all questions affecting Russia as will secure the best and freest cooperation of the other nations of the world in obtaining for her an unhampered and unembarrassed opportunity for the independent determination of her own political development and national policy and assure her of a sincere welcome into the society of free nations under institutions of her own choosing; and, more than a welcome, assistance also of every kind that she may need and may herself desire. The treatment accorded Russia by her sister nations in the months to come will be the acid test of their good will, of their comprehension of her needs as distinguished from their own interests, and of their intelligent and unselfish sympathy.

7. Belgium, the whole world will agree, must be evacuated and restored, without any attempt to limit the sovereignty which she enjoys in common with all other free nations. No other single act will serve as this will serve to restore confidence among the nations in the laws which they have themselves set and determined for the government of their relations with one another. Without this healing act the whole structure and validity of international law is forever impaired.

8. All French territory should be freed and the invaded portions restored, and the wrong done to France by Prussia in 1871 in the matter of Alsace-Lorraine, which has unsettled the peace of the world for nearly fifty years, should be righted, in order that peace may once more be made secure in the interest of all.

9. A readjustment of the frontiers of Italy should be effected along clearly recognizable lines of nationality.

10. The peoples of Austria-Hungary, whose place among the nations we wish to see safeguarded and assured, should be accorded the freest opportunity to autonomous development.

11. Romania, Serbia, and Montenegro should be evacuated; occupied territories restored; Serbia accorded free and secure access to the sea; and the relations of the several Balkan states to one another determined by friendly counsel along historically established lines of allegiance and nationality; and international guarantees of the political and economic independence and territorial integrity of the several Balkan states should be entered into.

12. The Turkish portion of the present Ottoman Empire should be assured a secure sovereignty, but the other nationalities which are nWow under Turkish rule should be assured an undoubted security of life and an absolutely unmolested opportunity of autonomous development, and the Dardanelles should be permanently opened as a free passage to the ships and commerce of all nations under international guarantees.

13. An independent Polish state should be erected which should include the territories inhabited by indisputably Polish populations, which should be assured a free and secure access to the sea, and whose political and economic independence and territorial integrity should be guaranteed by international covenant.

14. A general association of nations must be formed under specific covenants for the purpose of affording mutual guarantees of political independence and territorial integrity to great and small states alike.

In regard to these essential rectifications of wrong and assertions of right we feel ourselves to be intimate partners of all the governments and peoples associated together against the Imperialists. We cannot be separated in interest or divided in purpose. We stand together until the end.

For such arrangements and covenants we are willing to fight and to continue to fight until they are achieved; but only because we wish the right to prevail and desire a just and stable peace such as can be secured only by removing the chief provocations to war, which this programme does remove. We have no jealousy of German greatness, and there is nothing in this programme that impairs it. We grudge her no achievement or distinction of learning or of pacific enterprise such as have made her record very bright and very enviable. We do not wish to injure her or to block in any way her legitimate influence or power. We do not wish to fight her either with arms or with hostile arrangements of trade if she is willing to associate herself with us and the other peace- loving nations of the world in covenants of justice and law and fair dealing. We wish her only to accept a place of equality among the peoples of the world, – the new world in which we now live, – instead of a place of mastery.

Prime Minister Lloyd George on the British War Aims

When the Government invite organized labour in this country to assist them to maintain the might of their armies in the field, its representatives are entitled to ask that any misgivings and doubts which any of them may have about the purpose to which this precious strength is to be applied should be definitely cleared, and what is true of organized labour is equally true of all citizens in this country, without regard to grade or avocation. "When men by the million are being called upon to suffer and die, and vast populations are being subjected to the sufferings and privations of war on a scale unprecedented in the history of the world, they are entitled to know for what cause or causes they are making the sacrifice. It is only the clearest, greatest and justest of causes that can justify the continuance even for one day of this unspeakable agony of the nations, and we ought to be able to state clearly and definitely, not only the principles for which we are fighting, but also their definite and concrete application to the war map of the world.

We have arrived at the most critical hour in this terrible conflict, and before any government takes the fateful decision as to the conditions under which it ought either to terminate or continue the struggle, it ought to be satisfied that the conscience of the nation is behind these conditions, for nothing else can sustain the effort which is necessary to achieve a righteous end to this war.

I have, therefore, during the last few days taken special pains to ascertain the view and the attitude of representative men of all sections of thought and opinion in the country. Last week I had the privilege, not merely of perusing the Declared War Aims of the Labour Party, but also of discussing in detail with the labour leaders the meaning and intention of that declaration. I have also had an opportunity of discussing this same momentous question with Mr. Asquith and Viscount Grey. Had it not been that the Nationalist leaders are in

Ireland engaged in endeavoring to solve the tangled problem of Irish self-government, I should have been happy to exchange views with them, but Mr. Redmond, speaking on their behalf, has, with his usual lucidity and force, in many of his speeches, made clear what his ideas are as to the object and purpose of the war.

I have also had the opportunity of consulting certain representatives of the great dominions overseas.

I am glad to be able to say, as a result of all these discussions, that, although the Government are alone responsible for the actual language I propose using, there is national agreement as to the character and purpose of our war aims and peace conditions, and in what I say to you to-day, and through you to the world, I can venture to claim that I am speaking, not merely the mind of the Government, but of the nation and of the empire as a whole.

We may begin by clearing away some misunderstandings and stating what we are not fighting for. We are not fighting a war of aggression against the German people. Their leaders have persuaded them that they are fighting a war of self-defence against a league of rival nations bent on the destruction of Germany. That is not so. The destruction or disruption of Germany or the German people has never been a war aim with us from the first day of this war to this day. Most reluctantly, and indeed quite unprepared for the dreadful ordeal, we were forced to join in this war in self-defence. In defence of the violated public law of Europe, and in vindication of the most solemn treaty obligation on which the public system of Europe rested, and on which Germany had ruthlessly trampled in her invasion of Belgium, we had to join in the struggle or stand aside and see Europe go under and brute force triumph over public right and international justice. It was only the realization of that dreadful alternative that forced the British people into the war.

And from that original attitude they have never swerved. They have never aimed at the break-up of the German peoples or the disintegration of their state or country. Germany has occupied a great position in the world. It is not our wish or intention to question or destroy that position for the future, but rather to turn her aside from hopes and schemes of military domination, and to see her devote all her strength to the great beneficent tasks of the world. Nor are we fighting to destroy Austria-Hungary or to deprive Turkey of its capital, or of the rich and renowned lands of Asia Minor and Thrace, which are predominantly Turkish in race.

Nor did we enter this war merely to alter or destroy the imperial constitution of Germany, much as we consider that military, autocratic constitution a dangerous anachronism in the Twentieth Century. Our point of view is that the adoption of a really democratic constitution by Germany would be the most convincing evidence that in her the old spirit of military domination had indeed died in this war and would make it much easier for us to conclude a broad democratic peace with her. But, after all, that is a question for the German people to decide.

It is now more than a year since the President of the United States, then neutral, addressed to the belligerents a suggestion that each side should state clearly the aims for which they were fighting. We and our allies responded by the note of the tenth of January 1917.

To the President's appeal the Central Empires made no reply, and in spite of many adjurations from their opponents and from neutrals, they have maintained a complete silence as to the objects for which they are fighting. Even on so crucial a matter as their intentions with regard to Belgium, they have uniformly declined to give any trustworthy indication.

On the twenty-fifth of December last, however, Count Czernin, speaking on behalf of Austria-Hungary and her Allies, did make a pronouncement of a kind. It is, indeed, deplorably vague. We are told that it is not the intention of the Central Powers to appropriate forcibly any occupied territories or to rob of its independence any nation which has lost its political independence during the war. It is obvious that almost any scheme of conquest and annexation could be perpetrated within the literal interpretation of such a pledge.

Does it mean that Belgium, and Serbia, Monte-negro and Roumania will be as independent and as free to direct their own destinies as the German or any other nation? Or does it mean that all manner of interferences and restrictions, political and economic, incompatible with the status and dignity of a free and self-respecting people, are to be imposed? If this is the intention, then there will be one kind of independence for a great nation and an inferior kind of independence for a small nation. We must know what is meant for equality of right among nations, small as well as great, is one of the fundamental issues this country and her Allies are fighting to establish in this war. Reparation for the wanton damage inflicted on Belgian towns and villages and their inhabitants is emphatically repudiated.

The rest of the so-called 'offer' of the Central Powers is almost entirely a refusal of all concessions. All suggestions about the autonomy of subject nationalities are ruled out of the peace terms altogether. The question whether any form of self-government is to be given to Arabs, Armenians or Syrians is declared to be entirely a matter for the Sublime Porte. A pious wish for the protection of minorities 'in so far as it is practically realizable' is the nearest approach to liberty which the Central statesmen venture to make.

On one point only are they perfectly clear and definite. Under no circumstances will the 'German demand' for the restoration of the whole of Germany's colonies be departed from. All principles of self-determination or, as our earlier phrase goes, government by consent of the governed, here vanish into thin air.

It is impossible to believe that any edifice of permanent peace could be erected on such a foundation as this. Mere lip-service to the formula of no annexations and no indemnities or the right of self-determination is useless. Before any negotiations can even be begun, the Central Powers must realize the essential facts of the situation.

The days of the Treaty of Vienna are long past. We can no longer submit the future of European civilization to the arbitrary decisions of a few negotiators striving to secure by chicanery or persuasion the interests of this or that dynasty or nation. The settlement of the new Europe must be based on such grounds of reason and justice as will give some promise of stability. Therefore, it is that we feel that government with the consent of the governed must be the basis of any territorial settlement in this war. For that reason also, unless treaties be upheld, unless every nation is prepared at whatever sacrifice to honour the national signature, it is obvious that no treaty of peace can be worth the paper on which it is written.

The first requirement, therefore, always put forward by the British Government and their Allies, has been the complete restoration, political, territorial and economic, of the independence of Belgium, and such reparation as can be made for the devastation of its towns and provinces. This is no demand for war indemnity, such as that imposed on France by Germany in 1871. It is not an attempt to shift the cost of warlike operations from one belligerent to another, which may or may not be defensible. It is no more and no less than an insistence that, before there can be any hope for a stable peace, this great breach of the public law of Europe must be repudiated and, so far as possible, repaired. Reparation means recognition. Unless international right is recognized by insistence on payment for injury done in defiance of its canons it can never be a reality.

Next comes the restoration of Serbia, Montenegro and the occupied parts of France, Italy and Roumania. The complete withdrawal of the alien armies and the reparation for injustice done is a fundamental condition of permanent peace.

We mean to stand by the French Democracy to the death in the demand they make for a reconsideration of the great wrong of 1871, when, without any regard to the wishes of the population, two French provinces were torn from the side of France and incorporated in the German Empire. This sore has poisoned the peace of Europe for half a century and, until it is cured, healthy conditions will not have been restored. There can be no better illustration of the folly and wickedness of using a transient military success to violate national right.

I will not attempt to deal with the question of the Russian territories now in German occupation. The Russian policy since the revolution has passed so rapidly through so many phases that it is difficult to speak without some suspension of judgment as to what the situation will be when the final terms of European peace come to be discussed. Russian accepted war with all its horrors because, true to her traditional guardianship of the weaker communities of her race, she stepped in to protect Serbia from a plot against her independence. It is this honourable sacrifice which not merely brought Russia into the war, but France as well. France, true to the conditions of her treaty with Russia, stood by her ally in a quarrel which was not her own. Her chivalrous respect for her treaty led to the wanton invasion of Belgium; and the treaty obligation of Great Britain to that little land brought us into the war.

The present rulers of Russia are now engaged without any reference to the countries whom Russia brought into the war, in separate negotiations with their common enemy. I am indulging in no reproaches; I am merely stating facts with a view to making it clear why Britain cannot be held accountable for decisions taken in her absence and concerning which she has not been consulted or had her aid invoked.

No one who knows Prussia nd her designs upon Russia can for a moment doubt her ultimate intention. Whatever phrases she may use to delude Russia, she does not mean to surrender one of the fair provinces or cities of Russia now occupied by her forces. Under one name and another – and the name hardly matters – these Russian provinces will henceforth be in reality part of the dominions of Prussia. They will be ruled by the Prussian sword in the interests of Prussian autocracy, and the rest of the people of Russia will be partly enticed by specious phrases and partly bullied by the threat of continued war against an impotent army into a condition of complete economic and ultimate political enslavement to Germany.

We all deplore the prospect. The democracy of this country means to stand to the last by the democracies of France and Italy and all our other Allies. We shall be proud to fight to the end side by side with the new democracy of Russia, so will America and so will France and Italy. But if the present rulers of Russia take action which is independent of their Allies we have no means of intervening to arrest the catastrophe which is assuredly befalling their country. Russia can only be saved by her own people.

We believe, however, that an independent Poland comprising all those genuinely Polish elements who desire to form part of it, is an urgent necessity for the stability of Western Europe.

Similarly, though we agree with President Wilson that the break-up of Austria-Hungary is no part of our war aims, we feel that unless genuine self-government on true democratic principles is granted to those Austro-Hungarian nationalities who have long desired it, it is impossible to hope for the removal of those causes of unrest in that part of Europe which have so long threatened its general peace.

On the same grounds we regard as vital the satisfaction of the legitimate claims of the Italians for union with those of their own race and tongue. We also mean to press that justice be done to men of Roumanian blood and speech in their legitimate aspirations.

If these conditions are fulfilled Austria-Hungary would become a power whose strength would conduce to the permanent peace and freedom of Europe, instead of being merely an instrument to the pernicious military autocracy of Prussia, which uses the resources of its allies for the furtherance of its own sinister purposes.

Outside Europe, we believe that the same principles should be applied. While we do not challenge the maintenance of the Turkish Empire in the homelands of the Turkish race with its capital at Constantinople, the passage between the Mediterranean and the Black Sea being internationalized and neutralized, Arabia, Armenia, Mesopotamia, Syria and Palestine are in our judgment entitled to a recognition of their separate national conditions. What the exact form of that recognition in each particular case should be need not here be discussed, beyond stating that it would be impossible to restore to their former sovereignty the territories to which I have already referred.

Much has been said about the arrangements we have entered into with our Allies on this and on other subjects. I can only say that as new circumstances, like the Russian collapse and the separate Russian negotiations, have changed the conditions under which those arrangements were made, we are and always have been perfectly ready to discuss them with our Allies.

With regard to the German colonies, I have repeatedly declared that they are held at the disposal of a conference whose decision must have primary regard to the wishes and interests of the native inhabitants of such colonies. None of those territories are inhabited by Europeans. The governing consideration, therefore, in all these cases must be that the inhabitants should be placed under the control of an administration, acceptable to themselves, one of whose main purposes will be to prevent their exploitation for the benefit of European capitalists or governments. The natives live in their various tribal organizations under chiefs and councils who are competent to consult and speak for their tribes and members and thus to represent their wishes and interests in regard to their disposal. The general principle of national self-determination is, therefore, as applicable in their cases as in those of occupied European territories.

The German declaration that the natives of the German colonies have, through their military fidelity in the war, shown their attachment and resolve under all circumstances to remain with Germany is applicable not to the German colonies generally, but only to one of them, and in that case (German East Africa) the German authorities secured the attachment, not of the native population as a whole, which is and remains profoundly anti-German, but only of a small warlike class from whom their Askaris or soldiers were selected. These they attached to themselves by conferring on them a highly privileged position as against the bulk of the native population, which enabled these Askaris to assume a lordly and oppressive superiority over the rest of the natives. By this and other means they secured the attachment of a very small and insignificant minority, whose interests were directly opposed to those of the rest of the population, and for whom they have no right to speak. The German treatment of their native populations in their colonies has been such as amply to justify their fear of submitting the future of those colonies to the wishes of the natives themselves.

Finally, there must be reparation for injuries done in violation of international law. The Peace Conference must not forget our seamen and the services they have rendered to, and the outrages they have suffered for the common cause of freedom.

One omission we notice in the proposal of the Central Powers, which seems to us especially regrettable. It is desirable and, indeed, essential, that the settlement after this war shall be one which does not in itself bear the seed of future war. But that is not enough. However wisely and well we may make territorial and other arrangements, there will still be many subjects of international controversy. Some, indeed, are inevitable.

The economical conditions at the end of the war will be in the highest degree difficult. Owing to the diversion of human effort to warlike pursuits, there must follow a world-shortage of raw materials, which will increase the longer the war lasts, and it is inevitable that those countries which have control of the raw materials will desire to help themselves and their friends first.

Apart from this, whatever settlement is made will be suitable only to the circumstances under which it is made and, as those circumstances change, changes in the settlement will be called for.

So long as the possibility of dispute between nations continues – that is to say, so long as men and women are dominated by passion and ambition, and war is the only means of settling a dispute – all nations must live under the burden, not only of having from time to time to engage in it, but of being compelled to prepare for its possible outbreak. The crushing weight of modern armaments, the increasing evil of compulsory military service, the vast waste of wealth and effort involved in warlike preparation, these are blots on our civilization of which every thinking individual must be ashamed.

For these and other similar reasons, we are confident that a great attempt must be made to establish by some international organization an alternative to war as a means of settling international disputes. After all, war is a relic of barbarism and, just as law has succeeded violence as the means of settling disputes between individuals, so we believe that it is destined ultimately to take the place of war in the settlement of controversies between nations.

If, then, we are asked what we are fighting for, we reply as, we have often replied: we are fighting for a just and lasting peace, and we believe that before permanent peace can be hoped for three conditions must be fulfilled; firstly, the sanctity of treaties must be established; secondly, a territorial settlement must be secured, based on the right of self-determination or the consent of the governed, and, lastly, we must seek by the creation of some international organization to limit the burden of armaments and diminish the probability of war.

On these conditions the British Empire would welcome peace; to secure these conditions its peoples are prepared to make even greater sacrifices than those they have yet endured.

APPENDIX 4

Ethnic Compositions

Ethnic Composition of the Austro-Hungarian Empire in 1911

Germans	12,006,521	23.36 per cent
Hungarians	10,056,315	19.57 per cent
Czechs	6,442,133	12.54 per cent
Serbo-Croats	5,621,797	10.94 per cent
Poles	4,976,804	9.68 per cent
Ruthenes	3,997,831	7.78 per cent
Romanians	3,224,147	6.27 per cent
Slovaks	1,967,970	6.27 per cent
Slovenes	1,255,620	2.44 per cent
Italians	768,422	1.50 per cent
Others	1,072,223	2.09 per cent
Total	51,390,223	100 per cent

From *The Habsburg Monarchy, 1809-1918* by A. J. P. Taylor

Ethnic Composition of the German Empire based upon the census of 1900

Germans	52,136,049	92.50 per cent
Poles	3,328,751	6.00 per cent
French	211,679	0.38 per cent
Danish	141,061	0.25 per cent
Lithuanian	106,305	0.19 per cent
Dutch	80,361	0.14 per cent
Czech	200,430	0.14 per cent
Frisian	20,677	0.04 per cent

Russian	9,617	0.02 per cent
Hungarian	8,158	0.01 per cent
Other	112,218	0.21 per cent
Total	56,355,306	100 per cent

Adapted from *Fremdsprachige Minderheiten im Deutschen* Reich, German national census of 1900.

Ethnic Composition of Yugoslavia in 1921

Serb (inc. Macedonians and Montenegrins)	5,271,500	44 per cent
Croats	2,884,700	24.1 per cent
Slovenes	1,020,000	8.5 per cent
Muslims (Bosnians)	755,300	6.3 per cent
Germans	505,800	4.2 per cent
Hungarians	467,700	3.9 per cent
Albanians	439,700	3.7 per cent
Romanians	231,100	1.9 per cent
Turks	150,300	1.3 per cent
Czechs and Slovaks	115,500	1.0 per cent
Ruthenes	25,600	0.2 per cent
Russians	20,600	0.2 per cent
Poles	14,800	0.1 per cent
Others	82,300	0.6 per cent
Total	11,984,900	100 per cent

From *Ethnic Groups and Population Changes in Twentieth Century Central Eastern Europe, History Data and Analysis*, Piotr Eberhardt, Routledge London and New York, 2015.

Ethnic Composition of Poland in 1921

Poles	17,789,287	69.23 per cent
Ruthenes (includes Ukrainians)	3,898,428	15.17 per cent
Jews	2,048,878	7.97 per cent
Belarussians	1,035,693	4.03 per cent
Germans	769,392	2.99 per cent
Lithuanians	24,044	0.09 per cent
Russians	48,920	0.19 per cent

'Locals'	38,943	0.15 per cent
Czechs	30,628	0.12 per cent
Others	9,856	0.04 per cent
Unknown	631	0.002 per cent
Total	25,694,700	100 per cent

Ethnic Composition of Czechoslovakia in 1921

Czechs	6,570,000	66 per cent
Slovaks	2,190,000	(Included in Czech figs)
Germans	3,124,000	23 per cent
Hungarians	745,000	5.6 per cent
Ruthenes	462,000	3.0 per cent
Jews	180,000	1.0 per cent
Poles	75,000	0.6 per cent
Total	13,346,000	100 per cent

Figures from *Czechoslovakia, Czechoslovakismus, and German National Minorities between the world wars*: Emmanuel Radl's Theory of a Nation and State, Tereza Novotna (Boston University).

Numbers of Jewish People Murdered during the Holocaust

	Prewar Population	Number Murdered	Percentage
Poland	3,259,000	3,000,000	92 per cent
Soviet Union	2,825,000	1,100,000	89 per cent
Hungary	725,000	569,000	79 per cent
Romania	441,000	287,000	65 per cent
Germany	240,000	210,000	86 per cent
Netherlands	112,000	105,000	94 per cent
Czechoslovakia	92,000	78,300	85 per cent
France	260,000	77,000	30 per cent

Note: Statistics cover selected countries and are not intended to be comprehensive. They are taken from various sources but are indicative of the overall numbers involved.

APPENDIX 5

Churchill's 'Something to Astonish You' Speech

Something to astonish you!
Mr Winston Churchill speaking in Zurich
19th September 1946.

I WISH TO SPEAK TO YOU TODAY about the tragedy of Europe.

This noble continent, comprising on the whole the fairest and the most cultivated regions of the earth; enjoying a temperate and equable climate, is the home of all the great parent races of the western world. It is the fountain of Christian faith and Christian ethics. It is the origin of most of the culture, arts, philosophy and science both of ancient and modem times.

If Europe were once united in the sharing of its common inheritance, there would be no limit to the happiness, to the prosperity and glory which its three or four hundred million people would enjoy. Yet it is from Europe that have sprung that series of frightful nationalistic quarrels, originated by the Teutonic nations, which we have seen even in this twentieth century and in our own lifetime, wreck the peace and mar the prospects of all mankind.

And what is the plight to which Europe has been reduced?

Some of the smaller States have indeed made a good recovery, but over wide areas a vast quivering mass of tormented, hungry, care-worn and bewildered human beings gape at the ruins of their cities and homes, and scan the dark horizons for the approach of some new peril, tyranny or terror.

Among the victors there is a babel of jarring voices; among the vanquished the sullen silence of despair.

That is all that Europeans, grouped in so many ancient States and nations, that is all that the Germanic Powers have got by tearing each other to pieces and spreading havoc far and wide.

Indeed, but for the fact that the great Republic across the Atlantic Ocean has at length realised that the ruin or enslavement of Europe would involve their own fate as well, and has stretched out hands of succour and guidance, the Dark Ages would have returned in all their cruelty and squalor.

They may still return.

Yet all the while there is a remedy which, if it were generally and spontaneously adopted, would as if by a miracle transform the whole scene, and would in a few years make all Europe, or the greater part of it, as free and as happy as Switzerland is today.

What is this sovereign remedy?

It is to re-create the European Family, or as much of it as we can, and provide it with a structure under which it can dwell in peace, in safety and in freedom.

We must build a kind of United States of Europe.

In this way only will hundreds of millions of toilers be able to regain the simple joys and hopes which make life worth living.

The process is simple.

All that is needed is the resolve of hundreds of millions of men and women to do right instead of wrong, and gain as their reward, blessing instead of cursing.

Much work has been done upon this task by the exertions of the Pan-European Union which owes so much to Count Coudenhove-Kalergi and which commanded the services of the famous French patriot and statesman, Aristide Briand.

There is also that immense body of doctrine and procedure, which was brought into being amid high hopes after the First World War, as the League of Nations.

The League of Nations did not fail because of its principles or conceptions. It failed because these principles were deserted by those States who had brought it into being. It failed because the Governments of those days feared to face the facts and act while time remained. This disaster must not be repeated. There is, therefore, much knowledge and material with which to build; and also bitter dear-bought experience.

I was very glad to read in the newspapers two days ago that my friend President Truman had expressed his interest and sympathy with this great design.

There is no reason why a regional organisation of Europe should in any way conflict with the world organisation of the United Nations. On the contrary, I believe that the larger synthesis will only survive if it is founded upon coherent natural groupings.

There is already a natural grouping in the Western Hemisphere. We British have our own Commonwealth of Nations. These do not weaken, on the contrary they strengthen, the world organisation. They are in fact its main support.

And why should there not be a European group which could give a sense of enlarged patriotism and common citizenship to the distracted peoples of this turbulent and mighty continent and why should it not take its rightful place with other great groupings in shaping the destinies of men?

In order that this should be accomplished, there must be an act of faith in which millions of families speaking many languages must consciously take part.

We all know that the two world wars through which we have passed arose out of the vain passion of a newly united Germany to play the dominating part in the world.

In this last struggle crimes and massacres have been committed for which there is no parallel since the invasions of the Mongols in the fourteenth century and no equal at any time in human history.

The guilty must be punished. Germany must be deprived of the power to rearm and make another aggressive war.

But when all this has been done, as it will be done, as it is being done, there must be an end to retribution. There must be what Mr Gladstone many years ago called 'a blessed act of oblivion'.

We must all turn our backs upon the horrors of the past. We must look to the future. We cannot afford to drag forward across the years that are to come the hatreds and revenges which have sprung from the injuries of the past.

If Europe is to be saved from infinite misery, and indeed from final doom, there must be an act of faith in the European family and an act of oblivion against all the crimes and follies of the past.

Can the free peoples of Europe rise to the height of these resolves of the soul and instincts of the spirit of man?

If they can, the wrongs and injuries which have been inflicted will have been washed away on all sides by the miseries which have been endured.

Is there any need for further floods of agony?

Is it the only lesson of history that mankind is unteachable?

Let there be justice, mercy and freedom.

The peoples have only to will it, and all will achieve their hearts' desire.

I am now going to say something that will astonish you.

The first step in the re-creation of the European family must be a partnership between France and Germany.

In this way only can France recover the moral leadership of Europe.

There can be no revival of Europe without a spiritually great France and a spiritually great Germany.

The structure of the United States of Europe, if well and truly built, will be such as to make the material strength of a single state less important. Small nations will count as much as large ones and gain their honour by their contribution to the common cause.

The ancient states and principalities of Germany, freely joined together for mutual convenience in a federal system, might each take their individual place among the United States of Europe. I shall not try to make a detailed programme for hundreds of millions of people who want to be happy and free, prosperous and safe, who wish to enjoy the four freedoms of which the great President Roosevelt spoke, and live in accordance with the principles embodied in the Atlantic Charter. If this is their wish, they have only to say so, and means can certainly be found, and machinery erected, to carry that wish into full fruition.

But I must give you warning. Time may be short.

At present there is a breathing-space. The cannon have ceased firing. The fighting has stopped; but the dangers have not stopped.

If we are to form the United States of Europe or whatever name or form it may take, we must begin now.

In these present days we dwell strangely and precariously under the shield and protection of the atomic bomb. The atomic bomb is still only in the hands of a State and nation which we know will never use it except in the cause of right and freedom. But it may well be that in a few years this awful agency of destruction will be widespread and the catastrophe following from its use by several warring nations will not only bring to an end all that we call civilisation, but may possibly disintegrate the globe itself.

I must now sum up the propositions which are before you.

Our constant aim must be to build and fortify the strength of the United Nations Organisation.

Under and within that world concept, we must re-create the European family in a regional structure called, it may be, the United States of Europe.

The first step is to form a Council of Europe.

If at first all the States of Europe are not willing or able to join the Union, we must nevertheless proceed to assemble and combine those who will and those who can.

The salvation of the common people of every race and of every land from war or servitude must be established on solid foundations and must be guarded by the readiness of all men and women to die rather than submit to tyranny.

In all this urgent work, France and Germany must take the lead together.

Great Britain, the British Commonwealth of Nations, mighty America, and I trust Soviet Russia – for then indeed all would be well – must be the friends and sponsors of the new Europe and must champion its right to live and shine.

Selected and Edited Articles from the Treaty of Rome

ARTICLE 3

The elimination, as between Member States, of customs duties and of quantitative restrictions on the import and export of goods, and of all other measures having equivalent effect;

The establishment of a common customs tariff and of a commercial policy towards third countries;

The abolition, as between Member States, of obstacles to the freedom of movement for persons, services and capital;

The approximation of the laws of Member States to the extent required for the proper functioning of the common market.

ARTICLE 48

Freedom of movement for workers shall be secured within the community by the end of the transitional period.

Such freedom of movement shall entail the abolition of any discrimination based on nationality between workers of the Member States as regards employment remuneration and other conditions of work and employment.

ARTICLE 53

Member States shall not introduce any new restrictions on the right of establishment in their territories of nationals of other Member States, save as otherwise provided in this Treaty.

ARTICLE 92

Save as otherwise provided in the Treaty, and aid granted by a Member State or through state resources in any form whatsoever which distorts or threatens to distort competition... [shall] be incompatible with the common market.

ARTICLE 100

The Council shall, acting unanimously on a proposal from the Commission, issue directives for the approximation of such provisions laid down by law... as directly affect the establishment or functioning of the common market.

ARTICLE 103
Member States shall regard their conjunctural policies as a matter of common concern. They shall consult each other and the Commission on the measures to be taken in the light of prevailing circumstances.

ARTICLE 104
Each Member State shall pursue the economic policy needed to ensure the equilibrium of its overall balance of payments...

ARTICLE 105
... Member States shall coordinate their economic policies. They shall for this purpose provide for cooperation between... their central banks...

ARTICLE 118
[Member States] ... shall have the task of promoting close cooperation... in matters relating to:

Employment
Labour Law and working conditions
Basic and advanced vocational training
Social security
Prevention of occupational accident and disease
Occupational hygiene
The right of association and collective bargaining between employers and workers

ARTICLE 123
... a European Social Fund... shall have the task of rendering the employment of workers easier and of increasing their geographical and occupational mobility within the Community.

ARTICLE 164
The Court of Justice shall ensure that in the interpretation and application of this Treaty the law is observed.
Article 210. The Community shall have legal personality.

Bibliography and Sources

Government Papers

CAB 1/27 Extracts from the French proposals for peace with Germany, 1 December 1918

CAB 1/28 Extracts from Fontainebleau Conference March 25, 1919

CAB 1/28 Extracts from report published in July 1919 on US public opinion towards the Treaty of Versailles and League of Nations

CAB 23/8 WC 484-5 Meeting held at 10 Downing Street, October 11,.1918

CAB 23/8 WC 485-6 Meeting held at 10 Downing Street, October 14, 1918

CAB 23/8 WC 486-7 Meeting held at 10 Downing Street, October 15, 1918

CAB 23/15/6 Meeting held at 10 Downing Street, March 4, 1919

CAB 23/15/23 Meeting held at 10 Downing Street, 5 August 1919

CAB 24/2/32 Suggested Basis for a Territorial Settlement in Europe, Ralph Paget and W. Tyrell, 7 August 1916

CAB/24/10/85 Memorandum on Proposals for Diminishing the Occasion of Future War, Internal Memorandum by Sir Robert Cecil, October 1916

CAB 24/67 – GT-6012-12, Memo on Pres. Wilsons speeches as a basis for negotiation, 12 October 1918

CAB 28 Fontainebleau Conference

CAB37/145/15

FO 1049/81

FO 374/19 Count Brockdorff-Rantzau speech 7 May, 1919

FO 211/517 Article 227 28 June, 1919

FO 211/517 Treaty of Versailles

GFM 33/1544 No. EO37850 German appeal for financial help to keep Germany afloat, 4 February, 1924

Original Documents, Articles and Publications

All Against One: The Congress of Oppressed Nationalities of Austria-Hungary (1918), Andrea Carteny, Department of Communication, University of Teramo, Working Paper No. 67, 2010.

Canadian-American Review of Hungarian Studies, vol v, No2 (Autumn 1978), Istvan Bethlen and Hungarian Foreign Policy, 1921-1931, Thomas Sakmyster.

Central Hungary: Magyars and Germans, Geographical Review, Volume 6, 11/1/1918 Wallis, B.C (207700.pdf).

Economic History of Europe: Twentieth Century, Selected Documents edited by Shepard B. Clough, Thomas Moodie, Carol Moodie, The Documentary History of Western Civilisation, Palgrave Macmillan, London – Melbourne, 1969.

Expulsion of the German Population from the Territories East of the Oder-Neisse Lone, Federal Ministry for Refugees and War Victims. Digital Library of India, Item 2015.183863.

Food Supply of the Republic of Austria end of 1919, Vienna, Salzer 1920.

France: Empire and Republic, 1850-1940, selected documents, edited by David Thomson, Palgrave Macmillan, London, 1968.

International Law Reports: Volume 6: Annual Digest of Public International Law Cases, 1931-1932. Edited by H. Lauterpacht MA Lld, Butterworth and Co. Ltd, Bell Yard, Temple Bar, London, 1945. Reprinted 1945 by Grotius Publications Ltd.

Legal Opinion on the Benes Decrees and the accession of the Czech Republic to the European Union.

Lloyd George's War Aims.

Makers of the New World (CU31924027876709) by One who Knows them, Cassell, London 1921.

Making the New Europe: European Unity and the Second World War, Edited by M. L. Smith and Peter M. R. Stirk, Bloomsbury, London and New York, 2016.

Markwell, Donald J., Keynes and Australia, Research Discussion Paper 2000-04, June 2000, Research Department, Reserve Bank of Australia and New College Oxford. Reserve Bank of Australia. A Paper presented at a seminar at the Reserve Bank of Australia on 18th September 1985.

Office of Military Government for Germany (US), Displaced Persons, Stateless Persons and Refugees (Cumulative Review), Report of Military Governor 1 October 1946-30 September 1947, No. 27.

Peace Treaty of Brest-Litovsk 1918, Internet Archive.

Poland Under the Germans, London, Sir Joseph Caulston and Sons Ltd. 1916.

Report of the Committee on Alleged German Outrages, Appointed by HMG, Rt Hon. Viscount Bryce, 1915.

Retaliation and Persecution on Yugoslav Territory During and after World War Two (1943-1950), Michael Portmann, Central and Eastern European Online Library, 1-2/2004.

Revanche ou Relevement, The French Peace Movement Confronts Alsace-Lorraine, 1871-1918, Michael Clinton, Canadian Journal of History, December 2005, pp. 431-448.

Serbian-Italian Relations: History and Modern Times, Ed: Bijana PhD. Ministry of the Education, Science and Technological Development of the Republic of Serbia, Belgrade 2015.

Stuttgart Speech: ('Speech of Hope') by J.F. Byrnes, US Secretary of State. Restatement of policy on Germany (Sept. 6 1946), reprinted in *Beata Ruhm von Oppen*, Edited Documents on German Occupation, 1945-1954, London and New York, OUP, pp. 52-60.

The Crimes of Germany, The Field and Queen (Horace Cox) Ltd, Special Supplement to *The Field* Newspaper.

The Croats Under Yugoslav Rule – A Visit of Investigation, October 1932, Riley Ben and Davies, Rhys MP Teasdale, Anthony.

The Fouchet Plan: De Gaulle's Intergovernmental Design for Europe, LSE, LEQS Paper No.117/2016, October 2016.

The Memory of the First World War in the Former Lands of Austria-Hungary, Christopher Brennan, Department of International History, London School of Economics.

The Oxford Handbook of International Trade Law, edited by Daniel Bethlehem, Donald McRae, Rodney Neufeld, Isabelle van Damme, OUP, 2009.

The Ruhr Problem – An Independent Rhineland-Westphalia Lecture delivered in February 1923 at Angers, Nantes, Lorient, Saint-Nazaire and la Roche sur Yon, by Maurice Schwob, editor of 'du Phare de la Loire', third impression, 1923.

The Truth About German Atrocities, Founded on the Report of the Committee on Alleged German Outrages, Parliamentary Recruiting Committee London, 1915.

The Treaty of Versailles – American Opinion – Old Colony Trust Co. Boston Mass. 1919. Speeches of Henry Cabot Lodge, Philander C. Knox, Gilbert M. Hitchcock, President Wilson.

Treaty of Versailles – the Avalon Project, Weimar Constitution.

Why France Wants Alsace-Lorraine, Stephane Lauzanne, Chief Editor of the Paris *Matin*, and member of the French mission to the US. Reprinted from the *Worlds Work*, with permission, 1919.

Woodrow Wilson's Fourteen Points.

Workers and Nationalism: Czech and German Social Democracy in Habsburg Austria, 1890-1918, OUP, 2017.

Websites

Avalon Project

Austria-Hungary from 1863 to 1914, Clemens, Jobst and Thomas Scheiber Oesterreichische Nationalbibliotek.

Osterreiche Nationalbank.

Central and East European Online Library

Foundation for Economic Education

France and the negotiations on the Treaty of Rome (1955-57), Laurent.
Worlouzet.www.cvce.eu
Holocaust Online.
Internet Archive.
Institute into Research of Expelled Germans.
Archive.org.
Margaret Thatcher Foundation.

Bibliography

Ambrose, Stephen, *Rise to Globalism: American Foreign Policy Since 1938* (London: Penguin, 1983)

Anderson, M. S., *The Ascendancy of Europe, 1815-1914* (Harlow: Pearson, 2003)

App, Austin J., *The Sudeten German Tragedy* (Maryland: Boniface Press, 1979)

Ardagh, John, *Germany and the Germans – After Unification* (London: Penguin, 1991)

Auty, Phyllis, *Tito* (London, Penguin, 1974)

Bakic, Dragan, *Britain and Interwar Danubian Europe: Foreign Policy and Security Challenges 1919-1936* (London: Bloomsbury, 2017)

Bamac, Ivan, *The National Question in Yugoslavia – Origins, History, Politics* (Cornell University Press, 2015)

Barnett, Margaret, *British Food Policy during the First World War* (London: Routledge, 2014)

Barraclough, Geoffrey, *From Agadir to Armageddon, Anatomy of a Crisis* (London: Weidenfeld and Nicolson, 1982)

Bascom, Barry Hayes, *Bismarck and Mitteleuropa* (Associated University Press, 1994)

Baycroft, Timothy & David Hopkin (eds), *Folklore and Nationalism in Europe during the Long Nineteenth Century* (Leiden: Koninkijke Bill NV, 2012)

Bayerlein, Henry, *Birth of Yugoslavia, Volume II* (London: Leonard Parsons, 1922)

Buell, Raymond Leslie, *Poland, Key to Europe* (London: Jonathan Cape, 1939)

Broehl, Wayne G., *Cargill: Trading the World's Grain* (Hanover: University Press of New England, 1992)

Beller, Steven, *Francis-Joseph: Profiles in Power* (New York: Longman, 1981)

Beller, Steven, *The Habsburg Monarchy: 1815-1918* (Oxford: OUP, 2018)

Bevan, Edwyn, *German War Aims* (New York and London: Harper, 1918)

Beevor, Antony, *Stalingrad* (London: Penguin, 1998)

Berend, Ivan T., *Decades of Crisis: Central and Eastern Europe Before World War Two* (Los Angeles, London: University of California Press, 1998)

Biondich, Mark, *Stjepan Radic, the Croat Peasant Party, and the Politics of Mass Mobilisation, 1904-1928* (Toronto: University of Toronto Press, 2000)

Blake, Robert, *The Conservative Party from Peel to Thatcher* (London: Fontana, 1985)

Bostridge, Mark, *Fateful Year, England 1914* (London: Penguin, 2014)

Brechtefeld, Jorg, *Mitteleuropa and German Politics: 1848 to the Present* (London: Palgrave Macmillan, 1996)

Bridge, Carl, *Makers of the Modern World, The Peace Conferences of 1919-1923 and their Aftermath* (Haus Publishing, 2011)

Calder, Kenneth J., *Britain and the Origins of the New Europe, 1914-1918* (Cambridge: Cambridge University Press, 1976)

Capo, Hrvoje, *Polity of the Kingdom of Serbs Croats and Slovenes, 1918-1941* (Zagreb: Croatian Institute of History, 2013)

Catchpole, Brian, *A Map History of the British People Since 1700* (London: Heineman, 1975)

Clark, Colin, *Australian Hopes and Fears* (London: Hollis and Carter, 1958)

Clark, Alan, *Barbarossa* (London: Cassell, 2002)

Clark, Christopher, *Sleepwalkers, How Europe went to war in 1914* (London: Penguin, 2013)

Clark, G. N., *Belgium and the War* (Oxford University Press, 1942)

Cook, Sir Theodore A., *The Crimes of Germany* (London: Speight and Sons, 1917)

Cord, Henry Meyer and Nyhoff, Martinus, *Mitteleuropa: In German Thought and Action 1815-1945* (The Hague: Springer, 1955)

Crampton, R. J., *Eastern Europe in the Twentieth Century – And After* (London and New York: Routledge, 1994)

Dockrill Michael L. & J. Douglas Goold, *Peace Without Promise: Britain and the Peace Conferences,1919-1923* (London: Academic and Educational Ltd, 1981)

Cornwall, Mark, *The Undermining of Austria-Hungary: The Battle for Hearts and Minds* (London: Palgrave Macmillan, 2000)

Davies, Evan, *Aspects of Modern World History* (London: Hodder and Stoughton, 1993)

Dell, Edmund, *The Schuman Plan and the British Abdication of Leadership in Europe* (Oxford: Clarendon Press, 1995)

Deutscher, Isaac, *Stalin* (New York: Penguin, 1982)

Dixon, Francis Graham, *The Allied Occupation of Germany, The Refugee Crisis, Denazification and the Path to Reconstruction* (London and New York: IB Tauris, 2013)

Donald, Robert, T., *The Polish Corridor and the Consequences* (London: Butterworth, 1929)

Douglas-Scott, Sionaidh, *Constitutional Law of the European Union* (Harlow: Longman Pearson, 2002)

Dredger, John A., *Tactics and Procurement in the Habsburg Military: 1866-1918* (London: Palgrave Macmillan, 2017)

Ducray Camille, *Clemenceau* (London: Hodder and Stoughton, 1919)

Duhem, Jules, *The Question of Alsace Lorraine* (London, NY, Toronto: Hodder and Stoughton, 1918)

Ellis, John and Cox, Michael, *The World War One Data Book* (London: Aurum Press, 2001)

Ellwood, David W., *Rebuilding Europe: Western Europe, America and Postwar Reconstruction* (New York and London: Routledge, 1992)

Emmerson, Charles, *Europe – The World before the Great War* (London: Vintage Books, 2013)

Falloden, Viscount Grey of, *The League of Nations* (Oxford: Oxford University, 1918)

Farmer, Paul, *Vichy Political Dilemma* (Columbia University Press, 1955)

Feldman, Gerald D., *The Great Disorder, Politics, Economics and Society in the German Inflation, 1914-1924* (Oxford: OUP, 1997)

Ferenz, Benjamin B., *Less Than Slaves: Jewish Forced Labor and the Quest for Compensation* (Indiana University Press, 2002)

Fink, Carole, *The Genoa Conference: European Diplomacy, 1921-1922* (Syracuse University Press, 1993)

Fisk, George, *Continental Opinion Regarding a Proposed Middle European Tariff Union* (Baltimore: John Hopkins Press, 1902)

Frentz, Christian Raitz von, *A Lesson Forgotten: Minority Protection under The League of Nations, The Case of the German Minority in Poland, 1920-1924* (New York: St Martin's Press, 1999)

George, David Lloyd, *War Memoirs of David Lloyd*, Volume 1 (London: Odhams Press Limited, 1938)

Gigliotti, Simone. *The Train Journey: Transit, Captivity and Witnessing the Holocaust* (New York: Berghahn Books, 2009)

Gilbert, Martin, *The Day the War Ended: May 8, 1945 – Victory in Europe* (New York: H. Holt, 1995)

Gilbert, Martin, *First World War* (London: Harper Collins, 1994)

Gilbert, Martin, *The Roots of Appeasement* (London: Weidenfeld and Nicolson, 1966)

Gilbert, Martin, *Churchill – A Life* (London: Minerva, 1992)

Gildea, Robert & Annette Warring, *Surviving Hitler and Mussolini: Daily Life in Occupied Europe* (London: Bloomsbury Academic, 2006)

Glenny, Misha, *The Balkans: Nationalism, War and the Great Powers* (London: Granta, 1999)

Graber, G. S., *History of the SS* (London: Granada, 1982)

Greenhalgh, Elizabeth. *Victory Through Coalition: Britain and France during the First World War* (Cambridge: CUP, 2005)

Gross, John T., *Neighbours – The Destruction of the Jewish Community in Jedwabne, Poland, 1941* (Princeton: Princeton University Press, 2003)

Grumbach, S., *Germany's Annexationist Aims*, translated by J. Ellis Banker (New York: EF Dutton and Company, 1917)

Hackett, Douglas, Monnet, Jean, *The Path to European Unity* (New York: Brinkley, St. Martin's Press, 1991)

Hackett, Clifford P., *Monnet and the Americans: The Father of a United Europe and his US Supporters* (Washington DC: Jean Monnet Council, 1995)

Hamann, Brigitte, *Hitler's Vienna: A Dictator's Apprenticeship* (Oxford: Oxford University Press, 1999)

Hardach, Gerd, *The First World War* (University of California Press, 1981)

Harrison, H. D., *The Soul of Yugoslavia* (London: Hodder and Stoughton, 1941)

Hastings, Max, *Armageddon: The Battle for Germany 1944–45* (London: Pan, 2005)

Hastings, Max, *Catastrophe, Europe goes to War 1914* (London: William Collins, 2013)

Hazen, Charles Downer, *Alsace-Lorraine Under German Rule* (New York: Holt, 1917)

Heater, Derek, *A History of Education for Citizenship* (London and New York: Routledge Farmer, 2004)

Heimann, Marie, *Czechoslovakia: The State that Failed* (Newhaven and London: Yale University Press, 2009)

Herwig, Holger H., *The First World War: Germany and Austria-Hungary 1914-1918* (Modern Wars; 2nd ed.) (London and New York: Bloomsbury, 2014)

Hill, David Jayne, *Impressions of the Kaiser* (New York and London: Harper and Brothers, 1914)

Hogan, Michael J., *The Ambiguous Legacy: US Foreign Policy in the 'American Century'* (Cambridge University Press, 1999)

Holbraad, Carsten, *Danish Reactions to German Occupation: History and Historiography* (UCL Press, 2017)

Horn, Martin, *Britain, France and Financing the First World War* (Montreal, Kingston, London: Kingston Press, 2002)

House, Edward M., *Intimate Papers of Colonel House into the World War* (Houghton Mifflin Co., 1928)

House, Charles Mandell & Charles Seymour, *What Really Happened at Paris; the story of the Peace Conference, 1918-1919, by American Delegates* (New York: Scribner's Sons, 1921)

Howard, Michael, *The Franco-Prussian War* (London and New York: Methuen, 1985)

Ingrao, W. & Francis A. J. Szabo, *The Germans and the East* (Lafayatte: Purdue University Press, 2008)

James, Harold, *Krupp: A History of the Legendary German Firm* (Princeton and Oxford: Princeton University Press, 2012)

James, Harold & Jakob Tanner, *Enterprise in the Period of Fascism in Europe* (London and New York: Routledge, 2017)

Jenkins, Roy, *Churchill* (London: Pan, 2001)

Kaplan, Karel C., *The Short March: The Communist Takeover in Czechoslovakia* (London: Hurst and Co., 1987)

Karsten, Peter (ed.), *Motivating Soldiers: Morale or Mutiny* (New York and London: Garland, 1998)

Kay, Alex J., *Exploitation, Resettlement, Mass Murder, Political and Economic Planning for German Occupation Policy in the Soviet Union, 1940-1941* (New York, Oxford: Berghahn Books, 2006)

Kershaw, Ian, *Hitler 1936-1945: Nemesis* (London: Penguin, 2001)

Kershaw, Ian, *To Hell and Back: Europe 1914-1949* (London: Penguin, 2016)

Keynes, John Maynard, *Economic Consequences of the Peace* (New York: Harcourt, Brace and Howe, 1919)

Kroll, Johannes, *Sudeten Germans in Austria after the First World War, Contemporary Austrian Studies*, Vol. 19 (Innsbruck University Press)

Lampe, John R., *Yugoslavia as History, Twice there was a Country* (Cambridge: Cambridge University Press, 1996)

Large, David Clay, *Germans to the Front: West German Rearmament in the Adenauer Era* (Chapel Hill and London: University of North Carolina Press, 1996)

Latowski, Paul, *The Reconstruction of Poland: 1914-1923* (New York: Palgrave Macmillan, 1992)

Lecom, George, *Georges Clemenceau: The Tiger of France* (New York, London: Appleton and Co., 1919)

Lentin, A., *Lloyd George and the Lost Peace: From Versailles to Hitler 1919-1940* (Basingstoke: Palgrave Macmillan, 2001)

Liddell Hart, Basil, *History of the Second World War* (London: Pan, 1982)

Lloyd George, David, *The truth About Reparations and War Debts* (London: Heinemann, 1923)

Lowe, Keith, *Savage Continent: Europe in the Aftermath of World War II* (New York: St. Martin's 2012)

Lowe, Norman, *Mastering Modern British History* (2nd ed.) (London: Macmillan, 1984)

Ludendorff, General Eric, *My War Memories, 1914-1918* (London: Hutchinson and Co., 1919)

Ludwig, Emil, *Kaiser Wilhem II: From Birth to Exile* (London and New York: Puttnam, 1926)

Macartney, C. A., *The Social Revolution in Austria* (Cambridge: Cambridge University Press, 2014)

Macmillan, Margaret, *Peacemakers: The Paris Peace Conference and Its Attempt to End War* (London: John Murray, 2001)

Mack Smith, Denis, *Mussolini* (London: Paladin, 1983)

Magnes, Judah L., *Russia and Germany at Brest-Litovsk, A Documentary History of the Peace Negotiations* (New York: The Rand School of Social Science, 1919)

Massie, Robert K., *Dreadnought – Britain, Germany and the coming of the Great War* (London: Pimlico, 1991)

Masur, Gerhard, *Imperial Berlin* (London: Routledge and Kegan Paul, 1971)

McMeekin, Sean, *July 1914, Countdown to War* (London: Icon Books, 2013)

Meinander, Henrik and J. A. Mangan, *The Nordic World: Sport in Society* (London, Portland: Frank Cass, 2006)

Melrose, Andrew, *The Real Kaiser: An Illuminating Study* (New York: Dodd Mead and Co., 1914)

Millen, Sarah Gertrude, *General Smuts*, The Second Volume (London: Faber and Faber,1936)

Nicholson, Harold, *Peacemaking 1919* (The Universal Library) (New York: Gossett and Dunlap, 1965)

Ousby, Ian, *Occupation, The Ordeal of France, 1940-1944* (London: Pimlico, 1999)

Ousby, Ian, *The Road to Verdun* (London: Pimlico, 2003)

Paikert, G. C., *The Danube Swabians: German Populations in Hungary, Romania and Yugoslavia and Hitler's impact on their Patterns* (The Hague: Martin's Nyhoff, 1967)

Paris, A. E., *The Question of Fiume* (Paris: Lang Blanchong and Company, 1919)

Pelt, Morgan, *Tobacco, Arms and Politics: Greece and Germany from World Crisis to World War* (Copenhagen: Museum Tusculanum Press, University of Copenhagen, 1998)

Peter, Laszlo, *Hungary's Long Nineteenth Century: Constitutional and Democratic Traditions in a European Perspective* (Leiden and Boston: Brill, 2012)

Pollock, Sir Frederick BT, KC, *League of Nations* (London: Stevens & Sons Ltd, 1922)

Porter, Ian and Ian D. Armour, *Imperial Germany 1890-1918* (London and New York: Longman, 1991)

Prazmowska, Anita, *Poland: A Modern History* (London: IB Tauris, 2013)

Ramet, Sabrina P., *The Three Yugoslavias: State building and Legitimation, 1918-2005* (Indiana University Press, 2006)

Reinkowski, Maurus & Gregor Thum, *Helpless Imperialists: Imperial Failure, Fear and Radicalisation* (Briston CT: Vandenhoek and Ruprecht, 2013)

Richie, Alexandra, *Faust's Metropolis: A History of Berlin* (London: Harper Collins, 1998)

Rielage, Dale C., *Russian Supply Efforts in America during the First World War* (Jefferson NC and London: McFarland and Company, 2002)

Roberts, J. M., *Europe 1880-1914* (3rd edition) (Harlow: Longman, 2001)

Roman, Eric, *Hungary and the Victor Powers, 1945-1950* (London: Macmillan, 1946)

Rose, Inbel, *Conservative and foreign Policy during the Lloyd George Coalition, 1918-1922* (London: Frank Cass, 1999)

Salisbury, Harrison E., *The 900 Days: The Siege of Leningrad* (London: Papermac, 1986)

Shamir, Haim, *Economic Crisis and French Foreign Policy, 1930-1936* (E. J. Brill, 1989)

Sharp, Alan, *The Versailles Settlement – Peacemaking in Paris 1919* (London: Macmillan, 1991)

Scherner, Jonas and White, Eugene N., *Paying for Hitler's War, The Consequences of Nazi Economic Hegemony in Europe* (Cambridge: Cambridge University Press, 2016)

Schieder, Theodor, *The Expulsion of the German Population from the Territories East of the Oder-Neisse-Line,* Translated by Prof Dr Vivien Stranders MA (Bonn: Federal Ministry for Expellees, Refugees and War Victims, 1954)

Schuman, Michael A., *Nations in Transition: Croatia* (New York: Facts on File Inc, 2004)

Shirer, William L. *The Rise and Fall of the Third Reich* (London: Pan, 1981)

Siebel-Achenbach, Sebastian, *Lower Silesia, from Nazi Germany to Communist Poland, 1942-1949* (London: Macmillan, 1994)

Sinclair, David, *Hall of Mirrors* (London: Century, 2001)

Singh, Chopra, *De Gaulle and European Unity* (New Delhi: Hardev Akhinav Publications, 1974)

Sluga, Glenda & Patricia Clavin, *Internationalisms: A Twentieth Century History* (Cambridge University Press, 2016)

Smuts, Jan Christian, *The League of Nations – A Practical Suggestion* (London: Hodder and Stoughton, 1918)

Snowden, Ethel, *A Political Pilgrim in Europe* (London: Cassel and Company, 1921)

Speer, Albert, *Inside the Third Reich* (London: Sphere, 1981)

Stachura, Peter, *Poland in the Twentieth Century* (London: Macmillan, 1999)

Stachura, Peter, *Poland, 1918-1945: An Interpretive and Documentary History of the Second Republic* (London and New York: Routledge, 2004)

Tardieu, Alan, *The Truth about the Treaty* (Indianapolis: The Bobbs-Merrill Company, 1921)

Taylor, A. J. P., *English History: 1914-1945* (London: Penguin, 1982)

Taylor, A. J. P., *The Origins of the Second World War* (London: Penguin, 1976)

Taylor, A. J. P., *The Habsburg Monarchy – 1809-1918* (London: Penguin, 1990)

Thompson, David, *England in the Twentieth Century* (London: Penguin, 1966)

Thorpe, Andrew, *A History of the Labour Party* (4th ed.) (London: Palgrave, 2015)

Thorsheim, Peter, *Waste into Weapons: Recycling in Britain during the Second World War* (New York: Cambridge University Press, 2015)

Tillman, Seth P., *Anglo-American Relations at the Peace Conference of 1919* (Princeton Legacy Library, 1961)

Tolstoy, Nikolai, *Victims of Yalta* (London: Gorgi, 1979)

Torp, Cornelius & Sven Oliver Muller, *Imperial Germany Revisited: Continuing Debates and New Perspectives* (New York and Oxford, Berghahn Books, 2013)

Trevor-Roper, H. R., *Hitler's War Directives – 1939-1945* (London: Pan, 1983)

Trifunovska, Snezana & Martinus Nijhoff, *Yugoslavia Through Documents, from its creation to its dissolution* (Dordrecht, Boston, London: Martinus Nijhoff, 1994)

Tuchman, Barbara, *August 1914* (London: Papermac, 1994)

Tung, Rosalie L. (ed.), *Learning from World Class Companies* (London: Thomson Learning, 2001)

Udenaren, John van, *Uniting Europe: an introduction to the European Union* (Lanham: Rowman and Littlefield, 2005)

Vonyo, Tomas, *The Economic Consequences of the War: West Germany's Growth Miracle after 1945* (Cambridge University Press, 2018)

Vujacic, Veljo, *Nationalism, Myth, and the state in Russia and Serbia: Antecedents of the Dissolution of the Soviet Union and Yugoslavia* (Cambridge University Press, 2015)

Wahlsatt, Evelyn Furstin Blucher von, *An English Wife in Berlin: A private memoir of politics and daily life Germany throughout the war, and the social revolution of 1918* (London: Constable and Company, 1920)

Walters, William and Jens Henrik Haahr, *Governing Europe: Discourse, Governmentality and European Integration* (London and New York: Routledge, 2004)

Weikert, Richard, *Hitler's Ethic: The Nazi Pursuit of Evolutionary Progress* (New York: Palgrave Macmillan, 2009:

Werth, Alexander, *De Gaulle* (London: Penguin, 1965)

Wheeler-Bennett, John, *Brest-Litovsk, The Forgotten Peace, March 1918* (London: Macmillan and Company, 1938)

Wheeler-Bennett, John W., and Anthony Nicholls, *The Semblance of Peace, The Political Settlement after the Second World War* (London: Palgrave Macmillan, 1974)

Whittle, Tyler, *The Last Kaiser* (London: Heinemann, 1977)

Williamson, D. G., *Bismarck and Germany* (London and New York: Longman, 1986)

Zartman, I. William, *Politics of Trade Negotiations Between Africa and the European Economic Community* (Princeton Legacy Library, New Jersey, 1971)

Acknowledgements

In researching and writing this book I had recourse to consult a range of sources, from government papers to printed books, articles and newspaper clippings. I should like to take this opportunity to recognise those sources as without them the writing of this work would certainly never have been possible. However, the revolution in internet technology since researching my last book, *Jihad: The Ottomans and the Allies*, has resulted in massive changes to the methodology I have been able to adopt in undertaking my preparation, planning and research.

In earlier projects, frequent treks to libraries, museums and other sources of material were required, followed by wading through documents, papers and books to identify and note the relevant information. Since then, the extensive digitisation of original documents and books, and their storage within a raft of internet libraries, archives and the websites of numerous specialist organisations has meant that researching this project has involved much less legwork.

I am therefore grateful for the free and unfettered access to repositories such as archive.org, which contains digitised copies of many of the books and original documents I have consulted, quoted from and referred to, saving me many trips to such institutions as the British Library, Imperial War Museum and National Archives in Kew.

The National Archives particularly, by modernising and digitising its vast collection of cabinet papers and other documents, has allowed me to investigate without the time and expense of a visit. Of course, there is nothing to compare with the experience of seeing and interacting with original materials, but when time is of the essence one must make those sacrifices.

This is therefore the briefest acknowledgement I have had to make in gratitude for the assistance I have received in producing a book. I would however, like to take this opportunity to thank all those bodies, institutions and organisations which I have consulted, however vicariously, to elicit the material I have needed.

Index

Also available from Amberley Publishing

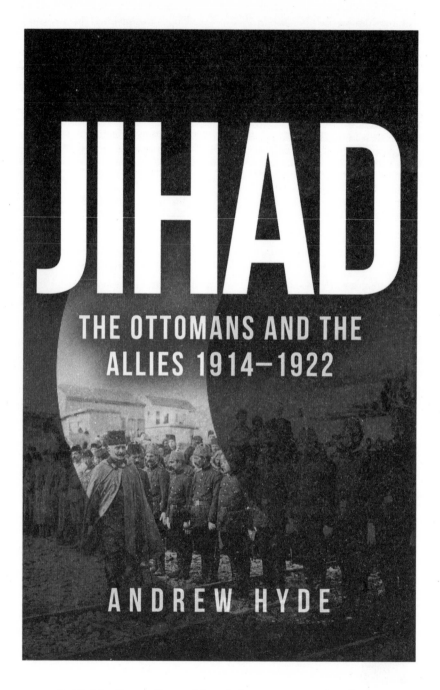

Available from all good bookshops or to order direct
Please call **01453-847-800**
www.amberley-books.com